India's Development Story

ECONOMIC DEVELOPMENTS IN INDIA

...A CONTINUING SERIES...

Editors :

RAJ KAPILA
Director,
Academic Foundation
New Delhi

UMA KAPILA
Senior Editor, Academic Foundation
Former Reader (retd.), Deptt. of Economics
Miranda House, University of Delhi

EDI—Two Hundredth Volume

India's Development Story

Editors:

RAJ KAPILA and UMA KAPILA

ACADEMIC FOUNDATION
NEW DELHI

www.academicfoundation.org
www.academicfoundation.com

First published in 2015
by

ACADEMIC FOUNDATION
4772-73 / 23 Bharat Ram Road, (23 Ansari Road),
Darya Ganj, New Delhi - 110 002 (India).
Phones : 23245001 / 02 / 03 / 04.
Fax : +91-11-23245005.
E-mail : books@academicfoundation.com
www.academicfoundation.org
www.academicfoundation.com

Cataloging in Publication Data--DK
Courtesy: D.K. Agencies (P) Ltd. <docinfo@dkagencies.com>

India's development story /
editors: Raj Kapila and Uma kapila.
pages cm
ISBN 9789332701830

1. Economic development--India. 2. India--Economic policy--1991- 3. Global Financial Crisis, 2008-2009. 4. Financial crises--India. I. Kapila, Raj, editor. II. Kapila, Uma, editor.

DDC 338.954 23

Typeset by Italics India, New Delhi.

Printed and bound by The Book Mint, New Delhi.
www.thebookmint.in

Contents

List of Tables and Figures 9

Contributors 13

Foreword by Vijay L. Kelkar. 21

Acknowledgements 23

Introduction 25

Section I

Growth and Social Development

1. Why Does India's Economic: Growth Process Falter?
   M.H. BALA SUBRAHMANYA 53

2. Two Issues in India's Growth Story
   C. RANGARAJAN 63

3. India: Economic Reforms and Growth Transition
   ARVIND VIRMANI 71

4. Transit Path for Indian Economy: Six Steps for Transforming the Elephant into a Tiger
   K.C. CHAKRABARTY 97

5. Indian Economy in Crisis: Assessment and Prospects
   A. VAIDYANATHAN 113

6. No Magic Wand: Why GDP Growth May Not Exceed 5.5 Per cent in FY 2015
BIBEK DEBROY 141

7. India's Three Arrows: How it Can Fire itself Back to High Growth
ALOK SHEEL 145

8. Economic Growth and Social Development: Synergic or Contradictory?
C. RANGARAJAN 149

9. Achieving Inclusive Growth: Recent Experience and Challenges Ahead
C.H. HANUMANTHA RAO 167

10. The Imperative of Distribution
PULIN B. NAYAK 183

11. Inclusiveness of Poor in Growth Akin to Mirage
N.A. MUJUMDAR 187

12. The Demographic Challenge and Employment Growth in India
JAYAN JOSE THOMAS 191

13. Finance and Opportunity in India
RAGHURAM G. RAJAN 201

14. Indian Inflation Puzzle
DEEPAK MOHANTY 211

15. Hold on to Interest Rates
ILA PATNAIK 225

16. Convergence: Have the Lower Income States 'Caught Up'?
C. RANGARAJAN, PADMA IYER KAUL and E.M. VIBEESH . . . 229

17. Funding States
INDIRA RAJARAMAN . . . 245

18. India's Economic Future: Moving Beyond State Capitalism?
VIJAY L. KELKAR . . . 249

19. India's Future: Opportunities and the Challenges
MANMOHAN SINGH . . . 305

20. Needed, a Growth Commission
C. RANGARAJAN . . . 313

21. Ten Myths of Indian Economic Policy
SHANKAR ACHARYA . . . 317

Section II

Globalisation and Global Financial Crisis

22. Financial Globalisation, Growth and Stability: An Indian Perspective
Y.V. REDDY . . . 321

23. India and the Global Financial Crisis: What Have We Learnt?
DUVVURI SUBBARAO . . . 329

24. Global Financial Crisis: Causes, Impact, Policy Responses and Lessons
RAKESH MOHAN . . . 345

Section III

Sectoral Development: Agriculture, Industry, Financial Sector and the External Sector

25. Changing Contours of Rural India: Causes and Consequences
V.S. VYAS 385

26. India's Second Green Revolution
ASHOK GULATI and SURBHI JAIN 399

27. The Industrial Recession: New or Ongoing?
C.P. CHANDRASEKHAR and JAYATI GHOSH 403

28. Indian Investments Abroad: What Explains the Boom?
R. NAGARAJ 411

29. The Five Pillars of RBI's Financial Sector Policies
RAGHURAM G. RAJAN 419

30. Capital Account Management and Macro-Prudential Regulation for Financial Stability and Growth
P. CHIDAMBARAM. 427

31. Indian Economic Crisis and the Fall of Rupee
MANMOHAN SINGH 431

32. What Saved the Rupee?
ARVIND SUBRAMANIAN 437

33. Recent Improvement in the Current Account Deficit: Is it Sustainable?
C. RANGARAJAN 443

List of Tables and Figures

Tables

2.1 Savings and Investment Rates 65

5.1 Recent Trends in Wholesale Price Index. 117

5.2 Trends in Secondary Sector GDP during the Reform and Pre-reform Periods. 127

5.3 Trends in Per Capita Private Consumption and its Inequality in Rural and Urban India 131

5.4 Average Earnings of Different Categories of Hired Labour 132

5.5 Growth of Non-wage and Non-self-employed Incomes in India 134

8.1 Social Sector Performance Indicators 151

8.2 Social Indicators: An Inter-country Comparison 153

8.3 Lorenz Ratio of Consumption Distribution 156

8.4 State-wise Analysis of Poverty Ratio 157

8.5 Decile-wise Growth in Per Capita Consumption (per cent per year, compound) 158

8.6 Under-5 Mortality Rate 159

8.7 Indian States Ranked with respect to HDI, 1999-2000 and 2007-08. 160

8.8 Per capita Public Expenditure on Health and Health Index 163

8.9 Per capita Public Expenditure on Education and Education Index 164

12.1 Net Increase in the Number of Workers in India, 1983 to 2011-12 192

12.2 Employment in India by Sectors: Estimates for 2011-12 and the Net Increase between 2004-05 and 2011-12. 195

12.3 Population in the 15-59 Age Group in India by Activity Status: Estimates for 2011-12 and the Incremental Change between 2004-05 and 2011-12 196

14.1 Global Inflation and Inflation in India. 212

14.2 Fiscal Deficit, Current Account Deficit, Agricultural Growth and Real Rural Wages 218

14.3 Real Bank Lending Rates and Real Policy Rate 222

18.1 India's Income Distribution (End-2004). 279

18.2 Occupational Structure of the Poor 282

24.1 Current Account Balance 349

24.2 Global Economic Outlook for 2009 353

24.3 Share of Banking Assets Held by Foreign Banks with Majority Ownership, 2006 360

24.4 Trends in Capital Flows 362

24.5 Key Fiscal Indicators of the Central Government 363

24.6 Key Indicators of Scheduled Commercial Banks in India 366

24.7 Activity in Money Market Segments (Average Daily Volume [One Leg]) 367

24.8 Actual/Potential Release of Primary Liquidity (Since Mid-September 2008) 373

24.9 Recent Behaviour of Monetary Aggregates in the US 375

24.10 Flow of Resources to the Commercial Sector 376

24.11 Measures of Inflation in India 378

27.1 Year-on-Year Growth of IIP for Particular Sectors 406

27.2 Year-on-Year Increase in Import Values for April-May 2008 408

Figures

2.1 Relationship between Growth and Inflation 69

3.1 Potential Growth Rate of Indian Economy 83

3.2 Post 1990 Trend and J Curve 83

8.1 Per capita GDP of India and China 165

14.1 WPI Inflation 215

14.2 Fiscal Deficits and Budget Estimates. 219

14.3 Non-food Manufactured Products Inflation. 220

14.4 Real Policy Rate and Monetary Policy Effectiveness 221

16.1 PCI Trend Growth Rates of 15 Major States 234

16.2 Trend in Gini Coefficient 237

16.3 Ratio of Average Growth Rates of States with Lowest PCI to Average Growth Rates of Different Categories of States 238

16.4 Relationship between Average Growth Rates in PCI of a State in Two Consecutive Periods 239

16.5 PCI in 1980-81 and Income Growth during 1981-82 to 1993-94 240

16.6 PCI in 1993-94 and Income Growth during 1993-94 to 2004-05 240

16.7 PCI in 2004-05 and Income Growth during 2004-05 to 2012-13 241

18.1 Growth of Output per Worker 253

18.2 Distribution of Total Annual Income in IRES (End-2004) . . . 281

18.3 Share of PSUs in Output of Large Firms. . . . 296

24.1 Effective Federal Fund Rate in the US . . . 347

24.2 Monetary Policy Rates: Deviation from the Taylor Rule . . . 347

24.3 Capital Flows to Emerging Market Economies . . . 355

26.1 Agri-GDP per Worker . . . 399

27.1 Index of Industrial Production . . . 404

27.2 IIP for Basic and Capital Goods . . . 405

27.3 IIP for Consumer Goods . . . 405

27.4 Exports and Imports . . . 407

32.1 Evolution of the Rupee (May 22 to October 13, 2013) . . . 438

32.2 Evolution of Five Fragile Emerging Market Currencies (May 22 to October 13, 2013) . . . 439

Contributors

Shankar Acharya is currently Member, Board of Governors and Honorary Professor, Indian Council for Research and International Economic Relations (ICRIER), New Delhi. He is also the Non-Executive Part-time Chairman of the Board of Directors of Kotak Mahindra Bank; besides serving on the governing boards of other national research organisations and the Advisory Committee on Monetary Policy of the Reserve Bank of India (RBI). He is a member of several advisory corporate boards, and writes a fortnightly column for the financial daily, *Business Standard*.

C.P. Chandrasekhar is Professor, Centre for Economic Studies and Planning, School of Social Sciences, Jawaharlal Nehru University (JNU), New Delhi. He has published widely in academic journals and is a regular columnist for *Frontline* (titled Economic Perspectives), *Business Line* (titled Macroscan) and the website of *The Hindu* (titled Economy Watch).

K.C. Chakrabarty, former Deputy Governor, RBI, started his career in teaching and research at the Banaras Hindu University. Earlier, he was Chairman of the Indian Bank and then Punjab National Bank. He has recently joined the board of Indiabulls Housing Finance Ltd (IBHFL) as an independent director.

P. Chidambaram, former Finance Minister, Government of India (GoI), is an Indian politician affiliated with the Indian National Congress. A corporate lawyer, he was earlier the Union Home Minister.

Bibek Debroy, a professional economist, has been recently appointed as a full-time member of the newly-created NITI Aayog or National Institution for Transforming India. Earlier, he was Director, Rajiv Gandhi Institute for Contemporary Studies, Rajiv Gandhi Foundation, New Delhi; Consultant to the Department of Economic Affairs, Ministry of Finance, Government of India (GoI); and Secretary General, PHD Chamber of Commerce and Industry (PHDCCI).

Jayati Ghosh is Professor of economics at JNU, New Delhi, and the Executive Secretary of International Development Economics Associates (Ideas). She was the Chairperson, Andhra Pradesh Commission on Farmers' Welfare (2004) and Member, National Knowledge Commission (2004-2009). She is a regular columnist for several Indian journals and newspapers and is closely involved with a range of progressive organisations and social movements.

Ashok Gulati is currently Infosys Chair Professor for Agriculture at ICRIER. Earlier, he was Chairman, Commission for Agricultural Costs and Prices (CACP), GoI; and Director, International Food Policy Research Institute (IFPRI). He also served as NABARD Chair Professor at the Institute of Economic Growth, and as Chief Economist at the National Council of Applied Economics Research (NCAER) in India. He has published widely in international and Indian journals, and is a prolific writer in media as well.

Surbhi Jain is Director, Commission for Agricultural Costs and Prices (CACP), Ministry of Agriculture, GoI.

Raj Kapila is Director, Academic Foundation. Earlier, he has been with Planning Comission, GoI; Ministry of Commerce and Industry; Industrial economist to Government of Punjab; Secretary, the Vanaspati Manufacturers Association of India; and Advisor, Hindustan Vegetable Oil Corporation. He has written extensively and has authored and edited several books.

Uma Kapila, author/editor of several books on Indian economy, retired as Reader, Department of Economics, Miranda House, University of Delhi. She has taught Indian economy to undergraduate students for more than 42 years and is the author of the widely-read book *Indian Economy since Independence*, currently into its 25th edition. Presently, she is Senior Editor, Academic Foundation.

Padma Iyer Kaul is Communication Controller of Accounts, Jammu and Kashmir, Department of Telecom, Ministry of Communication & IT, GoI. Earlier, she was working as Director, Economic Advisory Council to the Prime Minister.

Vijay L. Kelkar is currently Chairman of the Forum of Federations, Ottawa; India Development Foundation, New Delhi and Janwani—a social initiative of the Mahratta Chamber of Commerce, Industries and Agriculture (MCCIA) in Pune. Earlier, he was Chairman of the 13th Finance Commission; Advisor to the Minister of Finance (2002-2004); and is known for his role in economic reforms in India.

Rakesh Mohan, former Deputy Governor, RBI, is presently the Vice Chairperson of Indian Institute for Human Settlements. He was appointed in November 2012 as an Executive Director of the International Monetary Fund (IMF) for a three-year term. He remained an advisor to numerous ministries in GoI, including industry and finance. He will shortly be taking over as India's Executive Director at the IMF, Washington D.C.

Deepak Mohanty is Executive Director, RBI. The areas supervised by him are monetary policy, economic research and statistics. Earlier, he served in the IMF as Senior Advisor.

N.A. Mujumdar (late) was a distinguished economist who had wide interests in rural issues (particularly the food economy), monetary and fiscal policies, and international issues. He retired as Principal Advisor, Department of Economic Analysis and Policy, RBI, in 1988. He was also Editor of the *Indian Journal of Agricultural Economics*.

R. Nagaraj is Professor, Indira Gandhi Institute of Development Research, Mumbai. Earlier, he was Visiting Professor, Woodrow Wilson School, Princeton University, New Jersey, US; Visiting Professor, Hosei University, Tokyo; Visiting Fellow, Centre for International Studies, Princeton University, New Jersey, US; and Assistant Professor, Institute of Public Enterprise, Hyderabad.

Pulin B. Nayak is Professor of Economics at the Delhi School of Economics (DSE), University of Delhi. Earlier, he held the Agatha Harrison Fellowship at St Antony's College, Oxford; and was Director, Delhi School of Economics.

Ila Patnaik is Principal Economic Advisor to the GoI. Earlier, she was RBI Chair Professor at the National Institute of Public Finance and Policy (NIPFP), New Delhi and has worked at the NCAER, ICRIER and as Economics Editor of the *Indian Express*.

Indira Rajaraman was a Member of the 13th Finance Commission. Earlier, she held the RBI Chair at the NIPFP, Delhi; and was on the Economics faculty of the Indian Institute of Management, Bangalore. She writes regularly in the *Financial Press*.

Raghuram G. Rajan is Governor, RBI. Earlier, he was Chief Economic Advisor, Ministry of Finance, GoI. He was also chief economist at the IMF. For his book *Fault Lines: How Hidden Fractures Still Threaten the World Economy*, he was awarded the Financial Times-Goldman Sachs prize for the best business book in 2010.

C. Rangarajan, a distinguished former Member of Parliament and Ex-Governor of the RBI, was Chairman of the Prime Minister's Economic Advisory Council; served as the Governor of Andhra Pradesh and Chairman of 12th Finance Commission. Presently, he is Chairman, Madras School of Economics; President, Indian Statistical Institute; and Founding Chairman, C.R. Rao Advanced Institute of Mathematics, Statistics and Computer Science.

C.H. Hanumantha Rao is presently Chancellor, Hyderabad Central University; Chancellor, ICFAI Foundation for Higher Education (deemed to be University), Hyderabad; Honorary Professor, Centre for Economic and Social Studies (CESS), Hyderabad and Institute of Economic Growth (IEG), University of Delhi. He was a Fellow, IEG, University of Delhi, as well as its Director (1997-1980) and Chairman (2002-2008). One of the Founder-Members of CESS, Hyderabad, he was its Chairman during 1995-2007.

Y.V. Reddy, an Indian Administrative Service (IAS) officer of the 1964 batch, is Chairman of the 14th Finance Commission of India. Earlier, he was Governor, RBI. He has held the positions of Secretary (Banking) in the Ministry of Finance and Principal Secretary in the Government of Andhra Pradesh. He has also worked with the governments of China, Bahrain, Ethiopia and Tanzania.

Alok Sheel, IAS of the Kerala Cadre, has over 30 years of experience in public administration. Apart from extended stints in the finance departments in both Kerala and the GoI, he has interfaced with multilateral financial institutions such as the World Bank, IMF and UNDP, and also has anchored India's engagement with the G20. He is currently Additional Chief Secretary to the Government of Kerala.

Manmohan Singh was the 14th Prime Minister of India from 2004 to 2014. He began his bureaucratic career as an advisor in the Ministry of Foreign Trade. Over the 1970s and 1980s, he held several key posts in the GoI, such as Chief Economic Advisor (1972-1976), Governor, RBI (1982-1985) and Deputy Chairman, Planning Commission (1985-1987). In 1991, as Finance Minister, Dr Singh carried out several structural reforms that liberalised India's economy.

Duvvuri Subbarao, IAS officer of Andhra Pradesh cadre, was the 22nd Governor of RBI. Earlier, he worked as Joint Secretary in the Department of Economic Affairs, Ministry of Finance, GoI; Finance Secretary, Government of Andhra Pradesh; and lead economist in the World Bank.

Arvind Subramanian is Chief Economic Advisor to the GoI. He served as the Dennis Weatherstone Senior Fellow at the Peterson Institute for International Economics, Washington D.C., and Senior Fellow at the Center for Global Development, Washington D.C. Formerly an economist at the IMF, *Foreign Policy* magazine has named him as one of the world's top 100 global thinkers in 2011. He has published widely in academic and other journals, and contributes frequently to the *Financial Times* and *Business Standard*.

M.H. Bala Subramanya is Professor and Chairman, Department of Management Studies, Indian Institute of Science, Bangalore. His primary research interest is confined to industrial economics covering the wide spectrum of industry.

Jayan Jose Thomas is currently an Assistant Professor at Indian Institute of Technology (IIT), Delhi. He has previously held academic positions at the National University of Singapore, Indian Statistical Institute, Kolkata, Madras School of Economics and Central University of Kerala.

A. Vaidyanathan is Honorary Fellow at the Centre for Development Studies, Thiruvananthapuram. He has worked at NCAER, Planning Commission, as Professor at the Centre for Development Studies and Madras Institute of Development Studies (IDS), and as Economist, Food and Agricultural Organization and the World Bank.

E.M. Vibeesh was Senior Research Officer, Economic Advisory Council to the Prime Minister.

Arvind Virmani is President of the non-profit organisation Chintan, Member of RBI Technical Advisory Committee on monetary policy and Non-resident Senior Fellow, Global Economy and Development at the Brookings Institution. Previously, he served as chief economic advisor to the Indian government and executive director of the IMF. He has served as a member of the Telecom Regulatory Authority of India (TRAI) and of Appellate Tribunal for Securities and Exchange Board of India (SEBI); and Chief Executive of the ICRIER.

V.S. Vyas is Professor Emeritus, Institute of Development Studies (IDS), Jaipur. Earlier, he was Member, Economic Advisory Council to the Prime Minister; Director, Agro-Economic Research Centre, Vallabh Vidyanagar; Professor of Economics and Dean of Faculty of Humanities and Social Sciences, Sardar Patel University; Member, Agricultural Prices Commission of the GoI; Director, Indian Institute of Management, Ahmedabad; Senior Advisor in the Department of Agriculture and Rural Development of the World Bank, Washington D.C.; and Director, IDS, Jaipur. He has written extensively on key issues of agricultural policies and rural development.

Foreword

I am delighted to learn that Academic Foundation is publishing the 200th volume of its popular series: *Economic Developments in India* (EDI). Launched in 1998, *EDI* is brought out every month and covers the latest developments in Indian economy, including analytical articles by economists, policy makers and researchers, as well as the latest reports, documents and discussion papers, and current statistics.

EDI, being very user friendly covering practically everything latest on Indian economy, has made a seminal contribution towards promoting academic scholarship and research on Indian economy.

While there is no dearth of available material, both in terms of views and research presentations through various electronic media, a publication like *EDI* continues to be a precious resource for providing at one place, some of the best pieces of academic writing and also important reports and policy documents on different aspects of our country's economy. That is why *EDI* has also become an important source of policy ideas and analyses for the country's policy makers as well as opinion leaders.

The most important aspect of *EDI* is its eclectic approach in selecting material. You will find here outstanding work of scholars representing different schools of thought such as neo Marxist, Keynesian, neo liberal. I cannot over emphasise the value of such an open approach for nurturing scholarship in India.

I congratulate the editors, Raj Kapila and Uma Kapila, and the publisher, Academic Foundation, for bringing out this volume, as well as for their commendable efforts in academic publishing of high quality.

Pune —Vijay L. Kelkar

Acknowledgements

WE are grateful to all our authors who have been contributing regularly to Economic Developments in India, which has already run into 199 volumes, the present being the 200th volume.

The 33 articles in this volume, selected from EDI 101-199 have been contributed by eminent economists and experts. Our heartfelt thanks to the contributors of these articles.

We must express our deepest gratitude to Dr Vijay L. Kelkar for writing the Foreword for this special volume.

We take this opportunity to thank all our subscribers/readers for their support and encouragement which made it possible for us to bring out EDI month-after-month.

—Editors

Introduction

A few years ago, India was considered as one of the fastest growing economies in the world, and could do no wrong. Commentators talked of "Chindia" elevating India's performance to that of its northern neighbour. During the last two years, GDP (gross domestic product) growth slowed significantly dropping to as low as 4-5 per cent with high inflation and current account and budget deficits. Every commentator started highlighting India's poor infrastructure, excessive regulation, small manufacturing sector and a workforce with inadequate education and skills and that India could do no right.[1]

Such bipolar behaviour seems to apply to assessments of India's economy, with foreign analysts joining Indians in similar swings between over-exuberance and self-flagellation, similar to Indian cricket fans who are manic-depressive in the treatment of their favourite teams. They elevate players to God-like status when their team performs well, ignoring obvious weaknesses; but when it loses, as any team must, the fall is equally steep and every weakness is dissected. In fact, the team is never as good as the fans make it out to be when it wins, nor as bad as it is made out to be when it loses. Its weaknesses existed in victory, too, but were overlooked.[2]

Today again, Indian commentators and people in general as well as foreign analysists are over exuberant in their assessment that everything will turn right with the change in government.

Back to the cricketing analogy, India is an open argumentative society. But we are prone to mood swings, perhaps more so than

1. Rajan, Raghuram (2013). "Filtering Out the Real India", *RBI Bulletin*, November. Mumbai: Reserve Bank of India. Published in EDI 190, 2014.

2. Ibid.

other societies, in part driven by our excitable competitive and very young press. Stripping out both the euphoria and the despair from what is said about India—and from what we Indians say about ourselves—will probably bring us closer to the truth.[3]

The present book entitled *India's Development Story* (200th volume of *Economic Developments in India* [EDI]) is an humble attempt at filtering out the real India—stripping out both the euphoria and the despair, by selecting from over 500 articles published in the various volumes of EDI (from 101 to 199, 2006-2014), by some of our most distinguished economists who have contributed immensely to the analysis of India's economic conditions and policy formulation in their respective areas of expertise.

The selected articles are arranged in three sections. Section I narrates the growth story focusing on the post-Lehman crisis, particularly the deterioration in practically all aspects of country's economic performance during the last 2-3 years. Section II discusses the impact of globalisation and global financial crisis and section III looks into the sectoral issues relating to agriculture, industry, finance and the external sector.

I

The Growth Story

In chapter 1, Bala Subrahmanya narrates briefly what may be called an 'appropriate economic development path' for a developing economy, which was experienced by the developed countries and newly industrialised economies (NIEs), China and Malaysia. By and large, the developing economies are dominated by agriculture and supplemented by unorganised industrial and service sectors in terms of GDP composition. When economic growth takes place, industrialisation spearheads the whole process accompanied by agricultural development, followed by service sector development. Industrial development is characterised by a structural shift in the compositions of manufacturing value added (MVA) and industrial

3. Ibid.

employment. The growth of industry gives a fillip to the growth of organised sector in the entire economy. The economic transformation facilitated by industrial development also leads to a transformation of 'export basket', where the shares of agro and processed goods fall and are duly compensated by increase in the shares of manufactured goods, initially light manufactured goods but later the heavy manufactured ones. The countries which have pursued this path of economic development have achieved economic prosperity, current account surpluses, and have strong and stable currencies (such as NIEs, China and Malaysia).

Indian economic policy makers had precisely intended to pursue this path of development since independence, says Bala Subrahmanya. The composition of GDP changed: although agriculture contribution declined further from 33 per cent in 1990-91 to 16.17 per cent in 2011-12, the industrial contribution hardly improved (from 24.15% to 25.45% during the same period), implying that the declined contribution of agriculture has been duly compensated by the growth of service sector. What is more alarming has been the changes that occurred in the composition of MVA as well as the export basket and these are not along the desired path of economic development. The space vacated by the public sector (which spearheaded the role of transforming Indian economy on the desired path of economic development till 1991) was expected to be filled up more than adequately by the organised private sector (domestic and foreign), when the broad-based economic reforms were launched in 1991. According to Bala Subrahmanya, the much desired 'opening up' of the economy (which was hailed by the international institutions, the foreign media and the domestic industrial houses alike) did not trigger/accelerate the inflow of investments into the industrial sector (particularly capital goods industries) to generate more industrial employment, higher MVA and thereby contributing to the much needed shift in the export basket from light manufactured to heavy manufactured goods.

Perhaps it is here that our 'policy-making' has not produced desired results. We have not been able to decisively influence the flow of domestic and foreign private investments towards the desired direction so as to make an impact on the technology front of the global economy. It is imperative for the Indian economy to strive and achieve structural transformation of (manufacturing) industry by building-up the capital goods industry base and acquiring technological competence leading to the growing share of high-tech goods in the composition of total exports. This alone will lend strength and support to our currency in the international markets. Otherwise, our economy will continue to experience perennially CAD (current account deficit) and remain vulnerable resulting in even 'minor external vibrations' turning into 'shocks' more often than what we can afford.

In chapter 2, C. Rangarajan discusses two issues in relation to India's growth performance: (i) determination of the potential rate of growth of the Indian economy and (ii) threshold level of inflation—the level of inflation beyond which growth turns negative. Rangarajan believes that in the case of determining potential rate of growth of the economy, one can take the maximum growth rate achieved in the recent past as the lowest estimate of the potential. This assumption can be made if there is reason to believe that the maximum growth rate achieved in the recent past was not an one-off event and the growth rate achieved was robust. India achieved a growth rate of 9.5 per cent in 2005-06, followed by 9.6 per cent and 9.3 per cent in the subsequent two years. After declining slightly in the wake of international financial crisis, growth rate went back to 9.3 per cent in 2010-11. In many ways, the growth rate achieved in the high growth phase was robust. The gross domestic savings averaged 33.4 per cent of GDP and gross capital formation averaged 34.2 per cent. The CAD remained low at 1.1 per cent of GDP. Agricultural growth during this period averaged 5 per cent and the annual manufacturing growth was 11.5 per cent. CAD remained low and the accretion to foreign exchange reserves amounted to $144 billion. Thus on many dimensions, the growth rate was robust. It was not just fuelled by financial availability. Certainly, the external environment provided good support. This was the period during which the world economy was also booming.

The growth rate slowed to 6.2 per cent in 2011-12 and came down to 5.0 per cent last year, and this year also it is expected to be around the same level. The savings and investment rates have come down sharply from its earlier level. Gross fixed capital formation (GFCF) rate was around 30.6 per cent as against 32.9 per cent of GDP in 2007-08. Normally, keeping in view the recent trends in the ICOR (incremental capital-output ratio) which is around 4, we should have achieved a growth rate of 7.0 to 7.5 per cent, but the actual rate turned out to be 6.0 per cent. Economic growth has in fact declined much more steeply than what is warranted by the decline in investment, argues Rangarajan. This maybe because projects have not been completed on time or complementary investments have not been forthcoming or it could be due to non-availability of critical inputs such as coal and power. The fact that even today, savings and investment rates are at high levels re-assures us that if we are able to find ways to complete projects speedily, we shall be able to usher in rapid growth in income even in the short run. It is, however, to be noted that while the decline in overall GFCF rate from the peak reached in 2007-08 was only 2.2 per cent, the decline in the case of private corporate sector was as high as 4.6 per cent. Thus, the composition of investment has also played a role in the reduction in productivity of capital. Nevertheless, while the existing level of investment rate should enable us to grow at 7.5 per cent in the short run, a return to higher level of savings and investment can take us back to the very high levels of growth which we had seen earlier.

According to Rangarajan, to sustain a long-term growth rate of 8.5 per cent, three things need to happen: (i) CAD must be lowered, (ii) the domestic savings rate must pick up with much of it coming from fiscal consolidation and (iii) the productivity of capital should improve so that ICOR is maintained around 4:1. Given the performance of the Indian economy in the recent past, these are not impossible tasks. But this will require focused efforts on all the three fronts. Besides, we need to keep a watch on inflation which also has a bearing on the potential rate of growth when it exceeds a threshold level of inflation.

Arvind Virmani in chapter 3 has tried to explore the paradox between higher growth potential and the declining growth trend in India. The 1990s economic reforms including liberalisation of the external trade, investment and technology policy raised the potential growth of the Indian economy from around 5.5 to over 8.5 per cent per annum. Consequently, the economy grew at around 9.0 per cent per annum during the five years (2003-04 to 2007-08). The average growth rate fell to 7.7 per cent in the next four years (2008-09 to 2011-12) following the US financial crises of 2008. There are two factors in the slowdown. The first is the continuing financial crises and its accentuation of capital flow volatility into India, and the global economic slowdown and consequent global demand deficiency-excess capacity in tradable goods and services. The second is the negative fallout of India's growth acceleration and the political consequences of the V-shaped recovery from the 2008 global financial shock. More importantly, the growth acceleration has given rise to a number of economic bottlenecks and constraints and socio-political conflicts that must be resolved through economic policy and institutional reform if fast growth is to be sustained. These include conflicts related to land, water and natural resources. These conflicts can effect economic growth not just directly (e.g., inadequate supply of urban land), but also through their effect on the political system and its ability to act decisively in resolving issues not directly connected to them, such as macroeconomic response to external shocks and fundamental policy reforms.

According to Virmani, India has the potential to attain high growth economy (HGE) status by reversing the downward trend in its growth and going back to its underlying potential of per capita GDP growth of 7.0 to 7.5 per cent (GDP 8.5%+). This requires urgent policy actions to remove bottlenecks to growth, eliminate rents and facilitate removal of supply constraints. He outlines a range of policy actions to increase competitiveness in factor markets, agriculture and 'private goods infrastructure,' and separation of energy and other subsidies from debilitating price distortions and fiscal reforms, which can help in restoring India's growth trend. Some, if not all, policy reforms may require a reorientation/adjustment of the approach to political cooperation and competition.

In July 2011, Swaminathan Anklesaria Aiyar, wrote a paper for the Cato Institute, "The Elephant that Became a Tiger." In this paper, he persuasively argued that 20 years of economic reforms in India had transformed the Indian economy into a tiger. Later the same year, D. Subbarao (Haksar Memorial Lecture), Governor RBI, argued that India may be an elephants but even elephant can dance. The elephant dance was disrupted by the zoo party in the form of global financial crisis. He then suggested 10 steps to get back on course by re-jigging the elephant dance. In chapter 4, K.C. Chakrabarty argues:

> Growth in India has clearly slowed down since then to 6.5 per cent in 2011-12 and a likely 5.8 per cent in 2012-13, with significant downside risks. The twin deficits—fiscal and balance of payments—have compounded our problems. This may set us thinking on whether we are an elephant or a tiger or a goat, about to be devoured by global forces and our domestic inaction? So should we at all pursue the tiger dream? If yes, what do we need to do to earn the tiger tag?

In a very interesting style, Chakrabarty first explains what these metaphors elephant, tiger and dragon—often used for India mean and what steps need to be taken to turn the elephant into tiger. This according to Chakrabarty will require taking the following six steps: (i) preserve demographic dividends by investing in human capital, (ii) improve productivity and efficiency, (iii) revive infrastructure investments and harness natural resources better, (iv) improve governance at every level, (v) enforce accountability in all walks of life, and (vi) make finance more responsive to real sector and promote inclusive growth. He concludes:

> We need to learn from the East Asian tigers in our quest to become one. Growth acceleration in these tigers were supported by liberalisation, export-led growth, high investment in education, large share of educated workforce, high public and private savings rate and macroeconomic discipline and governance. We are pursuing some of these policies and can pursue some more of them. However, these tigers also failed to maintain their spurt because of some mistakes they committed. Some of them maintained high interest rate to attract foreign investments, others pegged currency arrangements

and many of them developed a vulnerable financial system. An unanticipated shock from banking and currency side, therefore, resulted in growth collapse for them during the East Asian crisis. Corporate failures added to the financial sector woes in some countries (especially Chaebols in Korea). While transforming the Indian economy into a tiger, we need to calibrate policies taking into account the lessons learnt during the East Asian crisis. Downturns come and go away as business cycles run their course. In our present predicaments with macroeconomic stabilisation, we must not lose sight of our larger goals, whether we walk at an elephant's pace or run like a tiger.

According to A. Vaidyanathan (chapter 5), the simultaneous deterioration of performance on three fronts—(i) balance of payment (BoP), (ii) wholesale price indices (WPI) and (iii) GDP growth—has led to a crisis of serious concern. After carefully examining the causes and consequences of this crisis—the factors that have contributed to the deterioration in each of these aspects—he has also commented on the prospects of reviving the economy, suggesting necessary corrective measures. To quote Vaidyanathan,

> My understanding of the evolving crisis and its denouement are clearly at odds with the optimism of many observers. Besides the various internal and external constraints (economic, political, and institutional), we have to reckon with the effect of over-exploitation of key natural resources (especially water and forests); the indiscriminate manner in which further expansion of land, forests, and minerals are sought to be promoted in the interests of rapid growth; and the cavalier way in which ecological, environmental, and social concerns are ignored and dismissed.

Talking about prospects of growth, Bibek Debroy (chapter 6) remarks:

> Growth is not a number conjured out of thin air. It means new jobs, lower poverty. NSS data for 2011-12 show, employment stagnates when growth tapers off. Three decades of inclusive intervention did not make much of a dent on poverty. Poverty declines have been sharper in states with higher growth, particularly in states where agriculture has done well. Will a new government in May wave a magic wand in June 2014 and propel growth back to 9 per cent? For 2014-15, 5.5 per cent is probably the best we can hope for.

Alok Sheel (chapter 7), on the other hand is of the view that although the prospects for a robust global recovery over the medium-term are still downbeat in view of the major demand re-balancings required, there is more cause for optimism regarding India for two good reasons. First, the two major drivers that recently pushed Indian growth trend from the 5.5-6.5 per cent into the 8.0-9.0 per cent trajectory are intact. The dependency ratio continues to decline, while the roughly 10 per cent increase in domestic savings as a share of GDP is largely intact but for some short-term damage to financial savings. Second, the rather startling fact is that in a demand-constrained world, India has the luxury of a domestic crisis caused by supply-side problems. Unlike other emerging markets, dependent on external levers for a return to high growth, our levers are mostly domestic. Since the supply-side crisis is of our own making and not a result of any major external shock, the solutions are also within our control. However, this will not be easy. Pulling these domestic levers is the big political challenge ahead.

The three critical levers, or the three big arrows that need to fire, according to Alok Sheel, are agriculture that targets the inflation problem, labour-intensive manufacturing that targets the CAD, and fiscal restructuring that targets the infrastructural deficit. If these three arrows can be fired accurately from a crossbow called good governance, they can address current macroeconomic imbalances and lay the foundations for return to a sustainable high growth trajectory.

Economic Growth and Social Development

The next six papers in this section (chapters 8-13) discuss the issues of economic growth and social development covering poverty inequality, inflation and regional disparities and convergence. According to C. Rangarajan (chapter 8), economic growth in a broader sense includes social development, what we call inclusive growth. In his paper, he has used the term social development for equity in growth. Analytically speaking on the relationship between the two, i.e., economic growth and social development, some key questions that arise are: Does social development come in the way of faster growth? Is social development possible without adequate economic growth? Is faster growth possible without equity? What are the synergies between social development and economic growth? Can expenditures on social sectors by themselves ensure better social progress? What are the organisational and motivational factors necessary to secure better returns from expenditure? What should be the role of the state and the private sector in relation to social development activities? Rangarajan's paper dwells on all these issues.

In his concluding remarks, he states:

> Development has many dimensions. It has to be inclusive, it must be poverty reducing and it must be environment friendly. We need to incorporate all these elements in the growth process. However, at our present stage of development, we cannot afford to sacrifice growth. It is key to improving the living standards of our people. Equity and growth should not be posed as opposing considerations. They must be weaved together to produce a coherent pattern of development. Therein lies economic statesmanship.

It is, therefore, necessary,

> to stress simultaneously economic development in the conventional sense of accelerating growth rate and social development in the sense of securing for everyone the basic needs. The two have a mutually interacting beneficial impact and the two must be pursued together. These are the two legs on which the country must walk. Any strategy of development, which ignores any one of the two legs, will only make the country limp along.

According to C.H. Hanumantha Rao (chapter 9), inclusive growth is not a new or a novel idea. Defined in the Eleventh Plan as a "growth process which yields broad based benefits and ensures equality of opportunity for all," it stands for "equitable development" or "growth with social justice," which have always been the watch words of development planning in India. Yet, since inclusive growth is so widely used these days by the reputed multilateral institutions as well as the policy makers in India, one wonders whether this usage acquires a special significance in the present context. Perhaps, it does. The belief that there is a significant 'trade-off' between growth and equity does not seem to be as widespread now as before. There is now a genuine and widespread recognition about the adverse social consequences of rising inequalities in the recent high growth phase, which do not seem to be mitigated through the so-called 'trickle-down' mechanism.

For about three decades, from the early 1950s to the early 1980s, when the country was experiencing a slow growth in GDP, or the so-called 'Hindu' rate of growth, the concern for accelerating GDP growth itself was uppermost, apart from ensuring equity. Inequalities did arise in the wake of growth then, but were not as prominent as in the recent phase of accelerated growth. With the GDP growth rate rising to 7-8 per cent, rural-urban divide, regional divide and rich-poor divide became glaring, which brought inclusive growth high on the policy agenda.

It is not inevitable that growth in GDP should bring about rise in inequalities in income—whether before or after the reforms. Much depends on the level and spatial distribution of physical infrastructure, human resource development, prevailing social structure, social policies and governance patterns. Therefore, the sharp rise in inequalities in the post-reform period cannot be attributed to economic reforms as such. Rather, they can be traced to the initial conditions obtaining in the pre-reform period itself. In China, for example, where land reforms were successful and infrastructure development was high in the pre-reform period, there was a rapid reduction in poverty following economic reforms and acceleration in GDP growth (Rao, 2005). The quality of reform package is, of course, important. It has to be such as to make good the infrastructural and other gaps inherited from the pre-reform period. It should also be effective in coping with the adverse social consequences that predictably result from the implementation of reforms under the given unfavourable initial conditions.

Inadequate physical and social infrastructure like irrigation, power, roads, transport and communications, education and health in the less developed regions and rural areas in general is a major factor responsible for the growing rural-urban and regional disparities in the country.

Rao has discussed the major achievements of the United Progressive Alliance (UPA) government since 2004 in respect of its promise of achieving inclusive growth. According to him, in the ultimate analysis, inclusive growth can be achieved only through inclusive politics. The social change underway in the country through the democratic process holds such a promise.

According to Pulin Nayak (chapter 10), the single most troubling aspect of our recent growth experience after onset of the reform process in 1991 is the dismal picture on the employment front described by many as the phenomenon of jobless growth.

Regarding the growth experience also, much of the impetus for growth has emerged from the high growth rate being experienced in the services and industry sectors, which account for 54 and 27 per cent of GDP respectively and agriculture, which is the mainstay of more than 60 per cent of the country's population, accounts for only 19 per cent. This share has fallen further and presently the share of agriculture in national income is around 14 per cent. This pattern of growth has obviously contributed to substantial accentuation of inequalities of incomes.

N.A. Mujumdar (chapter 11) has also emphasised on how extreme inequality is damaging and worrying for many reasons. It is morally questionable. It has a negative impact on growth and poverty reduction. It can multiply social problems. The wealthiest individuals and groups capture political institutions for their aggrandisement, at the expense of the rest of the society. If left unchecked, political institutions will become undermined and governments will overwhelmingly serve the interest of the economic elite to the detriment of ordinary people.

What is more disturbing is that economic inequality has increased in the last 30 years. In 24 out of 26 countries studied in Oxfam's briefing paper, "Working for the Few—Political Capture and Economic Inequality," the richest 1 per cent has increased their share of income. In the US, the wealthiest 1 per cent captured 95 per cent of the post-2008 growth, while the bottom 90 per cent became poorer. In India also, the findings of another study[4] is that at the national

4. Suryanarayana, M.H. and Mousmi Das (2014). "How Inclusive is India's Reformed Growth?", *Economic and Political Weekly* XLIX(6). 8 February.

level, disparities across social groups have increased and the relatively deprived social groups of scheduled tribes (STs) and scheduled castes (SCs) have been left out of the growth process. The study concludes: "Our findings, in general, suggest the inclusiveness of the poorest in the mainstream growth process is still a forlorn hope."

According to Jayan Jose Thomas (chapter 12), estimates by the World Bank (WB) show that the population aged 15-59 years is set to increase dramatically in India from around 757 million in 2010 to 972 million in 2030. This could potentially translate into an addition of over 200 million workers over the next two decades. On the other hand, during the same period, the working-age population is expected to decline in most developed regions of the world and even in China (where it would fall from 913 million to 847 million). In other words, India will contribute a substantial chunk of the increase in global labour supply over the coming years.

In India, the share of agriculture and allied activities in GDP declined from 35.1 per cent in 1983 to 14.0 per cent in 2011-12. The share of these sectors in the country's total employment also fell during this period from 68.2 to 47.5 per cent.

The shift of the workforce away from agriculture in India has occurred almost entirely among the younger age groups. Between 2004-05 and 2011-12, male agricultural workers in the age group of 5-24 years declined by 10.3 million, even as male agricultural workers who are 25 years and older increased by 5.6 million. A part of the reason for this shift is the rising enrolment of the young in educational institutions.

However, the generation of non-agricultural employment in the Indian economy has fallen behind the growth in supply of 'potential' non-agricultural workers. Additions made to the pool of potential non-agricultural workers come from two sources: growth of the working-age population and the shift of the workforce away from agriculture. At the same time, the growth in the number of students, who are not part of the labour force, tends to reduce the size of this pool.

To sum up, the generation of non-agricultural employment in India has accelerated after middle of the first decade of this century.

At the same time, the pace of job creation has been inadequate to absorb the rising supply of potential workers, especially females. With the movement of workers away from agriculture, with their rising education levels, this challenge will grow bigger in the coming years, particularly in the rural areas. Unless India's economic policies are geared towards a significant revival in the growth of decent jobs, the country risks losing its demographic dividend—the female part of this dividend in particular.

Raghuram Rajan in his paper, "Finance and Opportunity in India" (chapter 13) has very effectively argued that:

> The greatest dangers to the growth of developing countries is the middle income trap, where crony capitalism creates oligarchies that slow down growth. To avoid this trap, and to strengthen the independent democracy our leaders won for us 67 years ago, we have to improve public services, especially those targeted at the poor. A key mechanism to improve these services is through financial inclusion.

Financial inclusion and direct benefits transfer (DBT) can be a way of liberating the poor from dependency on indifferently delivered public services, and thus indirectly from the venal but effective politicians. However, it is not a cure-all but will help the poor out of poverty and towards true political independence. Financial inclusion can do more: by liberating the poor and the marginalised from the clutches of the moneylender, by providing credit and advice to the entrepreneur amongst the poor, and by giving households the ability to save and insure against accidents. It can set them on the road to economic independence, thus strengthening the political freedom that good public services will bring.

Rajan has also elaborated on how to make financial inclusion more effective by getting five 'Ps' right: product, place, price, protection and profit.

Inflation Puzzle and Threshold Level of Inflation

During the last three years, not only growth has slowed down but inflation has also been on the rise. The persistence of inflation in an environment of falling economic growth has come out as a 'puzzle.' India has been a moderate inflation country. For example, in the 62 years since 1950-51, average annual inflation rate as measured by changes in the WPI increased at a rate of 6.7 per cent per annum. That is certainly not a very high rate considering that many countries, both developed and developing, experienced very high inflation in their modern development history. In fact, more recently in the 1980s and 1990s, the world inflation averaged around 17 per cent per annum. It was only in the 2000s, that there was a sharp all-round moderation in global inflation. In the eight years period from 2000 to 2007, while the emerging and developing economies (EDEs) which traditionally had very high inflation showed an average annual inflation at 6.7 per cent, India's inflation performance was even better at 5.2 per cent as measured by WPI. However, there has been a pick-up in inflation and as of November 2014, it was 7.5 per cent. In this context, a question that has been raised is what is the acceptable or threshold level of inflation beyond which inflation has a negative impact on growth. The threshold level of inflation is that level beyond which inflation has a decisive negative impact on growth (C. Rangarajan, chapter 2).

Regarding the policy action to be taken to bring down inflation, Deepak Mohanty (chapter 14) remarks:

> While monetary policy action addresses the risk of unhinging of inflation expectations, attending to the structural supply constraints becomes important to ensure that these do not become a binding constraint in the long-run, making the task of inflation management more difficult. By ensuring a low and stable inflation, the Reserve Bank could best contribute to social welfare.

According to Ila Patnaik (chapter 15), "The impact of tighter fiscal and monetary policy on inflation is now visible in the recent price data. Inflation, measured both by the wholesale price index (WPI) and by the consumer price index (CPI), has come down." Rajan's strategy of an aggressive attack on inflation, despite the scepticism often voiced in the Indian monetary policy debate about effectiveness of the monetary policy, was a right strategy and is yielding results. Considering that inflationary expectations in India are high and persistent, and could take a while to come down, repo rate should not cut as yet. The fiscal and monetary contraction of the last 9 months, as well as the slowdown in the economy, have contributed to the reduction in inflation.

A further consideration in the decision about the stance of monetary policy, according to Ila Patnaik, would be global liquidity considerations. Low inflation, along with a low current account and fiscal deficit, would be a more prudent policy, as there could be sharp and sudden changes in the US and global liquidity conditions. This may prompt RBI to keep interest rates unchanged.

The next two papers by C. Rangarajan (chapter 16) and Indira Rajaraman (chapter 17) discuss the issue of convergence, how the lower income states have 'caught up' and the issue of funding states. As is well known, balanced regional growth is an important development objective in India and more importantly, an inclusive growth process is essential to promote social harmony and political stability. Differential natural resource endowments and skilled human resources result in wide variations in growth rates and hence incomes across states. While initially inter-regional disparity may increase in the process of development, it is expected that as growth gathers momentum and with specific policy initiatives, this divergence would attenuate. Convergence in per capita incomes (PCIs) will be driven by diminishing returns to capital, that is, states with a high initial income and presumably higher capital-labour ratio will, over time, have lower per capita income growth rates and *vice versa*. This process of convergence will be aided by redistribution of incomes in favour of poorer states through mechanisms such as the Finance Commission and grants from the Centre to the states (Rangarajan).

After a careful study of the empirical evidence on interstate disparities and convergence in the periods 1980-81 to 1993-94, 1993-94 to 2004-05 and most recent period, 2004-05 to 2012-13, Rangarajan comes to conclusion that strictly speaking the three periods do not show convergence. Absolute convergence in the sense of the PCIs of the different states converging to a single number has not happened. However, in the recent period, there is strong evidence of catching up by the lower income states. The median growth rate more than doubled in the recent period, increasing from 2.8 per cent during 1993-94 to 2004-05 to 6.3 per cent during 2004-05 to 2012-13. All the

15 states in the sample show higher growth rates in the recent period. States with lower PCI (1993-94) like Assam, Madhya Pradesh (MP), Uttar Pradesh (UP) and Bihar have made significant gains in growth rates in the recent period 2004-05 to 2012-13. Notwithstanding these gains, convergence did not happen in the recent period mainly because some states, especially Maharashtra, Gujarat, Kerala, Tamil Nadu and Haryana, which had high initial PCIs, also posted high growth rates (in the range of 7% and above). The declining trend in the positive values of the coefficients of divergence points towards increased catching up and greater convergence.

A recent report of the committee for a composite development index (CDI) for states, released in late September 2014, has attracted criticism for having been politically motivated to give a larger share to Bihar in fiscal flows from the centre (Indira Rajaraman, chapter 17).

In the past, outcome variables have been used in Plan schemes floated by the Centre, such as the Sarva Shiksha Abhiyan (SSA), whose objective was to even out the primary education deficit in deprived regions, or the Pradhan Mantri Gram Sadak Yojana (PMGSY), which provides last-mile connectivity for villages not so linked, thereby favouring states with a large number of marooned villages.

The report on CDI for states has two aspects, says Indira Rajaraman. It is an exercise along the lines of the Human Development Index (HDI), using outcome indicators to quantify and rank states on a scale. While HDI assigns high scores to high achievers, the CDI, on the other hand, assigns high scores to low achievers. The second aspect of the report is to quantify the relative entitlement of states in development funding from the centre, grounded in their low achievement. The CDI gives Bihar a 12.04 per cent share, as against what the report says was a 10.06 per cent share across tax shares and grants awarded by the 13th Finance Commission. According to Indira Rajaraman, the excess of the CDI over this revised tax share yields a rough and ready measure of the (accumulated) governance deficit in Bihar. The people of Bihar undeniably suffer from acute outcome deficits, which call for urgent redressal. But targeted interventions with measurable outcomes are a better way to confront consequences of accumulated governance deficits, rather than pouring more unconditional funding into them.

The next two papers by Vijay Kelkar (chapter 18) and our former Prime Minister Dr Manmohan Singh (chapter 19) talk about India's future.

Vijay Kelkar's paper[5] (chapter 18) is as relevant today, in fact I would say more relevant. At that time he had remarked "India is now on the threshold of a golden age of growth." But we cannot take this set of extremely attractive outcomes for granted. Achieving a golden age of growth crucially depends on the policy framework that we adopt. The window of opportunity, particularly of a grand demographic dividend, is available for a limited period of only next two decades or so. It is necessary that we choose wisely because wrong choices now can render all future generations poor forever. The choices that we make today will make a dramatic difference to India's future. If we seize this moment, India can transit out of poverty, and coming generations can enjoy an era of unprecedented prosperity and a decisive voice in shaping the global economic order and world politics.

But India on a growth turnpike is not inevitable destiny. It is only one possible future, that we have to step forward to make ours. If we continue down the slippery path of state capitalism, this can degenerate into populism and consequent economic stagnation, as has happened in the past.

State capitalism, which played a historic and creative role in the 1950s and 1960s, has run out of steam because of its inherent limitations. Hence, the choice is clear: we have to move beyond state capitalism and move towards a fullfledged advanced market economy by accelerating institutional reform, including rapid privatisation at the level of both Centre and states. In other words, we have to fully accept the institutional framework of modern capitalism as India's economic future.

In his concluding remarks, Kelkar says: "Public policy in India is at the crossroads. The old orthodoxy of socialism has decisively lost

---

5. Dr Gadgil memorial lecture, 26 October 2005. *Economic Developments in India*, Vol. 105.

ground in the minds of the younger generation, which is now the majority of the population. But a fully articulated alternative has not been articulated nor has it been internalised. While we should take great pride in the transformation that has been achieved in India in the last 20 years or so but something was missing and, I have tried to envision what India would look like as a modern market economy. There is an urgency for us to accelerate reforms; starting with transforming our mindset, and marching towards an advanced modern market economy by going beyond the paradigm of State Capitalism".

In Dwelling on India's Future (chapter 19), the former Prime Minister Manmohan Singh remarks,

> India is on the move. Indians are on the move. As India rises, there are challenges to deal with. Our real challenges are at home and ups and downs are part of life. We all know that. But we have never allowed ourselves to be overwhelmed by twists and turns in our lives. We have never allowed these challenges to weaken our faith in ourselves, in our democracy, in the principles that define our democracy and in India's destiny.

Needed a Growth Commission

There is a need to evaluate and restructure every organisation as circumstances change and the Planning Commission is no exception says C. Rangarajan (chapter 20). Restructuring an organisation can be of two types. One approach takes the functions of the organisation as a given function and proceeds to restructure it, making it more effective to fulfil those functions. The second approach is more fundamental. It questions the very basis of the organisation and focuses on relevance of the basic functions it has been performing. According to Rangarajan, "an organisation to look at the basic issues confronting the economy, and to prepare a broad framework on how long-term issues can be resolved, is still a necessity."

The last paper in this section (chapter 21) discusses the population myths of Indian economic policy. Economic policy in India, and perhaps in many other countries, is constrained by powerful prevailing myths and prejudices, says Shankar Acharya. Sometimes these myths simply reflect lazy thinking or an apparent immunity to facts. Sometimes they are shored up by strong vested interests. Sometimes all three. Whatever the reason, it is hard to dispute the potency of myths in economic policy making. Shankar Acharya talks about his 10 favourites ones—some old, some new, and also very effectively brings out the truth, an insightful reading indeed.

II

Globalisation and Global Financial Crisis

Section II looks into the issues of financial globalisation and global financial crisis. Y.V. Reddy (chapter 22) discusses an Indian perspective of financial globalisation, growth and stability. D. Subbarao (chapter 23) and Rakesh Mohan (chapter 24) look into the 2008-09 deepest financial crisis of our times, the causes, impact, policy responses and lessons we learnt. According to Subbarao, fundamental causes of all financial crises are the same—global imbalances, loose monetary policy and high levels of leverage driven by 'irrational exuberance'. In that respect, the crisis of 2008-09 has been no different. But where this crisis has been different, has been its manifestation. Most recent crises had occurred in individual emerging economies or regions, and they were, at their core, traditional retail banking or currency crises. The countries in trouble could be rescued by multilateral interventions; besides, the advanced countries provided a buffer for trade and financial support. In contrast, this crisis originated in the most advanced economy, the United States, and hit at the very core of the global financial system. With virtually no buffers to fall back on, the crisis rapidly engulfed the whole world. Much to their dismay, emerging market economies too were soon pulled into the whirlpool.

According to Rakesh Mohan, current global financial crisis has again shown that markets can fail and such market failures have huge costs. The financial system is prone to excesses, given the high leverage of banks and other financial institutions. Within the financial system, banks are 'special', whether locally or foreign-owned, because they effectively act as trustees of public funds through their deposit taking activities and are the lynchpins of the payment systems. The speed with which a bank under a run collapses is incomparable with any other organisation. A failure of one bank can have a strong contagion on the rest of the banks, even if they are healthy. In this age of globalisation, as the current crisis has revealed, the lack of confidence in banks in one country can also have a contagion on banks in the rest of the world.

The notion that markets will take care of weaknesses has once again been proven wrong. So far, the focus of banking regulation globally has been on capital adequacy. As this crisis has shown, liquidity issues are equally important and it is appropriate to note that, in India, we have focused our attention on these issues as well. Given the complex inter-linkages between banks and non-banks and the move towards conglomerates, it is important that regulatory arbitrage loopholes are fixed to avoid regulatory arbitrage. It is in this context that we have tightened the regulatory regime in regard to NBFCs over the past few years in a phased manner. It is, therefore, important that banks and other financial sector players are well-regulated, while permitting them the necessary flexibility to grow and expand and meet the financing needs of a growing economy. A host of other issues such as accounting, auditing and compensation have also received attention in the aftermath of the global financial crisis. All these issues are engaging the active attention of policy makers and academia alike around the world. In view of the fast pace of technological and financial innovations, regulatory authorities would have to follow an approach that would have to be dynamic and adjust in response to the changing economic environment.

III

Section III highlights some of the sectoral issues relating to agriculture, manufacturing, financial sector and the external sector.

Agricultural Transformation

V.S. Vyas (chapter 25) identifies some of the developments which have made profound impact on rural economy in our country, the strength they have imparted and distortions they have led to, and finally suggests the critical areas that need to be focused. Among several important forces of change, Vyas has focused on four major developments that are shaping the contemporary rural economy and society *viz*., (i) increased connectivity, (ii) spread of formal education, (iii) plethora of government programmes with large funds and numerous functionaries, and (iv) emergence of *panchayats* as powerful political institutions.

Agri-transformation that occurred during 2004-05 to 2011-12 was certainly the most remarkable change that happened since the beginning of economic reforms in 1991, and perhaps even one of the best spells for agriculture since Independence, demonstrate Ashok Gulati and Surbhi Jain (chapter 26).

The big-bang 51 per cent rise in agri-GDP per worker was presumably propelled by an even more impressive increase of 71.5 per cent in net fixed capital stock per worker in agriculture raising per worker productivity and agri-incomes with its salutary impact on rural poverty ratio, which decreased almost three times faster during 2004-05 to 2011-12 as compared to that during 1993-94 to 2004-05. Gulati and Jain try to decipher how it happened. "While the fastest increase in per worker agri-GDP and the fastest accumulation of capital in agriculture and most dramatic fall in rural poverty during 2004-2011 all go unnoticed, food inflation at double digits for the last five years seems to be taking a political toll."

Industry/Manufacturing

While agricultural sector performed well, the manufacturing sector has been a cause of concern. As Chandrasekhar and Jayati Ghosh (chapter 27) point out: "the industrial slowdown is now accepted as fact by most policymakers and observers of the Indian economy." After reaching a peak in March 2008, the index of industrial production fell quite sharply thereafter, and subsequently has been more or less flat at the lower level. This pattern essentially reflects behaviour of the manufacturing index, which accounts for around 80 per cent of the weight of the general index. The deceleration trend started even before outbreak of the global financial crisis. Thus, global crisis could not be a factor for the slow down.

The deceleration of industry, according to the authors, may have resulted from the inability of the government to ensure macro-management of the economy in a complex global situation.

The manufacturing slow down is still continuing. Raghuram Rajan in fifth *Bi-monthly Policy Statement 2014-15* has stated that despite uptick in September, the growth of industrial production slumped to 1.1 per cent in Q2. The persistent contraction in the production of both capital goods and consumer goods in Q2 reflected weak aggregate domestic demand.

While industrial growth has been slowing down, there has been boom in FDI (foreign direct investment) from India. According to R. Nagaraj (chapter 28), there are domestic reasons and international factors propelling outward flows. Industry-specific factors have also contributed to the trend. In an increasingly open world economy, large and efficient firms in India would want to expand overseas to secure external markets so as to extend their intangible assets like brand names into newer territories. For example, Asian Paints has emerged as the world's 10th largest producer operating in 24 countries. Nagaraj has also discussed the policy implications of growing outward investment from India.

Financial sector policies for promoting growth and stability in Indian economy, as is well known, are going through challenging times. Our industrial sector is no longer an infant that needs to be protected. While we should not enter into free-trade agreements that give foreign manufacturers an undue advantage, that is no reason for us to now respond by giving domestic manufacturers protection.

What is needed is developing a facilitating, though competitive, environment that will result in the emergence of the best solutions, says Raghuram Rajan (chapter 29). Rajan also discusses the five pillars over which RBI's developmental measures will be built *viz.*, (i) clarifying and strengthening the monetary policy framework; (ii) strengthening banking structure through new entry, branch expansion, encouraging new varieties of banks and moving foreign banks into better regulated organisational forms; (iii) broadening and deepening financial markets and increasing their liquidity and resilience so that they can help allocate and absorb the risks entailed in financing India's growth; (iv) expanding access to finance to small and medium enterprises, the unorganised sector, the poor, and remote and underserved areas of the country through technology, new business practices and new organisational structures, that is, we need financial inclusion and (v) improving the system's ability to deal with corporate distress and financial institution distress.

P. Chidambaram discusses the issue of capital account management and macro-prudential regulation for financial stability and growth (chapter 30). In India, we have experienced many systemic crises in finance—stock market scandal of 1992 extending to bond market as well. The Financial Sector Legislation Reforms Commission reviewed the scene and concluded:

> There are over 60 Acts and multiple rules and regulations that govern the financial sector. Many of the financial sector laws date back several decades when the financial landscape was very different from that seen today. For example, the Reserve Bank of India (RBI) Act and the Insurance Act are of 1934 and 1938 vintage respectively. Financial economic governance has been modified in a piecemeal fashion from time to time without substantial changes to the underlying foundations. Over the years, as the economy and the financial system have grown in size and sophistication, an increasing gap has come about between the requirements of the country and the present legal and regulatory arrangements.

The last three chapters look into issues relating to India's external sector. Former Prime Minister Manmohan Singh has discussed the sharp and sudden depreciation of the rupee, the causes, the effects and the steps taken by the government (chapter 31).

For understanding what happened to the rupee between May and October, what helped, what hindered, and the evolution of the rupee, Arvind Subramanian (chapter 32) has listed four hypotheses:

(i) Raghuram Rajan turned the rupee around.
(ii) External events, not domestic actions, played the decisive role.
(iii) Conventional defence of the rupee through monetary tightening failed.

(iv) Unconventional defence by lending foreign exchange to the public sector oil companies worked.

Why it worked in India as against international experience where it was ineffective or counterproductive was because the parties receiving the dollars—public sector entities—were liable to moral suasion by the government. Effectively, the RBI had become an import financing company, helping to pay for public sector imports with its foreign exchange reserves. Thus an India-centred perspective on the recent rupee crisis, according to Subramanian, offers two strong lessons. One, half-hearted and partial policy tightening in defence of the rupee was an unmitigated failure. Second, a very peculiar Indian case of sterilised intervention—which failed in other crises and is generally proscribed—actually worked.

The last chapter by Rangarajan analyses recent improvement and sustainability of the CAD. India's BoP has shown several interesting twists and turns in the last few years. In 2010-11, the CAD rose sharply from 2.8 per cent of GDP to 4.2 per cent in 2012-13. After reaching 4.8 per cent of GDP in the first quarter of 2013-14, it came down sharply and is estimated at 2.0 per cent of GDP. In this context, three important questions arise: (i) Is the improvement that has been seen in the last two quarters sustainable? (ii) In the light of our recent experience, what is the sustainable level of CAD? and (iii) What role does the exchange rate play in such a situation? Rangarajan has tried to provide an answer to these questions (chapter 33).

Summing Up

A recent OECD report[6] (November 2014) in its assessment of Indian economy has remarked, "India experienced strong inclusive growth between 2003 and 2011 with average growth rate about 8 per cent and the incidence of poverty cut down to a half." This according to the report reflected gains from past structural reforms, strong capital inflows up to 2007 and expansionary fiscal and monetary policies since 2009. However, these growth engines faltered in 2012. Stubbornly high inflation as well as large current and fiscal deficits

6. OECD (2014). *OECD Economic Surveys India*. New Delhi: Academic Foundation. November.

left little room for monetary and fiscal stimulus to revive growth. In 2014, however, the economy has shown signs of a turnaround.

Fiscal consolidation at the central government level has been accompanied by a decline in both inflation and the CAD. The ongoing reforms in the monetary policy framework, with more weight given to inflation has further boosted the confidence. Exports have revived. Reducing macroeconomic imbalances further is key to sustaining consumer and investor confidence and to containing external vulnerabilities. Addressing structural bottlenecks—in particular gaps in energy and transport infrastructure, overly stringent labour regulations, the shortage of skills, and market and institutional failures that keep women outside the labour force—will promote job creation and inclusive growth.

We have to make India a global manufacturing hub. Manufacturing should be the next big wave for us. We need to move the share of manufacturing in GDP from 15 per cent to 25 per cent. The growth of the manufacturing sector could contribute more to income, export and employment. In recent years, structural bottlenecks have affected the manufacturing sector more than the services. Labour and tax regulations are complex and raise cost of doing business above a certain size. Manufacturing firms, therefore, tend to be small and their productivity is low. The broad areas that we need to address are regulatory hurdles, infrastructure bottlenecks and developing talent. Creating more and better employment for women has a high growth potential.

Finally, there is need to improve health outcomes for all. The low level of public resources invested in health, the lack of health care professionals, poor regulation of health, services, inequality in access to health care are serious issues, in particular for the poor and those living in rural and urban slums. There is urgent need to increase public spending on health care with particular focus on prevention and primary care, especially in rural areas and urban slums. As rightly remarked by Nirvikar Singh in a recent paper,[7] "Perhaps the most

7. Singh, Nirvikar (2014). "India's Opportunities for Growth", *The Financial Express*, November, 13. New Delhi.

obvious place where the government needs to give its attention is in giving its citizens the initial conditions—basic health and education. There is a clear way forward for India—one that impliments the slogan of "minimum government, maximum governance".

Goldman Sachs has painted a bright future for the Indian economy. Indian economy is beginning a new growth cycle driven by reduced macro imbalances, benign global conditions (lower commodity prices) and structural reforms. Structural reforms and focus on reviving the economy is expected to boost India's GDP growth to 6.3 per cent in calender 2015 and 6.8 per cent in calender 2016. In contrast, it expects China to grow by 7 per cent in 2015 and 6.7 per cent in 2016. While India's growth is expected to accelerate in the coming years, China would witness a gradual slowdown in growth making India the fastest growing emerging market. Howerver, the biggest risk will came from the tardy implementation of reforms.

—Editors

1

M.H. BALA SUBRAHMANYA

Why Does India's Economic Growth Process Falter?

Introduction

Indian economy is currently undergoing difficult economic times. The much fanfare with which we embraced economic liberalisation and pursued it since 1991, which led to an acceleration of economic growth and attracted the global attention, is fading over. The much hyped higher economic (gross domestic product; GDP) growth did not translate into any kind of comfort on the trade front and India continued to be a perennial trade deficit economy even after 1991 (Ministry of Finance, 2013). Of course, the 'software earnings' did give us some comfort in some years, as we could earn surplus on the invisibles front but not good enough to generate surplus on the current account front (Ibid.). However, of late, both trade balance and current account balance are deteriorating, rather alarmingly. As a direct consequence of these, our currency has been depreciating against major international currencies led by the US dollar [Reserve Bank of India (RBI), 2013]. This poses a relevant question to Indian policy makers: where did we go wrong? What needs to be done to overcome the current economic situation?

The core objective of India's economic reforms introduced in 1991 and implemented since then gradually and consistently has been to enable Indian economy (in general and industry in particular) achieve international competitiveness (Ministry of Industry, 1991). The removal of industrial licensing, opening up of vast reserved areas for both domestic and foreign private investments, removal of restrictions on foreign direct investment (FDI) and foreign technology imports, disinvestment of public sector undertakings (PSUs), etc., are all part of the economic history now. Industrial liberalisation followed by trade liberalisation, and fine tuning of monetary and fiscal policies to suit the objectives of overall economic reforms have been undertaken. In the process, domestic private investment, and particularly, FDI inflows have grown dramatically, economic growth has picked up, and there were all-round cheers for Indian policy makers, particularly from abroad [Forbes, 2003; Ministry of Finance, 2013; Department of Industrial Policy & Promotion (DIPP) website, 2013]. Then why did not these achievements help us on the external front?

This article attempts to provide an answer to this question in a broader perspective.

Historical Path of Economic Development

At the outset, it is relevant to describe briefly what may be called an 'appropriate economic development path' for a developing economy, which was experienced by the developed countries, newly industrialised economies (NIEs), China and Malaysia (culled out from various sources). By and large, the developing economies are dominated by agriculture, supplemented by unorganised industrial and service sectors in terms of GDP composition. The occupational structure of the labour force (employment composition) would reveal that unorganised sector is predominant with a marginal presence of the organised sector. On the external front, such economies will be experiencing trade deficit and exports would comprise largely agro and processed products, supplemented by light manufactured goods. There will be hardly any presence of heavy manufactured goods in the export basket, for obvious reasons.

However when economic growth takes place, in which 'industrialisation' will spearhead the whole process, agricultural development takes place, thanks to industrial development, followed by service sector development. Industrial development will be characterised by a structural shift in the compositions of manufacturing value added (MVA) and industrial employment. The growth of industry will give a fillip to the growth of organised sector in the entire economy. Organised sector employment growth will outweigh that of unorganised sector employment. In the organised industry, the share of consumer goods industry will steadily decline duly compensated by a steady increase in the shares of capital goods, basic goods and intermediate goods industries. The economic transformation facilitated by industrial development leads to a transformation of 'export basket' as well where the relative shares of agro and processed goods will fall duly compensated by the increase in the shares of manufactured goods, initially light manufactured goods but later heavy manufactured goods. The countries which have pursued this path of economic development have achieved economic prosperity and such economies experience continuous trade surpluses, current account surpluses, and have strong and stable currencies (such as NIEs, China and Malaysia).

India's Initial Economic Objectives after Independence and Achievements

Indian economic policy makers had precisely intended to pursue this path of development, since Independence when they launched the Industrial Policy Resolution of 1948 and then the Industrial Policy Resolution of 1956, followed by a series of industrial controls and regulations, supplemented by five-year economic plans. In the process, we could develop agriculture in certain pockets, if not across the country. Organised industrial development progressed with a shift from consumer goods to capital goods, intermediate goods and basic goods industries, which also led to the development of organised service sector. The share of consumer goods industries in MVA decreased from about 49 per cent in 1960-61 to about 27 per cent by 1991, whereas the share of capital goods industries in MVA increased from about 12 per cent to almost 22 per cent during the same period (Bala Subrahmanya, 2009). The composition of GDP changed: agriculture which accounted for almost 54 per cent of the GDP in 1950-51 contributed 33 per cent in 1990-91, whereas contribution of industry to GDP increased from 14.35 per cent to 24.15 per cent during the same period, the rest emerging from the service sector (Ministry of Finance, 1998). Organised sector employment grew from 206.35 lakh in 1977 to 267.33 lakh in 1991, at an annual average growth rate of about 1.9 per cent (Ministry of Finance, 1992; 1998). But the organised sector employed only about 8 per cent of the total workforce in 1991. The export basket shifted from agro and processed goods towards manufactured goods, particularly the light manufactured goods. The agro and allied products which accounted for about 44 per cent of the total exports in 1960-61, contributed 19.40 per cent in 1990-91. The contribution of manufactured products which was about 45 per cent in 1960-61 increased to more than 79 per cent in 1990-91 (Ministry of Finance, 1998). Of course, manufactured exports primarily comprised light manufactured goods. However, the overall progress and shift from the early 1950s to the late 1980s were on the desired path of economic development.

Economic Reforms since 1991 and the Outcomes

The launching of broad-based economic reforms in 1991 has set the objective of facilitating Indian economy (in general and industry in particular) achieve international competitiveness. In the process, several key policy reforms were introduced to enable the integration of Indian economy with the global economy at large. The expectations were high. Freer trade and freer investment laws were expected to accelerate the achievement of desired path of economic development. How far have we come on the path of economic development today since 1991? The statistical figures are dismal and disappointing. The organised sector employment increased from 267.33 lakh in 1991 to 289.99 lakh in 2011 at the rate of 0.41 per annum. During the same period, public sector employment declined absolutely from 190.57 lakh to 175.48 lakh. Given the 'much sought-after' 'opening up' and 'gradual withdrawal' of public sector from the various economic and industrial spheres of the country (as part of the economic liberalisation process), this development may be natural and therefore justifiable. However, the growth of organised private sector employment (from 76.77 lakh in 1991 to 114.22 lakh in 2011 at the rate of 2% per annum) cannot be considered significant. The organised sector which employed about 8 per cent of the total workforce in 1991 employed less than 7 per cent of the total workforce in 2011. This brings out clearly that the larger chunk of the growing workforce has been absorbed by the unorganised sector and the growth of organised sector has miserably failed to make any 'dent' on the unorganised sector of our country. The composition of GDP changed: agriculture contribution declined further from 33 per cent in 1990-91 to 16.17 per cent in 2011-12 but the industrial contribution hardly improved (from 24.15% to 25.45% during the same period) implying that the declined contribution of agriculture has been duly compensated by the growth of service sector (Ministry of Finance, 2013).

What is more alarming has been the change that occurred in the composition of MVA as well as the export basket, which are not along the desired path of economic development observed earlier. Within the industrial sector, the relative share of consumer goods industries is growing with a dominant share emerging from non-durable consumer goods industries, and the base of 'much-needed' capital goods industries is shrinking. The share of consumer goods industries in MVA increased from about 27 per cent in 1991 to about 32 per cent in 2007, whereas the corresponding share of capital goods industries declined from about 22 per cent to about 19 per cent during the same period (Singh, 2013). The disturbing change in the structure of MVA is also reflected in the changing weights of sectors in the use-based classification of Indian industry (Ministry of Statistics and Programme Implementation website, 2013). Similarly, the much needed export basket diversification has not taken place at all. The share of agro and allied products increased from 19.40 per cent in 1990-91 to about 24.00 per cent in 1996-97 but declined to about 15 per cent in 2011-12. On the other hand, the share of manufactured goods in total exports declined from 79 per cent in 1990-91 to about 74 per cent in 1996-97 and further to about 61 per cent in 2011-12 (Ministry of Finance, 2013). In the meantime, the share of petroleum products which was nil in 1990-91 increased from <1.5 per cent in 1996-97 to >18.0 per cent in 2011-12. These are not domestic petroleum products rather they are imported crude but refined in India and then exported. The imported crude (for refining and exporting later) would have steadily accounted for an increasing share of the total petroleum products (petroleum, oil and lubricants; POL) imports in 2011-12. This is crudely reflected in the fact that the export value of petroleum products as a percentage of the total POL import bill increased from hardly 5 per cent in 1996-97 to almost 36 per cent in 2011-12 (Ibid.). Therefore, the entire increase in the POL import bill (since the mid-1990s) cannot be solely attributed to increased domestic consumption of petro products.

Overall, the kind of shift in the export basket experienced by other industrialising countries such as China, Malaysia and even Thailand from light manufactured goods to heavy manufactured goods did not take place in India at all. Domestic private sector has played a major role in those economies. To prove the point further, India, China and Malaysia were in the list of top 25 exporters of 'low-tech products' or 'resource-based exports' in 1985. Malaysia was also one of the top 25 'high-tech products' exporters. By 1998, China could enter the list of top 25 exporters of not only 'medium-tech products' but more importantly high-tech products and Malaysia could improve its rank in the list of top 25 high-tech products exporters from 19 to 10, whereas India could only improve its rank in the list of top 25 exporters of low-tech products (from 22 to 19) but could not enter even the list of top 25 medium-tech products leaving alone that of 'high-tech products' [United Nations Industrial Development Organization (UNIDO), 2003]. This is because, in India high-tech exports (comprising aerospace, computers, pharmaceuticals, scientific instruments and electrical machinery) accounted for hardly 4 per cent of the total manufactured exports in 1988 and 6 per cent in 2002, reached a maximum of about 9 per cent in 2009 but declined subsequently to about 7 per cent in 2010. In contrast, in China and Malaysia, high-tech exports accounted for 28 per cent and 45 per cent respectively of the total manufactured exports in 2010 (as against 24% and 58% respectively in 2002 and 26% and 40% respectively in 2008) (World Bank, 2013).

The above macroeconomic indicators bring out that India's economic growth experience since 1991 defies established economic growth theories, to the disadvantage of the country as a whole.

Why? The reasons for this development are not far to seek. The space vacated by the public sector (which spearheaded the role of transforming Indian economy on the desired path of economic development till 1991) was expected to be filled up more than adequately by the organised private sector (domestic and foreign) when we launched the broad-based economic reforms in 1991. The New Industrial Policy announced in July 1991 claimed, among others, that "Indian private entrepreneurship has come of age" (Ministry of Industry, 1991). They were anticipated to give a fillip to the industrial growth of the country and thereby transform the economy at an accelerated pace (than what was experienced during 1951-1991). However, that did not happen. This can be attributed to two factors: (a) FDI and multinational corporations (MNCs) have entered the service sector much more than the industrial sector, thanks to the favourable climate in the country for knowledge-intensive industries, housing and real estate, consultancy, and financial services (DIPP website, 2013), and (b) domestic private sector too entered the service sector covering wholesale and retail trade, communications and personal services, among others. This is also reflected in the fact that organised private sector employment grew by a meager 0.93 per cent per annum in the manufacturing sector during 1991-2011, whereas it grew by 4.15 per cent per annum in the service sector during the same period (Ministry of Finance, 2013).

The Real Challenge

The much desired 'opening up' of the economy (which was hailed by the international institutions, the foreign media and the domestic industrial houses alike) did not trigger/accelerate the inflow of investments into the industrial sector (particularly capital goods industries) to generate more industrial employment, higher MVA and thereby contributing to the much needed shift in the export basket from light manufactured to heavy manufactured goods. The formation of the National Manufacturing Competitiveness Council (NMCC) (set up in 2004) has hardly made an impact and the 'National Strategy for Manufacturing' (NMCC, 2006) has hardly taken off. The

National Manufacturing Policy of 2011 and the proposed national investment and manufacturing zones (NIMZs) are at their infancy.

Given this, what needs to be done is the next relevant question. The real challenge to our economy now is threefold:

- How to build-up the 'diluting' capital-goods industry base?
- How to develop and acquire indigenous technology base?
- How to transform the 'export basket' to comprise a growing share of high-tech products, similar to some of the industrialising south-east Asian countries (like Thailand), if not NIEs and China?

It is neither feasible nor desirable to reverse the ongoing trends of economic reforms by bringing the public sector to the centre stage. Therefore, the solution has to be found within the domain of private sector and private entrepreneurship, domestic and foreign both. But MNCs are more eager to deepen their presence in the ever-growing service sector where their superior technology, supply chain efficiency and managerial skills will generate more assured and sustainable profits. It is doubtful whether we can influence FDI inflow towards capital goods industries and make them contribute to the generation of high-tech exports. The other option is domestic private sector. But large domestic industrial houses (which have the financial muscle) too find more comfort in deepening their presence in the service sector to enjoy the relatively risk-free 'trade profits' rather than enter into risk-prone capital-intensive industries which would call for an increasing rate of R&D (research & development) investments.

Perhaps it is here that our 'policy making' has not produced desired results. We have not been able to decisively influence the flow of domestic and foreign private investments towards the desired direction to make an impact on the technology-front of the global economy. It is an irony that foreign investors (backed by/through international institutions and foreign media) demand more and more (favourable?) economic reforms (in the form of further 'opening-up' of the service sector) when they have not produced outcomes desirable to Indian economy through their participation in the already opened-up sectors (particularly manufacturing), and domestic captains of industry are not falling far behind. Acquisitions and takeovers abroad apart, it causes concern that none of our private large industrial houses could make a mark globally with any in-house developed high-tech product in the last two plus decades.

What Needs to be Done?

It is high time the captains of Indian private industry take the responsibility for driving the industrial growth of the country towards maturity with a renewed growth of capital goods industries to ensure that industry in particular acquires its own technological competence. The apex Chambers of Industry should take the lead in the interests of both industry growth and national economic growth. This should result in the tilting of country's export basket towards medium-tech and subsequently high-tech products and in turn favourably balancing the trade and current accounts to off-set the ever-growing import bill and strengthen Indian currency. (In this context, it is important to emphasise here that fiscal incentives and monetary policy actions will only provide short-term reliefs but not long-term solutions.)

To conclude, it is imperative for Indian economy to strive and achieve structural transformation of (manufacturing) industry by building up the capital goods industry base and acquire technological competence leading to the growing share of high-tech goods in the composition of total exports. This can be the most sustainable way in the long run to achieve trade surplus and thereby current account surplus. This alone will lend strength and stability to our currency in the international market. Unless and until we achieve this, our economy will continue to experience trade deficit perennially leading to current account deficit (CAD) and remain vulnerable resulting in even 'minor external vibrations' turning into 'shocks' more often than what we can afford.

References

Bala Subrahmanya, M.H. (2009). *Industrial Policy and Management*. Working Professionals Learning Project. Bangalore: Indian Society of Technical Education.

DIPP website (2013). *http://dipp.nic.in/English/Publications/FDI_Statistics/FDI_Statistics.aspx*

Forbes, N. (2003). "Doing Business in India: What has Liberalisation Changed?", in A.O. Krueger (ed.) (2003), *Economic Policy Reforms and the Indian Economy*. New Delhi: Oxford University Press, pp.129-67.

Ministry of Finance (1992). *Economic Survey 1991/92*, Part II. New Delhi: Government of India.

———. (1998). *Economic Survey 1997/98*. New Delhi: Government of India.

———. (2013). *Economic Survey 2012/13*. New Delhi: Government of India and Oxford University Press.

Ministry of Industry (1991). *Statement of Industrial Policy*. New Delhi: Government of India. July 24.

Ministry of Statistics and Programme Implementation website (2013). *http://mospi.nic.in/Mospi_New/upload/iip/IIP_main.htm?status=1&menu_id=89*

NMCC (2006). *National Strategy for Manufacturing*. New Delhi: National Manufacturing Competitiveness Council, Government of India.

NMCC website (2013). *http://www.nmcc.nic.in/Nmcc_background.aspx*

RBI (2013). *Macroeconomic and Monetary Developments: First Quarter Review 2013/14*. Mumbai: July 29.

Singh, A. (2013). *Structural Change in the Growth of Indian Industries (1991-2007): A Use Based Classification Approach*. Project Report. Bangalore: Department of Management Studies, Indian Institute of Science.

UNIDO (2003). *Industrial Development Report 2002/2003, Competing through Innovation and Learning* Vienna: United Nations Industrial Development Organisation.

World Bank (2013). *High-technology Exports (% of Manufactured Exports). http://data.worldbank.org/indicator/TX.VAL.TECH.CD*

Economic and Political Weekly, February 2014.

Economic Developments in India, Vol. 197.

2

C. RANGARAJAN

Two Issues in India's Growth Story

THIS article discusses two issues in relation to India's growth performance. One is on the determination of the potential rate of growth of the Indian economy and the other on the estimation of the threshold level of inflation, the level of inflation beyond which growth turns negative.

Potential Rate

The Indian economy is currently passing through a phase of relatively slow growth. However, this should not cloud the fact that over the eight-year period beginning in 2005-06, the average annual growth rate has been 8 per cent. Against this background, a frequently asked question is whether India has the potential to grow at a sustained growth rate of 8-9 per cent potential rate.

Normally, potential growth is measured using trends and filters like the Hodrick-Prescott (H-P). In one sense, these are backward looking measures, since they depend on historically observed data. In the case of measuring capacity utilisation, the maximum capacity is very often taken as the maximum output achieved in the recent period. In any case, in the case of determining the potential rate of growth of the economy, one can take the maximum growth rate achieved in the recent past as the lowest estimate of the potential. This assumption can be made if there is reason to believe that the maximum growth rate achieved in the recent past was not an one-off event and the growth rate achieved was robust. India achieved a growth rate of 9.5 per cent in 2005-06 followed by 9.6 per cent and 9.3 per cent in the subsequent two years. After declining a bit in the wake of international financial crisis, growth rate went back to 9.3 per cent in 2010-11. In many ways, the growth rate achieved in the high phase period of 2005-06 to 2007-08 was robust. The domestic savings rate during this period averaged 33.4 per cent of GDP (gross domestic product). Similarly, the gross capital formation rate averaged 34.2 per cent. The current account deficit (CAD) remained low with an average of 1.1 per cent of GDP. Agricultural growth during this period averaged 5.0 per cent and the annual manufacturing growth rate was 11.5 per cent. The capital flows were large but as CAD remained very low, the accretion to reserves amounted to $144 billion. Thus on many dimensions, the growth rate was robust. It was not just fuelled by financial availability. Certainly, the external environment provided good support. This was the period during which the world economy was also booming.

The growth rate slowed to 6.2 per cent in 2011-12, even though the rate may be revised upwards. It came down to 5 per cent last year and this year it is expected to be around the same level. The savings and investment rates have come down significantly from the peak reached in 2007-08, partly due to economic and partly because of non-economic factors such as perception towards governance and policy framework. Nevertheless, recent data indicate that in 2011-12, the gross fixed capital formation rate, a measure of the accumulation of fixed assets by business, government and households, was around 30.6 per cent as against 32.9 per cent of GDP in 2007-08 (Table 2.1). In normal conditions, keeping in view the recent trends in the ICOR (incremental capital-output ratio) which is around 4, this should have given us a growth rate of 7.0-7.5 per cent, but the actual rate turned out to be 6.0 per cent. Economic growth has in fact declined much more steeply than what is warranted by the decline in investment. This maybe because projects have not been completed in time or complementary investments have not been forthcoming.

In some cases, this could also be due to non-availability of critical inputs such as coal and power. The fact that even today, savings and investment rates are at high levels re-assures us that if we are able to find ways to complete projects speedily, we shall be able to usher in rapid growth in income even in the short run. It is, however, to be noted that while the decline in overall gross fixed capital formation rate from the peak reached in 2007-08 was only 2.2 per cent, the decline in the case of private corporate sector was as high as 4.6 per cent. Thus the composition of investment has also played a role in the reduction in productivity of capital. Nevertheless, while the existing level of investment rate should enable us to grow at 7.5 per cent in the short run, a return to higher level of savings and investment can take us back to the very high levels of growth which we had seen earlier.

Table 2.1

Savings and Investment Rates

(As a proportion of GDP)

	2007-08	*2011-12*	*Change over the Period*
Gross domestic savings rate	36.8	30.8	(-) 6.0
Households	22.4	22.3	(-) 0.1
Financial assets	(11.6)	(8.0)	(-) 3.6
Private corporate	9.4	7.2	(-) 2.2
Public sector	5.0	1.3	(-) 3.7
Gross Capital Formation	38.0	35.4	(-) 2.6
Public sector	8.9	7.9	(-) 1.0
Private corporate	17.3	10.6	(-) 6.7
Households	10.8	14.3	(+) 3.5
Valuables	1.1	2.7	(+) 1.6
Gross Fixed Capital Formation	32.9	30.6	2.3
Public sector	8.0	7.4	(-) 0.6
Private corporate	14.3	9.7	(-) 4.6
Households	10.6	13.6	(+) 3.0

To assess whether we will be able to get back to the high savings and investment rates of the previous period, we need to look a little more closely at some of the macroeconomic parameters during the low growth phase. The gross domestic savings rate fell by 6 percentage points between 2007-08 and 2011-12. However, the decline in the investment rate was less. It fell from 38.1 per cent in 2008-09 to 35 per cent in 2011-12 which is a decline of 3 percentage points. The lower decline in the investment rate is accounted for by the fact that the CAD rose from 2 per cent of GDP in 2007-08 to 4.2 per cent in 2011-12. Looking at the domestic savings rate of the decline of 6 percentage points, more than half was contributed by the decline in public sector savings. During this period, the fiscal deficit rose sharply. Within household savings, there was a sharp decline in the ratio of savings in financial assets to GDP by 3.6 percentage points, mostly due to high inflation. Going ahead, we should build in only a more modest CAD of about 2.5 per cent of GDP. Several studies have shown that this is the only sustainable level of CAD taking into account the normal capital flows. In fact, even a somewhat lower level of CAD will be desirable. Thus to get back to anything like 8.5 per cent growth rate, there has to be some pick up in the domestic savings rate from the current level. For this to happen, what is needed is fiscal consolidation. Thus with a modest CAD of 2.5 per cent of GDP and a savings rate of 32 per cent of GDP, one can expect the Indian economy to grow at 8.5 per cent. Thus to sustain a long-term growth rate of 8.5 per cent, three things need to happen: (a) CAD must be lowered, (b) the domestic savings rate must pick up with much of it coming from fiscal consolidation and (c) the productivity of capital should improve so that incremental capital output ratio is maintained around 4:1. Given the performance of the Indian economy in the recent past, these are not impossible tasks. But this will require focused efforts on all the three fronts. Besides, we need to keep a watch on inflation which also has a bearing on the potential rate of growth when it exceeds a threshold level.

Threshold Level of Inflation

During the last three years, not only growth has slowed down but inflation has been on the rise. Inflation as measured by the wholesale price index (WPI) stood at 10.9 per cent in April 2010, 9.7 per cent in April 2011 and 7.5 per cent in April 2012. As of April 2013, it came down to 4.8 per cent. However, there has been a pick up in inflation since then. As of November, it came to 7.5 per cent. It is, in this context, a question that has been raised as to the acceptable or threshold level of inflation. The threshold level of inflation is that level of inflation beyond which inflation has a decisive negative impact on growth.

A case for low and stable inflation has been persuasively made in the literature. The volatility of prices creates uncertainties in decision making. Rising prices adversely affect savings while they make speculative investments more attractive. Apart these, there is a crucial social dimension particularly in developing economies. High inflation adversely affects those who have no hedge against it and that includes all the poorer sections of the community. This is indeed a very strong argument in favour of maintenance of low inflation and price stability in emerging economies.

Empirical evidence on the relationship between growth and inflation in a cross-country framework is somewhat inconclusive because such studies include countries with an inflation rate as low as 1-2 per cent to those with inflation rate going beyond 200-300 per cent. These studies, however, clearly establish that growth rates become increasingly weaker at higher rates of inflation. However, in recent years, studies have been done to test the inflation-growth trade-off by using each country's time series data. There are two methods which are adopted. The first one is to regress the annual GDP growth on fundamental factors such as investment, coupled with inflation and square of inflation. The estimated equation is applied for different levels of inflation to find out inflection point or threshold beyond which inflation has negative impact on GDP. The alternative method uses, apart from fundamental factors such as investment, two variables related to inflation. One variable is the level of inflation and the other a dummy variable which takes on the value of 0 or 1 for different levels of inflation. Threshold level is that level of inflation which minimises the residual sum of squares of the regression equation. At that level, inflation has a significant negative impact on growth. Using the observations for the period 1982-2009, under the first method of estimation, the point of inflection occurs at 6.3 per cent. Under the second method also, the threshold level of inflation seems to fall between 6 and 7 per cent (see Annexure A-2.1). However, when it comes to the acceptable level of inflation for policy guidance, we need to work with a lower level of inflation for two reasons. First, the estimate of trade-off does not take into account the distributional implications of inflation. Second, this level of inflation is way above what other countries have treated as acceptable level of inflation. This will have implications for the exchange rate. While open economy helps to overcome domestic supply shocks, it also imposes the burden to keep the inflation rate in alignment with other countries.

Annexure A-2.1

*Estimating the Threshold Level of Inflation**

To estimate the non-linear relationship between inflation and growth, two methods have been adopted.**

Method 1

Here we used a model in which the inflation itself captures the non-linearity. The annual GDP growth is regressed on inflation, square of inflation and growth in gross domestic capital formation (GDCF).

$GDP\ growth = c+\beta_1 Inflation+\beta_2 Inflation+\beta_3 GDCF\ growth_t+\varepsilon_t.$

The estimated equation is applied for different levels of inflation to find out the inflection point, or threshold, beyond which inflation has a negative impact on GDP growth.

Using the data for the period 1982-2009, the following equation was estimated:

$$GDP\ growth_t = -2.29 + 1.90{*}Inflation_t - 0.150{*}Inflation^2_t + 0.30{*}GDCF\ growth_t+\varepsilon_t$$

SE	(3.2)	(0.86)	(0.06)	(0.03)
t-Value	(-0.73)	(2.2)	(-2.5)	(9.6)
R0Square	0.89			

* denotes significant at 5%

* I am grateful to Shri E.M. Vibeesh for his help in estimating the equations.

** Both the models presented here suffer from one limitation. They do not take into account explicitly the impact of inflation on variables such as exchange rate and income distribution.

Based on the equation, the relationship between growth and inflation in Figure 2.1 is derived.

Figure 2.1

Relationship between Growth and Inflation

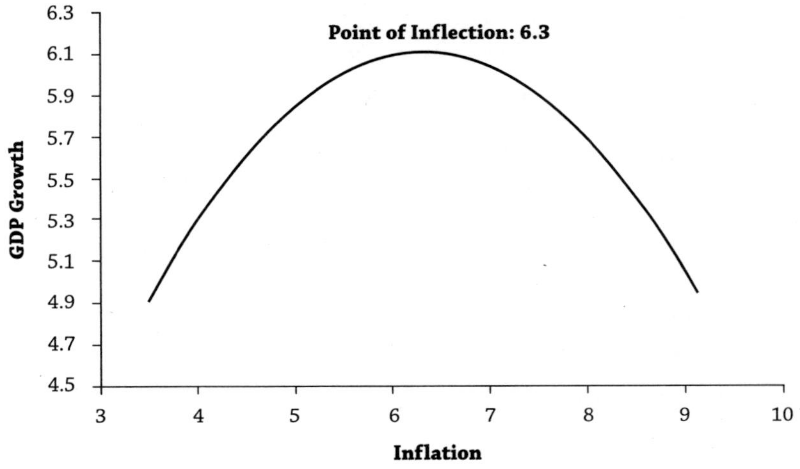

The point of inflection occurs at an inflation of 6.3 per cent.

Method 2

The method developed by Khan and Senhadji (2001) (by using GDP growth as endogenous variable and inflation and growth of GDCF as exogenous variables) is used to estimate the threshold level of inflation.

The equation estimated is of the following form:

$$GDP\ growth_t = c + \beta_1 GGDCF_t + \beta_2 Inflation_t + \beta_3 D_t(k) + \varepsilon_t$$

where $D_t(k)$ is a dummy variable defined as:

$$\left.\begin{array}{l} D_t(k)=1 \\ 0, \text{otherwise} \end{array}\right\} \text{if inflation}_t > k$$

The parameter k helps to determine the threshold inflation level. In the estimated relationship, β_2 captures the impact of the inflation on growth and β_3 explains the impact of inflation exceeding threshold on growth. At the threshold level of inflation, not only both β_2 and β_3

should be statistically significant, but also that β_2 should be positive, β_3 should be negative and sum of two coefficients ($\beta_2+\beta_3$) should be negative and statistically significant. While the value of *k* is given arbitrarily for the estimation, the optimal *k* is obtained by finding that value of *k* that minimises the residual sum of squares (RSS). Thus, the threshold level is that which minimises the RSS. Inflation at this level has a significant negative impact on economic growth.

Estimated equation for the period 1982-2010:

$$GDP\ growth_t = 2.8 + 0.29^{*}GGDCF_t + 0.20^{**}Inflation_t - 1.1^{*}D_t(7\%) + \varepsilon_t$$

SE	(0.86)	(0.03)	(0.12)	(0.27)
t-Value	(3.2)	(10.3)	(1.7)	(-3.9)
R0Square	0.88			

Minimum Residual Sum of Squares: 3.6

Test, $\beta_2+\beta_3 = 0$ Value: -0.87, *p* value: 0.01

*,** denotes significant at 5% and 10% level respectively

The sign of $\beta_2+\beta_3$ becomes negative when *k* crosses 6 per cent and reach the least RSS at optimum when $k = 7.0$ per cent. Therefore, we can conclude that the threshold level of inflation for this period was between 6 per cent and 7 per cent.

References

Khan, Mohsin and A.S. Senhadji (2001). "Threshold Effects in the Relationship between Inflation and Growth", *IMF Staff Papers* 48(1).

Pattaniak, Sitikantha and G.V. Nadhanael (2011). "Why Persistent High Inflation Impedes Growth? An Empirical Assessment of Threshold Level of Inflation for India", *RBI Working Paper Series*, W P S (DEPR) 17/2011.

Extracted from the address at the Golden Jubilee of the Indian Econometric Society held on 22 December 2013, at Mumbai.

Economic Developments in India, Vol. 193.

3

ARVIND VIRMANI

India: Economic Reforms and Growth Transition

SECTION 1

THIS section explores some of the issues that arose with respect to timing and phasing of liberalisation, about which formal economic theory had little to say, but were critical to (socio-political) success and sustainability of economic reforms.

Econometric studies have highlighted the importance of trade liberalisation in, "getting growth going, ...but also with sustaining it—particularly when combined with competitive exchange rates, current account surpluses and an external capital structure weighted toward foreign domestic investment" (Berg *et al.*, 2012). The Indian approach to (import) liberalisation during the 1990s[1] had precisely these goals in mind and the Indian experience confirms the importance of import liberalisation, foreign direct investment (FDI), exchange rate flexibility and a cautious approach to current account deficits (CAD).

The 1990s were marked by a broad array of reforms; the effects of some of which on aggregate growth were much more gradual than those of the more limited reforms during the 1980s.[2] There are a number of reasons for this. First, some of these reforms were dynamic in nature and were not expected to impact growth or total

---

1. As conceptualised by the professionals associated with it, India was perhaps less successful with respect to Berg *et al.*'s last conclusion, "Furthermore we find that export composition matters. The manufacturing share in exports and more generally, export product sophistication tend to predict prolonged growth spells."
2. See appendix of Virmani (2005a) for a comprehensive list of 1980s and 1990s reforms.

factor productivity (TFP) over the short term.[3] Such reforms may result in an increase in efficiency and/or equity leading to welfare improvements, but any growth impacts are likely to occur with a long and variable lag. The 1990s tax reforms (primarily income tax) were of this nature and were expected to lead to a sustainable increase in revenues.[4] Similarly financial reforms have improved the allocation of funds within the set of existing borrowers (static efficiency, welfare) and the health and stability of the financial system without endangering the financial system through external contagion effects. They do not, however, seem to have noticeably increased the supply of funds to new entrepreneurs, credit rationed small producers and (direct) investors.[5]

Second a sharp reduction in protection can give rise to a J curve of productivity and growth, an initial negative impact on measured productivity that is gradually exceeded by slowly rising factor productivity. There are several elements in the J curve of productivity and growth following major liberalisation. One, the rebalancing of historically distorted prices, which raise (lower) the relative price (weight) of previously slow (fast) growing sectors. Two, the immediate reduction in capacity utilisation in unprofitable product lines due to capital immobility, till depreciation eliminates the excess capacity ('adjustment costs'). Three, gestation lags in investment in newly profitable product lines and the S curve of technology diffusion that slows productivity improvements. Four, the resources and effort needed to adopt unfamiliar technology that may reduce the productivity of existing technology/capital (Section J Curve: Heuristic Theory).

3. Wacziarg and Welch (2003) show that only 1/5th of the effect of import liberalisation on growth comes through its effect on investment. The rest could be TFP etc. Some of their time patterns also support J curve effects.

4. Interestingly the polices that continued to worsen during the 1980s were also static in nature and therefore did not undermine the positive dynamic effects of decontrol policies.

5. The entry of private banks, both domestic and foreign, has been considerably liberalised, resulting in increased competition in consumer loans. However, the fact that 70 per cent of banking assets are still in public sector banks (>51% of equity) may have constrained competition in innovative lending.

Third, the increase in the pressure to compete has been higher, relative to the increase in access to the means to compete, in the 1990s than in the 1980s (Section Phasing of Liberalisation: Competition Dynamics). The sector liberalisation and its time pattern, and entry of private as against public producers, also affects the evolution of production and productivity, including J curve effects, at the sector level (Sections Timing of Sector Liberalisation and Public-Private Mix). Some of the imbalances may have been minimised if recommended factor market reforms (land, labour, risk capital and debt finance, bankruptcy law) had been implemented (Section Incomplete Reforms: Threat and Opportunity).

J Curve: Heuristic Theory

By definition, import liberalisation and reform changes relative prices from the distorted domestic ratios to world relative prices. Highly protected goods would have relatively higher prices and would grow faster in a distorted economy thus giving them a higher weight in production at the start of reforms. With liberalisation and opening of the economy, their prices and growth rate will fall, temporarily. At the same time the output and growth of previously under-protected goods would rise. Any Laspeyres type quantity indices will understate the (true change in) growth rate. Thus, conventionally measured growth rates may understate the true growth rate during the reform period. A shift in the base year to a post-reform year will raise the post-reform growth rate and reduce the pre-reform one, reflecting the effect of reforms more accurately.

If reforms are slow and gradual, as they were in India during the 1980s, relative prices change gradually and producers adapt by stopping investment in unprofitable product lines and initiating it in newly profitable ones. The former is limited on the negative side by the rate of depreciation and the latter by the pace of incremental technical change. If reforms are dramatic, the transitional effect on production and employment can be significant. In a heavily protected economy, a major import liberalisation can therefore initially slow measured productivity growth and result in its acceleration only after a lag.

Major import liberalisation, of the kind undertaken in India in the 1990s, can lead to a drastic change in product-specific competitive advantage. Because of capital immobility and 'adjustment costs', the capital employed in uncompetitive product lines becomes redundant and capacity utilisation falls. If productivity calculations use capital stock measures based on the accumulation method with no adjustment for capacity utilisation, calculated productivity will decline in these product lines. Although this will be partially offset by better capacity utilisation in lines that have become more competitive, full utilisation of the new potential requires adoption of new technology including investment in new capital goods (producing better quality output). The introduction of completely new (unfamiliar) technology will have short-term negative effects, while the positive productivity effects will take time to emerge, including the time taken to diffuse technology S curve. This results in what may be called the J curve of liberalisation-growth/productivity, by analogy with the J curve of the impact of exchange rate changes on trade. This is one of the reasons why the impact of the 1990s reforms was slow in manifesting itself at the aggregate level. It is also a potential cause of a fall in factor productivity growth slowdown at the sector and industry level.

We know from the innovation literature that incremental change can have a different effect from major ('drastic') inventions. The latter "can trigger an uneven growth trajectory, which starts with a prolonged slowdown followed by a fast acceleration" (Helpman, 2004). There are many possible reasons for this. Hornstein and Krusell (1996) and Greenwood and Yorokolgu (1997) argued that adoption of new technologies requires firms to learn how to use them and this slows down productivity growth. Helpman and Trajtenberg (1998) argued that it takes time and resources to develop complementary inputs, and during this time, the diversion of resources slows down growth. Helpman and Rangel (1999) argued that on-the-job training that raises the productivity of workers also means that technology-specific skills are lost when a new technology replaces an old one. Labour productivity would therefore decline temporarily. All these arguments have been used to explain the decline in productivity growth in the post-oil crises period (Helpman, 2004). The experience of Indian import liberalisation leads to the conclusion that major import liberalisation can have similar effects (Virmani, 2005a).

Phasing of Liberalisation: Competition Dynamics

The market reforms that appear to have had the strongest dynamic effects in India are those relating to production, investment and external sector. These are best understood through the prism of competition.[6] For this purpose, we distinguish three aspects of competition: the freedom to compete, the pressure to compete (competitive pressure), and the means and ability to compete. In a normal market economy, freedom to compete is taken for granted. India created a system of production and investment controls, and in some cases, price and distribution controls that restricted or eliminated the freedom of medium-large firms to compete with each other. As exploitation of economies of scale was an important characteristic of modernisation, limits on size effectively limited the freedom of such firms to compete globally.

The pressure to compete (competitive pressure) refers mostly to output markets and can come from two sources: domestic production or from imported supplies. In the first case, domestic production can be by indigenous entrepreneurs or through FDI. Entry of FDI can put competitive pressure on entrepreneurs, while imports can put pressure on both types of producers.

The threat of imports can sometimes be as powerful as actual imports. Thus the creation of artificial monopoly, an exclusive licence to produce non-tradable services or to produce a tradable good with a complete ban on imports, eliminates actual as well as potential competition. In contrast, a monopoly arising from market structure for instance a small market size relative to minimum efficient scale always has a potential competitive threat. Similarly, an import ban eliminates not just imports but the threat of imports. A very high tariff that makes current imports uncompetitive is preferable to a complete import ban as it maintains the threat of imports. Thus the

6. Porter (1990) had emphasised the importance of competition in developing and sustaining the competitiveness of firms on which the competitive strength of countries was built.

replacement of an import ban or quantitative restriction (QR) by an 'equivalent tariff' puts some competitive pressure on domestic producers. But reduction of QRs can also give rise to a paradoxical situation in which an overall liberalisation of import controls coupled with a rise in average tariffs can increase competitive pressure dramatically. The rise in tariffs on products subject to QRs by reducing rents, evasion and incentive for corruption, reduces transaction cost of imports and thus multiplies the positive effect of a liberalisation of these QRs. This is what happened during the 1980s.

The third dimension of competition is the means to compete. This has two aspects. One, competition requires access to the inputs and capital goods that a firm needs to increase its ability to compete. Liberalisation of product markets simultaneously increases both the pressure and ability to compete. Two, competition also requires access to factors (technology, capital, skills and land) and the flexibility to adjust them (unskilled labour). The lack of reforms in factor markets, such as urban land, supply of educated/skilled labour, has over time resulted in these factors becoming a constraint on sustaining fast growth.

Freedom to import inputs and capital goods not only puts competitive pressure on producers, but also expands the means available to the producer to compete. Freedom to import consumer goods on the other hand puts competitive pressure on producers but does not directly provide the means to compete in the short run. However, it increases the information flow about product innovations and enhances knowledge about new materials and technology that are incorporated in it, thus increasing competitive ability in the long run. As most of India's exports had access to duty-free imports of intermediate inputs and lower tariffs on capital good, even before the 1990s reforms, they were probably globally competitive even before the 1990s reforms.

The general effects of import liberalisation are modified by the phasing of sector liberalisation. Thus, exportable industries such as cotton textiles would tend to be relatively immune from the J curve effect. Their technology gap with global best practice would also be relatively low. In contrast, the technology gap would be expected to be highest in highly protected industries and would tend to show a stronger J curve effect.[7]

FDI that bundles technology, management, marketing skills (including export marketing) and capital can rapidly expand a country's access to all these factors. FDI improves not only the ability of the nation to compete, but also strengthens the ability of domestic entrepreneurs through spillover effects.[8] In contrast to abstract theoretical benefits of technology or exports, FDI demonstrates in practice the gains from new technology, management techniques, new products and new markets (exports). The spillover effects can therefore enhance the ability of domestic entrepreneurs to compete.[9] In a country with a relatively high number and quality of entrepreneurs, such as India, FDI is most effective in modern industries and new products. In other words, the positive effect of FDI is the highest where earlier controls/restrictions have created the largest gap between the domestic and global technology level. These are likely to be the industries and products which have had the largest technological change globally. This has been shown in the automobile sector in India. 'Technology' includes management and marketing techniques and system relevant to the industry/product. International spillover of knowledge is critical to the growth of all countries and the importance increases the less advanced the country. However, a competitive market and industrial environment is an essential prerequisite for obtaining these benefits.

Timing of Sector Liberalisation

A sub-sector aspect that would tend to offset or dilute the J curve effect is the time pattern of import liberalisation, particularly with respect to the manufacturing sector. Access to disembodied

7. See Virmani and Hashim (2011) for empirical evidence of the effect of phasing and timing of import liberalisation in different sub-sectors and industries and of public sector reform on the time pattern of output and TFP growth of 2 digit industry.
8. It may however also bias the modern sector towards excessive capital-skill intensive technology because the 'tunneling effect' of frontier technology that is more appropriate to the factor endowments of rich/advanced countries.
9. See Virmani (2005) or Virmani (2006b; 2006c) for empirical details of productivity enhancing effects of FDI.

technology and capital (FDI, equity and external commercial borrowing) was liberalised in the early 1990s followed by a more gradual opening of access to external long-term debt. Import controls/quantitative restrictions on intermediate and capital goods were eliminated in the early 1990s, while the QRs on manufactured consumer goods were not eliminated till the end of the 1990s to early 2000s (Virmani, 2003; 2005b). Although nominal tariff on consumer goods were reduced in line with those on other goods, the effective tariffs on consumer goods may actually have increased for much of the 1990s because the remaining import restriction/QRs kept the effective tariff on final consumer goods high.

Those consumer industries that used this period of protected profits to accelerate the introduction of new products using frontier technology and capital avoided any reduction in total factor productivity growth (TFPG) and may have accelerated it. Tariff reductions focused on reducing the peak or highest rate on all non-agricultural goods and were broadly proportional across the spectrum of goods, with a few notable exceptions. In the case of refineries, inputs on oil were deliberately maintained at a fraction of the average tariffs on the output of refineries, thus keeping effective protection high throughout the period. In the case of capital goods, an effort was made to keep import duties on major identifiable inputs such as steel well below the average tariffs on capital goods. This has likely resulted in some capital goods having a higher effective protection in the early sub- periods, with gradual convergence to neutrality by the end of the last sub-period.[10]

Public-Private Mix

Another important dimension affecting the J curve is the ability of the public sector to compete and the effect that 'regulatory arbitrage' has on private firms in the same industry, as the government departments managing the public sector are also the regulators for the industry in which the public sector operates. In several industries, such as steel, aluminum and refineries, the public

10. See Virmani and Hashim (2011) for empirical evidence.

sector had an important share of pre 1990-reform production. These industries were also characterised prior to the 1990s reforms, by controls/restrictions on capacity creation and licensing of new investment that adversely affected the private sector. Liberalisation of these controls and de-licensing allowed the private sector to raise its share of production, in some cases quite rapidly with minor investment in balancing equipment.[11] This would tend to raise the average productivity of the industry, if private efficiency was higher than that of the public sector. The same result would follow from the privatisation of loss-making public sector units. Thus the result of such reforms would be to offset the J curve effect.[12]

Incomplete Reforms: Threat and Opportunity

Import liberalisation largely bypassed the agricultural sector (Virmani, 2005b), partly due to entrenched political and ideological positions that favor certain pockets of agriculture production and trade at the expense of farmers as a group. This has slowed productivity improvements in production and supply.

FDI in manufacturing is virtually free except for the 26 per cent equity limit in defense industries. There are five significant service sectors in which their equity ceilings though only three have a major impact, namely multi-brand retail (26%), insurance (26%) and commercial airlines (49%). The limits on FDI in banking (74%) and telecom (74%) do not have a relatively lower impact than regulatory and security issues, which in these sectors are more important in determining foreign entry.[13] The latter issues arise even in the USA and other developed countries and tend to inhibit 100 per cent ownership from firms from many countries.

11. It is also speculated that their actual capacity was higher than the licensed and declared capacity.

12. See Virmani and Hashim (2011) for empirical evidence.

13. FDI in Internet and other parts of the communication and news media is also restricted for social and security reasons. FDI in crop agriculture and parts of the plantation sector remain prohibited because of issues connected with livelihood and land ownership by peasants.

The mining sector is also virtually open to FDI. However, public monopoly and restricted private entry (domestic and foreign) in sectors such as coal mining remains a serious problem.

Regulatory independence and objectivity remain serious concerns in infrastructure and related sectors in which the Government or public sector is a predominant producer/supplier (monopolistic) or buyer (monopsonistic). This is particularly so in 'private goods infrastructure' in which private production can realise the theoretical gains of competition, provided regulations and regulatory structures effectively implement this objective. Further, the welfare gains from public-private partnerships (PPPs) in 'public-goods infrastructure' can only be realised if the regulatory structure is more effective and efficient than government or public production and/or supply of these services.

Although financial sector liberalisation (both foreign and domestic) remains incomplete, the basic Indian approach of parallel and coordinated development of financial markets and products and regulatory expertise and systems remains valid. The risk minimising approach of phased opening of cross-border finance (FDI, LTD & equity, MTD, derivatives for hedging national risk) also remains valid. It has in fact been vindicated by the global financial crisis and the regulatory failures (*a la* layers of fraudulent behavior) that are still being exposed. The basic philosophy of Indian financial development should remain one of 'liberalisation with all deliberate speed', recognising that there are some fundamental differences between credit/financial markets and markets for goods and services in general.[14]

SECTION 2

DOMESTIC ENTREPRENUR-LED GROWTH

India's move from a low growth to a high growth economy has occurred in two stages, each higher stage being set of by economic

14. See Virmani (1995; 1996). The markets for education and health also require unbiased and effective regulation to function efficiently, because of asymmetric information and related problems.

reforms and liberalisation, first in the 1980s and then in the 1990s. What set it apart from many other growth accelerations, particularly in Asia are the role played by domestic entrepreneurs and the minimal direct role played by the government. The government's role in both sets of reforms was to lift controls and restriction on entrepreneurs and give them greater freedom. Its role in providing public goods and service, particularly 'public good infrastructure', has been highly inadequate compared to fast growing economies in Asia and elsewhere.[15] As FDI flows and stock are still a relatively small fraction of total investment and capital stock, the growth acceleration in both phases can therefore be largely attributed to domestic entrepreneurship, whence the term 'domestic entrepreneur led growth' has come. This contrasts with Korea and Taiwan Province of China, where the state played a much more active role in accelerating growth, Singapore where FDI was important in accelerating growth, though the state continued to play a critical role, and the role of the party and state in China.

Potential Growth

Till 2006, most academics and analysts were puzzled by the fact that the growth rate of the Indian economy appeared to have remained virtually unchanged after the 1990s reforms. One explanation proposed was a 'J curve of growth and productivity' arising from the dynamics between the negative and positive impact of reforms, as a result of which the acceleration of economic growth may take some time to materialise.[16] Based on the pre-1999-2000 NAS GDP data series it was predicted that,

> ... the underlying trend growth is currently about 6.3 per cent (6.25% to 6.35%). Thus the underlying medium term growth rate has been rising since the BOP crisis of 1990 and is now around 6.3 per cent.
>
> It is likely to rise to about 6.5 per cent over the next few years as the effect of the 1990s reforms works through the system as hypothesised in our analysis of the J curve of liberalisation' (Virmani, 2005a).

15. See Virmani (2005a).

16. Virmani (2005a; 2006a; 2006b; 2006c)

Once the new 1999-2000 based NAS GDP series became available in 2006, the rising growth trend was found to be statistically significant for aggregate growth, and the forecast for underlying growth was also revised upward. It was only post-2007 studies, which confirmed that Indian growth accelerated from 1992-93 and India entered the third more elevated stage of its growth history, following the 1991-92 reforms. In Virmani (2009), the potential growth rate of the Indian economy was estimated to be between 8.5 per cent and 9.0 per cent (Figure 3.1). Figure 3.2 is also based on GDP in 1999-2000 constant prices and shows the HP filtered growth trend (dotted line) relative to the linear trend growth line.

We test the J curve and other hypothesis using the new GDP data (at constant 2004-05 prices). The base model/equation of reforms and growth phases is re-estimated for 1980 to 2011 (i.e., excluding phase I). It shows a growth acceleration from 5.1 per cent in phase II (1980s to 1991-92) to 7.4 per cent in phase III (1992-93 to 2011-12) as a result of the 1990s reforms (Table 3). A test for J curve shows a net effect of -2.6 per cent points. Consequently the initial acceleration during the 1st sub-period of phase III (1992-93 to 2002-03) was from 5.5 per cent to 6.2 per cent with a long-term increase to 8.7 per cent per annum (seen in 2nd sub-period of phase III), with all significant at 1 per cent. This is depicted in Figure A3.1. Interestingly the investment-GDP ratio shows a significant J curve effect; the jump from 13.7 per cent in phase II to 22.8 per cent in phase III was held down (virtually unchanged) by a J curve effect of -7.1 per cent points.[17] An analysis of the J curve in manufacturing suggests that the initial gains in growth and TFP were from an increase in allocation efficiency, particularly from public to private production, partly offset by obsolescence (Virmani and Hashim, 2011). A significant proportion of the subsequent growth acceleration was probably the result of higher investment, including the effect of embodied technological change in sectors with large technology gap (Virmani, 2009: section 4; Virmani and Malhotra, 2010).

17. See Appendix 3. The base model shows a statistically insignificant effect of reforms (coefficient on dum1 and dum2) on the investment:GDP ratio.

Figure 3.1

Potential Growth Rate of Indian Economy

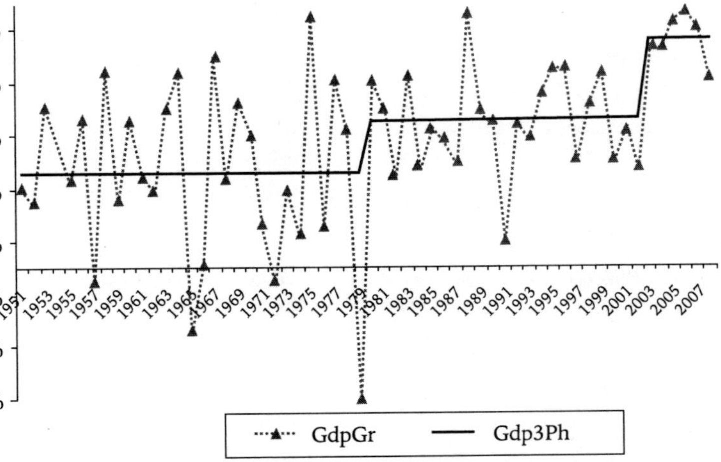

Figure 3.2

Post 1990 Trend and J Curve

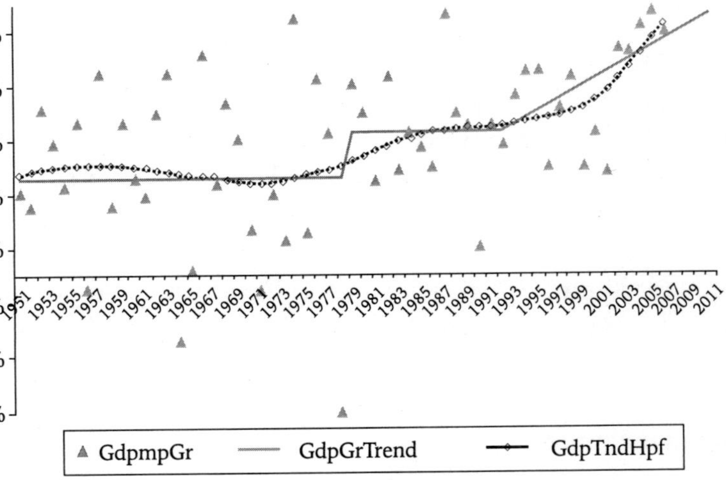

We also test two alternative hypotheses using the base model equation as well as the equation with J curve effects. One is the hypothesis that faster growth in India during 2003-04 to 2007-08 was due to faster world growth ("A rising global tide lifts all boats."). This is rejected in both the base model/equation and in the model/

equation with J curve effects present. In both cases, world GDP growth has the wrong sign and is not significant (Table 3). The second hypothesis that we test is that the disappointing performance of the Indian economy following the 1991 reforms was due to excessive monetary tightening, during 1992-93 to 2002-03 (the J curve period). The co-efficient for the real interest rate variable (call money rate – inflation of private consumption deflator) turns out to be significant at (10% level) in the base equation but insignificant in the equation with J curve effects.[18]

GDP growth averaged almost 9 per cent during 2003-04 to 2007-08 and 8.5 per cent during 2003-04 to 2010-11. In per capita terms, this translates to a growth rate of 6.9 per cent, a rate at which per capita income would almost double every decade. Even though India has grown at over 7 per cent for more than a decade in terms of GDP, India has still not completed one decade of per capita GDP growth of 7 per cent to become a high growth economy (HGE). Consequently, Virmani (2009) and the 2008-09 economic survey warned of complacency (Economic Division, 2009).[19] During the period 2003-03 to 2011-12 GDP, growth showed a declining trend (change) of (-) 0.16 per cent per annum, from about 8.75 per cent in 2003-04 to about 7.5 in 2011-12. It is valid to question whether this decline in the trend rate of growth will continue or it can be reversed to bring it back to a sustainable rate of around 8.5 per cent. In our view, once the fiscal-monetary policy mix is adjusted to take account of below trend growth and temporary shocks disappear, growth should return to this (declining) trend (see Table 4). A return to the medium-term trend of 8.5 per cent, however, requires determined, coherent and consistent policy reform action. From the economic perspective, it is still possible to reverse the declining trend (see below for policy recommendations).

18. This is consistent with the fact that in the base model, interest rates reduced growth by 0.54 per cent points, 0.61 per cent (8% of predicted) points and 0.22 per cent points during 1980-81 to 1991-92, 1992-93 to 2002-03 and 2003-04 to 2011-12 respectively. An increase in fiscal deficit reduces growth, but is not-significant at 10 per cent level.

19. As the author has made clear in numerous interactions with the media, speeches and in writings since 1995, the 1990s reforms raised growth potential of India from 8.5 per cent to 9 per cent.

SECTION 3

POLICY REFORMS FOR SUSTAINING GROWTH

The analysis of this paper leads to an identification of four broad areas for policy action in India to sustain growth:

(a) Macro-economic Stability and Sustainability

Inflation rates in India rose sharply in 2008, largely due to the global commodity price boom. Poor monsoons have contributed to food inflation. However, inflation seems to have persisted much longer than in previous episodes, while CADs have risen and the very welcome down-trend in fiscal deficits has been disrupted. At the same time, the global crisis has increased the volatility of capital flows and could at any time flare into a global liquidity freeze. Thus restoration of fiscal and current account balances to the trends prevalent before 2008-09, must be one of the priorities of economic policy.

(b) Market Reform to Increase Competition

Fast growth has accentuated and magnified the price distortions arising from existing supply bottlenecks and created new ones. Policy and regulatory reforms are needed to introduce and/or enhance competition in the markets for land, infrastructure services, agriculture and skills. With careful calibration, increased competition will stimulate increased supply, help accelerate productivity growth, reduce rents and rent seeking, and sustain inclusive growth.

(c) Institutional Reform and Conflict Resolution

Higher growth has also accentuated conflicts over land and natural resources, between rent accumulators and outsiders and between social and political groups. These must be resolved through economic policy and institutional reform, if fast growth is to be sustained. These conflicts can effect economic growth not just directly (e.g., inadequate supply of urban land) but also through their effect on the political system and its ability to act decisively in resolving issues not directly connected to them, such as macro-economic response to external shocks and fundamental policy reforms. Some of these require institutional change that will take time. Fortunately, affected economic agents do not expect perfect instantaneous solutions to institutional and social problems. They do expect the government and the political system to appreciate the importance of the problem and demonstrate that it is serious about addressing them i.e., take credible steps to address the problems.

(d) Social Equity and Inclusion

Innovative and imaginative approaches are needed to ensure that the goals of sustaining fast growth are not in conflict with inclusiveness and social equity and *vice versa*. The key is to identify the problems carefully, use the scientific method to link problems to potential solutions and choose the solutions that can be effectively implemented.

A number of urgent policy actions are identified keeping these in mind. Individual policy recommendations do not necessarily relate only to one of these aspects but aim to balance all four elements.

Oil/Energy

Globally oil price shocks have, since 1971, been a factor in the growth slowdown in many oil importing countries. Oil and energy import dependency in India is high and increasing. This results in implicit taxation-rent transfer to foreigners, which makes the people of the country as a whole worse off, the more the usage/import; long-term price trends are adverse (terms of trade effects) and the problem likely to get worse unless policy reforms are instituted. The solution is to separate and disconnect subsidy from pricing. Replace kerosene subsidy with free solar lanterns and cookers. Provide free training to village youth to service these items in rural areas. Replace diesel subsidy with subsidy for fuel efficient engines of all kinds (pump sets, generator sets, tractors, trucks, scooters/motor cycles). Give subsidy for adoption and development of new technology, including solar, but allow prices to reflect the global price of all energy items.

A medium-term objective must be to promote green cities: we must get the world's best designers and architects to come and design green buildings etc., suited to Indian climatic conditions (water, heat, etc.), construction materials and construction methods; publish and propagate these designs; train urban planning and regulatory officials in every state in planning work-residence zoning rules, public transport and public parking to minimise energy use.

Food Prices and Policy

Historically food inflation in India generally goes up following a bad monsoon and returns to normal rates following normal monsoon and the restoration of agricultural production to its trend growth of about 2.5 per cent per annum. This time around higher food inflation rates seemed to have persisted for an inordinately long time. As we noted earlier, agriculture is the only major sector that has seen little or no economic reform and import liberalisation. Consequently, it has not benefited from any of the aspects of competition that we analysed earlier. At the same time, there have been three significant changes on the domestic side (that we had identified in 2008-09). One is the doubling of the rate of growth of per capita income and its impact on growth of demand for food and its pattern (cereals to vegetables/fruit and milk products). Second is the boom in urban land prices and consequently on real estate prices and rents. The third is the increase in fuel prices and its effect on transport costs. The first and third would tend to increase the cost of food at all levels and the second would tend to increase the gap between the retail and wholesale levels. The small fragmented supply chains cannot cope with the increased demand for basic and new higher level foods. We need a revolution in the food supply chain—particularly fresh foods (from farm to retail). Governments' decade's old plans for cold chain, package of inputs, credit, output markets have not worked, given the institutional setting and context that exists. In fact, the institutions have in many cases deteriorated relative to what they were 20-30 years ago, so they are not able to cope even with normal increases, let alone unprecedented ones.

The only option left is to try what worked elsewhere—competition through FDI in grocery retail.[20] The entry of domestic large retail suppliers has made some difference in a few products and geographies. We need a (food) retail revolution to cope with the increased challenges. Opening of FDI in retail is the only solution we have not tried. This needs to be complemented by reforms of the Agricultural Produce Marketing Committee (APMC) acts and the Essential Commodities Act (ECA), for farmers to get the full benefit of increased competition.[21] We also need a more predictable import-export regime for farmers that balance the needs of consumers and farmers on a permanent basis rather than lurching from season to season from one extreme to the other. The economic survey of 2007-08 proposed price bands with variable import tariffs and export duties outside band. This would mitigate the effect of extreme high prices on consumers and of extreme low prices on farmers, while ensuring that the latter receive the right price signals to promote productivity and growth of production.

Urban Governance: Land Market

Despite some attempts by the central government, reforms to free up the land markets and introduce competition have been extremely limited, partly because most land-related policies come under the purview of the state governments. The basic most visible manifestation of the urban problem is the stratospheric price of land, equaling or exceeding that of countries that have more than 10 times our per capita GDP. This is due to the acute shortage of 'urban land', public transport (in metros) and basic urban public goods. The gap between demand and supply of urban land has started increasing

20. Because of local and regional tastes, there is a stronger inherent/natural incentive for large marketers to build domestic supply chains for food/grocery items. Thus it may be better to focus initially on allowing 74 per cent FDI in grocery/food retail as against 51 per cent FDI in general retail (including grocery), if the primary objective is to build an efficient food supply chain that benefits farmers and consumers.

21. For example, delisting of perishable commodities like fruits and vegetables and new nutritional items like soya, from schedule 1 of APMC acts. For poorer/less developed states/regions to benefit fully we also need a road grid connecting every village and a sustainable water/irrigation grid in every block.

rapidly since the rate of per capita GDP growth accelerated. The wider the gap, the sharper is the effect on wealth inequality, and more the opportunity for rent seeking and corruption. Only by increasing dramatically the supply of habitable and accessible urban land can we help the low income residents, reduce urban wealth inequalities and minimise corruption. Much of the extreme inequality noticed by foreign visitors is due to the abysmal supply of basic public goods and services (clean drinking water, sewerage, drainage, sanitation, public toilets, durable roads, primary education outcomes, public knowledge of nutrition and hygiene) that affects the bottom 20 per cent to 40 per cent of the population most acutely.[22]

Urban governance reform requires genuine decentralisation from state governments to the city governments and the modernisation of laws, policy and procedures for specifying/changing land use and for sale of land (through competitive auctions). This requires measures additional to the proposed land acquisition and relief and rehabilitation laws that are currently before parliament.

Human Capital: Skills

As has been widely reported, India is in the midst of its demographic transition. The demographic dividend can, however, only be actualised by providing usable skills built on sound primary education—recent surveys by government and Pratham show that only a fraction of secondary school students can read even at primary level. A fast growing lower middle income economy like India's needs intermediate skills in all kind of services (semi-skilled occupations). The provision of these skills in rural areas and to the poor in urban areas will also promote mobility and inclusive growth. The scale of the opportunity/problem is enormous. The government must and is trying to do whatever it can within its institutional capability

22. The simplest, most effective way to promote inclusive growth is by building a permanent road network that connects every habitation in India, a drinking water and sewage/sanitation grid that provides every town and all its residents a healthy environment and an irrigation-drainage (water sustainability) grid covering every block/village. More than finance, the greatest limitation is the lack of understanding and appreciation of the vital role that these simple public goods have played in the transformation of the USA and Europe from poor unequal societies to rich and relatively equal ones (at least till 1980).

and resources. A good strategy is to, "Let a hundred flowers bloom", under a sound regulatory framework that helps trainees understand what they are paying and what they are getting. The most critical direct role of the government is to educate the educators and train the trainers. It should encourage all other sectors (NGOs, private) to make whatever contribution they can. This is essential for providing equality of opportunity and thus promoting and sustaining inclusive growth.

Resource Rents and Corruption

As indicated, rents are giving rise to numerous conflicts, between different elements of society, within the business community, within the political class and between parties. Rent sucking (rent creation cum rent seeking) is the greatest source of inequality in income and wealth. A resolution of these conflicts is essential not only for social harmony, but for equitable growth. There are three major sources of rent that need to be addressed.

(a) Natural Resources (Minerals, Land, Spectrum)

Auctions with post-auction tradability between licensed holders. This can be complemented by capital gains taxation of such rights. Sound regulations and regulatory system are pre-requisite/ complement as otherwise; post-auction changes in terms in favour of the winner can vitiate the potential gains from the auctions.

(b) Land Use

The quality of land use planning and implementation has to be raised by training city officials and changing the rules. Involve stake holders in land use change decisions through land use hearings and appropriate change of land use based on these hearings, before acquisition starts. Once this is done, market price will reflect the true value of the land as long as government makes the information available to all land owners and potential land acquirers.

We must ensure that pending land acquisition and rehabilitation laws, level the playing field for all participants (land owners, land buyers and land users) while ensuring that there is no disincentive for economic development and growth.

(c) Government Procurement

A 'Public Accountability Information System (PAIS)' that insures that all information is put on a web site accessible to the public is needed. This would include the nature and scope of job/purchase, amounts paid and to whom.

Macroeconomics

Fiscal-Monetary Mix

Since the V-shaped recovery in 2009-10, Indian macro policy would have produced better results if the fiscal policy had been tighter and monetary policy looser, and supply bottlenecks had been directly attacked through policy reform. This remains true today. Virmani (2003) showed that even though a rise in the fiscal deficit and a 0.5 elasticity of the CAD with respect to the central fiscal deficit caused the 1991 balance of payment (BoP) crises, a flexible exchange rate (resulting in 30-40% devaluation) would have obviated the crisis. The government could then have had sufficient time for a textbook expenditure switching-expenditure reducing policy (of the kind adopted after the crises) to work.

Fiscal Deficit

Recent policy research suggests that the critical danger point for the government's debt-GDP ratio is between 60 per cent and 100 per cent, with the threshold being on the lower side for developing countries and on the upper side for developed countries. Large fiscal deficits and a high net international debt position make a country vulnerable to global financial shocks and terms of trade shocks (e.g., oil price spikes). As India's fiscal deficit is the primary reason for keeping its global credit rating perched on the border of investment grade, a total (centre + states) fiscal deficit around 2 per cent and a total debt-GDP ratio of 40 per cent (over the next 10 years) would be helpful in attaining a triple A rating and reducing dependence on unstable capital flows. The government's ability to deal with global adverse shocks and to exploit new global opportunities, while sustaining high domestic investment levels and lower inflation, would be greatly strengthened. Sustained fiscal reduction requires a return to the tax reform approach initiated in the 1990s and now represented by the Direct Tax Bill and the Goods and Service Tax (GST). The latter will help in creating a unified market in the country and facilitate greater competition. Government expenditure policies must also restore the balance between (a) public goods and human capital (skills, education, public health, communicable disease control) that promote equity and (b) income/consumption transfers and subsidies that incentivise dependency.

Infrastructure

Without a fair and rational policy and regulatory regime, no amount of infrastructure subsidies and Public sector bank lending to infrastructure will result in a sustained increase in infrastructure investment and supply. A policy-regulatory regime that promotes competition in 'private goods infrastructure' (e.g., coal, electricity generation, rail services) is an essential pre-requisite for eliminating infrastructure bottlenecks. Coal fields should be parceled into economic and viable mines and auctioned to a dozen producers (PSUs should also be permitted to bid in auctions). Benchmark competition in and open access to the distribution network is essential for effective competition in electricity generation.

A more focused push is also needed on 'public goods infrastructure'. The simplest, most effective way to promote social equity and inclusion is by building a permanent road network that connects every habitation in India, a drinking water and sewage/sanitation grid that provides every town and all its residents a healthy environment and an irrigation drainage (water sustainability) grid covering every block/village. More than finance, the greatest limitation is the lack of understanding and appreciation of the vital role that these simple public goods have played in the transformation of the USA and Europe from poor unequal societies to rich and relatively equal ones.

Investment Environment

Despite several aborted effort to simplify regulations, introduce automaticity, and remove the heavy hand of the bureaucracy on entrepreneurs, investors and producers, India remains close to the bottom on global indicators of 'investment environment.'

Financial Sector

Accelerate development of long-term debt markets to reduce dependency on volatile capital flows, increase financing for infrastructure and consequently improve the investment and growth environment.

Conclusion

Sustained, fast economic growth is the key to transforming a low income economy to a middle income one. Accelerating an economy's growth is not sufficient to get success in this transformation. What sets apart successful from unsuccessful countries is the time period during which growth is sustained. Too many countries' growth rate collapses after a period of fast growth; they are shooting stars that burn bright for a short period. The policy reforms needed to sustain fast growth are not necessarily the same as those needed to accelerate growth. One of the differences is that in the latter case, it is more important to focus on and address problems that are apparent and visible to all informed observers, and to do so in pragmatic problem-solving manner. An ideologically focus or theoretical obsession with historical problems can distract from and dissipate the limited room for manoeuver a government may have at any given time. This does not rule out a clear focus on long-term policy and institutional reform objectives to ensure consistency in reforms, while addressing the immediate problem. The latter is more important to sustaining growth than long-standing constraints that the system has adapted to. If growth is allowed to fall back to slower levels, there is unlikely to be much net benefit from addressing these long-term problems.

The paper explored the paradox between the higher growth potential and the declining growth trend in India. It had three interlinked goals:

- To analyse the experience of fast growing economies and learn about the policies that helped sustain fast growth. Maintaining growth at high levels requires alertness and a timely and flexible response to: (a) external and exogenous shocks that can derail macrostability and (b) new bottlenecks and conflicts that arise as a result of faster growth or are accentuated by it. If allowed to fester too long, they can eventually derail growth. Faster revenues growth, consequent to growth acceleration, is not a licence to fiscal irresponsibility or to reverse the policies (or policy direction) that raised the growth potential in the first place.
- To show that economic reforms of the 1990s have raised the trend growth rate of the Indian economy, i.e., the former is the cause of the latter and that the faster growth is not the result of the global boom. This analysis also helps understand the nature of successful policies and their mechanism and to identify a set of potential policies that could act as growth drivers.
- To apply the lessons from the experience of fast growing economies and its own earlier reforms, to the current Indian situation, by identifying the bottlenecks and problems that must be addressed, if Indian growth is to be sustained at the trend rate identified earlier and to suggest policy and institutional reforms to deal with them.

The 1990s economic reforms (structural reforms), including the liberalisation of the external trade, investment and technology policy, raised the potential growth of the Indian economy from around 5.5 per cent per annum to over 8.5 per cent. Consequently, the economy grew at around 9.0 per cent per annum during the five years 2003-04 to 2007-08. The average growth rate has fallen to 7.7 per cent in the next four years (2008-09 to 2011-12) following the US financial crises of 2008. There are two factors in the slowdown. The first is the continuing financial crises and its accentuation of capital flow volatility into India, and the global economic slowdown and consequent global demand deficiency-excess capacity in tradable goods and services. The second is the negative fallout of India's growth acceleration and the political consequences of the V-shaped recovery from the 2008 global financial shock. These induced complacency in policy and the economic and political elites of the country. More importantly the growth acceleration has given rise to a number of economic bottlenecks and constraints and socio-political conflicts that must be resolved through economic policy and institutional reform if fast growth is to be sustained. These include conflicts related to land, water and natural resources. These conflicts can effect economic growth not just directly (e.g., inadequate supply of urban land) but also through their effect on the political system and its ability to act decisively in resolving issues not directly connected to them, such as macro-economic response to external shocks and fundamental policy reforms.

There is a significant probability of external shocks during the next two years, such as euro melt-down and sharp spike in oil prices. Emerging market economies (EMEs), such as China and India, have the policy options and ability to minimise the effect of the continuing global financial crisis on their economies and resume/sustain growth at close to its potential in each country. There are currently eight countries with an average growth rate of per capita GDP of more than 6 per cent over the previous decade (2002-2011). Seven of these are in Asia: three in South Asia (India, Bhutan and Maldives), three in Association of Southeast Asian Nations (ASEAN) (Vietnam, Cambodia and Myanmar) and one in East Asia (China). Of these, the fast growth rate of four countries, all in Asia (China, India, Cambodia and Maldives), is not fuelled by natural resource riches and resource rents. History shows that there is an over 1/5th probability of India's decadal per capita growth rate falling below 6.0 per cent, if the pace of (real/genuine) economic reforms remains at the level prevailing during the last five years or so. If India learns and adopts the lessons from the highly successful HGEs and pHGEs of Asia, it still has the potential to attain HGE status by reversing the downward trend in its growth and going back to its underlying potential of per capita GDP growth of 7.0 per cent to 7.5 per cent (GDP 8.5%+). This requires urgent policy actions to remove bottlenecks to growth, eliminate rents and facilitate removal of supply constraints. This paper outlines a range of policy actions to increase competitiveness in factor markets, agriculture and 'private goods infrastructure', separation of energy and other subsidies from debilitating price distortions and fiscal reforms, that can help in restoring India's growth trend. Some, if not all these policy reforms may require a reorientation/adjustment of the approach to political cooperation and competition.

Excerpted from IMF Working Paper WP/12/185 Arvind Virmani (July 2012). *Accelerating and Sustaining Growth: Economic and Political Lessons,* sections 4, 5, 6 and 7. In this volume, these sections have been marked as 1, 2, 3 and 4 respectively and accordingly the footnote numbering.

Economic Developments in India, Vol. 189.

4

K.C. CHAKRABARTY

Transit Path for Indian Economy

Six Steps for Transforming the Elephant into a Tiger

TRANSFORMING the elephant into a tiger can mean different things to different people. In reality, the state of the art in genetic engineering still cannot contemplate such a modification. An Ang Lee or a Steven Spielberg can, of course, use computer-generated special effects to bring about such a transformation. But it is time to get real—given that the metaphor of elephant is used to denote the Indian economy and deals with our lives and the future of our children.

In 2007, Dr Shashi Tharoor wrote an enchanting book, *The Elephant, The Tiger and The Cellphone: Reflections on India—The Emerging 21st Century Power*. The book, ingrained in history, culture and socio-economic change, criss-crosses the Indian life from Ajanta-Ellora and cricket to cellphones and call centres, and makes a simple point of Indian growth effecting change in daily lives and imparting confidence to the Indian people. In December 2008, *The Economist* of London published a special report that India was elephant, not a tiger. It noted that for all its chaos, bureaucracy and occasional violence, India has had a remarkably successful past few years. But, it wondered how it will cope with an economic downturn and the general elections that were about to follow. It added that the democracy tax was rising and storm clouds were gathering. The prognosis, however, were proven to be off beam by the events that followed. The elections removed uncertainty and the Indian economy staged a V-shaped recovery clocking 8.4 per cent growth during 2009-10 and 2010-11. Yet, we lost steam and the chinks in the tiger skin that we tried wearing, got exposed.

In July 2011, Swaminathan Anklesaria Aiyar wrote a paper for the Cato Institute, "The Elephant that Became a Tiger". In this paper, he persuasively argued that 20 years of economic reforms in India had transformed the Indian economy into a tiger. Later the same year, the Reserve Bank Governor Dr Subbarao, while delivering the Haksar Memorial Lecture, argued that India may be an elephant, but even elephant can dance. The elephant dance was disrupted by the zoo party in the form of global financial crisis. He then suggested 10 steps to get back on course by re-jigging the elephant dance.

Growth in India has clearly slowed down since then to 6.5 per cent in 2011-12 and a likely 5.8 per cent in 2012-13, with significant downside risks. The twin deficits—fiscal and balance of payments (BoP)—have compounded our problems. This may set us thinking on whether we are an elephant or a tiger or a goat, about to be devoured by global forces and our domestic inaction. So should we at all pursue the tiger dream? If yes, what do we need to do to earn the tiger tag?

The Elephant and the Tiger: Which One Should We Prefer?

Before I touch upon what we need to do, the first step is to understand what these metaphors mean. So let me upfront visit the key attributes of elephants and tigers. There are four key attributes of an elephant: the size, the herbivorous nature, its perceived moderate pace and its anatomy that includes large ears, the trunk and the tusks. Tiger, on the other hand, is not as large as the elephant, but is largest of the cat species. It is carnivore, and is known for its speed and agility. Its anatomy includes the stripes, the powerful jaws and razor sharp teeth, sharp claws and a flexible backbone. But, what conclusively differentiates the two is the tiger's killer instinct.

I think, in terms of size, the Indian economy is, of course, an elephant. It is also herbivorous by habit given its democratic structure, unlike the carnivourous habits of tigers and dragons. In terms of speed, many people have a misconception that elephants can't run or walk fast. The fact is that elephants can walk as fast as 25 miles per hour (mph), while tigers can run only a shade faster. Bengal tigers can run at 35 mph, but for short spurts and they can't keep this pace for long.

Therefore, in my view, it is not axiomatic that one should try transforming the elephant into a tiger. Yes, we could do with an added bit of speed but what we should really aim at is developing a tiger's killer instinct. These, together with a better use of our anatomy or resources, both human and capital, would help us achieve what the dragons and the tigers have achieved, perhaps, with a smaller downside. For this to happen, in my view, we need to take the following six steps.

Preserve Demographic Dividends by Investing in Human Capital

India's demographic dividend presents the country with a great opportunity to enhance its growth and seek convergence of per capita incomes with that in the developed world. India's birth rate has fallen from 45.6 per 1000 in 1951 to an estimated 21 currently, but still remains highly driven by a slowly falling infant mortality rate (IMR) that remains high at about 46 per 1000. The death rate has fallen dramatically from 37.2 per 1000 birth in 1951 to an estimated 7 currently, but has still not caused population ageing. Median age for India's population is about 27 years compared with over 40 for most Organization for Economic Co-operation and Development (OECD) economies. It will add significantly to its labor pool, and even as the median age bucket rises, it will still be at a relatively young 30-34 age bracket by 2026. India's age-dependency ratio (ratio of dependents—people younger than 15 or older than 64—to the working-age population) is currently about 54. This is already lower than Japan and France.

Most developed countries would see a rapid ageing of their population over the next 2-3 decades putting severe pressure on their social security systems with the rise in dependency ratio. The overall median age of these countries rose from 29.0 in 1950 to 37.3 in 2000, and is forecast to rise to 45.5 by 2050.

Many developing countries like China, Brazil and Thailand too face issues of ageing population having passed through the demographic transition. Over the last 60 years, China has experienced demographic change at a historic pace that had a profound impact on its population structure. Baby boom began in the mid-1960s after the period of 'Great Leap Forward' saw famines and a sharp rise in death rate and a fall in birth rate. China is now a 'post-transitional' society, where life expectancy has reached new heights, fertility has declined to below-replacement level, and rapid population ageing is expected over the next few decades. China's population will start to shrink after reaching a peak of about 1.4 billion by 2025 A.D. The median age of its population could touch 50 years by then. India's population would overtake that of China at that point. Its population is expected to peak only at 1.7 billion by 2060 A.D.

Clearly, India has a potential advantage of demographic dividend over its emerging market peers. But this demographic dividend could be a boon or a curse depending upon how we exploit it, for the time to reap these gains is finite. By the turn of this century, India would be facing a demographic discount rather than dividend because India's population would have aged and the developed countries' population would be much younger. So what do we need to do to reap the demographic dividend while they exist?

The very first thing is to invest in the resources that are expected to give us advantage. India invests much less than it should in its human capital. The combined spend of central and state governments in education is just about 3.3 per cent of GDP (gross domestic product), while that on health is another 1.3 per cent of GDP. In contrast, the European Union (EU) countries spend from their general government account 5.5 per cent of their GDP on education and 7.5 per cent of their GDP on health, i.e., nearly three times more of their GDP. Canada's public spending on health alone is over 11 per cent of their GDP and that on education is nearly 5 per cent. India needs to step up its public spending on education and health considerably over the next five years. However, spending alone does not guarantee high quality human capital. We also need to focus on the quality of this spending and think whether we can achieve better outcomes with less spending.

The second step we need to take is for right skilling of our work force. There is shortage of trained manpower for the industry, both at the bottom of the pyramid and higher up the ladder. India is often considered to be a source for skilled labour supply to the rest of the world, given its sheer size of manpower. It is often not recognised that over four-fifth of our rural population and over half of our urban population remain unskilled. Women participation rate in the labour market remain poor. The biggest problem is the lack of focus on technical education that could absorb a large chunk of unskilled labour, if backed by greater push to primary education. Less than 11 per cent of the job-seeking population in the age group of 15-29 receives any form of vocational training in India and only one of every three who do get vocational training receives it from specialised training institutes. Furthermore, even in the value added segment, where we have the largest pool of skilled manpower i.e., in the area of information technology (IT), real wages are rising at a pace that may impact our competitiveness.

The biggest challenge is to ensure jobs for additional supply of labour that comes in to join the workforce. On a rough basis, about 10 million people would need a job every year for the next 15 years. Although disguised unemployment in agriculture sector has reduced over the years, it may not be possible for the sector to provide additional jobs given the rising rural wages and the need to shift to a corporate, more mechanised and capital-intensive model of farming. While the services sector has led India's growth and employment story for some time now, India's growth pace may not be sustained unless the manufacturing sector also becomes more competitive and creates lot more jobs. This poses a significant challenge in employment generation and skilling our workforce.

Improve Productivity and Efficiency

Productivity is an important driver of growth. Productivity depends on the efficiency with which scarce resources are allocated—be it your time, work effort, natural resources, capital or any other inputs. A great deal of the growth for most countries can be explained by productivity growth, especially total factor productivity growth (TFPG). Factor accumulation (such as increase in labour or capital) explains a smaller part of the growth. Given this experience, if India were to become a tiger, it would need to focus on technological developments to improve its rate of TFPG. Capital deepening may also help, but the key lies in overall productivity enhancements.

In India, output per worker has increased at an impressive rate in the services sector after the reforms initiated in early 1990s. In this period, TFPG has also been impressive for this sector, though I will eschew quoting precise numbers as the growth accounting research generally gives varied quantitative estimates. TFPG growth has also improved for the manufacturing sector since the 1980s. So, progress is being made. However, the rate of this technical change, still, has been lower than that for the East Asian economies during the period in which they earned the tag of being East Asian tigers.

I would rather focus on the issue of larger policy initiative that would be necessary in the quest to transform India into a tiger. In this context, I would make four suggestions. First, improving agriculture productivity is necessary as, clearly, increase in area under cultivation is just not practical and, therefore, increasing demand for cereals, pulses, fruits and vegetables would need to be met by improving yields. Substantial productivity enhancements are possible on the farm through adoption of precision farming techniques, better cultivars and optimal water management. Better adoption of modern technologies in the area of biotechnology, genomic tools, cost-effective and eco-friendly integrated pest management technologies, seed-supply chains and systems, regionally adapted varieties and hybrids, would help.

Second, we need to focus on issues confronting our small and medium enterprise (SME). SME sector accounts for over a third of our industrial output and contributes an equal share of our total merchandise exports. In the current downturn, SMEs are facing adverse business climate with rising receivables, inadequate credit and high cost of credit. SME sector does not enjoy the economies of scale and scope that a large corporation enjoys. It also cannot fully reap the benefit of IT as it has high sunk cost and a high rate of obsolescence. Although having strong links with large firms, institutional mechanisms for transfer of technology to SMEs are lacking. If SMEs are to effectively integrate with supply chains, we need to ensure that links of finance and technology with large firms work at all times.

Third, as I mentioned a little earlier, India's next growth push has to come from manufacturing sector. We had a missed century of opportunities. India cannot boast of one big 'home grown' global brand while much smaller nations like South Korea, Taiwan, etc., have plenty of them. Our abundant human capital has not been effectively channelised for supporting the manufacturing growth. But what I would really blame for this is a lack of 'R&D' (research & development) culture that we suffer from. Globally, India figures at near the bottom in terms of R&D intensity. It spends less than one percentage of its GDP on R&D expenditure, countries like Israel, Finland, Sweden, Korea, Japan, the USA and Germany have R&D intensities that are higher by three times or more.

Fourth, a key issue related to productivity is our attitude to work. It is strange that India, that epitomised the dignity of labour in the early Vedic period, has imbibed a culture that does not respect workers. We have forgotten Swami Vivekananda's contribution in equating work to worship. No form of work whether manual or intellectual is less inferior to the other. As a nation, we have been steadily neglecting our respect for dignity of labour. Since the manual labour does not receive the same respect as an intellectual work in India, work efforts are lost. This results in lower GDP and lower welfare. Individuals idle away than take up a manual job. What else would explain the fact that labourers from poor states like Bihar, Orissa, Uttar Pradesh (UP), etc., migrate and work hard in the agricultural farms in Punjab and Haryana, while refusing to do the same in their own locality where the land is more fertile and same amount of labour would be much more productive. We must emulate the western society in this regard where no form of labour is discriminated against. If President Cleveland could accept dignity of labour in 1894, more than a century down the line, it is time that we give respect to casual labour that operates around us—be it our maids, our drivers or the workmen in our factories—a due recognition and respect. If we do so, more women and men would join the workforce. Unemployment would be reduced and Indian industry would become more competitive globally.

Revive Infrastructure Investments and Harness Natural Resources Better

Much has been said about India's infrastructure deficit and rightly so. India does not have sufficient roads, nor sufficient power. When I was growing up, I was taught that India is a land of poor, but is rich in resources. Today we have made a giant leap in lowering poverty and still remain abundant in natural resources. Yet, we have not learnt to optimally utilise them. Take for example coal, which accounts for India's 55 per cent of energy needs. We have hard coal reserves of around 246 billion tonnes, of which 92 billion tonnes are proven. Yet, we are able to produce only 530 million tonnes of coal, leaving supply shortages of over 150 million tonnes. Coal shortages are constraining our power generation, and though about 55 GW of new capacity was created during the 11th Five Year Plan (FYP), a large part of it remains unutilised due to coal shortages. Private sector has failed to develop most of the new coal blocks that were allotted to them. We ended up with inadequate planning and poor execution in this area. We are now planning to create even more thermal power capacity during the 12th FYP, but remain unsure of coal supplies. At the same time, banks have heavily extended themselves into lending to power sector both on generation and distribution side. On the distribution side, the state distribution companies (discoms) are sitting on huge losses and bank debt that is threatening to go bad. The end result is a loss of business confidence that has brought the investment boom to a premature halt.

What is most important in this context is to revive the confidence for investing and lending to the infrastructure sector. The government, in recent period, has taken several steps to facilitate this. The broad contours of the New Fuel Supply Agreements (FSAs) have been worked out, though some thorny issues such as price pooling of imported and domestic coal are still to be resolved. These pending issues must be solved quickly. Similarly, a debt restructuring package for the discoms has been worked out. The private sector must seize the initiative and rekindle the Schumpeterian spirit at this juncture. Banks also need to perform their core banking business while balancing risk assessment with the functional need to support growth.

We also need to harness our natural resources much better. Take the simple example of water. We are a country blessed with water resources with a network of perennial rivers and abundant rainfall. The rainfall provides four times the water that we use annually. Yet, water is a scarce resource in India. We haven't harnessed our resources enough and haven't planned the storage and distribution of water efficiently. India's per capita storage capacity is significantly lower than that of other countries. For example, the quantum of water that can be stored as a proportion of average river run-off for India is just 50 days of average run-off with wide variations—from 220 days in the Krishna to just two days in the Brahmaputra/Barak Basin. The comparable figures for the Colorado River Basin and Australia's Murray-Darling Basin are 900 days, while for South Africa's Orange River Basin it is 350 days. Better water management could radically alter the agriculture situation in India.

India also needs to utilise its mining, spectrum and air resources better. The importance of clean air is often not recognised. We need to strike a right balance between our development needs and environmental commitments to ensure long-run growth sustainability. We are not among the world's top polluters. It needs to be recognised that average per square kilometre carbon dioxide (CO_2) pollution in Japan is 7.5 times more than in India. Similarly, per capita CO_2 emission by India is amongst the least globally. Nevertheless, we also need to note that air pollution has serious health costs and India ranks fourth in the list of the largest CO_2 pollutants after China, the USA and Russia. As such, if we want to ensure not just fast growth but also good quality growth sustainable for a fairly long period of time, we must continue to make efforts to exploit natural resources in an environmentally friendly way.

Improve Governance at Every Level

The World Bank's Worldwide Governance Indicators 2006-2011 place India below average on key parameters of governance. It scores about 15 per cent on political stability and absence of violence, 40 per cent on control on corruption as well as regulatory quality, 55 per cent on rule of law as well as government effectiveness, while 60 per cent on vice and accountability. Clearly, there is lot of scope for improvement on these parameters. Both our overall governance and corporate governance needs improvement. In fact, we need better governance at every level—from hospital and schools to polity, firms, non-profit institutions, sports, banking and finance, regulation, land records and even in our daily lives.

Our governance deficit, in some form, is reflected in our ranking on ease of doing business. According to the International Finance Corporation (IFC)-World Bank Report 2013 released this year, India ranks 132nd on the index measuring 'ease of doing business' amongst 185 economies. Singapore and Hong Kong got the top and second spots overall. In its sub-components, India stands at an impressive 23rd on the criteria of ease of getting credit and 49th in terms of protecting investors. However, it figures at 173rd in terms of starting a business, 182nd in terms of dealing with construction permits and 184th in contract enforcement.

According to the same report, on an average, in India it requires 173 days to start a business, 196 days for obtaining a construction permit and 67 days to get electricity. In Singapore, one needs just 3 days to start a business, 26 days for construction permit and 36 days for getting electricity. All other East Asian tigers also have a far superior record than India on these parameters.

If we aspire to become a tiger, we must become more business friendly, both for domestic and foreign firms, traders and tourists. We, of course, have an enviable record of a democratic system, a responsive government, an active media and an independent judiciary. However, the risk of dealing with India must come down further. We have to reach where the East Asian tigers reached. It is for this reason that we advocated the adoption of Singapore model in the last Reserve Bank of India (RBI) Annual Report. In a limited way, this is being attempted in the form of National Investment Board (NIB). A well-functioning NIB can go a long way in cutting project delays. However, in our federal structure, NIB would still have some limitations. It will not have jurisdiction over project clearances that are required at sub-national levels. The Singapore model is a step further. It requires all concerned agencies to sit together in a time bound manner to clear or reject projects, failing which the clearance is deemed to be automatic. We must make doing business easy, to unleash entrepreneurship and venture capitalism in India.

We also need to improve our record of corporate governance in both financial and non-financial firms. Barriers to entry must collapse and a more competitive environment needs to be generated. However, we must develop a framework and inculcate practices of arms length relationships that do not permit connected lending and business relationships that may promote 'looting' behaviour as described by Akerlof (awarded the Nobel Prize in 2001) and Romer. They argued that an economic underground can come to life if firms have an incentive to go broke for profit at society's expense (to loot) instead of to go for broke (to gamble on success). Bankruptcy for profit will occur if poor accounting, lax regulation, or low penalties for abuse give owners an incentive to pay themselves more than their firms are worth and then default on their debt obligations. There is still a large gap arising from our nominal compliance of good corporate governance in accordance with regulatory provisions and real compliance of practicing it in law and spirit. We need to bridge this gap.

Enforce Accountability in All Walks of Life

All the other five steps that I talk of in this address, including real compliance of good governance, cannot be achieved unless we enforce accountability. Just as we need better governance at every level, we also need to enforce accountability in all walks of life. Our accountability structures, especially in public sector, are weak. In administration, the civil servants are insufficiently incentivised for the risks they take, are seldom rewarded for successful completion of their goals and are, at best, merely transferred for poor implementation. Mangers in public sector enterprises face similar problems in addition to bureaucratic interventions that delay decisions or require them to move away from policies which may be in the best interests of a public sector unit. It is difficult to enforce accountability in this climate.

On corporate accountability, the principal-agent relationship between the management or those who wrest ownership and control and the shareholders as actual owners is rather weak. We have seen asset stripping and bankruptcies in this weak environment. This has been especially true where a complex web of companies within business groups prevail. There is a strong case for simplifying these structures that are often developed to evade taxes, indulge in regulatory arbitrage and to strip assets of the firm for personal use. In recent period, we have come across instances where corporate debt restructuring is sought but ownership commitment of those who have control is rather left weak. We must enforce accountability in such cases by forcing such business entities to bring in more of their capital. There are, sometimes, grave cases of businessmen launching new firms, renaming firms or indulging in M&As (mergers and acquisitions) to garner fresh public money after they misused funds in the first instance. The concept of the modern firm based on limited liability principle requires care to prevent such practices.

Our political process ensures a fair deal of accountability through our democratic institutions. Yet, there is debate on whether a right to recall should exist. A more fragmented polity and existence of coalitions and minority governments, sometimes, make matters worse. Accountability at the municipal levels is also lacking. This, in turn, impacts the upkeep of our infrastructure that gets built. Roads seldom last more than a year. Drainage systems choke.

What is, therefore, necessary in this climate is to do four things. First, stakeholder engagement must be intensified in all institutions—public or private. Furthermore, there should be a principle of inclusivity in stakeholder engagement so that any sort of regulatory capture by interest groups is avoided. Second, individuals, rather than committees or groups, should be made accountable even where a collegiate approach is adopted. Such accountability should not be time barred by transfers of jobs or retirements. Third, financial accountability must be enforced for all. For enhancing fiscal transparency, the budgetary processes should be made tighter so that slippages are eliminated. Similarly, financial accountability needs to be promoted for firms and non-profit institutions. Fourth, accountability should be codified to the degree it can be done and a periodic evaluation must be done to assess achievement, failures and correctives.

Make Finance More Responsive to Real Sector and Promote Inclusive Growth

Let me, at last, cover the role of finance in India's transformation from elephant to tiger. I have kept this for the end because this is where finance should belong to. In recent period, finance has become big and rather than responding to the real sector needs, it is leading the real sector. Too-big to fail syndrome, firms depending on other incomes to shore up their accounts, market herd behaviour driven by noise rather than fundamentals are all examples of finance sector becoming too big for its boots. Yet, the finance to support real activity is still inadequate. Firms and businesses still get crowded out by information asymmetry. Financial frictions and financial constraints come in the way of investment and growth in the economy. For want of collaterals, the poor cannot access even elementary banking services, resulting not only in some potential saving getting lost but leaving the society more unequal and polarised with insufficient support for Pareto superior outcomes just because gainers can't compensate the losers.

Finance must be regulated more tightly. This does not require more regulations but perhaps less and newer regulations with greater effectiveness. At the same time, those who engage in finance must have an obligation towards promoting financial inclusion, without which inclusive growth cannot be achieved. Banking should have a human face for it is the households who provide the base for all banking activities. They are the only ones with financial surpluses which can be intermediated to corporate and public sectors that run financial deficits. It has been my endeavour to push policies on bank lending with a view to encourage credit flows to the vulnerable section of the population that would otherwise get financially excluded.

Over the years, this has been the ethos of the RBI. The branch licensing policy and the directed lending route have been the two pillars on which the efforts for financial inclusion have rested for a long time. The bank licencing policy, mandating a certain ratio of rural bank branches for each license for urban branch, has often been criticised by banks as coming in the way of their business interests. However, there is strong research evidence to suggest that this social banking experiment in India has been successful in improving the credit flows to the rural population and even in lowering poverty as a result. The priority sector lending (PSL) stipulation has also improved the flow of credit to certain productive sectors of the economy that would otherwise have been crowded out of the bank credit market due to information asymmetries. There are reasons to believe that with proper planning and use of technology-enabled efficient delivery channels, banks can pursue financial inclusion in a profitable way.

Our approach should not be seen as being interventionist. In practice, RBI has deftly balanced objectives of equity and efficiency so that financial inclusion is furthered, but banks' financial health is not impaired. In more recent period with which I have been associated, we have redoubled our efforts at financial inclusion. For instance, the prescription for PSL in respect of foreign banks has been raised from 32 per cent to 40 per cent in the case of those banks which have 20 or more branches. We have also imparted a more human touch to basic banking for those who did not have bank accounts.

Conclusion

Let me end by talking about something we need to learn from the East Asian tigers in our quest to become one. Growth acceleration in these tigers were supported by liberalisation, export-led growth, high investment in education, large share of educated workforce, high public and private savings rate, and macroeconomic discipline and governance. We are pursuing some of these policies and can pursue some more of them. However, these tigers also failed to maintain their spurt because of some mistakes they committed. Some of them maintained high interest rate to attract foreign investments, others pegged currency arrangements and many of them developed a vulnerable financial system. An unanticipated shock from banking and currency side, therefore, resulted in growth collapse for them during the East Asian crisis. Corporate failures added to the financial sector woes in some countries (especially Chaebols in Korea). While transforming the Indian economy into a tiger, we need to calibrate policies taking into account the lessons learnt during the East Asian crisis.

Downturns come and go away as business cycles run their course. In our present predicaments with macro-economic stabilisation, we must not lose sight of our larger goals, whether we walk at an elephant's pace or run like a tiger. Let me assure you that as a society, if we can inculcate an aggressive and tenacious urge to attain a set goal- the killer instinct of the tiger—we would definitely earn our rightful place under the sun.

References

Aiyar, Swaminathan Anklesaria (2011). "The Elephant that Became a Tiger: 20 Years of Economic Reform in India", *Development Policy Analysis no. 13*, July 20. Cato Institute.

Akerlof, George A. and Paul M. Romer (1993). "Looting: The Economic Underworld of Bankruptcy for Profit", *Brookings Papers on Economic Activity* 2: 1-73.

Bosworth, Barry and Susan M. Collins (2007). "Accounting for Growth: Comparing China and India", *NBER Working Paper* No. 12943, February.

Tharoor, Shashi (2007). *The Elephant, the Tiger and the Cellphone: Reflections on India: The Emerging 21st Century Power*. New York: Arcade Publishers.

Subbarao, Duvvuri (2011). "Rejigging the Elephant Dance", Haksar Memorial Lecture delivered by Dr Duvvuri Subbarao, Governor, Reserve Bank of India at the Centre for Research in Rural & Industrial Development, Chandigarh, November 25, 2011, reprinted in *RBI Bulletin*, December 2011, pp.2041-8.

World Bank and IFC (2012). *Doing Business 2013: Smarter Regulations for Small and Medium Enterprises*. Washington: The World Bank.

Address delivered at the interaction with members of Delhi Chapter of the Young Presidents Organization at New Delhi, December 7, 2012.

Economic Developments in India, Vol. 180.

5

A. VAIDYANATHAN

Indian Economy in Crisis

Assessment and Prospects

THE last two to three years have witnessed a deterioration in practically all aspects of the country's economic performance.

- After a decade of being in a healthy state, India's balance of payments (BoP) has worsened sharply in the last three years. The current account deficit (CAD) has increased in absolute terms from an average of $18 billion in 2006-2008 to nearly $55 billion and from less than 3 per cent to nearly 6 per cent as a proportion of the gross domestic product (GDP). The country's ability to finance the deficit has declined.
- Domestic wholesale price indices (WPIs), which increased at an average rate of 5 per cent per annum during 2000-2010, have recorded a progressive increase to double-digit levels, and consumer prices are rising at a faster rate.
- GDP growth in the country, which reached historically unprecedented levels of 9 per cent to 10 per cent per annum during the last decade, has come down to 5 per cent and less in the last two years.

The simultaneous deterioration of performance on these key fronts has led to a crisis of serious concern. This article examines the causes and consequences of this. We will explore the factors that have contributed to deterioration in each of these aspects, and comment on the prospects for reviving the health and growth momentum of the economy.

Balance of Payments

The surge in the CAD until 2012-13 was accounted for by the widening trade deficit because export growth has been increasingly outpaced by growth of commodity imports, and there has been no sustained or significant rise in net inflows of non-factor services (mostly software exports), remittances and invisibles.

Commodity exports have maintained a healthy rate of growth under a regime of more or less constant and stable exchange rates despite the recession in developed countries. But this has been slower than the surge in imports during the last three years. The bulk of increase in imports is accounted for by the growing demand for crude oil and higher prices for it; fertilisers; metals and minerals to meet shortfalls in domestic production; capital goods needed for capital formation; electronics; and materials for export industries. These items account for about 70 per cent of the increase in the value of total imports. The balance goes in meeting requirements of imports for other domestic production and consumption, including gold. The rapid growth in import of gold, which has risen nearly threefold since 2008-09, has emerged as a significant element in total imports, now comprising nearly one-eighth of them. The CAD grew from $16 billion in 2007-08 and $28 billion in 2008-09 to $78 billion in 2011-12. It has since been brought down to around 3 per cent of GDP because of slower growth and restrictions on gold imports.

In the pre-reform era, the CAD was largely financed by drawing down reserves, and using foreign aid and non-resident Indian (NRI) deposits. Capital inflows were severely restricted. Heavy reliance on commercial borrowings during the 1980s culminated in a severe payments crisis that triggered the liberalisation reforms of the 1990s. Since then, restrictions on external capital flows have been substantially relaxed to encourage foreign direct investment (FDI), investments by foreign institutional investors (FII) and through commercial borrowings. These measures, combined with the abundant availability of cheap funds in world financial markets, and the relatively higher returns to investments in stock markets, real estate and bank deposits in India, led to large inflows of foreign capital that were more than adequate to cover the CAD. This helped the country to increase its foreign exchange reserves to $307 billion by 2007-08.

The situation has since changed dramatically due to a conjunction of external and internal factors. The meltdown of the world financial system in 2008, followed by deep and continuing recession in the economies of developed countries, have had a significant impact on the Indian economy through shrinking markets for exports, increases in world market prices for key imports and declining capital inflows. These factors were compounded by the slowing down of investment and growth rate of the domestic economy; a rapid rise in the CAD; persistently high rates of inflation; and concerns about the country's ability to finance the widening CAD and meet impending large obligations for repayment of external commercial borrowings (ECBs). The decline in foreign reserves and sharp reduction in the rate of overall growth fuelled pessimism, inducing extreme volatility in both the stock market and the exchange rate. The situation has been contained by intervention of the Reserve Bank of India (RBI) at the cost of substantial depreciation of the rupee. The underlying concerns about the future prospects of both growth and BoP remain.

The reduction in imports during the last year will be reversed when growth revives. Containing it within the comfort level of 3.0 per cent to 3.5 per cent level of GDP calls for narrowing the difference between the rates of growth of exports and imports. The recent depreciation goes some way to this, but its efficacy is likely to be limited by several factors. While it obviously increases the profitability of export industries, the extent of the increase varies depending partly on the extent to which export production depends on imported inputs, and the ability of entrepreneurs to exploit the competitive advantage by increasing production and aggressive marketing.

The impact on imports depends on the extent to which their higher costs are passed on to users, and on the price sensitivity of domestic demand to prices. In the case of oil, oil products and fertilisers, which are widely used by other sectors in production but are supplied at highly subsidised rates, only a small part of the increase in import prices is passed on to users. There are indications that this will change in the near future. In these cases, users have little incentive to economise on the use of these inputs. In some cases, notably metals and coal, import is determined by shortfalls in domestic production. Removal of bottlenecks to investment for expansion of capacity and for underutilisation of available capacity would substantially reduce the need for imports. The demand for gold is price insensitive. Altogether, about a third of total imports belong to the above categories. The demand for the rest, which have to bear the full impact of higher import prices, can be expected to dampen the growth of demand and also induce greater import substitution.

Prospects of FDI

The reliance on unstable sources of finance clearly needs to be reduced. Direct investment in projects in the country is obviously preferable because it goes with the acquisition of a permanent stake in enterprises and contributes directly to improvement of technology and production. Interest in encouraging FDI increased during the reform era and it became a major element of policy. Government attempts to woo FDI have become a highly contentious domestic political issue. Faced with severe opposition, the approach to liberalising the FDI policy has been cautious and limited to a few selected spheres, notably automobiles, telecom, finance, real estate and software. The proportion going into greenfield investments has been relatively small compared to mergers and acquisitions (M&A) and for buying into the equity of existing enterprises. With significant exceptions such as automobiles, components and software (both capital and technologically intensive), their focus has been on the domestic market. Overall, the scale of inflows has been relatively small.

Inflation

Persistent high rates of inflation are another major cause for concern. Analyses and discussions of causes and remedies of inflation in academia, policy and political forums are based on the official WPI and CPI (consumer price index). By these indices, inflation has significantly increased since 2004-05 compared to the previous decade—the average rate of increase in the WPI during the decade ending 2004-05 was around 5 per cent per annum, while in the subsequent seven years it averaged 6.6 per cent. Moreover, while there was no significant trend in the rate in the earlier period, it has increased significantly after that—from 8 per cent in 2006-07 to a peak of 17 per cent in 2009-10. Although it has since dipped, it still remains at 9 per cent to 10 per cent. There are significant differences both in the rate and pattern of price increases across sectors (Table 5.1).

Table 5.1

Recent Trends in Wholesale Price Index

	Overall	*Indices of WPI, 2004-05 =100*				*Ratio of Food/*
		Food	*Manufactures*	*Fuel*	*Minerals*	*Manufactures*
Average 1994-2005 to 2004-05	5.0	5.0		4.0		
2005-06	104.5	105	115	102	114	1.01
2006-07	111.4	116	137	108	121	1.08
2007-08	116.6	126	153	118	121	1.07
2008-09	126	135	187	120	135	1.13
2009-10	130.8	155	203	123	132	1.26
2010-11	143.3	180	253	130	148	1.40
2011-12	156.1	193	321	140	169	1.38
Average 2004-05 to 2011-12	6.6	10	16.7	5.1	7.9	

Source: Based on estimates of averages for months for various years in *Economic Survey 2012-13*; 1993-2005 estimates based on series with 1983-84 as base; those for 2005-2011 based on 1993-94 base.

Changes in the indices for several key sectors do not reflect the state of balance between supply and demand in the domestic market. They are influenced to a significant extent by direct government intervention in the market through administered prices as well as the effect of changes in the world market. The prices of several key inputs (energy, fertilisers and rail transport) are determined administratively and not through the market. Ideally, these should be fixed at levels that enable the total revenue to cover the overall costs of producing and distributing them for various uses, allowing for discrimination between uses on the basis of social and strategic considerations. Costs have varied around a strong rising secular trend. But governments have followed a conscious policy of not charging prices to end-users to ensure full cost recovery. In many cases, issue prices have been unchanged or even reduced to prevent causing hardship to users, especially socially and economically vulnerable people. Because of this, the official price index tends to suppress the true extent of inflationary pressures in the economy.

A striking feature is a sharp break in the trend behaviour of agricultural prices relative to those of manufactures before and after 2004-05. During the decade before 2004-05, they rose at an average rate of 5 per cent per annum, roughly at the same rate as the overall index and slightly more than that of manufactures. Their ratio does not show any significant trend. But in the subsequent seven years, while the overall index rose by 6.6 per cent per annum on an average and that of manufactures rose by 5 per cent per annum, the index for agriculture increased by 10 per cent per annum. Since then, and especially during the last five years, the ratio of agricultural to manufacturing prices has shown a sustained rise.

Besides well-known deficiencies such as the coverage and reliability of prices, especially of products in the unorganised sector, the official WPI does not adequately capture the impact of major changes in patterns of production and consumption; the introduction of numerous new products; and changes in their quality. Over time, especially during the last two decades, the proportion of private consumption expenditure spent on food has steadily declined even as the proportion devoted to non-food items has grown rapidly. Among non-food items, the share of services has grown much faster than of manufactures. These patterns are evident in both rural and urban areas, more markedly so in the latter.

In the case of agriculture, we have a situation in which the government's policy of raising the minimum support price (MSP) for staple crops and accumulating larger stocks of food grains has had a significant impact on open market prices. But prices of non-MSP crops (which include practically all fruits, vegetables and animal products) are left wholly to the market. The production of all crops being significantly dependent on rainfall, they are inherently volatile. The trend growth rate of output (overall) has remained more or less constant throughout, even as accelerated urbanisation, worsening income distribution and changing consumption patterns have led to a slower growth in demand for food despite much higher growth of incomes.

The relative constancy of food to non-food prices during the 1980s and 1990s suggests that the growth of overall food supply was in a rough balance with decelerating demand growth. The subsequent sharp increase in food to non-food prices points to a major change with aggregate supply growth falling increasingly short of the slower pace of demand growth. The increase in prices of non-cereal food is far more marked than for cereals, which points to an increasing shortfall of supplies relative to demand for animal products, vegetables and fruits. The possibilities of coping with this growing imbalance through imports to contain domestic prices is limited because of BoP constraints, and the non-availability of perishables on the scale needed to meet the overall demand. Under these conditions, in the absence of a significant turnaround in domestic agricultural growth, for which the prospects are far from promising, sluggish agriculture can become an important structural source of food inflation.

Inflation Control Mechanisms

Under these circumstances, control of inflation is handled at the macro-economic level through appropriate conventional fiscal, foreign exchange and monetary policies. The first two are the responsibility of the central government. Maintaining reasonable price stability and ensuring the stability of the financial system are the central mandate of the RBI. Monetary policy is meant to be decided and implemented by the RBI as an autonomous and professional organisation. As all three components of macroeconomic management are closely interrelated, coordination between them to ensure mutual consistency is important. While, by law, the RBI board is free to decide on matters falling within in its domain, the necessity for coordination requires consultation and discussions with the central government. There are inbuilt mechanisms, both formal and informal, to facilitate the process and arrive at a consensus. These mechanisms have worked fairly well so far. In the process, the RBI is exposed to covert and overt pressures from the government and business interests, but has managed to assert and retain its autonomy.

The ability of the RBI to fulfil its mandate is severely constrained by the government's fiscal deficit, which is both chronic and frequently beyond prudent limits. The inability of the government to control the deficit forces the RBI to carry the brunt of responsibility for inflation control by regulating the volume and terms of credit overall and for different sectors, and at the same time ensuring stability of the financial system. The bank seeks to achieve these objectives primarily by adjusting the rates of interest permissible on different types of deposits; the repo and reverse repo rates for RBI lending to banks; and the provisioning norms for different kinds of loans depending on the emerging trends in the economy.

But the scope for using these instruments is constrained partly by the need to balance concerns about containing inflation without hurting growth, and that the demand for credit from large sections (especially agriculture, a wide range of intermediate goods, imports and the public sector) is not sensitive to interest rates on loans. The room for manoeuvre is constrained by mandatory targets of lending at concessional rates for priority sectors, and that large unorganised segments of the economy are beyond the reach of banks and institutions over which the RBI has control.

Going forward, it is clear that the efficacy of monetary policy for inflation management and maintaining stability of the financial system is severely limited unless combined with appropriate fiscal and foreign exchange policies. The exchange rate has been kept reasonably stable for much of the last decade along with significant accretion to reserves thanks to substantial inflows of foreign funds. But recent volatility of these flows in response to disturbances in the world markets and their impact on the exchange rate of the rupee and on domestic economic growth gives cause for concern. On the fiscal front, the government has been unable to control the burgeoning fiscal deficit, and its adverse impact on inflation, public sector development outlays and growth.

Subsidies

The persistently high and rising fiscal deficit touched a high of 6.5 per cent in 2009-10 and is around 3.0 per cent to 4.0 per cent now. This has severely impaired the government's capacity to maintain the holy trinity in balance and led to rampant inflation. The major part of the fiscal deficit is because of the conscious state policy of supplying a wide range of goods to different sections of the population at prices well below their cost.

Much the larger part of subsidies and their rapid growth currently is for energy, water, fertilisers and other intermediate products used in the process of production. The supply of these products and their costs of production and distribution are determined by world market conditions for some resources, and constrained by the level and efficiency of investments for expanding domestic capacity. In the absence of independent and effective regulatory authorities, the pricing of these products is subject to political pressures to keep them low despite supply constraints and rising costs. This results in a chronic cycle of excess demand and conflicts over access to, including illegal appropriation of, available supplies. Subsidies on these inputs not only cut deep into the resources available for growth, but also cause enormous collateral damage to sustainable development. Subsidisation of commercial energy for domestic use and private motorised transport, which is mostly concentrated among middle and upper-income groups, can hardly be justified in the interests of social equity. Supply at low prices encourages faster growth of demand for imports and, if world markets for oil continue to be tight, sustained pressure on public authorities to not increase prices.

These tendencies cannot be corrected by appropriate adjustments in prices in the face of concerted user pressure for keeping prices low and the political class' propensity to succumb to it. This has caused distortions in the patterns and efficiency of use throughout the system, posing serious threats to sustainability of growth with equity. The undesirable consequences of these policies are best illustrated by the effect of water and fertiliser pricing policies.

The expansion of irrigation, increased fertiliser use and introduction of improved varieties with a genetically higher yield potential have been the key factors that have contributed to the growth of agricultural production. Each individually and in combination contributes to increased production by more intensive cropping, a shift to higher-yielding crop patterns and higher yields of individual crops. Their combined impact is to increase the overall productivity of land and return to cultivation compared to rainfed farming. But there are strict diminishing returns to increasing their quantum. The optimum results depend on how much inputs are applied, in what combination, and when. Individual farmers neither have the knowledge nor the means to determine and observe this. Their tendency is to focus on getting more water to irrigate larger areas as the main pre-condition for increasing productivity. The large difference in yields between irrigated and rain-fed land gives rise to a strong demand for expansion of irrigation facilities.

The government has responded to these pressures by undertaking massive investments for constructing large-scale surface irrigation works; infrastructure for expansion of groundwater irrigation; and by keeping water charges and energy for pumping groundwater very low. Under these circumstances, farmers' focus is on somehow getting access to water and not its optimal management. Nor are administrative agencies of the government responsible for water management. On the contrary, their pricing policies seriously erode incentives for prudent and efficient use of both water and fertilisers. As a consequence, the yield impact of irrigation both per unit of land and, more so, per unit of water use are much below that demonstrated under controlled research conditions.

Low water rates have led to the demand for water outstripping the increase in available supplies, and increasing conflicts between uses and users. In many areas, over exploitation of groundwater has led to a progressive lowering of the water table. In surface irrigated areas, overuse of water has resulted in increased waterlogging and salinity, and degradation of land. Large-scale leaching of nutrients into water sources due to excessive and imprudent use of fertilisers has become a major reason for pollution and qualitative deterioration of water sources, making them unfit for potable and agricultural uses.

Rationalisation and reduction of subsidies is essential to reduce, if not eliminate, dysfunctional subsidies, which do not contribute to reducing inequalities and/or have adverse effects on the efficient and sustainable use of resources. This will release resources available to the exchequer for growth of output and employment in a manner that is inclusive and equitable. Many of the existing subsidies do not help mitigate socio-economic inequalities, tend to benefit the better-off segments, and are ineffective from the viewpoints of efficiency, equity and sustainability.

Sustaining rapid economic growth under conditions of reasonably stable domestic price levels and the CAD depends, at present, on reducing the fiscal deficit. That a high level of explicit and implicit subsidies is being borne by the budget is a major reason for the persistence of high levels of budget deficits. Reducing the burden of subsidies is therefore both necessary and urgent for restoring the economy to a higher but stable growth trajectory. That there is ample scope for this should be apparent from the foregoing discussion. But it is also obvious that any attempt to exploit this potential will face strong opposition from varied and widespread interests that have been beneficiaries of the existing system.

This calls for a strategy that focuses initially on rationalisation of the existing subsidy regime so that larger revenues can be generated without raising rates. Thus more resources can be released for productive investment. This is possible because a considerable amount of revenue is foregone because of the pervasive under-assessment of dues and underrecovery of assessed dues. The potential for this is quite substantial in the case of water and electricity.

Steps are also necessary to narrow the differential between issue prices and costs. But this has to be done in a phased manner by setting targets for raising prices by specified degrees over the medium and long term. In doing so, it is necessary that this done transparently and on the basis of clearly stated principles. The changes must be based on a credible professional analysis documenting the loss of efficiency and the inequities of the present system, and the consequences of not taking corrective action. An essential condition is to assure users that they will not bear the burden of high costs due to mismanagement and/or corruption; that the increases will be phased in moderate steps and in a progressive manner; and that it will find ways (through differential and discriminatory changes) to reduce the impact on poor and vulnerable segments.

The ultimate objective is a radical restructuring of the institutional arrangements for developing and managing these programmes. It must be insulated from government/political interference except for laying down the basic policy framework, and run by autonomous professional managers, subject to independent audit. Decisions on pricing must be subject to review and approval by independent regulatory agencies.

Growth

The performance of the economy during the last two decades in terms of overall growth and structural transformation is obviously both unprecedented and impressive. During much of the last decade, the economy maintained a high rate of growth of domestic output and investment. Foreign trade and capital inflows at relatively low rates of inflation from 2000-01 to 2007-08 received a major shock in the wake of the meltdown of the financial system in 2008 and the recession in developed countries. India's growth rate dipped sharply in 2008-09. Although it recovered in the next two years to a level comparable to the levels reached in mid-decade, the impact of the continuing world recession, and the rise in oil and commodity prices has since led to a slowing down of domestic growth rates in most key sectors.

The trend rate of increase in agriculture continues to fluctuate around the long-term historical trend of 2.5 per cent per annum, and industrial growth has averaged around 7.0 per cent per annum since 2008-09, compared to more than 9.0 per cent per annum earlier. The overall growth of tertiary sector GDP increased progressively from less than 7.0 per cent in 2001-02 to more than 11.0 per cent in 2005-

06, but fell to 9.0 per cent in 2011-12. The growth rates of transport, communications, construction and business services—the 'sunrise' sectors that drove growth over this period—have also slowed down. There are, however, concerns about the sustainability of the nature and pace of volatility of sectoral growth rates, with robustness of growth based so heavily on the tertiary sector and the increased vulnerability of the economy to the external economic environment. The social and political consequences of inequalities and the growing power of big corporations (domestic and foreign) in the economy and polity, and the pursuit of a pattern of growth unmindful of its environmental consequences and sustainability are additional sources of concern.

Agriculture

Except for liberalisation of foreign trade in farm products, there has been no significant change in the strategy for promoting agricultural growth during the last two decades. The domestic agricultural development strategy continued to focus on increasing public investments in irrigation and land improvement; research to develop varieties and techniques to raise the yield of crops and livestock; providing key material inputs at subsidised prices; and substantial increases in farm support prices. The overall impact has been limited because of the adjustments mandated by the World Trade Organization (WTO).

The scale of resources devoted to various components of development programmes has grown manifold without making much of a difference to the growth of output. This is largely due to technological, institutional and economic constraints. The expansion of irrigation has slowed down despite massive investments by both the public and private sectors. In the public sector, problems caused by inordinate delays in implementation and uncontrolled cost escalations of surface water works have been aggravated. Private investment, mostly for exploiting groundwater, goes increasingly into deepening wells and installing more powerful pumps. Programmes for soil conservation and land improvement, which are critical for raising the productivity of rainfed lands, are inadequate both in scale and effectiveness. Progress in improvement of crop varieties and agronomic practices has been uneven across regions and crops, and more so between rainfed and irrigated crops. The functioning of public systems responsible for the management and regulation of common pool resources, research and input supply have deteriorated. But there is no sign of recognition among the political class and policy makers of the implications of the persistence of these trends and their underlying causes. The prospects of any significant improvement in terms of sustained growth rates of farm output overall, and of its ability to meet rapidly diversifying patterns of consumption are therefore very dim. That the socio-economic consequences of allowing present trends to continue will be serious is already manifest in widening disparities between rainfed and irrigated tracts, and between rural and urban areas.

There are growing social tensions and agrarian distress in the rural economy, and signs of growing disinclination among the newer generation of large and even medium farm households to continue in agriculture. These problems are likely to accentuate as the gap between the agricultural and non-agricultural sectors continues to widen. With the long-term trend growth of agriculture being only slightly more than population growth, and signs of greater volatility during the last decade, droughts and natural calamities can have a disproportionately large impact on shortfalls, which in turn would adversely affect the ability to manage the new food security programme and ensure reasonable price stability of non-cereal food items.

Secondary Sector

The performance of secondary sectors during the reform period has been quite uneven. The pace of increase in GDP from mining, manufacturing and utilities during the last two decades has been faster than in the previous two decades. However, closer scrutiny of the trajectories of changes in different sub-sectors over the period shows considerable unevenness. Growth in mining and utilities during the reform period turned out to be much slower than earlier, with no sign of sustained improvement over the period.

The progressive increase in rates of capital formation following liberalisation was reflected in the faster and quickening growth of construction activity and in the slight rise (from 6.8% to 7.8%) in its share in GDP over the period. Given that the main focus of reforms was on freeing industry from the earlier regime of direct controls, freer markets and more scope and opportunity for the private sector should have had a big impact on production and investment in this sector. But this expectation has been belied.

Manufacturing output during the last two decades did increase 3.7 times compared to 2.6 times in the earlier two decades. However, this was only marginally higher than the overall GDP growth rate. The share of manufacturing in total GDP rose, but marginally from 15 per cent to less than 16 per cent over the period. Moreover, even the limited liberalisation reforms initiated during the 1980s had a sizeable impact in the latter half of that decade. The rate of increase in manufacturing GDP in the reform period turns out to be only marginally higher than that during the second half of the 1980s. Nor is there any indication of a sustained quickening in the pace of growth over the last two decades. During this period, manufacturing output more or less kept pace with the overall economy. There was no significant increase in the share of this sector in total GDP or its increment (Table 5.2).

Table 5.2

Trends in Secondary Sector GDP during the Reform and Pre-reform Periods

	1988-1990	*1998-2000*	*2008-2010*	*1990-2010*
Mining	429	675	1,039	142
Manufacture	1,919	3,409	7,167	274
R	1,125	2,100	4,894	335
UR	813	1,314	2,273	180
EGW	251	504	874	248
Construction	873	1,468	3,574	309

Note: R: registered, UR: unregistered, EGW: electricity gas and water. Estimates in rupees billion at constant 2004-05 prices are based on the Central Statistical Office's national accounts statistics.

The rate of increase in manufacturing GDP in the reform period turns out to be only marginally higher than during the second half of the 1980s. Nor is there any indication of a sustained quickening in the pace of growth over the last two decades.

This is widely attributed to tardy implementation of programmes to expand infrastructural support; lukewarm responses to efforts to attract FDI; delays in land acquisition and getting environmental clearances for major projects; concerns about the scope, pace and social impact of liberalisation; and the quality of entrepreneurial response to emerging opportunities.

Given that India was and still is a low income country, one would expect domestic consumer demand for manufactures relative to incomes to be relatively high. However, according to national income estimates, private consumption of manufactured goods has grown roughly at the same rate as aggregate consumption expenditure. The available data from consumer surveys suggest that per capita expenditure on manufactures in urban areas is around twice the level reported in rural areas. Given the rapid pace of urbanisation, overall consumer demand for manufactures must have risen faster than total private consumption expenditure. This tendency would be reinforced by rising per capita incomes and worsening income distribution between (and within) rural and urban areas. While the reasons for this discrepancy need to be investigated, it is worth noting that national income estimates are based on inadequate data on physical output of manufactures and their disposition, especially in the unorganised sector.

With rising rates of capital formation, the demand for machinery, cement and construction material used for investment has increased faster than total national income. Exports of manufactures have also recorded unprecedented growth during the last two decades. Overall, the aggregate domestic demand for manufactures has grown rapidly. The full impact of the growth of aggregate demand for manufactures was, however, not been realised by domestic industry because an increasing proportion of it (especially of capital goods) is met by imports. The recent sharp reduction in industrial growth to near stagnation levels reflects a slowdown of investment, exports and domestic consumer demand.

Exports of manufactures, which were relatively small and did not increase much during the 1970s and 1980s, recorded a phenomenal expansion in the last two decades. The performance has, however, been neither consistent nor comparable to the record of several other developing countries, including China.

Tertiary Sector

The tertiary sector consists of a mixed bag of diverse activities with widely varying growth. Several segments (personal services, entertainment, real estate services and rentals) have grown much slower than aggregate GDP, and largely cater for private consumption. Public administration and defence have grown roughly at the same rate as overall GDP. Activities that cater for domestic demand and have grown somewhat faster than average include trade, transport, education and medical services provided by both the private and public sectors.

- The growth of trading activity is related to the expansion in the total volume of commodities being produced and the proportion that is traded in domestic and international markets.
- Expansion of transport reflects the growth of freight traffic (which is a function of commodity production) and the rapid increase in private demand for travel by all modes.
- The rapid expansion in demand for education and health services being met by the public sector and increasingly by the private sector is reflected in the relatively rapid growth of GDP generated by these sectors.

Together, all these activities accounted for the bulk (85%) of tertiary sector GDP in 1988-1990. Their output has now quadrupled to account for nearly 70 per cent of its increment over the period. Given the economic slowdown in developed countries, the rapid growth of IT services is unlikely to be sustained, as also the growth in telecom and domestic business services. On this basis, and given the modest growth of agriculture and industry, the overall growth rate may be around 7 per cent per annum.

Inequality

Concern over the persistence of social and economic inequality and the need for purposive action to reduce it has been a continuing feature of public and political discourse in India. These concerns have been heightened by the widespread impression that these inequalities have increased in the era of liberalisation. Inequalities exist across several dimensions—between castes and communities, classes, rural and urban areas, individuals, and in terms of income, wealth, consumption levels, and living standards. Data from household consumption surveys conducted by the National Sample Survey (NSS) give some idea of trends in inequality in private consumption expenditures in rural and urban India, across states and social groups, in the post-reform period.

They show that at the all-India level, overall per capita consumption expenditure was consistently higher in urban areas than in rural areas, and the disparity has been growing progressively since the early 1970s. This trend has been more remarked in the reform period (1987-88 to 2009-10). Interpersonal inequality in the distribution of consumption—measured by the Gini coefficient—is considerable and persistent in both rural and urban areas. Inequality in urban areas is consistently higher than in rural areas.

Over the last two decades, the extent of inequality has not shown any sustained trend in rural areas, but it shows a sustained rising trend in urban areas. The rural-urban difference has also widened progressively, especially in the reform period. With urban pre-capital private consumption expenditure (PCE) being higher and increasing faster than in rural areas, inequality in the distribution of private consumption for the population as a whole is increasing (Table 5.3).

Trends estimated from household consumption surveys are apt to understate the degree of inequality because NSS estimates of total PCE are consistently lower than National Accounts Statistics (NAS) estimates and the difference progressively widened from about 36 per cent in 1987-88 to 50 per cent in 2009-10. This points to an increasing underestimation bias in NSS estimates of private consumption. The downward bias in NSS estimates reflects the unwillingness and inability of households to give complete and accurate information on their consumption expenditures. Field experience suggests that this is more pronounced among upper-income households, especially in urban areas. If allowance is made for these differences, the NSS estimates of inequality (Gini coefficient) substantially understate the true extent of inequality and upward trends in it. It is, however, difficult to pin down the extent of this downward bias in NSS estimates.

Table 5.3

Trends in Per Capita Private Consumption and its Inequality in Rural and Urban India

		1972-73	*1977-78*	*1983*	*1987-88*	*1993-94*	*1999-2000*	*2004-05*	*2009-10*
Mean PCE	Rural	44.2	68.9	112.3	158.1	286.1	486.1	558.8	927
	Urban	63.3	96.1	165.8	250	464.3	854.9	1052.4	178.5
	U/R	1.43	1.4	1.48	1.58	1.62	1.75	1.88	1.92
Gini coefficient of PCE	Rural	.302	.337	.298	.291	.281	.28	.297	.27
	Urban	.341	.345	.330	.352	.340	.343	.373	.381
	U/R	1.13	1.02	1.11	1.21	1.21	1.23	1.26	1.41

Note: Estimates are at current prices. After adjusting for differences in the rate of inflation (consumer price index for agricultural labourers, or CPIAL, for rural, and index for non-manual workers in urban areas), the rural-urban gap in mean consumption shows a sharper rise since the late 1980s.

Source: Rattanchand (2006).

Incomes generated in the process of economic activity consist of two components: wages and salaries paid to hired labour or imputed for labour provided by the self-employed and employers, and income from real and financial assets owned by entities. Inequalities in the former reflect differences in the extent and quality of employment, and the rates at which workers of different categories and skills are remunerated. Unskilled casual wage labour is paid the least; workers with full time, regular employment get more; and wages increase with the level of education and experience (Table 5.4).

For the economy as a whole, average wage rates of casual wage labour are consistently low in rural areas, followed by urban areas. The average for all workers with regular employment is much higher. During the post-reform period, both the level of employment and average wage rates of both casual and regular workers have increased significantly. Casual labour wages have increased significantly and at a faster rate in rural areas. Urban wage rates for regular workers are also consistently higher than in rural areas and the rate of increase is higher. Therefore the rural-urban differential is progressively widening. This rising wage trend has gone with a sustained rise in both the level and the degree of diversification of employment during the reform period. Over the last two decades, the entire increase in the labour force has found employment in non-agricultural activities and involuntary unemployment rates are low.

Table 5.4

Average Earnings of Different Categories of Hired Labour

		1987-88	*1999-2000*	*2009-10*
Casual rural manual	₹ per day	11.2	45	102
Casual urban manual	₹ per day	17.9	63	132
Regular RM	₹ per day	34.9	127	249
Regular UM	₹ per day	34.9	170	377
Factory workers	₹ per day	53	193	411
Factory workers	000 ₹/year	15.8	57	125
Government employees	000 ₹/year	20.1	113*	
Central PSUs	000 ₹/year	32.5	168	610
Banks	000 ₹/year	48.3	403*	
ICT companies	000 ₹/year		5,300**	
BPOs	000 ₹/year		1,000-1,200**	

Source: * Figure reported in Ghosh, Arijit (2003). *Determinants of Executive Compensation in Emerging Evidence from India's Economy*. Mumbai: IGIDR.

** Reported in Pratap, Surendra (2010). *Challenges for Organising the BPO Workers in India*. Hong Kong: Asia Monitor Resource Centre.

However the rate of increase varies hugely across different categories of employment in a manner that increases inequality in wage incomes at the point of generation. At the bottom of the pile are casual wage labourers, who constitute more than a quarter of the total workforce. Their average wage rates and total earnings per year are the lowest and remain so despite significant increases over time. Overall, their relative position has worsened compared to regular workers.

The advent of IT, communications, and specialised business services generated demand for personnel with high levels of technical and professional training, which commanded a worldwide market. This led to salary levels getting aligned with international rates, which are far higher than in domestic sectors. The fact that the growing demand could not be fully met with available supplies of personnel led to a rapid increase in emolument levels. This phenomenon had a spillover effect on other organised enterprises. The available evidence suggests that this affected salaries at the professional/managerial levels more than others. For instance, in the factory sector of industry, the average emoluments of employees other than process workers are invariably higher than the average for workers in both non-corporate and corporate establishments. Interestingly, the disparity between the two has increased during the last two decades, the tendency being much pronounced in the private corporate sector. The cumulative effect of these trends is to increase the inequality in the distribution of wage and salary incomes among workers. This tendency is likely to be further aggravated by the progressive increase in the proportion of organised sector workforce hired on a contract or temporary basis. Given the importance of these phenomena, it is surprising that so little attention is given to ensuring reliable and sufficiently detailed data on the composition of employment and the basis and levels of remuneration of different classes of employees in different sectors and types of enterprises.

Non-wage incomes consisting of the incomes of the self-employed and employers of unincorporated enterprises and the profits of the organised sector have also grown. The former has increased at roughly the same rate as wages and salaries of hired labour. Little is known about the degree of inequality in its distribution within that class. But the distribution of profits of other enterprises, especially corporate enterprises, is heavily skewed in favour of the higher income classes. The higher the proportion of profits earned by the private sector (operating surplus in national income terminology), the higher is the overall inequality in income distribution. During the last decade, profit incomes have grown far faster than total wage and mixed incomes. The increase in their share in total private incomes from 14.7 per cent in 1993-94 to 19.4 per cent in 2009-10 must have led to a significant increase in overall inequality (Table 5.5).

Table 5.5

Growth of Non-wage and Non-self-employed Incomes in India

	1993-94			*2009-10*		
	Total	*PSUs*	*Private*	*Total*	*PSUs*	*Private*
NDP	6,990	1,629	939	54,490	11,115	12,400
Employee compensation	2,390	1,107	433	34,868	9,056	3,600
Mixed incomes	3,548	–	–	24,178	–	–
Operating surplus	1,028	522	506	10,690	2,159	8,740
% of NDP	14.7	31.5	53.8	20	19.4	70

Note: PSU = public sector enterprises; Private = enterprises in the organised private sector.

Source: National accounts estimates; all figures are in billions of rupees at current prices.

Strategy for Reducing Inequality

Reducing, if not eliminating, socio-economic inequalities figured prominently in both political and policy rhetoric in the early part of the post-Independence era. For nearly two decades, inequalities in income and wealth were sought to be reduced through land reforms; encouraging cooperative forms of production; nationalising key sectors; progressively increasing the proportion of income and wealth generated by the public sector; and progressive taxation. But none of them was pursued seriously and at any rate had little effect on the ground reality of persistent inequality, slow growth and an unacceptably high incidence of mass poverty and unemployment.

The 1950s and 1960s were marked by growing concern over the slow pace of improvement in average living standards and in basic social amenities; per capita incomes; the persistence of high levels of unemployment and underemployment, especially among poor segments of the population; declining real wages; and indications of increasing concentrations of incomes and wealth. Efforts to achieve faster growth being unsuccessful, attempts to cope with growing restlessness veered towards ways of directly ameliorating the conditions of the poor and the unemployed, who constituted a large majority of the electorate. The idea of an employment guarantee scheme mooted during this phase was rapidly expanded as an important part of national strategy. Indira Gandhi used this along with bank nationalisation and abolition of privy purses as socialistic measures to win elections. Ever since, the idea of anti-poverty programmes has come to be widely accepted and pursued by practically all political parties. Expanding the scope and differentiated packaging of its elements to garner wider support has become an endemic feature of electoral strategy in this era of competitive politics.

These trends have continued in the post-reform era in an even more intensified form. With sharp increases in the growth of both overall and average per capita GDP during this period, the entire increase in the labour force has been absorbed outside agriculture at rising real wage rates. Thus the incidence of poverty has declined appreciably. While pro-reformers saw this as justifying liberalisation and carrying it further, those opposed highlighted the slow pace of improvement in living standards of the rural population, largely reflecting the persistent slow growth of agriculture; the aggravation of inequalities in living standards between rural and urban areas; and the unsatisfactory access to and quality of basic social amenities.

National Pro-poor Programmes

The scope, scale and range of national programmes for employment guarantee, universal basic education and health care, rural infrastructure, security and pensions for the poor, aged and disabled, and public housing have been widened. This restructuring as well as the passage of legislation on the right to work, education, health and food were made with the concurrence of the states by the National Development Council. The programmes are wholly funded by the centre. While the responsibility for implementation rests with the states, they are expected to observe central government guidelines on implementation and monitoring.

The outlays on these flagship programmes have tripled over the last decade: from ₹ 92 billion in 1999-2000 to ₹ 280 billion in 2009-10. In addition, the revamped food security programme has vastly expanded the scope and scale of subsidised public distribution of food grains. This led to a significant shift in public sector plan allocations—the share of social services in total public sector plan outlay increased from 24 per cent in 1990-2001 to 54 per cent in 2009-10.

Central government outlays on these revamped and expanded flagship programmes is projected to grow manifold over the next decade. It is possible, though very unlikely, that the result of the 2014 elections will lead to a drastic departure from these programmes or a significant reversal of recent trends in outlays. Both the scale of these programmes and the rationale for the strategy underlying them will continue to be centres of controversy.

Criticism of poverty alleviation programmes as the main if not the only cause of the fiscal crisis and erosion of resources available for development is highly misleading. This is based on a comparison of the expenditures on these programmes with the fiscal deficit reported in the central budget, which is but a small fraction of numerous explicit and implicit subsidies provided in the production/distribution of various goods and services by/through central and state governments. In 2009-10, central government outlays on flagship programmes accounted for only half the amount of explicit subsidies reported in the budget. This proportion would be much smaller when implicit non-merit subsidies on account of non-departmental enterprises (such as water and electricity) and other handouts by state governments are taken into account. Reducing these subsidies will make a far bigger contribution to the fiscal situation and release more resources for capacity augmenting investments than trimming pro-poor programmes. It will contribute to reducing the current bias in the distribution of costs and benefits between classes, and have a hugely beneficial impact in terms of efficient and sustainable use of resources. But public discussion and debate on reform of pricing and deficiencies of governance is quite limited. The need for a significant increase in rates and measures to improve efficiency of production and distribution hardly figures in it. This is not surprising because, if seriously pursued, these measures will adversely affect the middle and upper classes in whose favour the current system is heavily biased.

This is not to suggest the current strategy and programmes for achieving greater equity are all well conceived, implemented effectively, and have the desired impact. They are a mixed bag. Of these, the employment guarantee and the food security programmes are the largest in terms of coverage and claims on public funds. The rationale for the former and its achievements in terms of additional employment generated for the rural poor and its impact on their bargaining power in the rural labour market are widely recognised. So are its main weaknesses: it is unevenly spread across the country; all the poor are not covered and all those covered are not poor; the works undertaken are of poor quality and do not significantly augment durable and productive social assets; and the programme is marked by significant leakages and corruption. There are widespread complaints that the programme has not only raised wage rates, but also adversely affected the availability of labour for normal economic activities and reduced the quality of work. But these aspects have not been rigorously examined and documented.

The rationale for a food security programme focusing exclusively on the highly subsided supply of food grains (including the not so poor) and its efficacy in raising food intake and quality to nutritionally satisfactory levels is also questionable. Past experience shows that among the poorest segments of the population, even in regions with a well-functioning public distribution system (PDS), the actual intake of grains remains well below nutritional norms and has remained stagnant despite increases in incomes and subsidies of various kinds. The huge difference between the price at which grains will be supplied to beneficiaries and prevailing market rates gives tremendous scope for leakages and corruption. Direct cash transfers to PDS traders—not an easy task—can take care of leakages but not provide arbitrage opportunities for beneficiaries.

General eco-development programmes (like rural and agricultural development, education and health) seek to ensure a sustained increase in income and employment in rural areas and to enable the socially and economically underprivileged to take advantage of employment and income opportunities. Measures to narrow differences in the average duration and quality of education, and affirmative action to enable underprivileged segments acquire higher skills, and access capital to engage in entrepreneurial opportunities are necessary to make a significant and sustained reduction in inequality of income and opportunity.

In the areas of agricultural and rural development, social services, social protection, and employment guarantee, the responsibility for planning and implementing programmes rests entirely with the states. Several of the elements of the present national programmes in these fields were originally pioneered at the state level. These programmes have over time become increasingly important in determining the scale, content and financing of states' plans in domains over which they are supposed to have dominant, if not exclusive, authority. The Planning Commission is given the authority to work out the operational details, procedures and scale of overall funding; the distribution between the states; and the guidelines that they have to follow. This arrangement has led to a situation in which states' role in devising strategies and financing programmes in areas of their core responsibility has been largely replaced by centrally-sponsored national programmes.

Problems and Solutions

The design and guidelines of these programmes have been rightly criticised for adopting a 'one size fits all' approach, with the guidelines allowing little room for the flexible adaptation of programmes to local conditions. However states chose to acquiesce in the arrangement because it opened up a large and increasing source of funds, thereby giving them greater freedom to use their own resources to pursue other priorities.

States have not paid serious attention to building effective implementation mechanisms to ensure that the selection of beneficiaries is fair, and that the various physical works at the ground level meet a minimum standard. Elected *panchayats* are the appropriate agencies to handle these tasks with account ability. But the upper tiers of the political class and bureaucracy are loathe to empower *panchayats*. Instead, they have everywhere taken control over what schemes are to be taken up where, who gets contracts, and who will receive benefits. The scope and design of these programmes, and institutional arrangements for their implementation, leave much scope for improvement. Despite considerable simplification and rationalisation, centrally sponsored schemes are still far too numerous and rely on central government directives, funding, and oversight, all of which are neither conducive to efficiency nor effective in ensuring accountability.

The necessary corrective measures include the following:

- Shifting the locus of effective authority and responsibility for deciding and implementing all local development works from the state government bureaucracy to the appropriate tiers of elected local governments at the district and subdistrict levels.
- Ensuring that funds allocated in the national and state plans for such works are placed at the disposal of elected local bodies, leaving them free, subject to general guidelines regarding prudent use of resources, to decide their priorities and their implementation.
- Vesting elected local bodies at different levels with accountability for the observance of rules and outcomes of expenditures.
- Switching from financial audit to independent social audit of realised outcomes relative to the targets decided by elected bodies.
- Combining audits with inbuilt mechanisms (of which periodic elections are most important) as well as external inducements (by making the scale and composition of future funding commitments contingent on past and current performance) to make elected local governments function in a transparent and efficient manner.

Conclusions

My understanding of the evolving crisis and its denouement are clearly at odds with the optimism of many observers. Besides the various internal and external constraints (economic, political and institutional), we have to reckon with the effect of over-exploitation of key natural resources (especially water and forests); the indiscriminate manner in which further expansion of land, forests and minerals are sought to be promoted in the interests of rapid growth; and the cavalier way in which ecological, environmental, and social concerns are ignored and dismissed.

Economic and Political Weekly XIIX(24), June 14, 2014.

6

BIBEK DEBROY

No Magic Wand

Why GDP Growth May Not Exceed 5.5 Per cent in FY 2015

THERE will be a new government in May 2014. Irrespective of its political composition, economic management will be tough. The mess is known, getting out of the morass is easier said than done. Let's take growth. While a decimal point here and there doesn't matter, 2013-14 will have real growth of 4.9 per cent, that is, sub-5 per cent. That's the new baseline. Manna doesn't descend from heaven because 4.9 per cent is higher than 2012-13's revised 4.5 per cent. Nor does inching up from 4.5 per cent to 4.9 per cent signify confidence in a recovery.

There is an apocryphal story about John Maynard Keynes. Apparently, he was once asked, "How is your wife?" He responded, "Compared to whose wife?" The point being that many things in life are relative. Therefore, 4.9 per cent is better than 4.5 per cent, but is a far cry from the 9 per cent India aspires for.

Low Growth Hurts Jobs

Growth is not a number conjured out of thin air. It means new jobs, lower poverty. National Sample Survey (NSS) data for 2011-12 show employment stagnates when growth tapers off. If poor households spend on education, this means there are expectations of better jobs, outside farming.

For those in jobs, growth means increments, increases in nominal income and an ability to service loans. Such nominal income increases mean one resents inflation, less.

Even if one expects government to spend in social and other sectors, growth generates revenue. While distribution of gains from growth is important, any suggestion that inclusion should be interpreted as lower growth, unless gains are proportionately distributed, is a no-brainer.

Without getting into debates about poverty lines and NSS data, with the same poverty line, around 1950, 50 per cent of India's population was below the poverty line. Around 1980, it continued to be 50 per cent.

No Magic Wand

Three decades of inclusive intervention didn't make much of a dent on poverty, not in terms of this indicator. With the new Tendulkar methodology, poverty ratio was 21.9 per cent in 2011-12. As a trend, poverty began to drop when growth began to pick up in the 1980s.

Poverty declines have been sharper in states with higher growth, particularly in states where agriculture has done well. If one doesn't like poverty based on expenditure cut-offs alone, one can consider something like the human development index (HDI). Even there, HDI improvements have followed growth.

Will a new government in May wave a magic wand in June 2014 and propel growth back to 9 per cent? Growth of 9 per cent requires a benign external environment and the present one is anything but that. However, there are plenty of local sources of growth and slack to drive growth up to 7.5 per cent or 8 per cent. In the western world, June is regarded as a good time for weddings.

There are many reasons for this, some historical. But there's one reason I want to flag. During the Middle Ages, people didn't bathe during the winter. You didn't want prospective marriage partners to stink. Hence, marriages in June, after baths and cleansing of bodies.

Why has growth slackened? The answer doesn't lie in pointing a figure at the external world. Like the story of the blind men and the elephant, there are different ways of diagnosing the problem. In parts of the western world, John Godfrey Saxe's poem partly made the story famous. "The disputants, I ween, Rail on in utter ignorance, Of what each other mean, And prate about an Elephant, Not one of them has seen." It isn't quite that for our growth slowdown.

Sagging Private Investment

Here is a list most people will agree on. Widening deficits, driven by unproductive revenue expenditure, have crowded out private investments and also contributed to inflation.

They have also reduced financial savings. Where investments have happened, the efficiency of capital has worsened. The Finance Minister mentioned this in the Interim Budget speech. He didn't give specific numbers. But at one point, incremental capital-output ratio (ICOR) had fallen to 3.6. ICOR depends on nature of investments and investments in infrastructure lead to increases in ICOR; there is no reason why ICOR should be 6.5, as it is now.

It should not be above 4 and infrastructure expenditure as a share of GDP should be 10 per cent, not the present 6 per cent. Why have investments? For roads and power, it has been land, forest and environmental clearances. These can be streamlined.

Why have decisions not been taken? Land, natural resources, capital and labour markets have been messed up. Where are sources for growth? In the short run, how does one shrink deficits without privatisation and removal of tax exemptions? How does one cut government spending and reorient it towards capital expenditure?

Bathing a physical body is simpler. Cleansing this is no mean task. Beyond rehabilitating administrative decision-making, I don't see any quick-fixes. Hence, I am extremely sceptical of growth projections of 6.5 per cent in 2014-15. Perhaps in 2015-16. For 2014-15, 5.5 per cent is probably the best we can hope for.

The Economic Times, February 28, 2014.

Economic Developments in India, Vol. 194.

7

ALOK SHEEL

India's Three Arrows

How it can Fire itself Back to High Growth

THE Indian economy is in trouble. India recently lost its traditional rank of the second fastest growing G20 economy to Indonesia. With major imbalances and a sharp decline in growth, the challenges facing it are daunting. However, it needs to be understood that these are quite different from those of other major emerging markets. While the imbalances have declined over the last few months, this is largely because growth has settled at a much lower trajectory than in the recent past. For these reasons, unlike 1997 and 2008, India recently found itself within the polar vortex of the currency crisis sweeping emerging markets in the wake of the quantitative easing 'taper tantrums.'

What are the critical factors underlying a sustainable recovery to high growth over the medium term? Although the prospects for a robust global recovery over the medium term are still downbeat in view of the major demand re-balancings required, there is more cause for optimism regarding India, for two good reasons. First, the two major drivers that recently pushed Indian growth trend from the 5.5-6.5 per cent into the 8-9 per cent trajectory are intact. The dependency ratio continues to decline, while the roughly 10 per cent increase in domestic savings as a share of GDP is largely intact but for some short-term damage to financial savings. Second, the rather startling fact is that in a demand-constrained world, India has the luxury of a domestic crisis caused by supply-side problems. Unlike other emerging markets, dependent on external levers for a return to high growth, our levers are mostly domestic. Since the supply-side crisis is of our own making and not a result of any major external shock, the solutions are also within our control. This will not be easy. Pulling these domestic levers is the big political challenge ahead.

The three critical levers, or the three big arrows that need to fire, are agriculture that targets the inflation problem, labour-intensive manufacturing that targets the current account deficit (CAD), and fiscal restructuring that targets the infrastructural deficit. If these three arrows can be fired accurately from a crossbow called good governance, they can address current macro-economic imbalances and lay the foundations for a return to a sustainable high growth trajectory.

At a time when inflation trends are becoming globally aligned, the persistence of high inflation in India seems a trifle puzzling. The global trend is presently deflationary. If food inflation is the villain of the piece, it is worth noting that global food prices have been subdued. Why is India an outlier?

Indian food prices have traditionally been lower than global prices. International trade cannot therefore be expected to dampen domestic food inflation. The roots of Indian food inflation are domestic, the result of market failure. This should not come as a surprise, because agriculture is the one sector which has yet to reap the efficiency gains from the opening up and liberalisation of the Indian economy since the early 1990s.

Cereal inflation has increased because of repeated sharp spikes in the administered support prices for, and public stocks in, the large-scale procurement programme. This has negated the deflationary pressures from the demand shift away from cereals to non-cereal food items on account of rising incomes. Non-cereal inflation has increased because of an antiquated marketing system and infrastructure that leads to low levels of productivity, large amounts of wastage and big mark-up in prices between the farm and final consumer. The price signalling mechanism that equates supply and demand is consequently weak. The agriculture arrow needs to address these fatal flaws in the agricultural sector and working of agricultural markets. Controlling for technology, Indian agriculture has a global comparative advantage that is waiting to be unlocked.

The second arrow should create a conducive environment to leverage India's comparative advantage in labour-intensive manufacturing. This would facilitate the transfer of large numbers of underemployed workers stuck in low-productivity agriculture to high-productivity manufacturing, thereby raising incomes and absorbing the large projected additions to its labour force. India enjoys the same advantage as China in manufacturing, with the added advantage of stronger private entrepreneurship and more developed capital markets. With competitive frameworks in land, labour, tax, skill development, education and governance, there is no reason why Indian manufacturing cannot plug into globalisation the way China has. This would also help address India's current account imbalance.

The third *brahmastra* is fiscal reform that targets not so much the level as the composition of India's structural budget deficit. There is avoidable confusion regarding fiscal reform in India because we do not distinguish between cyclical and structural budget deficits. *Ceteris paribus*, falling growth increases the budget deficit through a negative revenue shock, and *vice versa*. In either case, the structural balance does not change. The last thing that policy makers should do is aggravate an economic slump by cutting back government demand when private demand is slack, or increase expenditure when growth is above trend, to keep the nominal fiscal deficit unchanged.

However, on the high side, India's structural fiscal deficit has not led to a runaway deterioration in the public debt-to-GDP ratio. High growth in the early stages of development creates its own fiscal space for the large-scale investment in physical and social infrastructure necessary to sustain high growth and improve human well-being. Historical experience indicates that private investment can at best supplement this on the margins in a conducive policy environment, and that public investment has the potential to crowd in more private investment. If this policy space is squandered instead by offering low levels of public goods and services at subsidised cost, growth as well as the productivity of capital employed are bound to suffer, and eventually also consumer welfare.

Fiscal restructuring would involve tax reforms, such as the Goods and Services Tax (GST), the Direct Tax Code and improved tax administration, to improve revenue buoyancy to GDP. On the expenditure side, it would involve a shift from non-targeted subsidies to stepping up public investment in infrastructure, both physical and social. Extant social compacts would need to be renegotiated by the political executive, as reforms can be painful over the short-run. As Chancellor Gerhard Schroeder showed in Germany a decade ago, they can be made more palatable through greater, rather than less, fiscal support during the critical phase through well-designed and targeted social safety nets.

Business Standard, March 1, 2014.

Economic Developments in India, Vol. 195.

8

C. RANGARAJAN

Economic Growth and Social Development

Synergic or Contradictory?

ECONOMIC growth, as it is normally understood, means an acceleration of the output of goods and services. Equity in growth or social development, on the other hand, implies that every citizen would have his or her basic needs such as food, clothing and shelter met. Economic growth in a broader sense includes social development. We have come to describe it as 'inclusive growth.' However, analytically speaking, social development, which is the term used here for equity in growth, and economic growth are two separate concepts and there is need to understand fully the implications of each one of them. On the relationship between the two, some key questions that arise are: Does social development come in the way of faster growth? Is social development possible without adequate economic growth? Is faster growth possible without equity? What are the synergies between social development and economic growth? Can expenditures on social sectors by themselves ensure better social progress? What are the organisational and motivational factors necessary to secure better returns from expenditure? What should be the role of the state and the private sector in relation to social development activities?

Evolution of Thinking on Growth

The relative importance of growth and human development in the development process has been dealt with in great detail by two recent publications (Drèze and Sen, 2013; Bhagwati and Panagariya, 2012). One can see five stages in the evolution of thought on economic growth. The chronological sequence is not without some overlap. In the first stage, the major concern was simply to accelerate economic growth. Growth was identified with the increase in the availability of material goods and services and was to be achieved through capital formation facilitated by greater savings. In the words of Lewis (1954), "the central issue for development economics was to understand how a country which saves 5 per cent of its income is transformed into one which saves 20 per cent of its income." Better life was identified with enhanced production of goods and services. Eradication of poverty was to be achieved through faster economic growth. In the second stage, a distinction was made between growth and development. A greater concern with the distribution of income emerged. Development was seen as going beyond mere economic growth and bringing about changes in the structure of the economy. Equitable distribution of the benefits of economic growth became an independent goal. Balanced regional development also became a concern in large economies like ours. In the third stage, the concept of equity was interpreted to mean the provision to everyone of what came to be described as 'basic needs' which included the minimum requirements of life such as food, education, safe drinking water, sanitation and health services (Jolly, 1976). Thus in many countries, the satisfaction of basic human needs became the over-riding objective of national development policy. The fourth stage in the evolution of economic thinking on growth was the emergence of the concept of 'sustainable development' which became relevant in the context of the environmental degradation caused in the process of economic growth. Sustainable development focuses attention on balancing today's concerns with tomorrow's requirements. In the current and fifth stage of thinking on growth, the concept of basic needs has been widened and the objective of growth is set as 'human development' which means an improvement in the quality of life of the people. Enhancement of human development should lead on the one hand to the creation of human capabilities through improved health, knowledge and skills and on the other the opportunities for the people to make use of these capabilities. In a broader sense, human development implies human rights and participation and freedom of choice. Under this approach, economic growth becomes only one aspect of human development.

Performance of the Indian Economy

The performance of the Indian economy since Independence as measured by the normal indicators of economic growth has been impressive. The Indian economy was literally stagnant during the first half of the 20th century. With population growing fast, the per capita income showed a steady decline. The growth momentum started with the attaining of Independence. The annual growth rate in GDP (gross domestic product), however, remained below 4 per cent until the end of 1970s. It was only in the 1980s that the annual growth rate crossed the 5 per cent figure. Between 1981-82 and 1990-91, the growth rate of the economy was 5.6 per cent per annum. In the post-liberalisation period between 1992-93 and 2012-13, the average annual growth rate was 6.9 per cent. In the eight-year period beginning 2005-06, the average annual rate of growth has been 8.0 per cent, even though the current phase of slowdown in growth is causing concern.

Obviously the growth in national income and per capita income is reflected in a number of social performance parameters such as rise in the literacy rate, the availability of medical and health facilities, expansion in education, etc. The literacy rate has gone up from 30.7 per cent in 1951 to 73.0 per cent currently . Similarly, expectation of life at birth for males has increased from 37.1 years to 62.6 years and for females from 36.1 years to 64.2 years (Table 8.1).

Table 8.1

Social Sector Performance Indicators

Parameter	*1951*	*1981*	*1991*	*2001*	*Current Level*
Literacy rate	30.7	43.1	51.6	64.8	73.0
Dropout rate in school education	64.9	58.7	42.6	40.7	27.0
Crude Birth Rate (per 1,000 population)	39.9	37.2	32.5	24.8	22.5
Crude Death Rate (per 1,000 population)	27.4	15.0	11.4	8.9	7.3
Infant mortality rate	146.0	110.0	80.0	66.0	44.0
Total fertility rate	6.0	4.5	3.6	3.1	2.6
Expectation of life at birth (in years)					
Male	37.1	54.1	60.6	61.8	62.6
Female	36.1	54.7	61.7	63.5	64.2

As measured by the social indicators, the performance of the country is less impressive. No wonder Drèze and Sen (2013) describe India's performance as 'An Uncertain Glory'. India ranks low in the Human Development Index (HDI). As per the *Human Development Report 2013* of the United Nations Development Programme (UNDP), India's rank was 136 among a total of 187 countries. It is, however, to be noted that India, with the HDI value at 0.554, is included among the medium human development countries. The three components of the HDI are life expectancy, education and per capita GDP. Of these three, India's life expectancy index at 0.72 is near the world average of 0.79. But with respect to education and per capita GDP, our indices at 0.46 and 0.52 are much lower than the world average of 0.62 and 0.68 respectively. Admittedly, the computation of these indices is debatable. The HDI also does not take into account many other aspects of social development as well as institutional dimensions like the freedoms enjoyed by people in making political and economic choices. The index may thus understate somewhat India's achievements. However, the deprivation in India in terms of health and education facilities has been documented by several studies. Around 20 per cent of the children in the 6-14 years age group were not attending school even in 2005-06 (*India Human Development Survey*, 2005). Fifty-nine per cent of the deliveries were non-institutional in nature and 56.5 per cent of the children were not fully immunised [National Family Health Survey-3 (NFHS), 2005-06]. Around 14 per cent of our population still does not have access to safe drinking water (*Economic Survey*, 2012-13) and around 25 per cent of the households (in 2008-09) did not have electricity (*India Human Development Report*, 2011). Infant mortality rate in India is 44 per thousand live births as compared to 37 for Bangladesh, 14 for Brazil and 13 for Mexico. Similarly, under-5 mortality rate was lower in Bangladesh, Brazil and Mexico than in India. The number of people living below the poverty line is close to 270 million. Table 8.2 compares India's performance with those of Bangladesh, Brazil and Mexico. While in one sense there has been significant progress in the provision of medical and educational facilities as reflected in the improvement in life expectancy and in literacy rates, we still have a long way to go before we can claim a satisfactory level of performance in meeting basic needs.

Table 8.2

Social Indicators: An Inter-country Comparison

Indicators	*India*	*Bangladesh*	*Brazil*	*Mexico*
Percentage of population below poverty line	21.9 (2012)	31.5 (2010)	21 (2009)	51.3 (2010)
Out-of-school children (million)	4.8	NA	<1	<1
Primary school dropout rate (%)	28.9	34.9	19.5	9.4
Under-5 mortality rate (per 1,000 live births)	55 (2012)	46 (2011)	16 (2011)	16 (2011)
Infant mortality rate (per 1,000 live births)	44 (2012)	37 (2011)	14 (2011)	13 (2011)
Maternal mortality rate (per lakh live births)	200 (2010)	240 (2010)	56 (2010)	50 (2010)
Access to sanitation: urban (%)	87.4 (2011)	55	87	90
Access to sanitation: rural (%)	50.2 (2011)	52	37	68
Women 15-49 with anaemia (%)	55.3	NA	NA	NA
Children 6-59 months with anaemia (%)	69.5	47.5	5.7	7.5

Notes: The poverty lines are national poverty estimates.

Source: UN Statistical Division for Bangladesh, Brazil and Mexico.

Interaction between Growth and Human Development

At a fundamental level, there is no conflict between economic growth and social or human development. Economic growth implies improvement in the material well-being of people which necessarily includes better health, education and sanitation. However, there are two possible routes to achieve the end of social development. One is to let the economy grow and expect the consequential benefits to accrue to all segments automatically. This approach is often described as 'trickle down.' However, for this to happen, the economy needs to grow strongly. Any moderate rate of growth, as we have had in this country particularly in the first three decades after Independence, is unlikely to have a significant impact on the bottom deciles of population. The alternative strategy of development is to focus directly on social infrastructure facilities such as health, education, sanitation and drinking water. No country including India has adopted an exclusive approach. Poverty alleviation programmes of various types were introduced from time to time, besides focusing on providing basic facilities like primary education and health.

While it is true that nutrition, health and education can and should be treated as ends in themselves, there is no assurance that improved health and education will automatically result in higher economic growth. They only create conditions under which growth in the sense of rise in national income can be accelerated. However, enhanced human development expenditures cannot be sustained over a long period unless supported by accelerated economic growth. There are examples of regions and countries where substantial improvements in human development indicators have not necessarily resulted in higher economic growth. When there is a dichotomy between human development indicators and economic development, it can be a source of social tensions. For example, as education spreads, the economy must have the ability to productively absorb the growing number of educated. To think of social development or greater equity independent of economic growth is unrealistic. Economic growth and social development must move in tandem so as to reap the synergic effects of the two moving together.

Needless to say, equity and growth can be mutually supporting. There is enough cross-country evidence to show that economic growth leads to reduction in poverty. By the same token, equity through creating equality of opportunities can accelerate growth by enabling the deprived to reach their full potential (Drèze and Sen, 1995). However, in the short-run, there could be possibilities of trade-off which then should be managed in a manner that the long-run potential both for growth and equity is not undermined. The design of policies has, therefore, to perform a delicate balancing act. The pro-poor policies necessary as they are to widen the opportunities and capabilities of the poor must be so fashioned as to promote growth in the long run. Pro-poor polices should include not only income transfers which by their very nature have to be limited, but also flow of investment to sectors and areas where poor work and live. Rural development including agricultural growth thus assumes major importance.

On the relationship between economic growth and social development, there are certain questions which need to be answered not only at a theoretical level but also at an empirical level. What is the historical record on the relationship between the two? Does growth result in the reduction of poverty and improvement of social indicators? What light does the recent Indian experience throw on this issue?

Growth leads to improvement in social development (Bhagwati and Panagariya, 2012). This can happen through two possible routes. As a country grows particularly at a faster rate, there happens the percolation effect and all sections of the society do benefit, even though, perhaps, some sections may benefit more than others. As the saying goes, a rising tide lifts all boats. But the effect may be stronger or weaker depending on the rate of growth and the pattern of growth. Second, in a fast growing economy, more resources are available for the government to provide for various kinds of social safety nets. Therefore, the ultimate impact depends on the pattern of government expenditures as well. It was Simon Kuznets who had argued in a famous paper in 1955 that in the early period of economic growth, distribution of income tends to worsen and that only after reaching a certain level of economic development, an improvement in the distribution of income occurs. It may be worthwhile to point out in this context that measuring inequality is not the same as measuring the changes in level of poverty defined in terms of some minimum consumption expenditure or the enjoyment of certain socioeconomic benefits. Inequality coefficient may rise despite the fact that citizens are in general provided with the minimum requirements of food, clothing and shelter. Economic development in the 20th or 21st century cannot be compared with development in the previous centuries. There is a greater awareness among the people even, if they are poor, of the entitlements. Economic growth and social development cannot be kept in two separate compartments or sequenced in a particular way. In that sense, faster growth is not possible unless accompanied by measures aimed at ensuring a certain minimum for all. The society cannot wait for growth to reach a certain level before looking for improvement in socioeconomic indicators. At the same time, at very low levels of per capita income, distribution by itself is no solution. Motivation for growth must be part of the development process.

The period 1993-94 to 2011-12 provides some interesting insights into the question of the relationship between growth and reduction in poverty ratio which is taken as a summary indicator of social development. (The poverty ratios looked at here are according to the Tendulkar methodology. This is only taken as a convenient reference without going into the merits and demerits of the methodology.) The annual rate of growth in per capita income in the period 1993-94 to 2004-05 was 4.3 per cent and the growth rate for the period 2004-05 to 2011-12 was 6.7 per cent. The annual rate of decline in the poverty ratio in the first period was 0.7 per cent and 2.18 per cent in the second period. This has happened in the backdrop of an unchanged inequality in rural areas and somewhat of an increase in inequality in urban areas (Table 8.3). Perhaps, it is not far fetched to draw the inference that the faster decline in poverty ratio was mainly due to the faster growth of income. It may also be noted that the period 2004-05 to 2011-12 saw also a sharp increase in the growth rate of agriculture. The average annual growth rate in agriculture during this period was 3.61 per cent. A state-wise analysis confirms a similar trend. Without exception, in all states the decline in poverty ratio is much stronger in the second period than in the first period (Table 8.4).

Table 8.3

Lorenz Ratio of Consumption Distribution

	Rural	*Urban*
1993-94	0.28	0.34
2004-05	0.30	0.37
2011-12	0.30	0.38

Table 8.4

State-wise Analysis of Poverty Ratio

Sl. No.	State\UT	Annual Average Growth in Per Capita NSDP at Constant Prices		Average Decline in Poverty Annual Ratio (Percentage Points)	
		Between 1993-94 and 2004-05	Between 2004-05 and 2011-12	Between 1993-94 and 2004-05	Between 2004-05 and 2011-12
1	Andhra Pradesh	4.62	7.57	1.34	2.96
2	Arunachal Pradesh	3.41	4.82	2.13	-0.51
3	Assam	1.43	4.57	1.58	0.35
4	Bihar	2.82	7.76	0.55	2.95
5	Chhattisgarh	2.46	5.60	0.14	1.35
6	Delhi	4.33	8.45	0.24	0.46
7	Goa	4.91	5.62	-0.38	2.84
8	Gujarat	5.28	8.77	0.55	2.17
9	Haryana	4.32	7.29	1.07	1.85
10	Himachal Pradesh	5.28	5.64	1.06	2.12
11	Jammu & Kashmir	1.82	4.21	1.19	0.41
12	Jharkhand	4.73	5.14	1.40	1.19
13	Karnataka	5.01	6.64	1.46	1.78
14	Kerala	4.62	7.80	1.05	1.81
15	Madhya Pradesh	1.99	6.79	-0.36	2.42
16	Maharashtra	3.51	8.23	0.88	2.96
17	Manipur	4.13	3.66	2.46	0.16
18	Meghalaya	4.33	6.33	1.74	0.60
19	Mizoram	2.85	7.02	-0.32	-0.73
20	Nagaland	2.26	5.17	1.04	-1.41
21	Odisha	3.82	4.63	0.17	3.52
22	Punjab	2.19	4.95	0.14	1.81
23	Rajasthan	4.33	6.56	0.35	2.81
24	Sikkim	3.95	16.64	0.06	3.27
25	Tamil Nadu	4.45	9.67	1.43	2.52
26	Tripura	6.68	7.15	-0.70	3.79
27	Uttar Pradesh	1.57	5.00	0.68	1.64
28	Uttarakhand	3.49	10.75	-0.06	3.06
29	West Bengal	4.79	5.58	0.46	2.05
30	Puducherry	8.38	7.92	1.53	0.63
	All India	4.34	6.72	0.74	2.18

The impact of higher growth on poverty reduction can also be seen from the decile-wise growth in per capita consumption expenditure. In the period 2004-05 to 2011-12, an increase in per capita consumption had taken place across all the 10 deciles of the population both in rural and urban areas. Table 8.5 gives a comparison of the growth rate of per capita consumption (in real terms) during the periods 1993-94 to 2004-05 and 2004-05 to 2011-2012. It shows that the average growth of per capita consumption of the top five deciles is more than that of the bottom five deciles. However, the ratio of the average growth rates of the two periods is higher for the bottom five deciles as compared to the top five. It implies that the expansion of consumption of the lower deciles of the population was more than the upper deciles.

Table 8.5

Decile-wise Growth in Per Capita Consumption
(per cent per year, compound)

Decile	*1993-94 to 2004-05*		*2004-05 to 2011-12*	
	Rural	*Urban*	*Rural*	*Urban*
1. First Decile	0.70	0.66	2.91	2.96
2. Second Decile	0.49	0.54	3.00	3.28
3. Third Decile	0.56	0.66	3.15	3.39
4. Fourth Decile	0.55	0.91	3.17	3.42
5. Fifth Decile	0.54	1.00	3.17	3.41
6. Sixth Decile	0.55	1.24	3.30	3.35
7. Seventh Decile	0.52	1.36	3.40	3.30
8. Eighth Decile	0.61	1.35	3.45	3.40
9. Ninth Decile	0.71	1.47	3.48	3.45
10. Tenth Decile	1.61	2.30	3.71	4.52
A. Bottom Five Deciles	0.57	0.75	3.08	3.29
B. Top Five Deciles	0.80	1.54	3.47	3.60

Note: The growth rates are in real terms and derived from uniform recall period (URP) consumption data.

Within India, among states, there is a wide diversity in relation to performance on the social front. In general, it appears that states with higher per capita income have done better on social development indicators (Tables 8.6 and 8.7), even though there are some exceptions. The exceptions clearly point to factors other than growth in income which have an impact on social development. The high degree of correlation between income and social development does not by itself establish the direction of causation. Perhaps it is fair to assume that in the short run, the causation runs from income to social development. Over the long run, it can run both ways.

Table 8.6

Under-5 Mortality Rate

(Per 1,000 live births)

States	*Per capita NSDP at Current Prices (2008-09)*	*Under-5 Mortality Rate 2008*	*Under-5 Mortality Rate 2009*	*Under-5 Mortality Rate 2010*
Delhi	111756	40	37	34
Haryana	67388	65	60	55
Maharashtra	62234	41	36	33
Punjab	55315	49	46	43
Gujarat	55068	60	61	56
Tamil Nadu	54137	36	33	27
Kerala	53046	14	14	15
Himachal Pradesh	49903	50	51	49
Karnataka	48084	55	50	45
Andhra Pradesh	46345	58	52	48
West Bengal	35487	42	40	37
Chhattisgarh	34360	71	67	61
Odisha	31416	89	84	78
Rajasthan	31279	80	74	69
Jammu & Kashmir	30212	55	50	48
Madhya Pradesh	25278	92	89	82
Jharkhand	25046	65	62	59
Assam	24099	88	87	83
Uttar Pradesh	20422	91	85	79
Bihar	13728	75	70	64
All India	40775	69	64	59

Table 8.7

Indian States Ranked with respect to HDI, 1999-2000 and 2007-08

States	Health Index		Income Index		Education Index		HDI	
	2000	2008	2000	2008	2000	2008	2000	2008
Andhra Pradesh	12	14	15	15	15	16	15	15
Assam	23	23	17	14	9	10	17	16
Bihar	14	15	20	23	22	23	19	21
Chhattisgarh	22	22	18	22	19	17	21	23
Delhi	2	2	1	1	1	2	1	2
Goa	20	7	2	6	3	3	3	4
Gujarat	11	10	8	9	10	14	10	11
Haryana	8	11	7	7	10	11	6	9
Himachal Pradesh	3	3	6	4	4	4	4	3
Jammu & Kashmir	16	16	5	5	12	13	11	10
Jharkhand	17	18	20	20	22	21	23	19
Karnataka	9	11	13	12	13	12	12	12
Kerala	1	1	3	2	2	1	2	1
Madhya Pradesh	20	21	18	19	19	18	20	20
Maharashtra	5	7	10	11	5	6	6	7
NE (excluding Assam)	9	5	9	8	8	7	9	6
Odisha	19	20	23	21	16	19	22	22
Punjab	4	4	4	3	7	8	5	5
Rajasthan	13	13	11	16	21	22	14	17
Tamil Nadu	7	9	12	10	6	5	8	8
Uttar Pradesh	18	19	15	18	17	20	18	18
Uttarakhand	15	16	15	13	17	9	16	14
West Bengal	6	7	14	17	14	15	13	13

Human Development Expenditure and its Efficacy

A comparison of the performance of the Indian economy in terms of social development with some of the neighbouring countries does raise some issues whether a different focus would have resulted in better performance of these indicators. Usually, a comparison is made between India and Bangladesh in this respect. The per capita income of Bangladesh is lower than that of India. But in some of the parameters such as infant mortality rate and literacy rate, Bangladesh has done better. Obviously, even with limited resources, a more focused attention and emphasis do give better results (Drèze and Sen, 2013).

The *Human Development Report*, 1991, introduced the concept of the human expenditure ratio (HER) which measures the percentage of national income devoted to human priority concerns such as elementary education, preventive health care, nutrition, water supply and sanitation to analyse how public spending on human development can be designed and monitored. According to the report, the HER may need to be around 5 per cent, if a country wishes to do well in human development.

This approach to the analysis of human development expenditure has been criticised on the ground that it implies that all human development expenditure needs to be incurred by the government which is neither correct nor desirable. There is a role for private initiative even in areas of social development programmes. In fact, there is evidence to show that in our country, in some of the regions where educational facilities have spread enormously, private educational institutions have played an important part. Besides stressing on the ratio, the report added: "what probably matters more than the HER is human development spending per person in absolute terms. This helps to place the ratio in proper perspective."

Cross-country comparisons on human development expenditure do throw interesting light on the effectiveness of expenditures incurred. According to the *Human Development Report*, 1991, both Sri Lanka and India had a similar human expenditure ratio of 2.5 per cent of the GDP. Human expenditure per capita in 1988 was $10 for Sri Lanka, while it was $9 for India. However, in the ranking of the HDI, Sri Lanka occupied the 75th rank, whereas India was lower down at the 123rd rank. Part of the reason for the difference in the ranking could be enhanced expenditure at a certain level over a longer period. The *Human Development Report* itself admits: "Even Government expenditure cannot be considered in isolation. Its impact depends on not just how much money is spent but on how and in what environment it was spent." While the human expenditure ratio provides a clue to the seriousness of efforts made, much depends on the efficiency with which the resources allocated are utilised.

It is important to think of an appropriate mechanism for the delivery of social services. While the state bears a major responsibility for the provision of basic social services such as health and education, the delivery system need not necessarily be through governmental administrative machinery. Public-private partnerships (PPPs) in the delivery of these services need to be explored. While taking advantage of the superior administrative efficiency of the private institutions, the larger public goals should not be sacrificed. PPP mode of delivery can thus supplement the direct delivery of services through government institutions. Non-governmental organisations (NGOs) can also be a useful supplement. In the AIDS (acquired immune deficiency syndrome) programme which has proved to be a success in India, NGOs have played an extremely useful role.

Conclusion

Social development and economic growth are not necessarily the same. That is why countries do not rank identically on the income scale and human development scale. Sometimes the differences in the rankings are quite striking. The rank correlation co-efficient between the real GDP per capita index and the HDI for all 187 countries is high at 0.95. This is to be expected since GDP-related index is one of the three factors included in the HDI. Also the other two components—life expectancy and education—are closely correlated with GDP. However, taking only medium human development countries, it is seen that the rank correlation coefficient with GDP index is lower at 0.37. There are several countries in this group which rank high on the real per capita GDP index but lower on the HDI and *vice versa*. However, in the case of India, the difference is small. India ranks 133 on per capita GDP index and 136 on HDI.

Nowadays, the HDI on the model of the global HDI is being computed for different states in India to understand inter-state differences in income and social development. We have figures available for 2000 and 2008. The rank correlation coefficient between the income index and the HDI across the states in India is unchanged and stood at 0.95 in 2000 and 2008 (Table 8.7). This figure is similar to the correlation seen globally. When we look at state-wise income and social indices and compare their values for 2000 and 2008, we see the positive relationship between the income and social indices getting stronger. The rank correlation between income index and health index was 0.6 in 2000 and it improved to 0.8 in 2008. Similarly the rank correlation between income index and education stood at 0.8 in 2000 which got stronger in 2008 and stood at 0.9. A comparison was also made of the performance of states in education and health with per capita public expenditure on these items (Tables 8.8 and 8.9). While the rank correlation between health index and per capita public expenditure was 0.46, it was slightly lower at 0.45 for education. These correlation coefficients indicate that performance in both education and health sectors is influenced not only by public expenditure but also by other factors.

Table 8.8

Per capita Public Expenditure on Health and Health Index

States	*Health Index*	*Per capita Public Expenditure (in ₹)*
Andhra Pradesh	0.580	191
Assam	0.407	162
Bihar	0.563	93
Chhattisgarh	0.417	146
Delhi	0.763	560
Goa	0.650	861
Gujarat	0.633	198
Haryana	0.627	203
Himachal Pradesh	0.717	630
Jammu & Kashmir	0.530	512
Jharkhand	0.500	155
Karnataka	0.627	233
Kerala	0.817	287
Madhya Pradesh	0.430	145
Maharashtra	0.650	204
Odisha	0.450	183
Punjab	0.667	247
Rajasthan	0.587	186
Tamil Nadu	0.637	223
Uttar Pradesh	0.473	128
Uttarakhand	0.530	280
West Bengal	0.650	173

Table 8.9

Per capita Public Expenditure on Education and Education Index

States	*Education Index*	*Per capita Public Expenditure (in ₹)*
Andhra Pradesh	0.553	710
Assam	0.636	848
Bihar	0.409	481
Chhattisgarh	0.526	593
Delhi	0.809	1152
Goa	0.758	2025
Gujarat	0.577	849
Haryana	0.622	3126
Himachal Pradesh	0.747	580
Jammu & Kashmir	0.597	11
Jharkhand	0.485	737
Karnataka	0.605	757
Kerala	0.924	1189
Madhya Pradesh	0.522	478
Maharashtra	0.715	721
Odisha	0.499	702
Punjab	0.654	807
Rajasthan	0.462	749
Tamil Nadu	0.719	4722
Uttar Pradesh	0.492	546
Uttarakhand	0.638	1690
West Bengal	0.575	654

As the nation looks ahead, growth is an important factor in generating employment and reducing poverty. With the population growth rate coming down, a strong growth will mean a substantial growth in the per capita income. If we grow at 9 per cent per annum, India's per capita GDP will increase from the current level of $1,600 to $8,000-$10,000 by 2025. Then we will become part of the middle income group of countries. Without a strong growth, we will not be able to provide employment to the growing number of young people who will join the labour force. Continued strong growth will help to accelerate the declining trend in poverty ratio. In the recent period, we have launched a number of schemes aimed at broadening the base of growth. These include employment guarantee scheme, universalisation of education, expansion of rural health and food security. All these programmes have made a substantial demand on public expenditure. This has been made possible only because of the strong growth that we have seen in recent years. Growth has facilitated raising more resources by the government.

China introduced economic reforms in the late 1970s. One can only speculate that had we also done so and initiated our reforms in the mid-1970s rather than early 1990s, we could have had the benefit of higher growth for an additional decade and a half. It is interesting to note that India's per capita GDP and China's per capita GDP were more or less the same until 1978. A strong pickup happened in China after 1978. India started narrowing the gap only after 1990-91 (Figure 8.1). A higher growth for a much longer period would have helped us to overcome poverty and other related problems (Bhagwati and Panagariya, 2012). Obviously growth is not the sole answer. With growth, there should be purposive action towards improving the conditions of the socially and economically vulnerable. Growth nevertheless is a necessary condition.

Figure 8.1

Per capita GDP of India and China

(In US$)

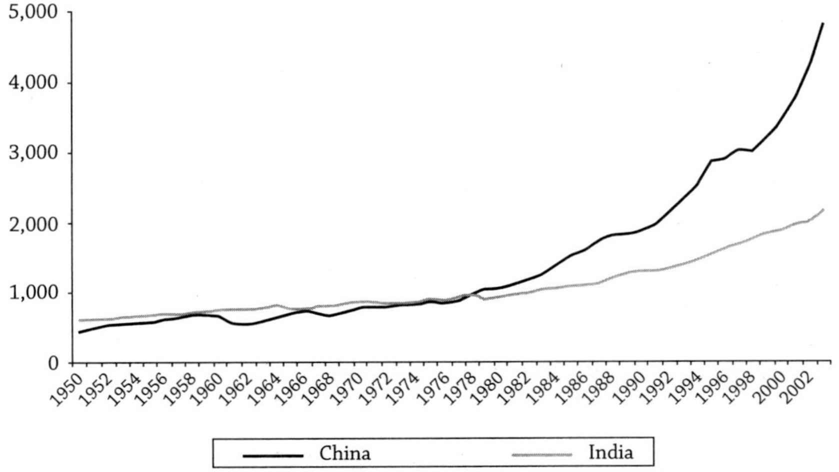

Development has many dimensions. It has to be inclusive, it must be poverty reducing and it must be environment friendly. We need to incorporate all these elements in the growth process. However, at our present stage of development, we cannot afford to sacrifice growth. It is key to improving the living standards of our people. Equity and growth should not be posed as opposing considerations. They must be weaved together to produce a coherent pattern of development. Therein lies economic statesmanship.

It is, therefore, necessary to stress simultaneously economic development in the conventional sense of accelerating growth rate and social development in the sense of securing for everyone the basic needs. The two have a mutually interacting beneficial impact and the two must be pursued together. These are the two legs on which the country must walk. Any strategy of development, which ignores any one of the two legs, will only make the country limp along.

References

Bhagwati, Jagdish and Arvind Panagariya (2012). *India's Tryst with Destiny: Debunking Myths that Undermine Progress and Addressing New Challenges*. Noida: Harper Collings Publishers India.

Drèze, Jean and Amartya Sen (1995). *India: Economic Development and Social Opportunity*. Oxford, Clarendon Press.

———. (2013). *An Uncertain Glory: India and its Contradictions*. Allen lane, London: Penguin Books Ltd.

India Human Development Survey (IHDS) (2005). Ann Arbor, United States: Inter-University Consortium for Political and Social Research (ICPSR).

Jolly, Richard (1976). "The World Employment Conference: The Enthronement of Basic Needs", *Development Policy Review*, Vol. A9. United States.

Kuznets, Simon (1955). "Growth and Income Inequality", *American Economic Review* 45.

Lewis, Arthur (1954). "Economic Development with Unlimited Supplies of Labour", *Manchester School of Economics and Social Studies* 22(2).

Ministry of Finance (2013). *Economic Survey 2012-13*. New Delhi: Government of India.

National Family Health Survey (NFHS)-3, (2005-06). International Institute of Population Sciences (IIPS), Mumbai.

Planning Commission (2011). *India Human Development Report 2011: Towards Social Inclusion*. New Delhi: Government of India.

———. (2013). *Press Note on Poverty Estimates, 2011-12*. New Delhi: Government of India.

Radhakrishna, R., C. Ravi and B. Sambi Reddy (2013). "Assessment of Well-being in Multidimensional Perspective in Post Reform India", *Indian Economic Review* 48.

UNDP (2013). *Human Development Report 2013, The Rise of the South: Human Progress in a Diverse World*. New York: United Nations Development Programme.

———. (1991). *Human Development Report 1991*. New York: United Nations Development Programme.

Economic Developments in India, Vol. 198.

9

C.H. HANUMANTHA RAO

Achieving Inclusive Growth

Recent Experience and Challenges Ahead

The Context

'Inclusive growth' is not a new or a novel idea. Defined in the Eleventh Plan as a "growth process which yields broad based benefits and ensures equality of opportunity for all," it stands for "equitable development" or "growth with social justice," which have always been the watch words of development planning in India. Yet, since 'inclusive growth' is so widely used these days by the reputed multilateral institutions as well as the policy makers in India, one wonders whether this usage acquires a special significance in the present context. Perhaps, it does. The belief that there is a significant 'trade-off' between growth and equity does not seem to be as widespread now as before. There is now a genuine and widespread recognition about the adverse social consequences of rising inequalities in the recent high growth phase, which do not seem to be mitigated through the so-called 'trickle-down' mechanism.

For about three decades from the early 1950s to the early 1980s, when the country was experiencing a slow growth in GDP (gross domestic product), or the so-called 'Hindu' rate of growth, the concern for accelerating GDP growth itself was uppermost, apart from ensuring equity. Inequalities did arise in the wake of growth then, but were not as prominent as in the recent phase of accelerated growth. With the GDP growth rate rising to 7-8 per cent, rural-urban divide, regional divide and rich-poor divide became glaring, which brought 'inclusive growth' high on the policy agenda.

Post-reform (Pre-2004) Experience

Growth rate of agriculture GDP, which was a little over 3 per cent per annum when the Green Revolution was in full swing in the 1980s and up to the mid-1990s, dropped to a mere 2 per cent during the Ninth and Tenth Plan periods. Worse still, the growth of food grains output fell short of population growth over much of this period. Since well over half the work force in the country is still dependent on agriculture, the difference in per capita incomes between agriculture and non-agriculture widened sharply. This led to rising rural distress and a large number of suicides by small and marginal farmers in several parts of the country.

The regional divide became similarly sharp. For example, the per capita gross state domestic product (GSDP) of Bihar—the poorest state in the country—which had steadily declined to a little over 30 per cent of the per capita GSDP of the richest state by 1993-94, dropped further to 20 per cent in 2004-05 (Planning Commission, GoI, 2008). The less developed states located in the central and eastern parts of the country account for over 60 per cent of population below the poverty line in the country. These rural-urban and the regional divides are basically responsible for the rise in inequalities in income or the rich-poor divide.

The proportion of people below the poverty line has no doubt been declining. Since poverty line is fixed in terms of a certain level of per capita expenditure, one should normally expect some decline in poverty when the average per capita income rises. It would be surprising if this does not happen. The issue really is: why has the pace of poverty reduction slowed down in the post-reform period despite the rise in per capita GDP at a faster rate? The rich-poor divide subsumes the 'social divide.' The population belonging to socially and economically disadvantaged sections like scheduled castes (SCs), scheduled tribes (STs) and backward classes, and women and children have benefited the least from growth and rising prosperity. The slow improvement in the various development indices for these sections and the slow rise in public expenditure targeted to them as well as for social sectors like health, education and poverty alleviation programmes, and greater vulnerability of the poor to various kinds of risks in this period have been documented extensively in the literature (Radhakrishna and Ray, 2005; Dev, 2008).

Economic reforms introduced in the country in the early 1990s released the initiative and enterprise of those adequately endowed with infrastructure, resources, skills, power and influence. Such sections are generally concentrated in states and regions that are relatively well developed and less so in other areas. People in the less endowed regions too have the spirit of enterprise, but in the absence of productive outlets and the requisite resources, they fail to display their initiative and enterprise. The situation turned worse for them as the post-reform policy failed to effectively counteract the adverse initial conditions by according greater priority for public investment in infrastructure, agriculture and social sectors in general, because of its faith in 'trickle-down' mechanism and the belief that greater role for the private sector can make good these gaps.

Economic polarisation was a logical corollary of such a policy. The climax of this was witnessed five years ago when the GDP growth rate was at its peak and the 'India Shining' campaign, then in full swing, co-existed with widespread rural distress and suicides by a large number of farmers in several parts of the country. The United Progressive Alliance (UPA) which came to power at the centre under these circumstances in 2004 came out with a National Common Minimum Programme articulating an economic and social policy which, for the first time after 15 years of economic reform, tried to integrate the objective of growth with social justice and promised to pursue reforms with a human face.

Inclusive Growth: The Issues

It is not inevitable that growth in GDP should lead to the rise in inequalities in income—whether before or after the reforms. Much depends on the level and spatial distribution of physical infrastructure, human resource development, prevailing social structure, social policies and governance patterns. Therefore, the sharp rise in inequalities in the post-reform period cannot be attributed to economic reforms as such. Rather, they can be traced to the initial conditions obtaining in the pre-reform period itself.

In China, for example, where land reforms were successful and infrastructure development was high in the pre-reform period, there was a rapid reduction in poverty following economic reforms and acceleration in GDP growth (Rao, 2005). The quality of reform package is, of course, important. It has to be such as to make good the infrastructural and other gaps inherited from the pre-reform period. It should also be effective in coping with the adverse social consequences that predictably result from the implementation of reforms under the given unfavourable initial conditions.

Inadequate physical and social infrastructure like irrigation, power, roads, transport and communications, education and health in the less developed regions and rural areas in general in the country is a major factor responsible for the growing rural-urban and regional disparities. This is also responsible for the slow growth of manufacturing and other activities in the rural non-farm sector, which explains the slow shift of labour force from agriculture and hence slow reduction in rural poverty. The highly stratified and hierarchical social structure characterised by inequalities in land holdings and other forms of wealth, status and power is the second major factor leading to the rise in income inequalities in the wake of growth. Because of this, achieving inclusive growth is far more challenging than stepping up the GDP growth rate *per se*. Finally, the governance pattern, that is, the working of our democracy under the prevailing social structure and the efficiency of implementation mechanisms or delivery systems, determines the actual outcomes on the ground from our planning exercises and policies. We shall look at the recent performance briefly and see what challenges confront the planners and policy makers on these three fronts.

Recent Experience

We shall briefly discuss the major achievements of the UPA government since 2004 in respect of its promise of achieving inclusive growth.

Acceleration in GDP Growth

Notwithstanding the externally induced economic meltdown in the recent days, the present UPA government can legitimately take credit for sustained high GDP growth, with strong recovery of manufacturing sector. This particular configuration has brought a boom in tax revenues for the government, led by the revenues from direct taxes, especially from the corporate sector. The tax-GDP ratio registered a significant rise recovering and even exceeding pre-reform levels both for the centre and the states. This has enabled governments to step up public investment in infrastructure and other expenditures on agriculture and social sectors. What is clearly on display, if indeed this was needed, is that high GDP growth, through improvement in revenues, can facilitate inclusive growth by enabling the governments to undertake the necessary investments and other expenditures. For a resource constrained economy, high GDP growth is a necessary, though not sufficient, condition for achieving inclusive growth.

Agricultural Growth

The UPA government was quick to address rural distress through a two-pronged strategy of reviving agriculture and putting in place a rural employment guarantee scheme. Public investment in agriculture which had declined from 5 per cent of agriculture GDP in the early 1980s to below 2 per cent in 2002-03 has now been stepped up to 3 per cent, with the target of raising it further to 4 per cent by the close of the Eleventh Plan. Together with private investment, the overall capital formation in agriculture is now 12 per cent of agriculture GDP which is the highest in the last 25 years (Planning Commission, 2008). By the end of the Eleventh Plan, this is expected to go up to 16 per cent—necessary for sustaining a 4 per cent growth in agriculture GDP. The target of doubling the supply of institutional credit to agriculture in three years has been exceeded. There have been concerted policy interventions such as launching of the National Food Security Mission and the Rashtriya Krishi Vikas Yojana.

As a result, there is a clear upturn in agriculture, the growth rate of agriculture GDP rising to over 3 per cent in the last four years with comfortable stocks of foodgrains—almost comparable to that achieved when the Green Revolution was in full swing. Needless to say, much more remains to be done towards strengthening the agricultural research system, regenerating dry land farming, and providing institutional support like credit and extension services to small and marginal farmers and women farmers among them. But the recent experience clearly demonstrates that there is considerable under-exploited potential in agriculture crying to be tapped and that a little extra effort can bring forth substantial results within a short period.

Rural Employment Guarantee

Rural Employment Guarantee Scheme has now been extended throughout the country. Most evaluations—official as well as non-official—show that the implementation of this scheme has been far more effective than any of its predecessor schemes in the country. In particular, the leakages have been reduced significantly in many places in respect of the number of days a worker is employed as well as wages paid. This is attributed mainly to the adoption of innovative methods like opening post offices and bank accounts for payment of wages to workers and the use of information technology (IT), apart from social auditing. The significant rise in the rural market wages reported from several parts of the country and the widespread demand from the farmers to reschedule the operation of the employment guarantee scheme from busy to lean season testify to the effectiveness of its implementation.

The encouraging experience is by no means uniform. In particular, planning and execution of works under the scheme needs considerable improvement by enhancing the technical and institutional capacity at the grass roots. But, coming against the backdrop of rural distress for over a decade, the scheme was successful in providing the much needed relief to the rural poor, apart from raising their awareness and bargaining power. Further, the recent experience shows that the Right to Information (RIT) Act being implemented in the country holds a great promise for improving the effectiveness of this and similar schemes designed to improve the lot of the poor.

Social Sectors

Major initiatives have also been taken in the social sectors like education and health through Sarva Siksha Abhyan (SSA) and National Rural Health Mission (NRHM). The allocations for the social sectors have been stepped up substantially in the Eleventh Plan compared to the 10th Plan. The allocation of funds to the poorer states from the centre during 2007-08 for programmes like NRHM, SSA and poverty alleviation was well above their share in population.

Challenges Ahead

We shall now attempt to bring out the major deficiencies in performance and the challenges confronting the planners and policy makers in the period ahead, including during the Eleventh Plan.

Deficiencies in Infrastructure and the Regional Divide

The Commission on Growth and Development, recently constituted by the World Bank, came out with the assessment that:

> No country has sustained rapid growth without also keeping up impressive rates of public investment in infrastructure, education and health. Far from crowding out private investment, this spending crowds it in....Unfortunately, we discovered, infrastructure spending is widely neglected (World Bank, 2008).

The Commission notes that public investment in infrastructure constitutes 5-7 per cent of GDP in fast growing Asia. Implying, presumably, that there is no sanctity to a particular number in this regard, the Commission specifically observes about India that, "now the government is trying to do more, making up for years of underinvestment in public infrastructure."

The performance of certain infrastructure industries has been far from satisfactory. For example, a basic input like electricity which had registered an annual growth rate of 8-10 per cent in the 1980s, showed a steady decline in its growth rate in the post-reform period reaching a low of about 3 per cent in 2002-03. Since then it has been recovering, its annual growth rate rising to a little over 7 per cent in 2006-07 (Reserve Bank of India [RBI], 2008). The Eleventh Plan, therefore, envisages a significant rise in public investment in infrastructure from a little over 4 per cent of GDP in the base year to over 6 per cent at the end of the Plan. Together with private investment, it is expected to rise from 5 per cent of GDP to 9 per cent over this period.

The Eleventh Plan claims to outline

> A comprehensive programme for development of infrastructure, especially in rural areas, and in the remote and backward parts of the country consistent with the requirements of inclusive growth at 9 per cent per year....what this plan seeks to do is to target the slower growing regions, and the backward areas within these states, for higher levels of public investment that will enable the backlog in physical and social infrastructure to be addressed (Planning Commission, 2008).

But from the information given in the Plan document, it is not possible to find out how the infrastructure planned is going to be spread over different states, on the one hand, and between agriculture and the non-farm sector including small towns, on the other.

The Tenth Plan, for the first time, specified targets for the growth rate in GSDP for each state in consultation with state governments, without specifying the corresponding investment rates. However, the growth rates actually achieved in the Tenth Plan in the less developed states like Bihar, Madhya Pradesh, Rajasthan and Uttar Pradesh fell considerably short of the target, the shortfall ranging from 1.5 (Bihar) to 3.35 (Rajasthan) percentage points. The Eleventh Plan has continued this practice of fixing state-wise growth targets. These targeted growth rates for GSDP show smaller divergence between the richer and poorer states than those achieved in the Tenth Plan. But the absence of targets in respect of investment rates casts doubt on the credibility of these growth targets.

There is no basis to believe that the divergence in the investment rates between the poor and better-off states would come down in the Eleventh Plan period. For one thing, the per capita plan outlays (including central assistance) of the poorer states have been declining relative to those of the richer states in the post-reform period. The poorer states have been handicapped basically by their own weaker resource position. Because of lower tax-GSDP ratios and higher debt-

GSDP ratios, their creditworthiness is lower, and so they have not been able to access borrowings adequately from the market. Private investment has been flowing basically to the high income states where infrastructure is well developed owing to higher per capita plan outlays (Rao, 2006).

The position has now become worse for the poorer states because of the centre's decision to do away with the loan component of the normal central assistance for state plans, following the recommendations of the Twelfth Finance Commission. No alternative mechanism has been put in place so far to enable the poorer states to easily access loans from the market. There is no increase in central assistance in the Eleventh Plan for infrastructure development of the backward regions through Backward Regions Grant Fund, Special Plan for Bihar and Action Plan for KBK (Kalahandi-Blangir-Koraput Districts of Odisha), which have only been protected at the Tenth Plan level. Such assistance constitutes less than 1 per cent of the total Eleventh Plan outlay for all states. It is not known how the performance of Bharat Nirman—a flagship programme designed to create infrastructure—is tilted in favour of the less developed states.

The Planning Commission notes that over the past several years, the share of public investment in the overall investment has been declining, reaching a little over 20 per cent in recent years. Therefore, according to the Commission, there is

> A very great limitation on the influence that fiscal quantities, allocations and strategy can directly exert on growth rates, especially at state level. States have, therefore, to focus on providing the necessary policy framework and supporting environment that makes economic activity possible and attractive enough for private sector investments. This would include the entire gamut of services.... right from maintaining law and order, providing quick and effective dispute resolution through an efficient adjudication system, avoiding an extortionate and distortionary tax system to enabling and empowering the general mass of population to take advantage of economic activity (Planning Commission, 2008).

While many of these measures for 'good governance' are desirable, they cannot be a substitute for the provision of adequate infrastructure through public investment. There is a case for revisiting the whole area of infrastructure development in the less developed regions and the rural areas in general.

Social Structure and Social Policy

While the UPA government, facing a crisis-like situation when it came to power, did address rural distress by taking steps to revive agriculture and introducing rural employment guarantee scheme, it has not been able to evolve a comprehensive and active social policy for providing safety nets to cope with the adverse consequences of non-inclusive growth under the prevailing iniquitous social structure. A comprehensive social policy at this stage should have four major elements, *viz.*, land policy, rehabilitation and resettlement policy, social security for the unorganised sections of labour, and financial inclusion.

Land Policy

'Land to the tiller' was the overarching principle of land policy in the early post-Independence period. While this policy continues to be relevant, especially for tribal areas, half a century of development has brought some new concerns to the forefront. With growing industrialisation and urbanisation, the rising demand for land for industrial purposes, including special economic zones, and for housing in expanding urban areas is posing an inevitable threat of a reverse movement of land from tillers. While raising agricultural productivity is a must to cope with the shrinkage of agricultural land, the very slow growth of non-farm opportunities for employment and livelihoods and lack of social security for small holders argue for a careful and calibrated approach for land acquisition.

Land alienation continues to be a serious problem in tribal areas. The enactment of Scheduled Tribes and Other Traditional Forest Dwellers (Recognition of Forest Rights) Act, 2006, is a major step towards protecting the rights of STs and other traditional forest dwellers. However, past experience suggests that the implementation of this act is going to be extremely challenging. A pre-requisite for effective implementation is improvement in land administration in tribal areas by putting in place field machinery with adequate staff, and effective monitoring and review, backed by necessary political will to counter the pressures from the vested interests. The efforts in this respect so far do not seem to match the challenges involved.

Policy for Rehabilitation and Resettlement

Willingness to part with land by the farmers for development projects has to be the guiding principle for making the sale transaction just and humane. Government and industry should, therefore, supplement the principle of fixed 'compensation' at a point of time with mechanisms for assuring original land owners adequate stake, on a secure footing, in the new establishments. This is essential because, in the present context of rising land values and high input-intensity of farming with increasing uncertainty, traditional norms for compensation and forms of rehabilitation and resettlement (R&R) of displaced persons are proving to be unviable. Therefore, while the R&R policy should give a primacy of place to land-for-land, it should also address the alternative of ensuring adequate stake in the new projects and enterprises, including those in special economic zones (SEZs), for the displaced persons. Such a course of action would be fully justified by the high profitability of new ventures.

Social Security

As in the previous plans, the Eleventh Plan proposes targeted livelihood support programmes aimed at increasing productivity and incomes of the poor in several low income occupations, such as small and micro enterprises, weavers, artisans, craftsmen, etc. But the lack of concern at the state and the lower levels for the plight of these unorganised sections renders many of these programmes in-fructuous. The recent spate of suicides of weavers in certain parts of the country reflects this lack of concern.

In this context, the recommendations on social security made by the National Commission for Enterprises in the Unorganised Sector, headed by Dr. Arjun K. Sengupta (NCEUS, 2006), assume significance. The UPA government has introduced schemes to provide social security coverage through life cover, health insurance and extension of old age pension on the lines recommended by NCEUS but by restricting coverage to sections of below the poverty line (BPL) households. The government has introduced an Unorganised Workers Social Security Bill, 2007, putting on a statutory footing the above-mentioned social security schemes as well as some other social security schemes for unorganised workers.

Financial Inclusion

Financial inclusion is a policy priority even in the developed countries. While liberalisation there improved financial products and services for the few, it accentuated denial of services for many. The same happened in India following the introduction of economic reforms in the early 1990s when there was a retrogression on several indices of financial inclusion reflecting a severe setback to the objectives with which major commercial banks were nationalised in the late 1960s. This experience has prompted renewed policy attention to the issues of financial inclusion in India in recent years. These have been examined by the Committee on Financial Inclusion appointed by the Ministry of Finance, under the chairmanship of Dr C. Rangarajan (GoI, 2007), and another Committee on Financial Sector Reforms constituted by the Planning Commission under the Chairmanship of Dr Raghuram G. Rajan (Planning Commission, 2008).

Financial inclusion should be measured not only by the number of bank accounts held by the weaker sections, as brought out by the above committees, but also by the amounts borrowed by them, which show a more dismal picture. For example, the share of direct accounts with a credit limit of less than ₹ 25,000 in total direct accounts declined from 97 per cent in 1990 to 67 per cent in 2005, while their share in outstanding direct credit declined from 0.66 per cent to 0.23 per cent in the same period (Planning Commission, 2007). Financial inclusion is no doubt inhibited by the higher transaction costs of dealing with a large number of small accounts rather than a small number of large accounts. But such costs can be reduced through organisational innovations or, where necessary, met through explicit subsidies. Unduly lower ceiling on interest rates for bank loans could also encourage exclusion, which need not be insisted upon, as the small borrowers are interested in adequate supply of credit rather than such lower rates of interest, the benefit of which, in any case, may not accrue to them but to the middle men.

But the basic cause for financial exclusion, often missed—including by the Raghuram Rajan Committee, is a mindset lacking in social concerns. This has to be faced squarely if appropriate institutional arrangements are to be made for checking the prevailing distortions in bank lending. The experience with the linkages of banks with micro finance institutions and self-help groups (SHGs) clearly demonstrates that the poor are bankable: even when margins are low, high volumes can make the business profitable (Joshi, 2008). Innovative institutions and methods for the delivery of credit, including those recommended by the above committees, are called for. Also, the targets for inclusion should be set in terms of the number of accounts as well as the amount of credit to be extended.

Inclusive Governance

Governance is not simply a matter of particular administrative arrangements, procedures, monitoring, etc. In view of the all-pervading influence of the prevailing social structure on decision-making as well as implementation processes, governance has to be viewed and shaped in the context of ongoing social change through the functioning of our democratic system. It is wrong to attribute the deficiencies in decision-making and tardiness in implementation to the prevailing democratic system as such. Rather, they can be traced to the way the functioning of our democracy has been twisted and moulded by the pulls and pressures from various interest groups. The solution lies in broadening and deepening our democracy by effectively extending it to the grass roots.

Experience has amply demonstrated that participatory or inclusive governance is indispensable for achieving inclusive growth. This is woefully lacking at the grass-roots levels where the formulation of schemes is not quite in keeping with the local needs and circumstances, and administration is not accountable to the people. It is precisely to cope with such challenges that Panchayati Raj was visualised by the late Prime Minister Shri Rajiv Gandhi.

Thanks to the 73rd and 74th Amendments to the Constitution, elected *panchayats* have been in place. But they are deprived of necessary functions, finances and functionaries. No serious effort has been made so far to devolve such powers, not to speak of any effort to build up local capabilities by training the elected functionaries. This is explained solely by the resistance from the entrenched interests to part with their powers. Therefore, the change in attitudes has necessarily to be driven through the political process.

It is indeed ironical that governments at the centre and the states owing allegiance to Rajiv Gandhi have not taken any major initiative—political or administrative—in this direction showing tangible results on the ground. On the contrary, certain state governments, owing allegiance to Rajiv Gandhi, have been active in pursuing top-down development and governance by floating numerous schemes and parallel implementation structures which cut at the very root of Panchayati Raj Institutions—on the top of it by naming such schemes after Rajiv Gandhi. In a situation riddled with formidable socio-political obstacles to decentralisation, the Planning Commission's proposal to provide incentives to encourage the states to devolve functions by evolving "a suitable Devolution Index called PRI-Empowerment Index," though well meaning, may not take us very far.

Inclusive governance has a wider connotation encompassing inclusive politics or empowerment of social groups hitherto not having access to political power at different levels. In the ultimate analysis, inclusive growth can be achieved only through inclusive politics. The social change underway in the country through the democratic process holds such a promise.

References

Mahendra Dev, S. (2008). *Inclusive Growth in India—Agriculture, Poverty, and Human Development*. New Delhi: Oxford University Press.

Government of India (2007). *Report of the Committee on Financial Inclusion*. New Delhi: Ministry of Finance.

Joshi, Deepali Pant (2008). *Financial Inclusion*. Cambridge University Press, India Private Ltd., forthcoming.

Planning Commission (2007). *Report of the Steering Committee on Agriculture and the Allied Sectors for the Formulation of the Eleventh Five Year Plan (2007-2012)*. New Delhi: Government of India.

———. (2008). *Eleventh Five Year Plan (2007-2012)*, Vols. I & III. New Delhi: Government of India.

———. (2008). *Draft Report of the Committee on Financial Sector Reforms*. New Delhi: Government of India.

Radhakrishna, R. and Shovan Ray (eds.) (2005). *Handbook of Poverty in India—Perspectives, Policies, and Programmes*. New Delhi: Oxford University Press.

Rao, C.H.H. (2005). *Agriculture, Food Security, Poverty, and Environment—Essays on Post-Reform India*. New Delhi: Oxford University Press.

———. (2006). "Growing Regional Disparities in Development in India—Post-Reform Experience and Challenges Ahead", Lecture dedicated to the Memory of Professor A.M. Khusro, delivered at the 88th Annual Conference of the Indian Economic Association, held at Visakhapatnam, 27-29 December 2005; published in *The Indian Economic Journal* 54(I), April-June.

Reserve Bank of India (2008). *Handbook of Statistics on the Indian Economy*. Mumbai.

World Bank (2008). *Report of the Commission on Growth and Development*. Washington.

Shri Chandra Shekhar Memorial Lecture, Institute for Studies in Industrial Development, New Delhi, 5 December 2008, published in *Economic and Political Weekly*, 28 March to 3 April 2009.

Economic Developments in India, Vol. 136.

10

PULIN B. NAYAK

The Imperative of Distribution

IF there is a single clear economic yardstick by which one might wish to characterise the first three years of the United Progressive Alliance (UPA) government, then it would have to be the consistent high growth trajectory that the Indian economy seems to have hit upon. The average growth rate of GDP (gross domestic product) in the past three years has been around 8.6 per cent, and there would seem to be no serious reason to fear that the growth rate one might achieve in the remaining two years is going to dip below the 8 per cent mark. And this for the reason that gross domestic savings rate in 2005-06 was 32.4 per cent of GDP, the gross domestic investment rate for the same year was 33.8 per cent, and with a capital output ratio of somewhere around 4, one is broadly talking of a growth potential of 8.0 per cent-plus in the foreseeable future.

For any observer of the Indian economy, this should be a matter of no small comfort. But one must immediately qualify this by noting that while growth is important, growth alone cannot be the end-all of any developmental process. There has to be proper distribution and it is here that the shortfall is discomforting. There are alternative ways of computing the poverty ratio, but in terms of a major one among them, the National Sample Survey (NSS) 61st round for the year 2004-05 reveals that the ratio at the national level is as high as 27.8 per cent. After nearly 60 years of our avowed commitment to planned economic development, why the number of the absolutely poor in India should be so staggeringly high must remain a conundrum for any serious social scientist.

The single most troubling aspect of our recent growth experience after the onset of the reform process in 1991 is the dismal picture on the employment front. Many have described this as the phenomenon of jobless growth. With an economy expanding at an unprecedented rate, obviously some jobs are clearly getting created. But most of these are not in the formal organised sector. We have a situation where the vast bulk of the jobs that are getting created are typically in the urban informal sector. There is a massive increase in the casualisation of the workforce even as jobs in the formal sector are not increasing quite as fast, or even possibly shrinking in some sectors.

The official figures corroborate the above account. The number of unemployed as per the usual principal status has increased from about 9 million in 1993-94 to some 13.1 million as in 2004-05. The unemployment rate as a proportion of the labour force has increased during the same period from 2.6 to about 3.1 per cent. It hardly needs belabouring that increase in unemployment has a direct impact on poverty and destitution.

It is in this context that the National Rural Employment Guarantee Act (NREGA) assumes a very special importance. This seeks to improve the lives of the rural poor by providing one member from each of the country's 150 million rural households to get at least 100 days of employment at minimum wages. This may possibly be the single most profound piece of pro-poor legislation that has been enacted in post-Independent India. But this initiative of the UPA has had more than its fair share of naysayers from its very conceptual stage.

More than a year and a quarter after the implementation of the scheme from February 2, 2006, it is by and large having to put up with unenthusiastic public administrators who are not accustomed to any kind of empathetic public dealing. Any firm conclusion would be unwarranted, but the scanty evidence that is now available suggests that in those pockets where the administration is responsive to the needs of the populace, the impact of NREGA seems to be encouraging.

The posture of the influential tribe of well-heeled economists has almost uniformly been against the NREGA. The usual argument is that this would be a huge fiscal waste. Most of the proponents of this view are those who routinely subscribe to what is known as the 'Washington consensus'. A myth has been created that the NREGA is a 'demand-driven' scheme relating to water conservation, land development, drought-proofing, rural connectivity in terms of all-weather roads, etc. The implication is that if there is low demand for this scheme, then the government would need to make that much less allocation. Why all these activities cannot be considered under supply side management with firm governmental action is not clear. But the latter would require government officials in the districts to actually engage in developmental work with active public participation, which may be asking for too much from a class of *babus* only interested in pleasing their superiors.

Returning to the growth experience, much of the impetus for growth has emerged from the high growth rate being experienced in the services and industry sectors, which grew at 11.2 per cent and 10 per cent respectively during 2006-07. These sectors now account for 54 and 27 per cent of GDP respectively. Agriculture, which accounted for about 60 per cent of GDP just after Independence, now accounts for only around 19 per cent. It has lately been growing only around 2.3 per cent per annum, while it continues to be the mainstay of more than 60 per cent of the country's population.

This has obviously contributed to a substantial accentuation of inequalities of income. On the one hand, there are the young and upwardly mobile market-savvy graduates from leading business schools who command huge salaries and are idealised by the upper middle-class globalised India. On the other, there are the surging masses of the less fortunately placed in remote drought-prone areas and tribal belts who are unemployed for long periods and many of whom are led to Naxalism. While globalisation might have brought in rewards to several classes in, say, the top-end IT (information technology) and banking sectors, there are also the unfortunate farmers in Vidarbha and in remote parts of Andhra Pradesh who, unable to repay paltry loans, are led to committing suicide.

The killing fields of Kalinganagar and Nandigram have once again raised the question of the inevitable tensions between a brutal and insensitive state determined to push the agenda of industrialisation at the cost of the aspirations of common village folk. Powerful ministers in the upper echelons of the UPA government still do not tire of yearning for the growth rate of Indian economy to be pushed to double digit figures regardless of its social consequences. This proclivity needs to be checked.

The great advantage of the 8-9 per cent growth rate that the economy already seems to have achieved is that the government can now afford to be responsive to the bottom rungs of the population. Indeed, this is the imperative of the present day. The Prime Minister has very rightly emphasised the need to make economic growth more socially inclusive and regionally balanced. If in order to achieve this we have to accept the growth rate going down a notch or two, we should have the good sense to accept it.

Hindustan Times, May 31, 2007.

Economic Developments in India, Vol. 113.

11

N.A. MUJUMDAR

Inclusiveness of Poor in Growth Akin to Mirage

DURING the last two months, three international institutions have drawn our attention to extreme economic inequality: Oxfam, the World Economic Forum and the International Monetary Fund (IMF). Of these, Oxfam's briefing paper, "Working for the Few—Political Capture and Economic Inequality," is the most perceptive document and it should be compulsory reading for all Indian policy makers. Extreme economic inequality is damaging and worrying for many reasons. It is morally questionable. It has a negative impact on growth and poverty reduction. It can multiply social problems. The wealthiest individuals and groups capture political institutions for their aggrandisement, at the expense of the rest of the society. Extreme economic inequality and political capture are interdependent. If left unchecked, political institutions become undermined and governments overwhelmingly serve the interest of the economic elite to the detriment of the ordinary people.

Let us look at some basic facts. Almost half the world's wealth is now owned by just one per cent of the population. The bottom half of the world's population owns the same wealth as the richest 85 persons in the world.

What is more disturbing is that economic inequality has increased during the last 30 years. In 24 out of 26 countries studied, the richest one per cent increased their share of income. In the US, the wealthiest one per cent captured 95 per cent of the post-2008 growth, while the bottom 90 per cent became poorer.

Data in the following low-income countries—Indonesia, India, Pakistan and Nigeria—show that the richest 10 per cent of the population acquired a much greater share of national income than the poorest 40 per cent, over the past 30 years. The trend is set to continue.

The World Economic Forum's *Global Risk Report* has identified the large and chronic income gap between the richest and poorest citizens as the biggest risk factor to human progress and the one thing that could wreck the greatest havoc in the coming decade.

It is against this global background that developments in India need to be judged. In the past decade, the number of billionaires in India increased from less than 6 to 81. This means the concentration of some $250 billion among a few dozen people, in a country of 102 billion. The share of the country's wealth held by the elite minority, soared from 1.8 per cent in 2003 to 26.0 per cent in 2008.

The source of such acquisition is also interesting. Half of India's billionaires acquired their wealth in what are called 'rent thick sectors.' This means sectors where profits are dependent on access to scarce resources, made available exclusively through government permission, and therefore susceptible to corruption by powerful actors—as opposed to the creation of wealth. Such sectors include real estate, construction, mining and telecommunications. It is well known that property development is India's most opaque business, where enormous sums of illegal money exchanges hands and little tax is collected. Wealth accrued from rent is made possible by the coaction of the government and powerful groups.

While such incredible gains are made by a few dozen people, poverty and inequality remain rampant. Nor is the government compensating the poor by high public spending for their welfare. Public spending on health care is just one per cent of the GDP (gross domestic product). The Asian Development Bank's (ADB) 'Social Protection Index', which assesses a country's expenditure on poor and economically vulnerable groups, ranks India 23 out of 35 countries in the region. Even among the 19 low- and middle-income countries, India ranks in the bottom half.

Corruption and loopholes mean that revenues necessary to support public expenditure are too low. Another paper by Oxfam demonstrates that ending the inheritance tax in 1985 and limiting the wealth tax to non-productive assets, thereby excluding financial assets, has resulted in a low tax-to-GDP ratio. The tax structure in India is highly regressive, with only 38 per cent of total taxes coming from direct taxes on income, profits and capital gains.

Delivering the Richard Dimbleby Lecture in London, on February 4, IMF Managing Director Christine Lagarde stated that the net worth of the billionaire community in India increased 12-fold in the last 15 years: this wealth is enough to eliminate poverty in the country twice over. She was highlighting the rising economic inequality across the world, including India. Calling for urgent solutions to the growing problem of inequality, Lagarde said it was imperative to draw up policies that promote inclusive growth and shut out corruption and cronyism. Inclusion should be given as much weight as growth in our policy-mix. More inclusion and opportunity in economic life means less cronyism and corruption.

The general public perception about worsening economic plight of the masses has led the Government of India (GoI) to declare its commitment to the *aam admi*—common man—and the 'poorest of the poor.' The policy response has been to provide for a variety of rights-based programmes, like the Mahatma Gandhi National Rural Employment Guarantee Act (MGNREGA), Right to Education Act and more recently, the National Food Security Act. But it is pertinent to pose the question. How far have the poorest of the poor benefited from inclusive growth?

A recent study has sought to assess the outcomes of these policies of inclusive growth. The study uses the National Sample Survey (NSS) data on household consumption distribution across social groups ("How Inclusive is India's Reformed Growth?", *Economic and Political Weekly*, February 8, 2014).

Its finding is that at the national level, disparities across social groups have increased and the relatively deprived social groups of scheduled tribes (STs) and scheduled castes (SCs) have been left out of the growth process. The study concludes: "Our findings, in general, suggest the inclusiveness of the poorest in the mainstream growth process is still a forlorn hope."

Free Press Journal, March 03, 2014.

Economic Developments in India, Vol. 196.

12

JAYAN JOSE THOMAS

The Demographic Challenge and Employment Growth in India

THE recent survey on employment and unemployment in India, conducted by the National Sample Survey Office (NSSO), has attracted considerable media attention. This was mainly due to the wide fluctuations in overall employment growth as shown by these surveys. Overall employment in the country rose markedly by 59.4 million between 1999-2000 and 2004-05. But during the next five years, 2004-05 to 2009-10, net employment generated fell sharply to only 4.7 million, leading to the suggestion that this was a period of 'jobless growth.' Employment growth recovered subsequently, with 10 million new jobs registered between the surveys held in 2009-10 and 2011-12. (All estimates in this article, unless otherwise specified, are based on the usual principal status (UPS) and the usual subsidiary status (UPSS) of worker.) (see Table 12.1).

However, an exclusive focus on the growth of overall employment—which is the sum of employment in agricultural and the non-agricultural sectors—can be misleading for a developing country like India. With economic development, employment in agriculture is expected to decline, both in relative terms as well as in absolute numbers.

However, agricultural employment in India increased by 17.4 million between 1999-2000 and 2004-05, and some studies have attributed this increase to rural distress, that is people were driven to find work to supplement household incomes during a difficult period (Table 12.1). On the other hand, between 2004-05 and 2009-10, agricultural employment declined absolutely by 20.4 million, leading

The author is grateful to Seema for useful suggestions and assistance in research.

also to the deceleration in overall employment growth. This decline in agricultural employment was, at least partly, a reversal from the 'distress employment' created during the previous five-year period (Thomas, 2012). Agricultural employment declined further by 12.9 million between 2009-10 and 2011-12 (Table 12.1).

Table 12.1

Net Increase in the Number of Workers in India, 1983 to 2011-12

(Numbers in million)

Period	*Net Increase*			*Net Annual Increase*	
	All Workers	*Agricultural Workers*	*Non-agricultural Workers*	*All Workers*	*Non-agricultural Workers*
1983 to 1993-94	71.1	32.4	38.7	6.8	3.7
1993-94 to 2004-05	83.4	18.2	65.2	7.9	5.9
2004-05 to 2011-12	14.7	-33.3	48	1.4	6.9
1993-94 to 1999-2000	24	0.8	23.2	4.0	3.9
1999-2000 to 2004-05	59.4	17.4	41.9	11.9	8.4
2004-05 to 2009-10	4.7	-20.4	25.1	0.9	5.0
2009-10 to 2011-12	10	-12.9	22.9	5.0	11.5

Note: Refers to the usual principal and usual subsidiary status (UPSS) workers. Size of the workforce (in any year) is obtained by multiplying workforce participation rate (WPR) from the NSSO reports with the population figures from the Census of India. There are some differences between the estimates of workers reported in this article and those in Thomas (2012). This is because the population figures for 2004-05 and 2009-10 used in Thomas (2012) were projections based on the Census of India data until 2001. In this paper, these population figures have been revised using data from the Census of India 2011.

Source: Estimates based on the Survey on Employment and Unemployment, NSSO, 38th, 50th, 55th, 61st, 66th and 68th rounds.

The creation of non-agricultural employment in India was at the rate of 8.4 million a year between 1999-2000 and 2004-05, which slowed down to 5.0 million a year between 2004-05 and 2009-10, but rose again to 11.5 million a year between 2009-10 and 2011-2012. Notably, the rate of generation of non-agricultural employment in the country improved from 5.9 million a year between 1993-94 and 2004-05 to 6.9 million a year between 2004-05 and 2011-12 (Table 12.1). Therefore the suggestion, based on trends in overall employment, that India's employment growth decelerated after the mid-2000s is without basis.

However, a more pertinent question is whether the pace and nature of employment generation in India is adequate given the challenges on the labour supply front. This question is addressed in the rest of the paper.

Demographic Transition

Estimates by the World Bank (WB) show that the population aged 15-59 years is set to increase dramatically in India from around 757 million in 2010 to 972 million in 2030. This could potentially translate into an addition of over 200 million workers over the next two decades. On the other hand, during the same period, the working-age population is expected to decline in most developed regions of the world and even in China (where it would fall from 913 million to 847 million). In other words, India will contribute a substantial chunk of the increase in the global labour supply over the coming years.

Shift Away from Agriculture

In India, the share of agriculture and allied activities in gross domestic product (GDP) declined from 35.1 per cent in 1983 to 14.0 per cent in 2011-12. The share of these sectors in the country's total employment also fell during this period, from 68.2 per cent to 47.5 per cent.

An absolute fall in the size of the agricultural workforce was witnessed for the first time in India in the NSSO survey held in 2009-10. But then this decline was observed only in the case of females. It was in the NSSO survey in 2011-12 that the size of the male agricultural workforce registered an absolute decline for the first time in the country (Table 12.1).

Of course, there have been strong factors that may have pushed workers out of low-productivity agriculture, which in recent years has become non-remunerative in many parts of the country. At the same time, there have been 'pull' factors too that caused workers to move away from agriculture. Important among the latter is the expansion of casual employment in public works, which (as per the current weekly status) rose from only 0.9 million in 2004-05 to 6.6 million in 2009-10 and 6.7 million in 2011-12. These included employment created through the Mahatma Gandhi National Rural Employment Guarantee Act (MGNREGA), which accounted for 2.4 million in 2009-2010 and 2.9 million in 2011-12. Notably, casual employment in public works accounted for 69 per cent (3.7 million out of 5.4 million, as per the UPSS) of the incremental non-agricultural employment generated for rural females during the 2004-05 to 2011-12 period.

Further, between 2004-05 and 2011-12, 20.5 million new jobs were generated in rural areas in the construction sector (Table 12.2). Almost 50 per cent of this job creation occurred in the less-developed and chiefly agrarian states of Uttar Pradesh, Rajasthan, Bihar and Madhya Pradesh.

The shift of the workforce away from agriculture in India has occurred almost entirely among the younger age groups. Between 2004-05 and 2011-12, male agricultural workers in the age group of 5-24 years declined by 10.3 million, even as male agricultural workers who are 25 years and older increased by 5.6 million. A part of the reason for this shift is the rising enrolment of the young in educational institutions.

There has been a remarkable improvement in the ratio of students to population (SPR) among persons aged 15-19 years in India after the mid-2000s, pointing to an expansion of higher education in the country. SPR among rural males and females in this age group increased by 20 percentage points between 2004-05 and 2011-12, and reached the levels of 64 per cent and 54 per cent, respectively, by 2011-12.

Between 2004-05 and 2011-12, as India's total population (aged 15-59 years) increased by 113 million, the population of students among them increased by 41.5 million—that is, 37 per cent of the incremental population. The proportion of students to the incremental population was considerably higher at 45 per cent in rural areas (Table 12.3). As noted earlier, large numbers of the young in rural areas left agriculture to join educational institutions.

The growth in the population of students who are 15 years and above reduces labour supply for now, but raises the numbers of educated persons who would be demanding high quality jobs in the future.

Table 12.2

Employment in India by Sectors: Estimates for 2011-12 and the Net Increase between 2004-05 and 2011-12

(Numbers in millions)

Sectors	2011-12					Net Change (2004-05 to 2011-12)				
	RM	*RF*	*UM*	*UF*	*All*	*RM*	*RF*	*UM*	*UF*	*All*
1. Agriculture and allied activities	139.1	76.2	6.2	3.0	224.4	-5.6	-26.7	0.6	-1.6	-33.3
2. Manufacturing	19.1	10.0	24.4	7.9	61.3	1.9	-0.4	2.9	0.7	5.1
2a. Textiles, garments, leather	4.3	3.7	8.5	4.3	20.9	-0.2	0.3	1.1	0.5	1.6
3. Construction	30.5	6.7	11.6	1.1	49.9	15.7	4.8	3.2	0.1	23.9
4. Trade, repair, hotels	20.1	3.0	29.9	3.6	56.6	2.3	0	4.3	0.4	7.0
5. Transport, communication	9.8	0.1	11.1	0.3	21.3	1.5	-0.1	1.2	0	2.6
6. Financing, insurance, real estate, business services	2.4	0.2	9.1	1.6	13.5	0.9	0.3	3.7	0.9	5.8
6a. Computer and related	0.1	0.0	2.0	0.4	2.6	0.1	0.0	1.2	0.3	1.7
7. Community, social and personal services	11.4	5.0	14.4	9.6	40.4	0.1	0.4	1.4	1.5	3.4
7a. Public admnistration and defence	2.4	0.3	4.9	0.7	8.3	-0.2	0	-0.4	-0.1	-0.7
7b. Education	4.3	2.7	3.9	3.6	14.5	0.8	0.6	0.7	0.7	2.8
7c. Other services and private households	2.7	1.3	2.5	3.8	10.4	-0.4	-0.4	0.3	0.4	-0.2
Total non-agricultural	95.3	25.5	102.9	24.4	248.1	22.4	4.9	17.0	3.8	48.0
Total employment	234.4	101.6	109.1	27.4	472.5	16.8	-21.8	17.6	2.1	14.7

Note: RM, RF, UM and UF refer to rural males, rural females, urban males and urban females, respectively. Also see under Table 12.1.

Source: Estimates based on the Survey on Employment and Unemployment, NSSO, 61st, 66th and 68th rounds.

Table 12.3

Population in the 15-59 Age Group in India by Activity Status: Estimates for 2011-12 and the Incremental Change between 2004-05 and 2011-12

(Numbers in millions)

	2011-12				Net Increase (2004-05 to 2011-12)			
	RM	*RF*	*UM*	*UF*	*RM*	*RF*	*UM*	*UF*
Employed in agriculture	120.9	69.6	5.2	2.7	-5.7	-24.6	0.4	-1.5
Employed in non-agriculture	89.9	23.5	97.9	23.2	21.1	4.6	16.3	3.8
Employed, total	210.9	93.1	103.1	25.8	15.5	-19.9	16.7	2.3
Unemployed	4.0	1.7	3.3	1.5	0.6	-0.5	-0.2	-0.4
Labour force	214.9	94.8	106.4	27.3	16.1	-20.5	16.5	1.9
Students	37.1	24.1	21.9	16.9	16.4	11.9	7.1	6.1
Attending domestic duties	1.0	128.2	0.3	76.8	0.2	39.3	0	17.6
Population	257.3	250.4	131.5	123.0	32.9	30.7	23.7	26.0

Note: See notes under Tables 12.1 and 12.2.

Source: Same as Table 12.2.

Growth of Labour Demand

Between 2004-05 and 2011-12, total non-agricultural employment in India increased by 48 million. Jobs in construction, which rose by 24 million, accounted for half of this increase (Table 12.2). These construction jobs, which were overwhelmingly in the rural areas, were likely to be of poor quality.

In contrast, employment in manufacturing increased by just 5.1 million in India during the seven years after 2004-05 (Table 12.2). And the rate of job creation in this sector decelerated from 1.2 million jobs a year between 1993-94 and 2004-05 to 0.7 million jobs a year between 2004-05 and 2011-12. Manufacturing employment had, in fact, declined in absolute numbers, by 3 million, between 2004-05 and 2009-10. However, staging a recovery, 8 million manufacturing jobs were added in the country during the next two years (2009-2012).

The traditional service sector activities—comprising trade and repair services, hotels, transport and communication, and community, social and personal services—together generated 13 million jobs in India between 2004-05 and 2011-12 (Table 12.2). The rate of employment generation in these sectors, combined, declined from 3.2 million a year between 1993-94 and 2004-05 to 1.9 million a year between 2004-05 and 2011-12.

Other than construction, the only sector in which job creation accelerated in the country after the mid-2000s was finance, insurance, real estate and business services, which also include computers and related activities. This relatively high productivity sector added 5.8 million new jobs between 2004-05 and 2011-12 (Table 12.2).

Quality Only for Urban Males

Men in urban areas benefited disproportionately from the growth of non-agricultural employment in India in sectors other than construction. Urban males accounted for only 16 per cent of India's total population, but 77 per cent of all jobs in computer and related activities in 2011-12, and 60 per cent or even more of the incremental employment (between 2004-05 and 2011-12) in manufacturing and in finance, real estate and business services (Table 12.2).

On the other hand, for people in rural areas, construction has virtually been the only source of non-agricultural employment after the mid-2000s. For rural males, it accounted for 70 per cent of the net increase in non-agricultural employment (15.7 million out of 22.4 million) during 2004-2012 (Table 12.2).

Women, including urban women, received only a marginal share of the better quality employment generated in India. The share of females in incremental employment (between 2004-05 and 2011-12) was only 21 per cent in finance, real estate and business services, 18 per cent in computer and related activities, and 3 per cent in trade, repair, hotels, transport and communication combined (Table 12.2).

Demographic Dividend Lost?

Overall, the generation of non-agricultural employment in the Indian economy has fallen behind the growth in the supply of 'potential' non-agricultural workers. Additions to the pool of potential non-agricultural workers come from two sources: the growth of the working-age population and the shift of the workforce away from agriculture. At the same time, the growth in the number of students, who are not part of the labour force, tends to reduce the size of this pool.

Between 2004-05 and 2011-12, the population of rural males aged 15-59 years in India increased by 32.9 million, almost half of whom (16.4 million) were students (Table 12.3). Including the 5.7 million who shifted out of the primary sector, the net addition to the potential non-agricultural workforce on account of rural males during 2004-2012 was 22.2 million (32.9 million+5.7 million–16.4 million). During the same period (2004-2012), 21.1 million new non-agricultural job opportunities were generated in the country for rural males (Table 12.3).

Thus, in the case of rural males, the demand seems to be broadly in line with the supply of non-agricultural workers, but this may not be so in the future. With the rise in education levels, India's rural workers will demand better quality jobs in the coming years—outside agriculture and outside even construction.

In the case of females, the supply of potential non-agricultural workers far exceeds the demand. For instance, between 2004-05 and 2011-12, the population of urban females (aged 15-59 years) in India increased by 26.0 million, out of which 6.0 million were students. Including the 1.5 million who exited from agriculture and allied activities, the number of urban females who could potentially work for industry and services increased by 21.5 million in India during 2004-2012 (26.0 million + 1.5 million – 6.0 million) (Table 12.3).

On the other hand, industry and services sector together generated a meagre 3.7 million new jobs for urban females between 2004-05 and 2011-12. During the same period (2004-2012), as many as 17.6 million out of the incremental population of 26.0 million urban females were attending domestic duties in India (Table 12.3).

The low rate of female labour force participation is a severe obstacle to India's social and economic development. Highlighting this issue, Thomas (2012) showed that the proportion of females attending to domestic duties was relatively high among the better educated and among those belonging to the richer households.

While a variety of social and economic factors could be attributed to the low levels of female labour force participation in India, the discouragement effect arising from the low demand for labour is clearly the most important among them.

To sum up, the generation of non-agricultural employment in India has accelerated after the middle of the first decade of this century. At the same time, the pace of this job creation has been inadequate to absorb the rising supply of potential workers, especially females. With the movement of workers away from agriculture, with their rising education levels, this challenge will grow bigger in the coming years, particularly in the rural areas. Unless India's economic policies are geared towards a significant revival in the growth of decent jobs, the country risks losing its demographic dividend—the female part of this dividend in particular.

Reference

Thomas, Jayan Jose (2012). "India's Labour Market during the 2000s: Surveying the Changes", *Economic & Political Weekly* 48(51): 39-51.

Economic & Political Weekly, vol xlIx, no. 6, February 8, 2014.

Economic Developments in India, Vol. 196.

13

RAGHURAM G. RAJAN

Finance and Opportunity in India

WE are approaching the 67th anniversary of our Independence. Sixty-seven years is a long time in the life of a man—indeed, it is about the average Indian's life expectancy today. Since life expectancy was shorter at the time of Independence, it is safe to say that most Indians born just after Independence are now no more. It is useful to take stock at such a time. Did we achieve the dreams of our founding fathers for freedom's first children? Or have we fallen woefully short? What more do we need to do?

Clearly, our founding fathers wanted political freedom for the people of India—freedom to determine who we would be governed by, as well as freedom of thought, expression, belief, faith and worship. They wanted justice and equality, of status and opportunity. And they wanted us to be free from poverty.

We have made substantial progress in achieving political freedom. Our democracy has matured, with people confidently choosing to vote out governments that lose touch with their needs. Our institutions protecting the freedom to vote have grown stronger, with the Election Commission and the forces of law and order ensuring free and largely fair elections throughout the country. Political parties, NGOs (non-governmental organisations), the press and individuals exert checks and balances on public policy. And the judiciary has taken important steps to protect individual freedom.

Our economy is also far richer than it was at the time of independence and poverty has come down substantially. Of course, some countries like South Korea that were in a similar situation then are far better off today but many others have done far worse. Indeed, one of the advantages of a vibrant democracy is that it gives people an eject button which prevents governance from getting too bad.

Democracy has probably ensured more stable and equitable economic growth than an authoritarian regime might have.

Yet a dispassionate view of both our democracy and our economy would suggest some concerns. Even as our democracy and our economy have become more vibrant, an important issue in the recent election was whether we had substituted the crony socialism of the past with crony capitalism, where the rich and the influential are alleged to have received land, natural resources and spectrum in return for pay-offs to venal politicians. By killing transparency and competition, crony capitalism is harmful to free enterprise, opportunity and economic growth. And by substituting special interests for the public interest, it is harmful to democratic expression. If there is some truth to these perceptions of crony capitalism, a natural question is why people tolerate it. Why do they vote for the venal politician who perpetuates it?

A Hypothesis on the Persistence of Crony Capitalism

One widely held hypothesis is that our country suffers from the want of a 'few good men' in politics. This view is unfair to the many upstanding people in politics. But even assuming it is true, every so often we see the emergence of a group, usually upper middle class professionals, who want to clean up politics. But when these 'good' people stand for election, they tend to lose their deposits. Does the electorate really not want squeaky clean government? Apart from the conceit that high morals lie only with the upper middle class, the error in this hypothesis may be in believing that problems stem from individual ethics rather than the system we have. In a speech I made before the Bombay Chamber of Commerce in 2008, I argued that the tolerance for the venal politician is because he is the crutch that helps the poor and underprivileged navigate a system that gives them so little access.[1] This may be why he survives.

Let me explain. Our provision of public goods is unfortunately biased against access by the poor. In a number of states, ration shops

1. This idea was inspired from those in Richard Hofstadter's seminal book *The Age of Reform* on the difficulties of reform in the United States (US) around the early 20th century.

do not supply what is due, even if one has a ration card—and too many amongst the poor do not have a ration card or a BPL (below poverty line) card; teachers do not show up at schools to teach; the police do not register crimes, or encroachments, especially if committed by the rich and powerful; public hospitals are not adequately staffed and ostensibly free medicines are not available at the dispensary; ... I can go on, but you know the all-too-familiar picture.

This is where the crooked but savvy politician fits in. While the poor do not have the money to 'purchase' public services that are their right, they have a vote that the politician wants. The politician does a little bit to make life a little more tolerable for his poor constituents—a government job here, an First Information Report (FIR) registered there, a land right honoured somewhere else. For this, he gets the gratitude of his voters and, more important, their vote.

Of course, there are many politicians who are honest and genuinely want to improve the lot of their voters. But perhaps the system tolerates corruption because the street smart politician is better at making the wheels of the bureaucracy creak, however slowly, in favour of his constituents. And such a system is self-sustaining. An idealist who is unwilling to 'work' the system can promise to reform it, but the voters know there is little one person can do. Moreover, who will provide the patronage while the idealist is fighting the system? So why not stay with the fixer you know even if it means the reformist loses his deposit?

So the circle is complete. The poor and the underprivileged need the politician to help them get jobs and public services. The crooked politician needs the businessman to provide the funds that allow him to supply patronage to the poor and fight elections. The corrupt businessman needs the crooked politician to get public resources and contracts cheaply. And the politician needs the votes of the poor and the underprivileged. Every constituency is tied to the other in a cycle of dependence, which ensures that the *status quo* prevails.

Well-meaning political leaders and governments have tried, and are trying, to break this vicious cycle. How do we get more politicians to move from 'fixing' the system to reforming the system? The obvious answer is to either improve the quality of public services or reduce the public's dependence on them. Both approaches are necessary.

But then how does one improve the quality of public services? The typical answer has been to increase the resources devoted to the service, and to change how it is managed. A number of worthwhile efforts are underway to improve the quality of public education and health care. But if resources leak or public servants are not motivated, which is likely in the worst governed states, these interventions are not very effective.

Some have argued that making a public service a right can change delivery. It is hard to imagine that simply legislating rights and creating a public expectation of delivery will, in fact, ensure delivery. After all, is there not an expectation that a ration card holder will get decent grain from the fair price shop, yet all too frequently grain is not available or is of poor quality.

Information decentralisation can help. Knowing how many medicines the local public dispensary received, or how much money the local school is getting for mid-day meals (MDMs), can help the public monitor delivery and alert higher-ups when the benefits are not delivered. But the public delivery system is usually most apathetic where the public is poorly educated, of low social status and disorganised, so monitoring by the poor is also unlikely to be effective.

Some argue that this is why the middle class should enjoy public benefits along with the poor, so that the former can protest against poor delivery, which will ensure high quality for all. But making benefits universal is costly, and may still lead to indifferent delivery for the poor. The middle class may live in different areas from the poor. Indeed, even when located in the same area, the poor may not even patronise facilities frequented by the middle class because they feel out of place. And even when all patronise the same facility, providers may be able to discriminate between the voluble middle class and the uncomplaining poor.

So if more resources or better management are inadequate answers, what might work? The answer may partly lie in reducing the public's dependence on government-provided jobs or public services. A good private sector job, for example, may give a household the money to get private health care, education and supplies, and reduce their need for public services. Income could increase an individual's status and increase the respect they are accorded by the teacher, the policeman or the bureaucrat.

But how does a poor man get a good job if he has not benefited from good health care and education in the first place? In this modern world where good skills are critical to a good job, the unskilled have little recourse but to take a poorly paying job or to look for the patronage that will get them a good job. So do we not arrive at a contradiction: the good delivery of public services is essential to escape the dependence on bad public services?

Money Liberates and Empowers

We need to go back to the drawing board. There is a way out of this contradiction, developing the idea that money liberates. Could we not give poor households cash instead of promising them public services? A poor household with cash can patronise whomsoever it wants, and not just the monopolistic government provider. Because the poor can pay for their medicines or their food, they will command respect from the private provider. Not only will a corrupt fair price shop owner not be able to divert the grain he gets since he has to sell at market price, but because he has to compete with the shop across the street, he cannot afford to be surly or lazy. The government can add to the effects of empowering the poor by instilling a genuine cost to being uncompetitive—by shutting down parts of the public delivery systems that do not generate enough custom.

Much of what we need to do is already possible. The government intends to announce a scheme for full financial inclusion on Independence Day. It includes identifying the poor, creating unique biometric identifiers for them, opening linked bank accounts and making government transfers into those accounts. When fully rolled out, I believe it will give the poor the choice and respect as well as the services they had to beg for in the past. It can break a link between poor public service, patronage and corruption that is growing more worrisome over time.

Undoubtedly, cash transfers will not resolve every problem, nor are they uncontroversial. A constant refrain from paternalistic social workers is that the poor will simply drink away any transfers. In fact, studies by NGOs like Self-employed Women's Association (SEWA) indicate this is not true. Moreover, one could experiment with sending transfers to women, who may be better spenders. Some argue that attaching conditions to cash transfers—for example, they will be made provided the recipient's children attend school regularly—may improve the usage of the cash. The danger of attaching conditionality is that if the monitor is corrupt or inefficient, the whole process of direct benefits transfers can be vitiated. Nevertheless, it will be useful to monitor usage carefully where automation is possible, and automatically attach further benefits to responsible usage.

A related concern is whether cash transfers will become addictive—whether they become millstones keeping the poor in poverty rather than stepping stones out of it. This is an important concern. Cash transfers work best when they build capabilities through education and health care, thus expanding opportunity, rather than when they are used solely for inessential consumption. The vast majority amongst the poor will seize opportunities, especially for their children, with both hands. Nevertheless, if there is evidence that cash transfers are being misspent—and we should let data rather than preconceived notions drive policy—some portion could be given in the form of electronic coupons that can be spent by the specified recipient only on food, education or health care.[2]

Another set of concerns has to do with whether private providers will bother to provide services in remote areas. Clearly, if people in remote areas have the cash to buy, private providers will find their

---

2. Eventually, we will have to find a way to wean those who start earning significant amounts from receiving such transfers. How to do this without providing disincentives to working and earning is a future problem born of success which is best left for another day. The US has dealt with the disincentive effects of getting off welfare with programmes like the earned income tax credit.

way there. Indeed, a particularly desirable outcome will be if some of the poor find work providing services that hitherto used to be provided by public servants. Moreover, implementing cash transfers does not mean dismantling the system of public delivery wherever it is effective—it only means that the poor will pay when they use the public service.

The broader takeaway is that financial inclusion and direct benefits transfer can be a way of liberating the poor from dependency on indifferently delivered public services, and thus indirectly from the venal but effective politician. It is not a cure-all but will help the poor out of poverty and towards true political independence. But financial inclusion can do more; by liberating the poor and the marginalised from the clutches of the moneylender, by providing credit and advice to the entrepreneurial amongst the poor, and by giving household the ability to save and insure against accidents, it can set them on the road to economic independence, thus strengthening the political freedom that good public services will bring. This is why financial inclusion is so important.

Five Ps of Financial Inclusion

Let me end with a vision of how the Reserve Bank of India (RBI) can speed up and enhance financial inclusion of the kind I have just outlined. Financial inclusion in my view is about getting five things right: product, place, price, protection and profit.

If we are to draw in the poor, we need products that address their needs: a safe place to save, a reliable way to send and receive money, a quick way to borrow in times of need or to escape the clutches of the moneylender, easy-to-understand accident, life and health insurance, and an avenue to engage in saving for old age. Simplicity and reliability are key—what one thinks one is paying for is what one should get, without hidden clauses or opt-outs to trip one up. The RBI is going to nudge banks to offer a basic suite of 'products' to address financial needs.

Two other attributes of products are very important. They should be easy to access at low transactions cost. In the past, this meant that the place of delivery, that is the bank branch, had to be close to the customer. So a key element of the inclusion programme was to expand bank branching in unbanked areas. Today, with various other means of reaching the customer such as the mobile phone or the business correspondent, we can be more agnostic about the means by which the customer is reached. In other words, 'place' today need not mean physical proximity, it can mean electronic proximity or proximity *via* correspondents. Towards this end, we have liberalised the regulations on bank business correspondents, encouraged banks and mobile companies to form alliances, and started the process of licensing payment banks.

The transactions costs of obtaining the product, including the 'price' and the intermediary charges, should be low. Since every unbanked individual likely consumes low volumes of financial services to begin with, the provider should automate transactions as far as possible to reduce costs, and use employees that are local and are commensurately paid. Furthermore, any regulatory burden should be minimal. With these objectives in mind, the RBI has started the process of licensing small local banks, and is re-examining KYC (know your customer) norms with a view to simplifying them. Last month, we removed a major hurdle in the way of migrant workers and people living in makeshift structures obtaining a bank account, that of providing proof of current address.

New and inexperienced customers will require 'protection.' The RBI is beefing up the Consumer Protection Code, emphasising the need for suitable products that are simple and easy to understand. We are also working with the government on expanding financial literacy. Teaching the poor the intricacies of finance has to move beyond literacy camps and into schools. Banks that lend to the entrepreneurial poor should find ways to advise them on business management too, or find ways to engage NGOs and organisations like the National Bank for Agriculture and Rural Development (NABARD) in the process. We are also strengthening the customer grievance redressal mechanism, while looking to expand supervision, market intelligence, and coordination with law and order to reduce the proliferation of fly-by-night operators.

Finally, while mandated targets are useful in indicating ambition (and allowing banks to anticipate a large enough scale so as to make investments), financial inclusion cannot be achieved without it being 'profitable.' So the last 'P' is that there should be profits at the bottom of the pyramid. For instance, the government should be willing to pay reasonable commissions punctually for benefit transfers, and bankers should be able to charge reasonable and transparent fees or interest rates for offering services to the poor.

Let me conclude. One of the greatest dangers to the growth of developing countries is the middle income trap, where crony capitalism creates oligarchies that slow down growth. If the debate during the elections is any pointer, this is a very real concern of the public in India today. To avoid this trap, and to strengthen the independent democracy our leaders won for us 67 years ago, we have to improve public services, especially those targeted at the poor. A key mechanism to improve these services is through financial inclusion, which is going to be an important part of the government and the RBI's plans in the coming years.

Address delivered by the Governor, RBI, at the Twentieth Lalit Doshi Memorial Lecture, Mumbai, 11 August, 2014.

RBI Bulletin September 2014.

14

DEEPAK MOHANTY

Indian Inflation Puzzle

OVER the last three years, the persistence of inflation in an environment of falling economic growth has come out as a 'puzzle'. In this paper, I propose to address the following questions: What do I mean by a 'puzzle'? Why do we need to worry about inflation? What is the nature of the current inflation process? How did monetary policy respond to the recent bout of inflation? I conclude with some thoughts on the way forward to achieve price stability.

Current Inflation Puzzle?

First, let me begin by giving the context. India is a moderate inflation country. For example, in the 62 years since 1950-51, average annual inflation rate as measured by changes in the wholesale price index (WPI) increased at a rate of 6.7 per cent per annum. That is not a very high rate considering that many countries, both developed and developing, experienced very high inflation in their modern development history. In fact, more recently in the 1980s and 1990s, the world inflation averaged around 17 per cent per annum. In the 2000s, there was a sharp all round moderation in global inflation.

In the eight-year period from 2000 to 2007, the world inflation averaged 3.9 per cent per annum. Even the emerging and developing economies (EDEs) which traditionally had very high inflation showed an average annual inflation at 6.7 per cent. India's inflation performance was even better at 5.2 per cent as measured by WPI and 4.6 per cent measured by the consumer price index (CPI-IW). In 2008, the global financial crisis struck following which inflation rose sharply both in advanced countries and EDEs as commodity and oil prices rebounded ahead of a sharp 'V' shaped recovery. Thereafter, inflation rate moderated both in advanced economies and EDEs. In India too, the inflation rate rose from 4.7 per cent in 2007-08 to 8.1 per cent in 2008-09 and fell to 3.8 per cent in 2009-10 (Table 17.1). However, the inflation rate backed up and stayed near double digits during 2010-11 and 2011-12 before showing some moderation in 2012-13. Given India's good track record of inflation management, the persistence of elevated inflation for over two years is apparently puzzling.

Table 14.1

Global Inflation and Inflation in India

(In Recent Years India's Inflation Rate has been Higher than World Average)

(Year-on-year in per cent)

	2000-2007	*2008*	*2009*	*2010*	*2011*	*2012*	*2008-2012*
	Average			*Annual*			*Average*
Global Inflation							
World	3.9	6.0	2.4	3.7	4.9	4.0	4.2
EDEs	6.7	9.3	5.1	6.1	7.2	6.1	6.8
Inflation in India							
WPI	5.2	8.1	3.8	9.6	8.9	7.6	7.6
WPI-Food	3.8	8.9	14.6	11.1	7.2	9.1	10.2
WPI-NFMP	4.3	5.7	0.2	6.1	7.3	5.2	4.9
CPI-IW	4.6	9.1	12.2	10.5	8.4	9.9	10.0

Note: Indian inflation data pertains to financial year, EDEs: emerging and developing economies, WPI: wholesale price index, NFMP: non-food manufactured products, CPI-IW: consumer price index for industrial workers.

Second, the deceleration of growth and emergence of a significant negative output gap has failed to contain inflation. It is understandable if inflation goes up in an environment of accelerating economic growth. There could be a situation when the real economy is growing above its potential growth that could trigger inflation what economists call an overheating situation. It is like an electric cable exploding if we overload it with appliances beyond its capacity. But, that is not the case. The Reserve Bank of India (RBI) estimates suggest that the potential output growth of the Indian economy dropped from 8.5 per cent pre-crisis to 8.0 per cent post-crisis and it may have further fallen to around 7.0 per cent in the recent period. Even against this scaled down estimate of potential growth, actual year-on-year GDP (gross domestic product) growth has decelerated significantly from 9.2 per cent in the fourth quarter of 2010-11 to 5.3 per cent in the second quarter of 2012-13. The loss of growth momentum that started in 2011-12 got extended into 2012-13.

During a boom, economic activity may for a time rise above this potential level and the output gap becomes positive. During economic slowdown, the economy drops below its potential level and the output gap is negative. Economic theory puts a lot of emphasis on understanding the relationship between output gap and inflation. A negative output gap implies a slack in the economy and hence a downward pressure on inflation. So, India's current low growth-high inflation dynamics has been in contrast to this conventional economic theory. Real GDP growth has moderated significantly below its potential. Yet inflation did not cool off.

Third, the RBI raised its policy repo rate 13 times between March 2010 and October 2011 by a cumulative 375 basis points. The policy repo rate increased from a low of 4.75 per cent to 8.5 per cent. Still it did not help contain inflation. The critics of the RBI argue that monetary tightening rather than lowering inflation has slowed growth. Interest rate is a blunt instrument. It first slows growth and then inflation. But the growth slowdown has not been commensurate with inflation control.

The above three considerations will suggest that the recent persistence of inflation is a puzzle. I will come back to the causes of the recent bout of inflation, but before that, let me address the question as to why do we need to worry about high inflation?

Costs of Inflation

Inflation, though a nominal variable, imposes real costs on the economy. Let me elaborate.

First, inflation erodes the value of money. As I mentioned earlier, India is a moderate inflation country with the 62-year long-term average inflation rate being 6.7 per cent, notwithstanding occasional spikes in inflation. Yet during this period, the overall price level has multiplied 45 times. This means that ₹ 100 now is worth only ₹ 2.2 at 1950-51 prices. Since price stability is a key objective of monetary policy, central banks are obviously concerned with inflation.

Second, high and persistent inflation imposes significant socio-economic costs. Given that the burden of inflation is disproportionately large on the poor, and considering that India has a large informal sector, high inflation by itself can lead to distributional inequality. Therefore, for a welfare-oriented public policy, low inflation becomes a critical element for ensuring a balanced progress.

Third, high inflation distorts economic incentives by diverting resources away from productive investment to speculative activities. Fixed-income earners and pensioners see a decline in their disposable income and standard of living. Inflation reduces households' savings as they try to maintain the real value of their consumption. Consequent fall in overall investment in the economy reduces its potential growth. With a high inflation of over two years, we are already seeing a fall in household savings in financial assets, particularly in bank deposits. At the same time, households' preference for gold has increased. This is putting additional pressure on our balance of payments (BoP).

Fourth, economic agents base their consumption and investment decisions on their current and expected future income as well as their expectations on future inflation rates. Persistent high inflation alters inflationary expectations, and apprehension arising from price uncertainty does lead to cut in spending by individuals and slowdown in investment by corporates which hurts economic growth in the long-run.

Fifth, as inflation rises and turns volatile, it raises the inflation risk premia in financial transactions. Hence, nominal interest rates tend to be higher than they would have been under low and stable inflation.

Sixth, if domestic inflation remains persistently higher than those of the trading partners, it affects external competitiveness through appreciation of the real exchange rate.

Finally, as inflation rises beyond a threshold, it has an adverse impact on overall growth. The RBI's technical assessment suggests that the threshold level of inflation for India is in the range of 4 to 6 per cent. If inflation persists beyond this level, it could lower economic growth over the medium-term.

Causes of Recent Inflation Spike

Let me first identify the high inflation period. The WPI inflation rate accelerated from 7.1 per cent in December 2009 to a peak of 10.9 per cent by April 2010, thereafter it remained stubbornly close to double digits till November 2011. Thus, we experienced two years of high inflation between January 2010 to December 2011. During this two-year period, WPI inflation averaged 9.5 per cent per annum. All the major components of inflation contributed to this surge. The trigger for inflation first emanated from the failure of South-West monsoon of 2009, following which food prices rose sharply. Concurrently, the global economy made a sharp recovery from the recession of 2009. As a result, global commodity prices including oil rose substantially. India being a net commodity importer, particularly oil, the intermediate prices rose. This quickly spilled over to non-food manufactured products inflation, making the inflation process fairly generalised. In the subsequent one year between January 2012 to December 2012, the average WPI inflation moderated to 7.5 per cent led by all its major components except fuel and power (Figure 14.1).

Figure 14.1

WPI Inflation

(WPI Inflation has Moderated since December 2011)

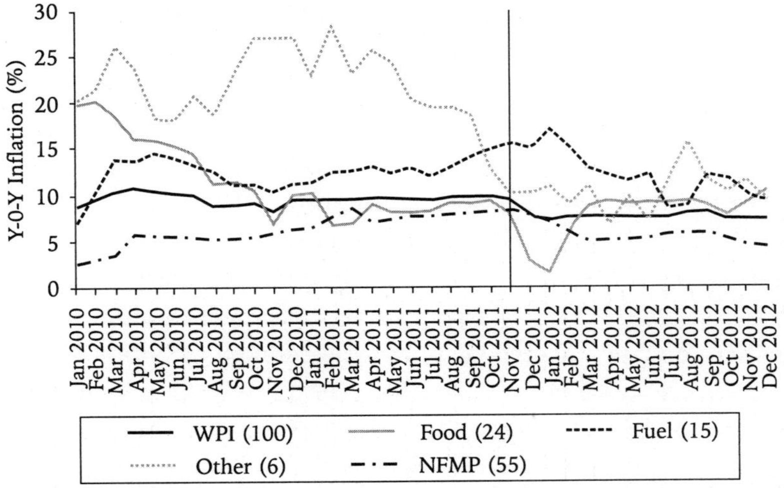

Note: Figures in brackets are the weights.

The high inflation during 2010 and 2011 was a combination of both adverse global and domestic factors as well as supply and demand factors.

First, crude oil and other global commodity price trends as well as exchange rate movements are increasingly playing an important role in defining domestic prices. With the gradual external liberalisation, the Indian economy is much more open and globalised now than ever before. Currently, over 85 per cent of demand for crude oil in India is met by imports. The imported Indian basket of crude oil price rose from US$ 49 per barrel in April 2009 to an average of US$ 79 per barrel in 2010 and further to US$ 108 per barrel in 2011 and remained high at US$ 110 per barrel in 2012. Global metal prices, reflected in the International Monetary Fund (IMF) index, rose by 48 per cent in 2010 and again by 14 per cent in 2011 before moderating by 17 per cent in 2012.

Moreover, the rupee depreciated from an average of 45.7 per US dollar in 2010 to 46.7 in 2011. The depreciation of the rupee was particularly sharp in 2012 as the rupee averaged 53.4 per US dollar. Empirical evidence suggests that one percentage point change in the rupee-dollar exchange rate has 10 basis points impact on inflation. While, during 2010 and 2011, global commodity prices had an adverse impact on domestic inflation, the depreciation of the rupee more than offset the beneficial impact of modest softening of global commodity prices on domestic inflation in 2012.

There is another important dimension of India's external sector linkage, particularly towards explaining high non-food manufactured product inflation. Analysis suggests that the pass-through from non-food international commodity prices to domestic raw material prices has increased in the recent years reflecting growing interconnectedness of domestic and global commodity markets. This trend is also corroborated by corporate finance data which show that the share of raw material costs as a percentage of both expenditure and sales has been rising. Therefore, as the economy is increasingly getting integrated, external sector developments are progressively becoming important for domestic price behaviour.

Second, while the growth in domestic agricultural production has stagnated around 3 per cent per annum, the demand for food has increased. Although the country currently has sufficient food grains stocks, it is not yet self-sufficient in pulses and oilseeds. Further, demand for protein-based products like meat, eggs, milk and fish as well as fruits and vegetables has increased substantially with rising per capita income. The protein inflation has assumed a structural character. This has also resulted in substantial divergence between WPI and CPI as food has a larger share in the CPI basket.

Further, with the increase in income, real consumption expenditure has grown significantly. Recently released key results of the NSSO 68th round survey (2011-12) on household consumption expenditure indicate that real per capita consumption expenditure in rural areas increased at an average rate of 8.7 per cent during 2009-2012 as compared with 1.4 per cent during 2004-2009. Similarly, urban real per capita consumption increased by 6.7 per cent as against 2.4 per cent in the corresponding period. The fact that real consumption expenditure expanded during a period of high food inflation indicates that the demand remains strong, feeding into higher price levels as supply elasticities remain low.

The high food prices are supported by increase in wages. The average nominal rural wage increase was of the order of 17 per cent during 2008-09 to 2012-13 so far. Even after adjusting for high rural consumer inflation, real wage increase over 6 per cent per annum was significant (Table 17.2). In the formal sector, company finance data suggest that the wage bill has risen at a faster rate since the middle of 2009-10. As wages increase, entitlement goes up, and consequently demand and preference for essential commodities increases.

Third, with the persistence of near double-digit inflation in 2010 and 2011, the medium- to long-term inflation expectations in the economy have risen, underscoring the role of higher food prices in expectations formation. If inflation is expected to be persistently high, workers bargain for higher nominal wages to protect their real income. This creates a pressure on firms' costs and they may in turn increase prices to maintain their profits. Independently, the producers' own inflation expectations also affect inflation directly by influencing their pricing behaviour. If companies expect general inflation to be higher in the future, they may believe that they can increase their prices without suffering a drop in demand for their output.

Table 14.2

Fiscal Deficit, Current Account Deficit, Agricultural Growth and Real Rural Wages

(In Recent Years both Fiscal Deficit and Current Account Deficit have Increased, while Agricultural Growth Stagnated, Real Rural Wages Increased Sharply)

(In per cent)

	2000-2008	*2008-09*	*2009-10*	*2010-11*	*2011-12*	*2012-13*	*2008-2013*
	Average			*Annual*			*Average*
Fiscal/External							
GFD/GDP	4.4	6.0	6.5	4.8	5.7	5.1	5.6
CAD/GDP	-0.04	-2.3	-2.8	-2.8	-4.2	-4.6	-3.3
Growth							
GDP	7.2	6.7	8.6	9.3	6.2	-	7.7
Agricultural GDP	3.0	0.1	0.8	7.9	3.6	-	3.1
Rural Wages							
Nominal	3.3	10.7	15.8	18.3	19.8	18.4	16.6
Real@	-0.4	0.6	2.1	8.3	11.5	9.2	6.3

Note: - : Not available, @: nominal wages adjusted for CPI for agricultural labourers, GFD: gross fiscal deficit of the centre, GDP: gross domestic product, CAD: Current account deficit.

Fourth, there has also been added stimulus from the crisis driven fiscal and monetary policy. Fiscal consolidation process was reversed in 2008-09 which impacted the macroeconomic conditions (Figure 14.2). Higher fiscal expansion also impedes efficacy of monetary policy transmission. The moderation in private demand resulting from anti-inflationary monetary policy stance is partly offset by the fiscal expansion. Let me now turn to the role of monetary policy in a little more detail.

Role of Monetary Policy

The current phase of high inflation followed the global financial crisis, which affected India's economy, though not with the same

Figure 14.2

Fiscal Deficits and Budget Estimates

(Fiscal Deficits have Overshot their Budget Estimate in Recent Years)

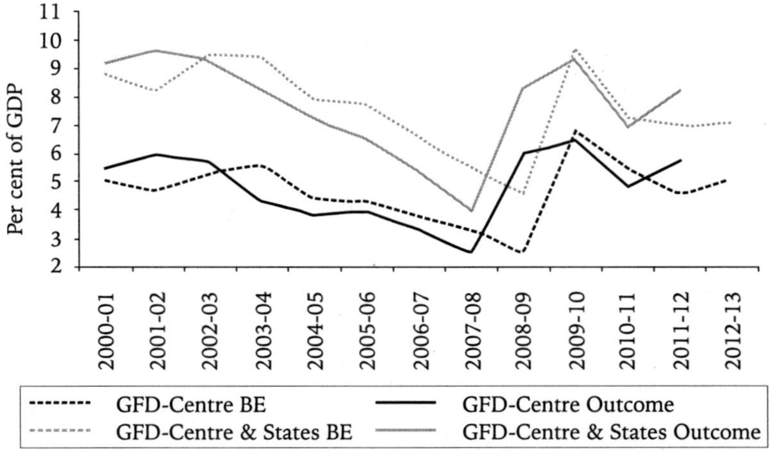

intensity as advanced countries. India, though initially somewhat insulated from the global developments, was eventually impacted significantly by the global shocks through all the channels—trade, finance and expectations channels. The RBI, like most central banks, took a number of conventional and unconventional measures to augment domestic and foreign currency liquidity, and sharply reduced the policy rates. In a span of seven months between October 2008 and April 2009, there was an unprecedented policy activism. For example: (i) the repo rate was reduced by 425 basis points to 4.75 per cent, (ii) the reverse repo rate was reduced by 275 basis points to 3.25 per cent, (iii) cash reserve ratio (CRR) of banks was reduced by a cumulative 400 basis points of their net demand and time liabilities (NDTL) to 5.0 per cent, and (iv) the total amount of primary liquidity potentially made available to the financial system was over ₹ 5.6 trillion or over 10 per cent of GDP. The government also came up with various fiscal stimulus measures.

The RBI, in October 2009, highlighted the need for exit from crisis-time monetary policy stimulus. But it was not easy to exit from the excessively accommodative monetary policy stance for two main reasons. First, the year-on-year headline WPI inflation had just barely turned positive and was entirely driven by food inflation (Figure 14.3). Industrial production had started to pick up but exports were still declining. Hence, recovery was not assured. Second, globally, most central banks were in favour of continuing stimulus. On the other hand, domestically, consumer price inflation was high, households' inflation expectations were rising and surplus liquidity was substantial. These developments had inflationary consequences.

Figure 14.3

Non-food Manufactured Products Inflation

(Inflation Moderation since November 2011 is Accompanied by Easing of Non-food Manufactured Products Inflation)

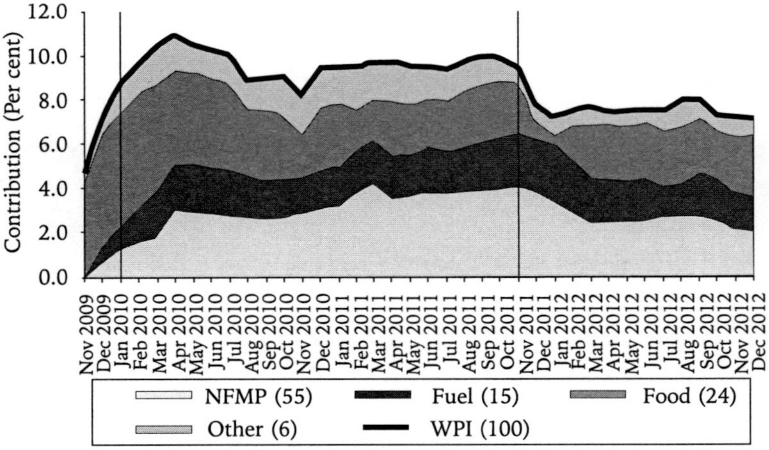

Note: Figures in brackets are the weights.

Nevertheless, the RBI withdrew the unconventional liquidity support measures and restored the statutory liquidity ratio (SLR) of banks to its pre-crisis level. At the same time, monetary policy had to recognise that the economic growth was recovering from the crisis time slowdown and any aggressive monetary tightening at that point would have affected the recovery. Subsequently, in January 2010, the CRR was raised by 75 basis points of banks' net demand and time liabilities (NDTLs), and policy rate was increased for the first time in March 2010 by 25 basis points. Between March 2010 and October

2011, the policy repo rate was raised by 375 basis points to contain inflation and anchor inflationary expectations. It may, however, be emphasised that policy rate was raised from a historically low level of 4.75 per cent. As inflation had already risen sharply, the real policy rate during this period was negative. Thus, monetary policy was still accommodative though the extent of accommodation was gradually closing (Figure 14.4 and Table 14.3).

Figure 14.4

Real Policy Rate and Monetary Policy Effectiveness

(Real Policy Rate has Turned Mildly Positive since November 2011 Improving Monetary Policy Effectiveness)

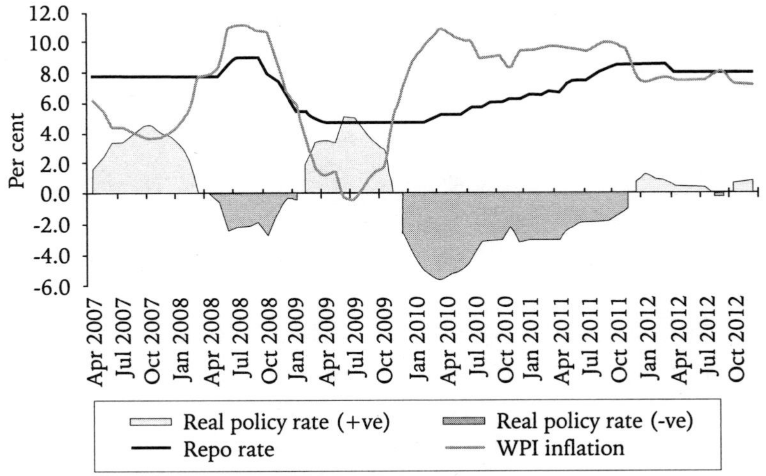

The policy rate was left unchanged at 8.5 per cent between October 2011 and March 2012. Consequently, the inflation rate started trending down from October 2011 and the real policy rate tuned positive since January 2012. This enhanced the efficiency of monetary policy which was reflected in easing of the inflation rate. Accordingly, the RBI reduced the policy rate by 50 basis points in April 2012 and again by 25 basis points in the last monetary policy review on 29 January 2013. Currently the CRR stands at a historically low level of 4 per cent of NDTL of banks and policy repo rate is at 7.75 per cent.

Table 14.3

Real Bank Lending Rates and Real Policy Rate

(In Recent Years while the Real Bank Lending Rates Remained Relatively Low, the Real Policy Rate Turned Mildly Negative)

(Year-on-year in per cent)

	2000-2008	*2008-09*	*2009-10*	*2010-11*	*2011-12*	*2012-13*	*2009-2013*
	Average			*Annual*			*Average*
Monetary Block							
Money Supply*	16.6	20.5	19.3	16.0	16.1	13.3	17.0
Non-food Credit*	23.8	24.5	14.6	21.2	18.7	16.5	19.1
Weighted Average Bank lending rate	12.9	11.5	10.5	11.4	12.6	-	11.5
Real Weighted Average lending rate@	7.7	3.4	6.7	1.8	3.7	-	3.9
Policy repo rate	7.0	7.4	4.8	5.9	8.1	8.0	6.8
Real Policy Rate@	1.7	-0.7	0.9	-3.6	-0.8	0.4	-0.8

Note: * Data for 2012-13 up to 11 January 2013, - not available,
@ Nominal rate adjusted for average WPI inflation.

Conclusion

While I have tried to unravel the inflation puzzle and provide some explanation why inflation remained entrenched despite output gap being negative, we know that sustained level of high inflation is bad for the economy as it imposes real costs which are borne disproportionately by the different segments of the economy. In order to bring inflation down on an enduring basis and anchor inflation expectations, there is a need for policy action on several fronts.

First, it is important to aim for nutritional security not only to harness the demographic dividend stemming from our sizeable young population but also to contain food prices. This will require addressing the supply-demand imbalance in the agricultural sector and modernising the supply chain.

Second, concerted efforts are required to secure energy security for the country. The bulk of our fossil fuel requirement is met by imports. A necessary step in this direction is market-related pricing of petroleum products to economise consumption and reduce the subsidy burden. This should be supplemented by step up in electricity generation so as to minimise fall back option of diesel generation of power.

Third, in a supply constrained economy, potential output is not a reliable gauge for inflation threshold as firms operate below capacity and yet retain the pricing power. Hence, reliability of power supply and availability of necessary industrial raw materials are important for industrial capacity utilisation and improvement in productivity. Besides moderating inflation, this will also reduce reliance on imports of products for which domestic capacity exists.

Fourth, it is imperative to maintain exchange rate stability to cushion transmission of international price pressures in commodities, particularly crude oil. This will require management of the current account in our BoP with the rest of the world at sustainable levels.

Fifth, fiscal consolidation is important for maintaining both domestic and external balance so that we avoid the risks of twin deficits. As our own high growth experience of 2003-2008 suggests, lower fiscal deficit not only encourages private investment but also helps in maintaining price stability.

Finally, while persevering with the steps to increase the depth of the financial market and addressing credit constraints, monetary policy needs to be calibrated to the evolving growth-inflation dynamics so that we move towards our potential growth in a non-inflationary manner. For a country at our stage of development with a vast labour supply, potential growth is not a constant. Only in an environment of price stability, a step up in investment accompanied by productivity improvements could bolster potential growth. Even when the supply side factors dominate the inflationary pressures, given the risks of spillover into a wider inflationary process, there is need for policy response. While monetary policy action addresses the risk of unhinging of inflation expectations, attending to the structural supply constraints becomes important to ensure that these do not become a binding constraint in the long-run, making the task of inflation management more difficult. By ensuring a low and stable inflation, the RBI could best contribute to social welfare.

Acceptance Speech in the function of Late Dr Ramchandra Parnerkar Outstanding *Economics Award 2013* at Mumbai, January 31, 2013.

Economic Developments in India, Vol. 183.

15

ILA PATNAIK

Hold on to Interest Rates

THE impact of tighter fiscal and monetary policy on inflation is now visible in the recent price data. Inflation, measured both by the wholesale price index (WPI) and by the consumer price index (CPI), has come down. It may still be too early to cut rates, but the Reserve Bank of India (RBI) Governor Raghuram Rajan can now afford to hold rates unchanged in today's monetary policy announcement. His strategy of an aggressive attack on inflation, despite the scepticism often voiced in the Indian monetary policy debate about the effectiveness of monetary policy, was the right strategy and is yielding results.

Considering that inflationary expectations in India are high and persistent, and could take a while to come down, Rajan should not cut the repo rate as yet. If the WPI inflation measure is the target, there is a case for cutting rates since this has come down sharply. However, the CPI, the target towards which the RBI sensibly appears to be moving, is still above 8 per cent and there is fear that it may go up due to unseasonal rains. Also, CPI-based inflation has not remained low long enough for inflationary expectations to fall.

The fiscal and monetary contractions of the last 9 months, as well as the slowdown in the economy, have contributed to the reduction in inflation. In this environment, effective communication by RBI that its focus will be on inflation control has played an important role. In addition, the setting up of the Urjit Patel Committee and its view that RBI should adopt inflation targeting has helped counter some of the traditional RBI views that monetary policy has no impact on inflation, that India has a weak monetary policy transmission mechanism so there is no point in trying to raise rates, that inflation in India cannot be measured properly and so on.

The war on inflation is still not won. The present dip in inflation must be sustained for many months before RBI can relax. Despite the fall in GDP growth, the consequent slowdown in demand, and the fall in commodity prices, Indian inflation is higher than what is seen elsewhere in the world. Inflation in food has contributed most, but inflation in non-food has also been sticky.

Looking forward, there is a contradiction between RBI's aggressive stance on inflation and its intervention in the foreign exchange market. RBI's stance on monetary policy could be undermined by its intervention in the foreign exchange market. In recent weeks, RBI appears to be intervening in the foreign exchange market to prevent the rupee from appreciating. The extent of intervention and its sterilisation is not known yet. If the intervention is unsterilised, then it would lead to an increase in liquidity and would pull down interest rates even without a monetary policy announcement. Indeed since RBI's monetary policy is not conducted only through the interest rate instrument, but also through its intervention and sterilisation, something that the Governor does not announce with the policy stance, it has been seen in the past that while actions on the policy rate move in one direction, the liquidity conditions in the market can move in quite the opposite direction. This was the story of the mid-2000s, when RBI was intervening in the foreign exchange market to combat rupee appreciation and raising the repo rate at the same time to fight inflation. Its intervention was only partly sterilised and was pumping liquidity into the system pushing up inflation. As a consequence, the policy rate hikes were ineffective.

Inflation targeting countries usually solve this problem by adopting a flexible exchange rate. In other words, the exchange rate is allowed to move, while inflation is stabilised. Sometimes there may be occasional sterilised intervention by the central bank. However, central banks that target inflation do not pursue pegged exchange rates for long periods. This means that they do not require resources for sustained sterilisation. While the Urjit Patel Committee has proposed that RBI should target inflation, it has also proposed that the central bank should get unlimited sterilisation powers. Occasional foreign exchange intervention and sterilisation to contain volatility do not require unlimited sterilisation capacity. If RBI is to move to an inflation targeting framework, it cannot plan to do unlimited sterilisation. The People's Bank of China, the Chinese central bank, which targets the exchange rate, has such powers. Other central banks do not have such powers, as these are inconsistent with the mandate of inflation targeting. In other words, if RBI is to seriously adopt inflation targeting, it must give up on pegging the exchange rate. Trying to target inflation and exchange rate simultaneously on a sustained basis is inconsistent.

A further consideration in the decision about the stance of monetary policy would be global liquidity considerations. Janet Yellen's recent comments suggest that the US Fed could start raising rates next year. As long as the US monetary policy remains unconventional, i.e., until the time comes when the FOMC discusses and decides policy interest rates rather than the purchase of bonds, it remains in uncharted territory. Low inflation, along with a low current account and fiscal deficit, would be a more prudent policy, as there could be sharp and sudden changes in the US and global liquidity conditions. This may prompt RBI to keep interest rates unchanged.

Financial Express, April 01, 2014.

Economic Developments in India, Vol. 196.

16

C. RANGARAJAN, PADMA IYER KAUL
and E.M. VIBEESH

Convergence

Have the Lower Income States 'Caught Up'?

Introduction

Balanced regional growth is an important development objective in India. More importantly, an inclusive growth process is essential to promoting social harmony and political stability. Differential natural resource endowments and skilled human resources result in wide variations in growth rates and hence incomes across states. While initially inter-regional disparity may increase in the process of development, it is expected that as growth gathers momentum and with specific policy initiatives, this divergence would attenuate. Convergence in per capita incomes (PCIs) will be driven by diminishing returns to capital, that is, states with a high initial income and presumably higher capital-labour ratio will, over time, have lower per capita income growth rates and *vice versa*. This process of convergence will be aided by redistribution of incomes in favour of poorer states through mechanisms such as the Finance Commission and grants from the centre to the states (Cashin and Sahay, 1996). Empirical evidence on convergence, largely based on PCI time series, has been the subject of a lot of debate and study. In this paper, we attempt to address this issue by examining the PCI data for the period 1980-81 to 2012-13.

The article is divided into six sections. Section I presents a brief literature survey on the empirical evidence and conclusions on inter-state disparities and convergence. Section II details the methodology underlying the study, while Section III analyses the gross state domestic product (GSDP) and net state domestic product (NSDP) data to examine the movements in inter-regional disparities in the period 1993-94 to 2004-05 and the more recent period, 2004-05 to 2012-13. Section IV uses some simple inequality measures and the Gini coefficient to examine the trends in inter-state inequality. Section V tests for absolute convergence using the technique of simple regression, taking the initial per capita income and the growth rates of states. Section VI makes some concluding remarks.

Section I

Literature Review

One can distinguish between two types of convergence in growth empirics: sigma convergence and beta convergence. When the dispersion of real PCI across a group of economies falls over time, there is sigma convergence and when the correlation between growth in income over time and its initial level is negative, there is beta convergence (Young, 2007). Beta convergence literature divides itself into two broad sets of studies. The first category pertains to 'absolute convergence,' which tests the hypothesis that states with low initial incomes experience higher growth rates, while states with high initial incomes experience some slowing down. The assumption here is that heterogeneity among states does not make a difference to this process. The second category pertains to 'conditional convergence,' which tests for the same process but controls for heterogeneity using variables like savings/investments (Aiyar, 2001), infrastructure (Nagaraj, 1998) and income redistribution (Cashin and Sahay, 1996).

A large number of studies have documented beta convergence of per capita state incomes in the pre-1990s. Cashin and Sahay (1996) find absolute and conditional convergence for the period 1961-1991. Purfield (2006) finds absolute convergence for the period 1973-2003 and estimates the rate of convergence at 1.5 per cent per annum, though the post-1991 pace of convergence was slower than that observed over the full sample period. The study also finds evidence for conditional convergence once controls that proxy for differences in the policies and economic structure are held constant. Bandyopadhyay (2006) finds 'twin peaked' dynamics over the period 1965-1997, that is, the Indian inter-state distribution has polarised into two income convergence clubs. He also finds that the association between infrastructural indicators (roads/power consumption in industrial sector) and economic growth is a significant one, especially for the lower income states. Nagaraj *et al.* (1998) find evidence of conditional convergence across states for the period 1960-1994 and observe that disparities are accounted for by differences in the structure of production, infrastructure endowments and state-specific factors. Ahluwalia (2000) found that the Gini coefficient, a measure of dispersion, was fairly stable up to 1986-87 but rose subsequently, indicating an increase in inter-state inequalities in the 1990s. This is however not inconsistent with the conditional convergence results of others. Ghosh (1998) records absolute divergence for the period 1960-61 to 1994-95, but unlike others, rejects the need for conditional convergence stating that "it is enough to look at the above regression as the states within a geopolitical boundary do share common characteristics. Interesting point is how 'divergence' appears in such homogeneous environment." Rao *et al.* (1999) find the existence of absolute and conditional divergence during 1965 to 1995 among 14 major states. They identify unequal private investment as contributing to divergence. Sachs *et al.* (2002) confirmed the above finding and found geographical variables to be responsible for this diverging trend.

There is similar lack of consensus for the more recent period. Ahluwalia (2011) finds the growth rates of the poorer states, notably the BIMARU[1] states, accelerated after 2000-01 and the process of 'catch-up' was clearly visible. However, he does not make any comments on convergence. Bhalla (2011) has shown that the extent of acceleration in growth in the post-reform period is negatively correlated with the level of per capita GSDP, that is, the poorer states have actually experienced faster growth rates relative to the richer states.[2] This is stated as being consistent with what one would expect

1. Acronym for Bihar, Madhya Pradesh, Rajasthan and Uttar Pradesh.

2. Bhalla comments on two periods, 1993-2002 and 2003-2009, to draw this conclusion. However, instead of using initial income, he uses initial growth rate and the difference between growth rates in the two periods to comment on convergence. It is important to note that states with low growth rates in 1993-2002 were not necessarily the ones with low initial incomes, e.g., Punjab and Haryana.

under conditional convergence. The mid-term appraisal of the 11th Five Year Plan finds similar results and notes: "Although growth rates continue to differ across states the variation has tended to decline." Arvind Subramanian (2012) explores two periods, 1993-2001 and 2001-2009, and finds evidence of divergence. However, the author does not share the regression results and is silent on the coefficients.

The rich literature on 'convergence' with significant variations in conclusions, often for similar periods, could probably be explained by the fact that the studies vary across various dimensions: sample period, coverage of states, data sources and estimation methodology. Ghosh (1998) uses a sample of 26 states, while a number of others use a sample of only 14 states. Some authors use annual growth rates directly, while others use compounded annual growth rates (CAGRs). The deflators used also vary between different studies; for instance, Ghosh (1998) uses state-wise consumer price index (CPI) (AL) to deflate nominal per capita NSDP, while others use all-India deflators. There are variations in the control variables used, which range from sector shares, infrastructure improvements and credit growth, to migration and literacy (Kalra, 2010).

Section II

Methodology

Some of the recent literature has used the terms 'catching up' and 'convergence' synonymously, but this is erroneous and a distinction needs to be made. 'Catching up' is a broad term. Loosely defined, it can mean that lower-income states are growing faster than earlier so that the gap between their growth rates and those of the richer states is reduced. 'Convergence' on the other hand would mean that the lower-income states have caught up and the PCIs of the states are converging towards the national mean. In other words, convergence can simply mean the successful culmination of the process of catching up by the lower-income states. We analyse the GSDP and NSDP data for 'catching up' using growth rates and dispersion indicators like max-min ratios, coefficient of variation and Gini coefficient. We also test for absolute convergence using initial income and growth rates for different periods.

We use per capita GSDP and NSDP time series data from 1980-81 to 2012-13 for 15 states: four in the south, *viz.*, Tamil Nadu, Karnataka, Andhra Pradesh and Kerala; three in the west, *viz.*, Maharashtra, Gujarat and Rajasthan; three in the north, *viz.*, Punjab, Haryana and Uttar Pradesh; one in the centre, Madhya Pradesh; and four in the east, *viz.*, Bihar, West Bengal, Assam and Odisha. Together these account for 95 per cent of the Indian population.[3] One of the major limitations of this data set is that it is not a single series. GSDP/NSDP data from the Central Statistics Office (CSO) is available in different series with different base periods, 1980-81, 1993-94, 1999-2000 and 2004-05. We use the unspliced NSDP data series for the growth and convergence analysis and spliced GSDP series at constant price (2004-05) for calculating inequality measures. To examine the growth performance of these major states, we divided the per capita NSDP data series into three periods, namely, 1980-81 to 1993-94, 1993-94 to 2004-05, and 2004-05 to 2012-13, in line with the different series provided by the CSO. The state-wise annual trend growth rates (ATGRs) of per capita NSDP (PCI) for these periods were estimated by fitting the exponential trend curves for each state.

Section III

Analysing GSDP Data

Figure 16.1 compares the growth performance of states for the latest two periods: 1993-94 to 2004-05 and 2004-05 to 2012-13. In the first period, 1993-94 to 2004-05, the ATGRs of PCI display large inter-state variations ranging from 0.9 per cent (Assam) to 4.7 per cent (West Bengal). The median growth rate in this period is 2.8 per cent (Rajasthan). In terms of per capita income, four states, *viz.*, Bihar, Odisha, Uttar Pradesh and Assam, had the lowest ranks

3. In the case of Bihar, Uttar Pradesh and Madhya Pradesh, in the post-bifurcation period, we have added the GSDP/NSDP of Jharkhand, Uttarakhand and Chhattisgarh to keep the data comparable.

in this period and even in terms of growth rates, they occupied the bottom positions. However, the four top ranking states in terms of PCI (Punjab, Maharashtra, Haryana and Gujarat) were not the fastest growing in this period. It is the middle income states like West Bengal, Karnataka, Andhra Pradesh and Kerala that grew the fastest at 4 per cent-plus. In the second period, 2004-05 to 2012-13, inter-state variations continued to be large, ranging from 4.5 per cent (Odisha) to 8.4 per cent (Tamil Nadu). However, in this period, the overall growth rate of the low-income group states was four times that of the previous period. Between these periods, the median growth rate more than doubled to 6.5 per cent (Madhya Pradesh). All the 15 states, across the different income levels, show higher growth rates in the second period compared with the first. Interestingly, the growth rate of 10 out of the 15 states under review doubled or more than doubled during the second period (Annexure Table A-16.2). The evidence of the 'catch-up' phenomenon for the lower-income states is quite striking in the period 2004-05 to 2012-13.

Figure 16.1

PCI Trend Growth Rates of 15 Major States

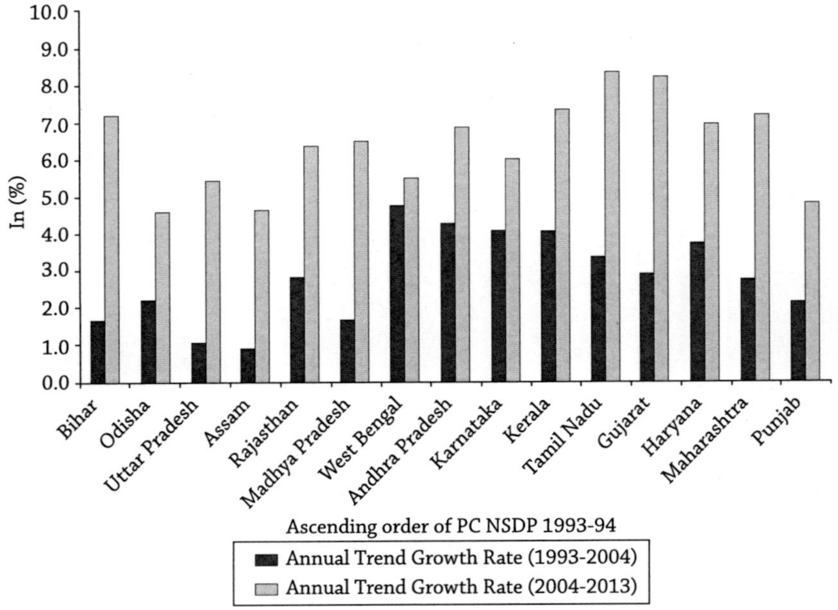

If instead of using the per capita figures, we look at GSDP for the period 2004-05 to 2012-13, the performance of the low-income-group states looks even better. Bihar, Madhya Pradesh and Rajasthan grew above, while Odisha was very close to, the all-India average of 7.8 per cent. Uttar Pradesh, a poor performer in the earlier periods, turned in a growth rate of almost 7 per cent, reflecting the buoyancy and resurgence in this period. Even Assam, which ranked last in this period, had a growth rate of 6.14 per cent—a significant improvement over its previous achievement. It is difficult to explain why low-income states grew faster in the period 2004-05 to 2012-13. Several factors appear to have been responsible. Improved law and order situation and greater commitment to efficient administration seem to have attracted more investment to these states. These states have also laid greater emphasis on education and infrastructure investment. However, more in-depth analysis of all the states is required to understand causality and to assess the role each of these factors has played in promoting growth.

Section IV

Measuring Inequality

There are a number of measures that can be used to analyse regional inequality. We use three measures in this paper, *viz.*, max-min ratio, coefficient of variation and Gini coefficient. These measures ignore the inequality within a state and assume that all individuals have an income equal to the PCI. The simplest of these, the max-min ratio, has the major advantage of ease of calculation. But on the flip side, it takes only the extreme values and disregards the remaining ones. This disadvantage can be somewhat neutralised if we use a population weighted coefficient of variation. This takes into account all the observations in the distribution and is the second measure adopted for our analysis. The third, the Gini coefficient, is a popular measure of inequality that gives an estimate of inequality between the states.

In the period 1980-81 to 1993-94, the max-min ratio of the per capita GSDP of the 15 states under review shot up from 2.4 to 3.1, increasing at an annual rate of 2.0 per cent, indicating an increasing divergence during the period. In the period 1993-94 to 2004-05, the ratio increased from 3.1 to 3.6, indicating a further increase in divergence. In this period, the CAGR of the max-min ratio was lower at 1.4 per cent. In the third period, 2004-05 to 2012-13, the max-min ratio displayed an increase in the first three years and then showed a declining trend,[4] finally reaching 3.6 in 2012-13.

The population weighted coefficient of variation (CV) also shows an increasing inequality in the per capita GSDPs of the 15 states during the periods 1980-81 to 1993-94 and 1993-94 to 2004-05. However, in the recent past, it has remained relatively constant in the range of 44-45 per cent. In the first period, 1980-81 to 1993-94, the CV increased from 23.2 per cent to 31.4 per cent, and in the next period, it further increased to 38.6 per cent. This result mirrors the trends shown by the max-min ratio. In the latest period, 2004-05 to 2012-13, the CV rose from 40.0 per cent to 45.0 per cent. There was a clear tendency towards divergence in these three periods. The only mitigating factor was that in the latter half of the third period, the CV appeared to have stabilised somewhat.

To understand the impact of growth on regional inequality, we construct a Gini coefficient[5] using the cumulative relative proportions of GSDP and population for the 15 states for the three periods under study (Figure 16.2). In the first period, 1980-81 to 1993-94, the Gini coefficient rose from 0.13 to 0.17 and in the second, it further increased to 0.22, indicating a rise in regional inequalities. Overall, in these two periods, the Gini coefficient shows a steadily increasing trend. In the latest period, 2004-05 to 2012-13, the Gini coefficient remained at a slightly elevated level of 0.25 as compared with the earlier two periods. Just like in the case of CV, a positive development

4. Except for the year 2009-10.

5. The Gini coefficients were calculated as $G = 1 - \frac{\sum_{k=1}^{n}(X_k - X_{k-1})(Y_k + Y_{k-1})}{10000}$

where $X_0 = Y_0 = 0$ and $X_n = Y_n = 100$

Y_k is the cumulative relative frequency of income of the kth state.

X_k is the cumulative relative frequency of population of the kth state.

in this period is that the coefficient seems relatively static for a fairly long period. Additionally, a slight declining trend is discernible in the recent past (Figure 16.2 and Annexure Table A-16.1).

Figure 16.2

Trend in Gini Coefficient

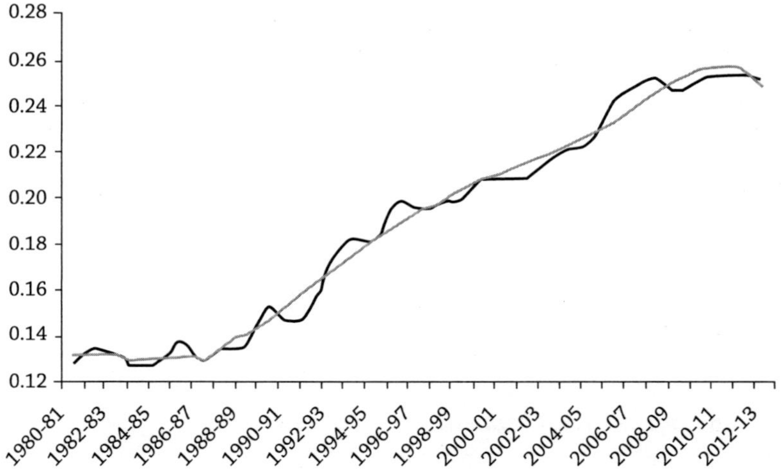

Section V

Test for Convergence/Divergence

Before going into the test for convergence in PCI, we may refer to the analysis in the 12th Five Year Plan document which looks at the average growth of the bottom five PCI states in relation to that of the remaining states, the top five PCI states and all-India. The ratios, average growth rate of the bottom five PCI states to the average growth rate of the remaining states, the top five PCI states and all-India, show an upward trend in the latest period, 2004-05 to 2012-13 (Figure 16.3). The ratio of the average growth rate of the bottom five PCI states to that of the top five PCI states rose from 0.59 (in 1980-81 to 1993-94) to 0.82 (in 2004-05 to 2012-13), showing a positive trend towards convergence.

In order to study the convergence in growth, we looked at the relationship between the average growth rates in PCI of a state in a

Figure 16.3

Ratio of Average Growth Rates of States with Lowest PCI to Average Growth Rates of Different Categories of States

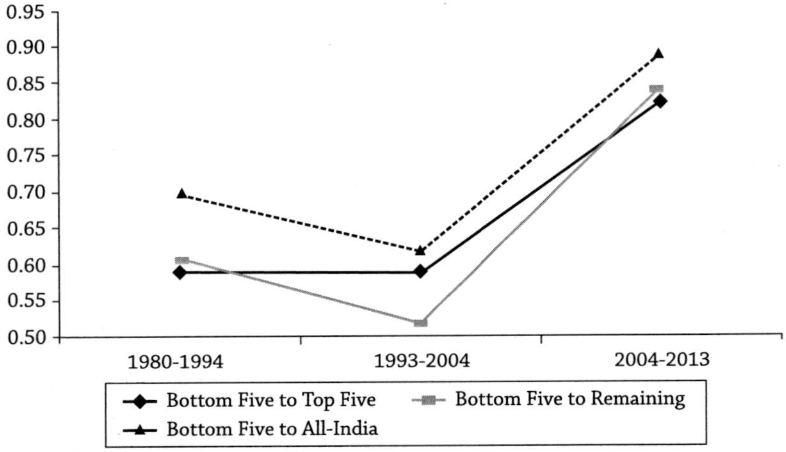

particular period with that of the previous period. Accordingly, we estimate two cross-sectional regression lines. First, the state-wise average growth rate of PCI in the period 1993-2004 is regressed on the average growth rate of PCI in the period 1980-1993. We get a statistically significant positive relationship (0.74) between the growth rates, that is, the states that had a high growth rate in the period 1980-1993 also had high growth rate in the period 1993-2004 and *vice versa*. A similar exercise relating the average growth rate of the period 2004-2013 to the average growth rate of the period 1993-2004 yields a positive relationship; the coefficient is however smaller at 0.37 and it is not statistically significant (Figure 16.4).

Theoretically, if the states were converging, the states with a low initial income would experience faster growth than the ones starting with a high initial income. In other words, convergence would translate into a negative relationship between growth rate and initial income, and a positive relationship would imply divergence. To test the absolute convergence in PCI between the 15 states under review for the three periods 1980-81 to 1993-94, 1993-94 to 2004-05 and 2004-05 to 2012-13, we regressed the state-wise average growth rate

Figure 16.4

Relationship between Average Growth Rates in PCI of a State in Two Consecutive Periods

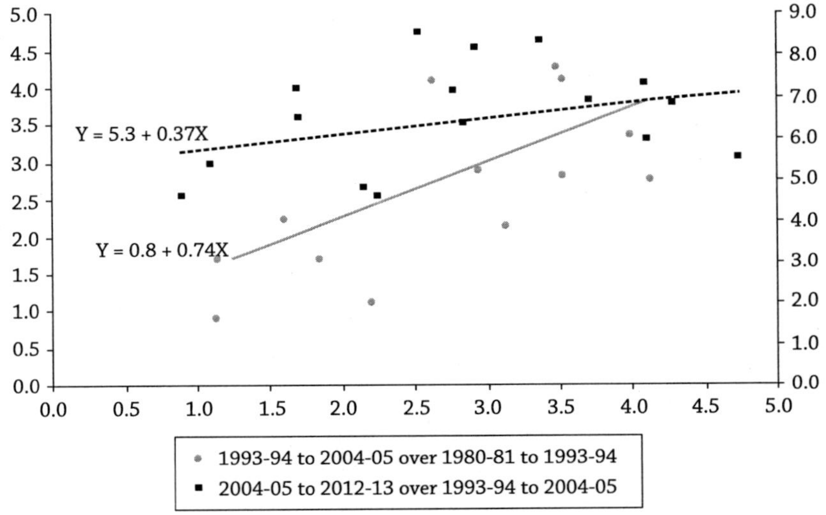

in per capita income of a period with the natural log of the initial per capita income of that period. As expected, the period 1980-81 to 1993-94 displays a statistically significant coefficient of divergence (coefficient of the log of initial PCI in the regressed equation) of 2.0. States with a lower initial income like Bihar, Odisha, Madhya Pradesh and Assam show low growth rates, ranging between 1 and 2 per cent, while the high initial income states like Maharashtra, Haryana and Punjab show relatively higher growth rates of between 3 and 4 per cent. In this period, there are some states like Rajasthan, Andhra Pradesh, Tamil Nadu and Karnataka which show a contrary trend with high growth rates exceeding 3 per cent despite a lower initial income. The overall trend however is of absolute divergence.

In the period 1993-94 to 2004-05, the picture is still of divergence (Figure 16.6). Some states like Bihar, Assam, Uttar Pradesh and Odisha continue to lag behind. However, in this period, we find that the coefficient of the log of initial per capita income in the regressed equation decreases to 1.4, even though it is not statistically significant, indicating that the divergence is somewhat attenuated.

More interestingly, in this period, one can clearly observe the formation of converging clusters of states at two different income levels, one at the lower income level (A) and the other at the middle and higher income levels (B).

Figure 16.5

PCI in 1980-81 and Income Growth during 1981-82 to 1993-94

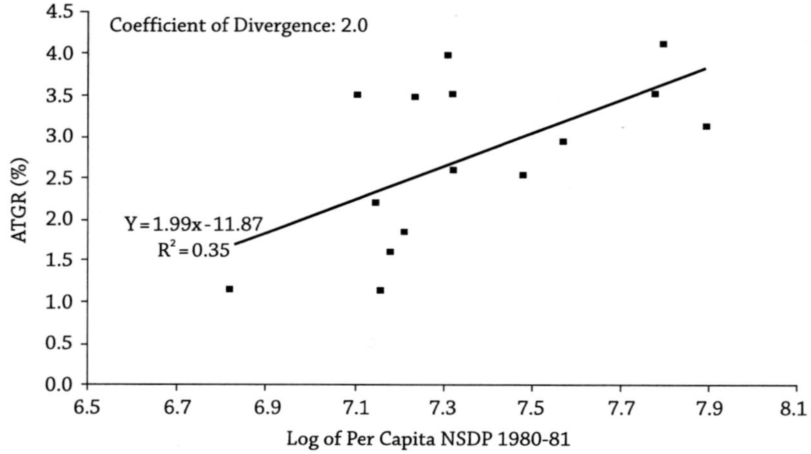

Figure 16.6

PCI in 1993-94 and Income Growth during 1993-94 to 2004-05

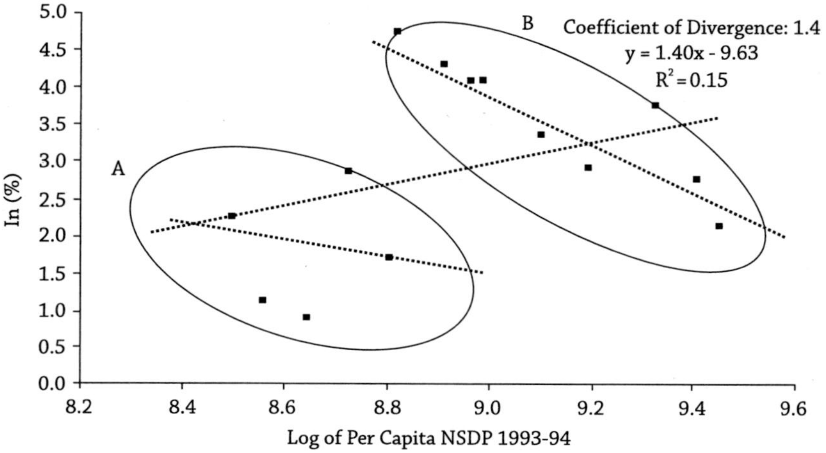

In the period 2004-05 to 2012-13, this phenomenon of clustering seems to have vanished (Figure 16.7). The low-income states of the earlier period like Uttar Pradesh and Assam show an increase in growth rates to 4-5 per cent, but this is inadequate for them to catch up with others like Maharashtra, Gujarat, Kerala and Haryana, which grew at 7-8 per cent despite starting out with high initial incomes. The major transformation happens in Bihar, Rajasthan and Madhya Pradesh, which manage to catch up by growing at 6-8 per cent in this period. The growth rates of these states more than tripled as compared with the first period. However, even in this period, the relationship between the log of initial per capita income (in 2004-05) and the growth rate in per capita income (in the period 2004-05 to 2012-13) continues to be positive. But the value of the coefficient of the log of PCI goes down to 1.1, though it is not statistically significant.

Figure 16.7

PCI in 2004-05 and Income Growth during 2004-05 to 2012-13

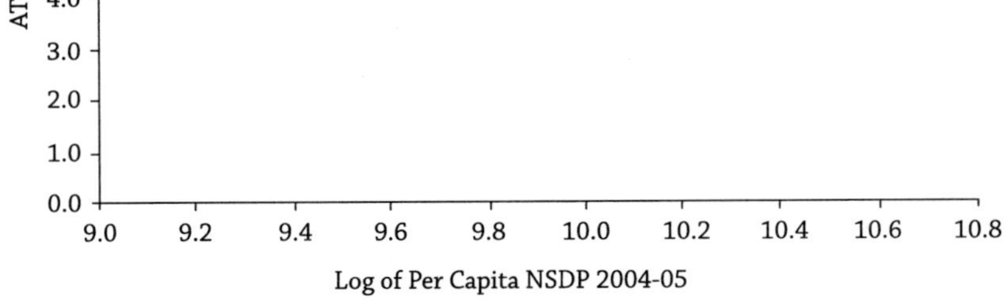

A comparison of the results for the three periods detailed above yields an interesting result. Even though the per capita incomes of these 15 states do not show convergence, over time, the tendency to diverge appears to be coming down, suggesting a move towards convergence. There is clear evidence of strong growth rates of the erstwhile lower income states in the recent period.

Section VI

Conclusion

A question posed in this analysis was: What, if any, is the evidence on convergence between states? Strictly speaking, the three periods 1980-81 to 1993-94, 1993-94 to 2004-05 and 2004-05 to 2012-13 do not show convergence. Absolute convergence in the sense of the PCIs of the different states converging to a single number has not happened. However, in the recent period, there is strong evidence of catching up by the lower income states. The median growth rate more than doubled in the recent period, increasing from 2.8 per cent during 1993-94 to 2004-05 to 6.3 per cent during 2004-05 to 2012-13. All the 15 states in the sample show higher growth rates in the recent period. States with lower PCI (1993-94) like Assam, Madhya Pradesh, Uttar Pradesh and Bihar have made significant gains in growth rates in the recent period 2004-05 to 2012-13. Notwithstanding these gains, convergence did not happen in the recent period mainly because some states, especially Maharashtra, Gujarat, Kerala, Tamil Nadu and Haryana, which had high initial per capita incomes, also posted high growth rates (in the range of 7% and above). The declining trend in the positive values of the coefficients of divergence points towards increased catching up and greater convergence.

Annexure Table A-16.1

Trend in Inter-state Inequality—1980-81 to 2010-11

Year	*Gini*	*CV*	*Max-Min Ratio*
1980-81	0.13	23.23	2.39
1981-82	0.13	24.23	2.48
1982-83	0.13	24.13	2.53
1983-84	0.13	22.99	2.40
1984-85	0.13	23.66	2.38
1985-86	0.14	25.32	2.51
1986-87	0.13	24.40	2.44
1987-88	0.14	25.12	2.67
1988-89	0.14	25.15	2.53
1989-90	0.15	27.87	2.75
1990-91	0.15	27.00	2.56
1991-92	0.15	27.65	2.79
1992-93	0.17	31.35	3.06
1993-94	0.18	32.87	3.11
1994-95	0.18	32.56	2.97
1995-96	0.20	35.14	3.39
1996-97	0.20	34.90	3.24
1997-98	0.20	35.05	3.16
1998-99	0.20	35.30	3.10
1999-2000	0.21	36.60	3.39
2000-01	0.21	36.38	3.27
2001-02	0.21	36.65	3.49
2002-03	0.22	38.20	3.42
2003-04	0.22	38.64	3.77
2004-05	0.22	39.51	3.60
2005-06	0.24	42.76	3.97
2006-07	0.25	43.84	4.10
2007-08	0.25	44.69	4.09
2008-09	0.25	43.60	3.95
2009-10	0.25	44.67	4.08
2010-11	0.25	44.95	3.84
2011-12	0.25	45.19	3.76
2012-13	0.25	44.94	3.60

Source: Calculated using State-wise PCI data from CSO, Ministry of Statistics and Programme Implementation (MoS&PI).

Annexure Table A-16.2

PCI Trend Growth Rates of 15 Major States

State	*PC NSDP 1980-81*	*Annual Trend Growth Rate (1980-1993)*	*PC NSDP 1993*	*Annual Trend Growth Rate (1993-2004)*	*PC NSDP 2004-05*	*Annual Trend Growth Rate (2004-2013)*
Andhra Pradesh	1380	3.5	7416	4.3	25321	6.9
Assam	1284	1.1	5715	0.9	16782	4.6
Bihar	917	1.1	4183	1.7	10503	7.2
Gujarat	1940	2.9	9796	2.9	32021	8.2
Haryana	2370	3.5	11079	3.7	37972	6.9
Karnataka	1520	3.5	7838	4.1	26882	6
Kerala	1508	2.6	7983	4.1	31871	7.3
Madhya Pradesh	1358	1.9	6693	1.7	16241	6.5
Maharashtra	2435	4.1	12183	2.8	36077	7.2
Odisha	1314	1.6	4896	2.3	17650	4.5
Punjab	2674	3.1	12710	2.2	33103	4.8
Rajasthan	1222	3.5	6182	2.8	18565	6.3
Tamil Nadu	1498	4	8955	3.4	30062	8.4
Uttar Pradesh	1278	2.2	5245	1.1	13516	5.4
West Bengal	1773	2.5	6756	4.7	22649	5.5

Source: Calculated using state-wise PCI data from CSO, MoS&PI.

ICRA Bulletin, Money and Finance, February 2014.

Economic Developments in India, Vol. 195.

17

INDIRA RAJARAMAN

Funding States

THE report of the committee for a composite development index (CDI) for states, released in late September, has attracted criticism for having been politically motivated to give a larger share to Bihar in fiscal flows from the Centre. Of greater interest than the motivation is how the committee addressed its task, and what its collective effort led it to.

The report has two aspects. In the first and most harmless, it is an exercise along the lines of the human development index (HDI), using an assortment of outcome indicators to quantify and rank states on a scale. Indeed, the report plots a scatter of its CDI against the HDI and finds a very high negative correlation of 0.9. Negative, because the HDI assigns high scores to high achievers, like any academic test. The CDI, on the other hand, assigns high scores to low achievers. That gets us to the second (and main) task of the report, which is to quantify the relative entitlement of states in development funding from the Centre, grounded in their low achievement.

This aspect of the report is more problematic. Even the dissenting member agrees with the committee's use of outcome variables for the ranking, rather than what they call background or process variables. He merely disagrees with inclusion of per cent scheduled caste (SC)/scheduled tribe (ST) population, because it is not an outcome variable, and with the use of per capita consumption rather than income.

Outcome variables have in the past been used in Plan schemes floated by the Centre, such as the Sarva Shiksha Abhiyan, whose objective was to even out the primary education deficit in deprived regions, or the Pradhan Mantri Gram Sadak Yojana, which provides last-mile connectivity for villages not so linked, thereby favouring states with a large number of marooned villages. There can be no legal challenge to such schemes, because the Centre is autonomous within the federation and therefore free to address particular outcome deficits across the country.

But when a whole bunch of these deficits are pooled together as a basis for determining overall state shares in development funding, that becomes an approach subject to legal challenge. Why does pooling become a problem, when funding a specific outcome deficit is not? Simply because this then becomes an unconditional fund flow, and thus mimics the statutory tax share prescribed by Finance Commissions, which similarly quantify unconditional relative state entitlements. When that happens, the formula must necessarily begin from a neutral construction of the relative needs of states. What the Constitution most certainly permits is adjustment of this neutrally obtained entitlement for the relative fiscal capacity of states to meet these needs themselves. Any measure of relative prosperity like per capita income comes in here not as a measure of poor outcomes, and hence higher entitlement, but as a measure of fiscal self-sufficiency (or lack thereof).

Per capita income is not the best indicator of fiscal capacity. I have written on how better measures of fiscal capacity are possible, and on the poor quality of the per capita income figures used. Once the Goods and Services Tax (GST) comes into being, we will have a readily available measure of relative tax capacity in place, and could then perhaps approach the Canadian ideal in respect of adjusting for fiscal capacity. The point here is that a poor state's claim to higher shares in central flows can only rest on its low fiscal capability to meet its needs itself. But the basic building blocks of need have to be neutral across states. The report acknowledges the perverse incentive properties of the CDI, and prescribes a one-quarter share in the final formula for improvements in performance (i.e., reductions in the CDI). But the CDI clearly overrides the performance component.

The very 'background' variables that the committee rejects for arriving at relative entitlement are in fact the only bases acceptable to states. They have also accepted adjustment for the cost disability posed by hilly terrain, although placing 11 states in a special category may have been a ham-handed way of dealing with it. I have written on how better measures of cost disability are possible ("Is Bihar a Special Category State?" *Business Standard*, April 24, 2012). The committee does use the basic cross-state neutral indicators of need, population and area, but merely as 80:20 weights to the CDI, which is constructed from outcome disparities on 10 indicators.

The requirement of neutrality, and the rejection of perverse outcome incentives, is taken so seriously in our country that the very terms of reference of Finance Commissions over the last 40 years have mandated the use of frozen population shares by the 1971 census, so as not to reward states that went easy on population control. This feature, just by itself, has reduced the share of Bihar relative to what it would have been with the use of current population. Only the current 14th Finance Commission has been given some leeway, by being allowed to consider "demographic changes subsequent to 1971".

The CDI gives Bihar a 12.04 per cent share, as against what the report says was a 10.06 per cent share across tax shares and grants awarded by the 13th Finance Commission. The 13th Finance Commission tax share, the more appropriate comparison, was 10.92 per cent. If the 13th Finance Commission share were reworked with current population, and with fiscal capacity more carefully assessed, it would easily cross 11 per cent.

The excess of the CDI over this revised tax share yields a rough and ready measure of the (accumulated) governance deficit in Bihar. The people of Bihar undeniably suffer from acute outcome deficits, which call for urgent redressal, in mission mode. Foremost among these must surely be the eradication of Japanese encephalitis, an annual visitor at this time of year, which leaves dead and disabled children in its wake in several districts of Bihar and Uttar Pradesh (UP). Targeted interventions with measurable outcomes are a better way by which to confront these horrific consequences of accumulated governance deficits, rather than more unconditional funding poured into those deficits.

Business Standard, October 21, 2013.

Economic Developments in India, Vol. 191.

18

VIJAY L. KELKAR

India's Economic Future

Moving Beyond State Capitalism

WE are today at a unique and important moment in India's history. A unique constellation of factors now objectively indicates that India is now on the threshold of a golden age of growth.[1] But we cannot take this set of extremely attractive outcomes for granted. Achieving a golden age of growth crucially depends on the policy framework that we adopt. The window of opportunity, particularly of a grand demographic dividend, is available for a limited period of only next two decades or so. It is necessary that we choose wisely because wrong choices now can mean all future generations would remain poor forever. The choices

---

This is a collaborative effort and I gratefully acknowledge the help of my valued colleague Ajay Shah.

It is a great honour and a privilege for me to be invited to give the D.R. Gadgil Memorial Lecture. Prof. Gadgil was one of the foremost economists of India, and perhaps the best economist from Maharashtra since Justice Mahadev Govind Ranade. He established the Gokhale Institute of Economics and Politics in Pune, which has become one of the great schools of economics in India. His intellectual interests within the field of economics were very wide. He wrote on urban economics, development issues, regional planning, economic history, cooperatives and agricultural sector. Most people may not be aware of his outstanding essay on the future of Bombay, written more than 50 years ago, numerous insights of which are still valid. He was not only a scholar, but also a man of praxis. His contributions to the cooperative movement are legendary, and his work in the Planning Commission as its deputy chairman is still remembered. Even today, the centre-state financial relations are guided by the "Gadgil formula"! I am truly honoured by this opportunity to pay my tribute to this great son of India.

His essay "Origins of the Modern Indian Business Class" is a seminal contribution towards understanding the history of Indian capitalism. This essay has inspired me to share my perspectives on contemporary Indian capitalism. My lecture today is exploratory, and many of the propositions are preliminary in nature. I have chosen the title of the lecture as "India's Economic Future: Moving beyond State Capitalism." I hope to offer a brief overview of the development of India's capitalism, and also outline it's possible future, that of marching towards a developed market economy.

that we make today will make a dramatic difference to India's future. If we seize this moment, India can transit out of poverty, and coming generations can enjoy an era of unprecedented prosperity and a decisive voice in shaping the global economic order and world politics.

But India on a growth turnpike is not inevitable destiny. It is only one possible future: that we have to step forward to make ours. If we continue down the slippery path of state capitalism, this can degenerate into populism and consequent economic stagnation, as has happened in the past. Populism seems to be a first cousin of state capitalism. Populism is, obviously, popular in the short run. But this path will mean enormous costs:

- Firstly, there are the costs of continued fiscal deterioration. Public debt has already reached very high levels in India. We need to reverse this trend, which continues to have the potential of inducing a lower quantity and quality of public goods, and the nightmare scenario of a debt trap.
- Fiscal pressure could lead to bouts of high inflation. High inflation is well known to be anti-poor. But it is also anti-growth, since it will contaminate the investment planning of firms, which requires an environment of macro stability.
- The ubiquitous presence of the public sector, and the consequent lack of competition, in the economy means that consumers will suffer. Through the well-known principal-agent problems embedded in state capitalism, this will imply an inefficient use of resources, both in a static and a dynamic sense. This would result in lower employment and a reduced growth rate, as state capitalism oscillates between the scylla of moral hazard and the chabrydis of the 'soft budget constraint'.
- Finally, state capitalism would reduce the supply of innovation due to the lack of incentives, thus denying the very sinews of growth in the knowledge economy. This would mean that India would lose out in this demanding age of globalisation.

State capitalism, which played a historic and creative role in the 1950s and 1960s, has run out of steam because of its inherent limitations. Hence, my choice is clear: that we have to move beyond state capitalism and move towards a full fledged advanced market economy, by accelerating institutional reform, including rapid privatisation at the level of both centre and states. In other words, we have to fully accept the institutional framework of modern capitalism as India's economic future.

While there can be a consensus about such a direction, we need to do more in translating this strategic framework into an operational blueprint. So far, a considerable focus has been on dismantling the mechanisms of state control on the economy. While this agenda is undoubtedly important, and a lot more needs to be done on that front, we also need a positive agenda of what kind of economy we seek to fashion. Thoughtful scholars such as Lester Thurow, Mitchele Albert and Esuki Sakakibara have argued that in the contemporary globalised economy there are three major models of capitalism: the Anglo-Saxon model, the Rhine-Alpine model and the East Asian model.

Each of the three models has it's own strengths and weaknesses. Each of these developed in a path-dependent way, owing to specific historical peculiarities. There are deep problems for each of these models. For the first, it is inadequate attention to equity and distribution issues, while in the second, is excessive reliance on entitlements which reduce incentives for high employment, high efficiency, and greater innovation and growth. In the East Asian model, there are dangers of crony capitalism and the implied anti-democratic features.

In India, we need to understand the strengths and weaknesses of each of these forms, and think about what our choice should be, given our circumstances and opportunities. We need to fashion our own *sui generis* model of capitalism so that we can move towards an advanced market economy, promoting inclusive growth and thus gain the benefits of enhanced efficiency, greater equity and better governance under liberal democracy.

Our Journey

I would like to begin with a historical review of the developments of the production system of the last 100 years. I think it is fair to say that in British India, the production system was a largely feudal system, with Indian capitalists trying to industrialise India inspite of an alien power ruling the country. What this meant was that the rate of primitive accumulation of capital and the pace of industrialisation was rather slow, although rudimentary capitalist institutions such as banks, stock markets and property rights were getting established.

After independence, India's industrialisation got a boost with the state actively supporting the domestic capital. In this first phase of state-led capitalism, there was little nationalisation. The emphasis was on the state becoming an entrepreneur to promote capital accumulation, on the creation of knowledge institutions e.g., Indian Institutes of Technology (IITs), Council of Scientific and Industrial Research (CSIR), etc., and on physical infrastructure. The main architect of this path was of course Jawaharlal Nehru, who wanted the national economy to gain independence from the metropolitan capital i.e., pursue an independent path of accelerated growth.

This led to an industrialisation strategy based on heavy industries and selectively delinking India from the world economy through high tariffs and import controls. These measures, alongwith encouraging domestic industry also meant that the terms of trade were turned against agriculture to facilitate primitive capital accumulation. This strategy, which was successful in many ways, ran into difficulties because of the relative neglect of agriculture with no decisive victory against feudal agriculture particularly in the Indo-Gangetic plains. The 1966 drought finally exposed these weaknesses.

Consequently, the next phase of capitalist growth involved agriculture where the Green Revolution played an important role of spreading the capitalist form of agriculture. Unfortunately, this phase was accompanied by a deteriorating state-led capitalist system, mainly due to populist and rent seeking economic policies. This led to stagnation of the national economy in the 1970s and also to retardation in the accumulation of capital, with subsidies mounting to 14-15 per cent of GDP (gross domestic product).[2] A series of nationalisation episodes led to a decline in private investment. This was some times described as the triumph of the 'intermediate regime'.

Growth of Output per Worker

A New Look at Our Growth Experience

Much attention has focused on India's GDP growth, and to a lesser extent, on India's GDP growth per capita. As is well known in growth theory, changes in GDP respond to changes in labour, changes in capital and changes in productivity. Out of these, changes in labour are caused by deeper demographic forces and, to a significant extent, are exogenous to economic policy choices. When thinking about economic policy, our prime interest is on higher productivity and building up a high stock of capital.

These aspects are effectively captured by measuring the growth of GDP per worker. This is a different series from either the growth of GDP or the growth of per capita GDP. It is the best 'report card' on how Indian economic policy is faring, shorn of demographic factors.

Measurement of the number of workers is not easy. Hence, we use the population between age 16 and age 64 as a proxy for the number of workers.

Figure 18.1

Growth of Output per Worker

Figure 18.1 shows this time series, with moving-window estimates over the latest one decade at every point in time. The first few data points relate to the early 1960s. For example, the value shown for 1962 is the average per capita growth from 1952 to 1962. Per capita GDP was then growing at a rate of roughly 2 per cent.

There is a dip corresponding to the two droughts and the China war, but the economy climbed out of that to get back to a one-decade growth of 2 per cent. After that, the policy environment changed, giving a sharp drop in the growth of output per worker. Most people tend to think of the drop in India's growth as having been caused by the wars and droughts of the 1962-1965 period. But this graph shows that India actually recovered out of that. Growth fell sharply in the 1970s, not in the early 1960s.

The next dip in the series is associated with the 1979 drought. Growth accelerated sharply from 1984 onwards, reflecting the Rajiv Gandhi liberalisation, and the consistent pace of further progress on economic reforms thereafter. A striking feature of the graph is that the 2 per cent rates of growth of per-worker GDP over the latest decade, which were lost after the early 1960s, were only regained in the mid-1980s.

Summary statistics for the three periods are as follows:

Period	*Average Growth of GDP per Worker*
1951-52 to 1964-65	2.02
1965-66 to 1976-77	0.58
1977-78 to 2004-05	3.09

The Recent Period

The process of dismantling of this phase of Indian state capitalism or of the 'intermediate regime' began in 1991, with the launching of economic reforms by P.V. Narasimha Rao and Manmohan Singh.

This also coincided with the collapse of the Berlin wall and the beginning of the new era of globalisation. The results have been extremely favourable, as India's growth rate has been increasing steadily and the economic system has taken new initiatives to move towards a market-based economic system.

Fortunately, in terms of deep determinants of growth, there is now a confluence of extremely favourable factors such as the demographic transition, with growing supply of human capital and of financial capital, openness of the economy giving access to larger markets to India's enterprises, economies of scale and scope, blossoming of entrepreneurship and availability of new technology (IT) and of 'network industries' making a positive impact on productivity growth. All these developments mean that India could embark on a golden age of growth. But to make this happen requires that we decisively break away from state capitalism which has an adverse effect on accumulation, governance, competition and innovation.

We have to choose between two alternatives today:

- to continue to follow the path of state capitalism under the banner of socialism, or
- to fashion our own model of capitalist growth towards an advanced market economy.

There is no task in India that is more important than that of clarifying our minds, and agreeing on the ideas that will make up India as a modern, advanced market economy.

Many people who work in one sector at a time have a clear understanding of how incentives can be reshaped, in that one sector, to obtain efficiency and rapid growth. But reforms at the level of one sector at a time are generally seen as isolated exceptions to the powerful 'background noise' of state capitalist rhetoric. I continue to be astonished as I encounter thoughtful people who have powerful and clear visions about one sector or social issue, but mechanically lapse into statist thinking for everything else.

There is a need of a fully articulated set of interlocking ideas about what India would look like, as a modern market economy. We in India are engaged in a very important new enterprise: we are in the midst of constructing a new kind of capitalism where we are going on our *sui generis* path. The trajectory of a country on such issues is imbued with a strong path-dependence. In addition, there is a need for us to best utilise the lessons of global experience, and avoid the mistakes of systems and processes in operation in other countries.

Hence, mechanical copying from the US or the UK of policies and institutional mechanisms is surely a wrong path to building India as a modern market economy. We need to think about each issue from first principles, and come up with uniquely Indian solutions to the questions that we face.

The sagacious advice of Prof Chakravarty suggests that markets are good servants but not always good masters. We have to be mindful that in a highly stratified society like ours, the State has an important role, particularly in promoting equity through inclusive growth.

My main goal in this lecture is to suggest some key building blocks for moving towards such an advanced market economy.

The Building Blocks

The key building blocks of India as a modern market economy, as I see them, are:

- We have to rethink all aspects of policy required in order to achieve India as a common market, where goods and services, labour and capital, are able to move freely across the country.
- We have to effect institutional change in government and in the financial system so as to be able to manage an open economy with an open capital account, and harness it's benefits in this age of globalisation.
- The equity market is now the dominant source of financing firms in the country. Commensurate with this, we need new concepts of corporate governance so as to ensure that the gigantic resources being intermediated through the equity market are handled effectively.
- We need a new focus on competition, which (in turn) requires a meta-architecture of the regulatory system, and substantial and rapid progress on privatisation of public sector enterprises including public sector banks.
- We need to fully rethink the mechanisms through which public goods are being produced. I propose to use education, both elementary education and higher education, as an

example to illustrate some ideas in how India can achieve the quality and quantity of public goods provided by a modern market economy.

- We need to find new ways of providing livelihood security through effective income transfers to the poorest 10 per cent to 15 per cent of the population so that the transfers genuinely reach the poor, and simultaneously do not distort economic policy on a macroeconomic scale.
- Cities are the engines of growth of the India of tomorrow. We need a wholly new approach to the governance of cities, so as to obtain sound urban public goods.

India as a Unified Market

India is a big country: 108 crore people, 3.3 million square kilometres. This ought to be a unique opportunity for us. Big countries ought to be able to harness economies of scale, and thus achieve per-person output and income which are the envy of small countries.

But India has built a complex system of myriad rules which impede the free movement within the country of goods and services, capital and labour. I believe a central piece of the puzzle in building a vibrant market economy is to build India as a single national market.

This will help reduce inter-state disparities, which have bedeviled India's growth experience, and could induce substantial political strains in the future. If goods and services labour, and capital are able to move freely across India, then factories will be built in low-wage areas, and people from low-wage areas will migrate to high-wage areas.

More importantly, it will set the stage for India to become a player in the global production chains that dominate manufacturing. East Asia has obtained labour-intensive export-oriented growth in this field, and India has been largely unable to replicate this growth. A key feature of this is taxation. Global corporations will bring a subassembly into India, add some value here, and send the result on to a next stage of production somewhere in the world. For such operations to be profitable, it is essential that India must have no taxes such as customs, entry tax, sales tax, etc. The international principle in these matters is that "you cannot and do not export your taxes".

A big part of the problem lies in the way states and local bodies impose taxes such as octroi or the entry tax. A new fiscal strategy needs to be found, which delivers adequate resources to local governments, but yet guarantees the fluency of inter-state commerce.[3] From the perspective of Bombay, we need to envisage a future where there will be no octroi, no entry tax and no stamp duty.

I believe the foundation of this is the Goods and Services Tax (GST), as articulated in the the FRBM Task Force report which I chaired in 2004. The GST proposal is sometimes misunderstood. What we proposed was not a single, centrally administered Value Added Tax (VAT) on all goods and services. What was proposed is a synchronised state-GST and a central-GST, with unified administration, so that each firm thinks it is dealing with a single taxman.

The GST would be neutral to the production, movement and consumption of goods all across the country, and correctly treat the problems of tax treatment of imports and exports. The FRBM Task Force recommended that the centre and states come together to voluntarily make a deal to implement this GST.

The 'Level I GST', as articulated by the FRBM Task Force, is one where there is a central GST and a state GST, which are distinct but synchronised. According to prominent experts on constitutional law, this is feasible today, provided there is an agreement amongst states to sign up into it. Thanks to our experience with TIN, this is now feasible in terms of administrative implementation.

A Level II GST is one where the constitution is modified to shift VAT to being a single national tax, administered by the centre, with resources shared through the Finance Commission. This is indeed desirable. But it is not the immediate destination.[4]

One of the most valuable aspects of the GST proposal is that once it is in place, there should really be only three taxes in the country: the income tax, the GST and the property tax. It will greatly reduce the compliance burden upon individuals and firms, if they have to deal with atmost three tax collectors.

Some concerns have been expressed about the potential difficulties that such a tax poses for the autonomy of states as enshrined in the constitution. There are a few perspectives that need to be brought to bear on this question.

Autonomy of taxation is far, far from being the binding constraint in improving governance. The idea of having taxing powers at the state level is supposed to be that the level of production of public goods can vary from state to state, depending on local preferences. While that may be a first best design, the reality in India is that the production of public goods is deficient in all states. Law and order, judiciary, drinking water, etc., are all highly unsatisfactory. The first order issue in obtaining better governance is not the question of autonomy. I would argue that if states were to lose their flexibility to modify tax rates tomorrow, there will not be the slightest worsening in the quality or quantity of public goods.

The choice that we face. The choice that we really face is one between poor states with autonomy of taxing powers, *versus* rich states without. Most citizens of the country would take the latter. There is probably just a thin fringe of people who value state-level taxing autonomy so much, that they would accept poverty as the price.

The autonomy that matters is that of being able to control expenditure on local public goods. The real autonomy that matters is autonomy of expenditure. Bihar should want to spend more on law and order, and Tamil Nadu more on water. Such genuine autonomy will be strengthened if pro-growth policies yield bigger resources at the state level. The choice we face is of a Tamil Nadu which has more money—which can choose how to spend it—as opposed to a Tamil Nadu which takes pride in autonomy of taxation but has less money to spend on water.

The illusion of tax autonomy. In a world with mobile capital and mobile high-skill labour, tax autonomy is being eroded every day. High taxation of wage income, and infirmities of taxation of corporations, leads to exit of firms and high-skill individuals from the country. This directly affects both income tax and VAT tax revenues. Thus, in the modern world, countries do not have tax autonomy.

If the tax autonomy of a country is itself limited, there can be no question about sanctifying tax autonomy at the level of a state.

I believe that it is now feasible to build a GST system based on voluntary participation by states. Under this, there can be a synchronised system of central GST and state GST operating in a coalition of willing states. One by one, as states see the virtue of this system, they will sign up.

The Twelfth Finance Commission has shown the way on overcoming constitutional barriers with their offering financial incentives for states who enact fiscal responsibility legislation.[5] In similar fashion, it is feasible and useful for the centre to put out financial carrots for states to voluntarily join the GST system. If the top 10 states sign up, we will have covered the bulk of GDP, and India will start reaping the benefits of the GST. Other states can come around gradually, based on their self-interest.

Many authors have criticised India's 'dysfunctional fiscal federalism'.[6] A shift from the existing pattern of taxation to the GST, through voluntary participation by a coalition of states, will do a great deal to address the consequences of the poorly designed fiscal system. In the future, a *de facto* common market can be translated into a *de jure* system by amending the constitution, based on shared principles and consensus prevalent at the time, and thus moving on to a Level II GST. However, the present structure of the constitution does not hold back building a Level I GST. I believe that is a top priority for Indian economic policy today.

India cannot be a modern market economy without a modern fiscal system. But it is not enough to only criticise our dysfunctional fiscal federalism, and bemoan the efficiency implications upon firms and households. We need to shift gears from anguish to action. The Level I GST is a fully articulated and actionable proposal.

Open Economy Macroeconomics

There is a deeply ingrained traditional belief in India that capital account convertibility is dangerous and should be viewed with great caution. Such fears are used to justify an extensive bureacratic apparatus of capital controls. It has repeatedly been claimed that

India escaped the East Asian Crisis of 1997-98 owing to having a closed capital account. This reading of the events is now widely understood to be less than correct. Governments meddling with the currency market was the foundation of the East Asian Crisis, not openness to capital flows.

Over the years, while we have tinkered away at an elaborate system of capital controls, the size of flows in the current account and the capital account has grown enormously. It is common to measure the 'trade/GDP ratio' as the sum of imports and exports divided by GDP. But this only focuses on goods. India has a substantial engagement with the world through invisbles, ranging from services trade to remittances. Hence, it is useful to measure the total size of the current account as the sum of inflows and outflows on the current account. Similarly, we measure the total size of the capital account as the sum of inflows and outflows on the capital account.

Current and Capital Account

	Billion Nominal USD		*Per Cent to GDP*	
	1992-93	*2004-05*	*1992-93*	*2004-05*
Current Account	59.9	323.1	25.1	45.4
Capital Account	36.7	182.6	15.3	25.7
Total	96.6	505.7	40.4	71.1

Note: India's engagement with the world: 1992-93 *versus* 2004-05.

The data reveal spectacular growth of India's engagement with the world, over the 12-year period from 1992-93 to 2004-05:[7]

- GDP expressed in nominal USD grew at a compound rate of 9.5 per cent. But the current account grew at a rate of 15.1 per cent and the capital account grew at 14.3 per cent.
- Gross flows on the current account and the capital account, put together, crossed half a trillion dollars in 2004-05. This was a rise of five times—in USD—over a short period of 12 years.

The large capital account shows that certain avenues for movement of capital across the border are fairly open. More importantly, the large current account—$323 billion in 2004-05—can be used for moving capital across the border. If someone sends a check for $10 million into some software company in India, who is to know what software was actually produced? If overinvoicing/underinvoicing is done to an extent of just 10 per cent, this could be used to move more than $ 30 billion in or out of the country in 2004-2005. As Jayanth Varma of IIM Ahmedabad says, the present Indian regime has convertibility for everyone except the honest resident individual.[8]

In this situation, capital controls are increasingly ineffective. When many avenues for moving capital across the border are available, closing down one merely forces individuals or firms shift to another. When 10 doors are open, closing one door achieves nothing. Closing down one avenue can only change the identity of who benefits from capital movements in and out of India, but transactions can always be routed through some avenue or the other. This calls into question the enormous effort that is now being put in, tweaking one capital control after another on a monthly basis.

What, then, do our capital controls achieve? Capital controls mean non-transparency, encourage corruption, increase transaction costs and distort resource allocation. Capital controls help the state dispense patronage. The private sector has to take permissions from the Reserve Bank of India (RBI), Securities and Exchange Board of India (SEBI) and Ministry of Finance (MoF) for doing various things, and there is nothing a bureaucrat likes more than to be asked for permission. An army of functionaries is kept busy operating the system of controls. Stringent licencing norms deliver rents to the few who are able to obtain licenses. The sellers of Participatory Notes (PNs) are earning huge profits, because we have made it difficult for many people to directly enter the Indian market. These sellers of PNs now have incentives to prevent others from getting licenses.

My main point is that capital controls can give you a lot of distortions.[9] But the enterprise of maintaining capital controls, and devoting great care to micro-management of the system of controls, is increasingly irrelevant in terms of macroeconomics.

Our present state of affairs is *de facto* convertibility. We are in the world of convertibility. But we have not yet changed our mindset to reflect this. In terms of economics, this requires a sea change of our mental models. All of us grew up in India doing an obsolete field called 'closed-economy macroeconomics'. What we now need is knowledge of a field called 'open-economy macroeconomics'. Growing integration with the global economy, in product and capital markets, is India's economic future. To manage such an economy, we need to practice 'open economy macroeconomics', as other advanced market economies do. This involves new ideas like understanding the currency regime, and new ways of thinking about monetary economics.

The most importance consequence of open economy macroeconomics is that India now faces a choice between currency policy and monetary policy. Once a capital account is open, a country loses autonomy of monetary policy to the extent that the country does trading on the currency market.

This forces every country to choose between the beneficiaries of an active monetary policy (i.e., everyone) *versus* the beneficiaries of an active currency policy (i.e., importers, exporters, foreign investors). It is like asking whether we want Alan Greenspan to be India's central bank governor, or whether we want our own central bank which genuinely does monetary policy based on the domestic business cycle.[10] It is our task to empower RBI to be our central bank. Towards this, RBI must have a clear mandate focused on monetary policy, and like the Bank of England or the US Federal Reserve (Fed), RBI must be fully empowered to autonomously pursue this goal, and it must be freed of the burden of other tasks which interfere with the core *dharma* of monetary economics.

The other big consequence of *de facto* convertibility is that we must stop treating capital flows as a threat. We must start harnessing the benefits of capital account convertibility. With half a trillion dollars moving across the border in a year, we are already paying the cost in terms of the risks induced by an open capital account.[11] We are not, at present, commensurately obtaining the benefits of convertibility, which is the greater competition in the financial sector.

The Indian financial sector stands between Indian households and Indian firms. The customers of finance—households and firms—are forced to only do business with the local financial sector. This is anti-competitive.

We watched how Indian manufacturing was transformed, and is now faring much better, because our firms were given competition from foreign firms. The producers are now healthier, and the consumers are much happier. Indian finance will be transformed in the same way by competition. This requires ending our policy of forcing Indian households and Indian firms to only do business with the Indian financial sector. Capital account reforms are important because they will do for the financial sector what trade reforms did for the industrial sector.

The Dharma of Competition

People Respond to Incentives

A central message of economics as a science is that 'people respond to incentives'. Across a wide range of fields, we are persistently astonished at how powerfully individuals reshape their behaviour in response to incentives. The vision of economics is one where humans are not pre-programmed by biology or culture or society; humans respond to incentives.

As Larry Summers summarises in one line: "In the whole history of the world, nobody ever washed a rented car". This is a defining achievement of economics as a profession: to shift from the belief that there is such a thing as "deepset and immutable Chinese fertility patterns" to a view that fertility behaviour of all humans is mutable, and is shaped by the incentives that are neutral to caste or creed.

Hence, Firms must Compete

When this idea, of people being mutable, of people responding to incentives, is applied to firms, it leads to a simple idea. The way to get lean and competent firms, producing high quality and low cost products, is through competition.

If firms have an easy time earning profits, the individuals who make up the firm will relax and produce shoddy, high-cost products. If firms are exposed to brutal competition, cost-minimisation will take place, and high-quality products will be produced. The modern view of economists is to always throw firms into the deep end, to never have a soft and motherly touch in economic policy which attempts to protect firms or help firms. Humans are mutable, so even though the competition may at first be very daunting, firms are able to move mountains and reinvent themselves, and write the story of their lives, when presented with competition.

The *dharma* of competition will be a defining issue in thinking about India's economic policy as India marches towards becoming an advanced market economy. Across a very wide range of issues, this single touchstone should guide policy thinking. When faced with policy A *versus* policy B, we must pick the one which induces greater competition.

Telecom

The best morality tale of this nature, which can be told about our recent experience, is about telecom reforms.

Our starting point was the Department of Telecommunications (DoT) which did everything in the field: it made policy and it produced telecom services. There was no clear thinking about what is a public good, and what was the role of the state that led to a lack of separation between policy, regulation and service provision.

The DoT had an obvious vested interest in preserving the status quo. If a new firm approached the DoT and requested permission to start cellular telephony, DoT would deny the request, since this would generate competition against its own staff. Vendors who requested permission from DoT to start mobile telephony were told that mobile telephony would, at an un-specified future date, be implemented by DoT, owing to which there was no need for a private provider. Entry into telecom was controlled by DoT, which would resort to scare-mongering arguments about safety/stability/security in order to block reforms.

The monopolistic framework worked well for the DoT and its public sector undertakings (PSUs), and badly for customers. India languished behind the world in every respect: number of telephones, reliability of telephones, prices of telecom services, sheer existence of new technologies such as mobile phones and Internet, and lack of availability of high speed lines.

This picture was irrevocably changed through halting steps at first, and then fundamental reforms in the late 1990s. Videsh Sanchaar Nigam Limited (VSNL) was privatised. Bharat Sanchar Nigam Limited (BSNL) was corporatised. Telecom Regulatory Authority of India (TRAI) was created. The private sector is now found competing in all aspects of the telecom business. The results have been simply dramatic. The profit margins of Mahanagar Telephone Nigam Limited (MTNL) and VSNL have collapsed. Prices paid by consumers have collapsed. Telecom is now a major force powering Indian economic growth.

India's experience with telecom illustrates the false trade-off between growth and equity. For years, telecom reforms were hobbled by the claim that a public-sector-dominated field was required in order to reach the underserved. A mere few years of a competitive market has exploded this myth. Today, access to telephony has pierced below the rich, and telephones are in more remote corners of the country, than was ever achieved by the erstwhile PSU system. We got more done for the poor, by pursuing the competition agenda for a few years, than we got done by pursuing a poverty agenda for decades.

Telecom reforms are not yet finished, for MTNL and BSNL are still PSUs, and the relationship of TRAI *vis-à-vis* DoT has yet to be fully clarified. But the basic message is clear. TRAI is an effective regulator because it has a clear mandate: to be a telecom regulator, without conflicts of interest. And the central issue in regulation is that of competition. TRAI's task is to always obtain a greater and greater degree of competition.

It is possible that at some point, owing to competition, a PSU like MTNL may become unprofitable. This would generate new fiscal demands to keep MTNL aloft. However, TRAI's task is not to cater to the interests of the exchequer, which would like to avoid such payments. TRAI's loyalty should be to the consumer.

The Competition Agenda

A healthy industry is one where there is a ceaseless Schumpeterian process of creation and destruction. An industry with a stable structure, with a few big firms that top the tables year after year, has a problem. A healthy competitive industry is one where there is a ceaseless churning, of new firms coming in, and old firms dying out or getting bought out. A modern regulator must revel in contestability of markets, and an active pace of change through birth and death. If some firms are not falling into distress every year, the market structure of the industry needs to be questioned.

We need to now cast a skeptical eye upon the entire Indian economic landscape, to look for barriers to entry, and engage in economic reforms which remove these barriers. This is the single unifying theme which has worked wonders for India in some sectors in the last 15 years, and where revolutionary gains stand to be obtained in the future. We have only begun on this agenda, and the small benefits of competition that we have tasted so far are only a small foretaste of the revolutionary gains that lie ahead.

I will briefly show the implications of this approach in some areas.

Trade Barriers

While India has made much progress on removing customs duties, high duties and non-tariff barriers continue to be with us. Competition from the quasi-infinite world market is a powerful way to check monopolies in India, and thus constantly expose Indian firms to the highest levels of competition.

Removing trade barriers requires removing existing non-tariff barriers, implementing the GST with a proper treatment of VAT on imports and zero-rating of exports, and then going to a uniform customs duty with a tariff such as 2 per cent on all goods.

Privatisation

There is a deep link between competition policy and privatisation.

As the telecom story illustrates, the erstwhile framework of public ownership generated poor incentives for firms. What is worse, public ownership generates conflicts of interest. It is not easy for the DoT to advocate sound pro-competition economic policy measures when it is the owner of a telecom company.

All of us would be extremely unhappy if the CEOs of top firms attended cabinet meetings and shaped policy discussions. We would consider that an unacceptable conflict of interest; we would ask that public policy should focus on the interests of the people at large, and not the interests of a few companies. But this is exactly the predicament that we are faced with owing to PSUs. The concerned minister, who is like a CEO's CEO where PSUs are concerned, attends cabinet meetings and advocates the interests of his PSUs. Privatisation is required to remove this conflict of interest from policy making and thus provide a level playing field for all firms.

At present, the Ministry for Civil Aviation has to engage in a complex juggling act, trying to cater to the broader interests of sound economics, but simultaneously worrying about protecting Indian Airlines and Air India. When the two airlines are privatised, the ministry's sole interest will be that of maximising competition that is in the interest of consumers. This highlights the idea that privatisation is needed in order to align the interests of the state with the interests of the people.

Petroleum Products

In the petroleum sector, we must focus on the international market access of the consumer. If a trading firm wishes to import petrol from Dubai or Singapore and sell it to a consumer in Vishakhapatnam, it should be able to do so. The present barriers on distribution need to be removed, along with a shift to market pricing for petroleum products.

Once this is done, the global market will exert competitive pressure on the domestic industry. This will deliver immediate benefits to the economy. In parallel, a slow effort for resolving the existing oligopolistic and PSU structure, through privatisation and entry, needs to be undertaken.

Railways

In the case of roads, the road is a natural monopoly. But multiple transport companies compete to move goods and people using the roads. Similarly, airports are a natural monopoly. But airlines can be a normal competitive industry.

This same insight needs to be directly applied to railways. The rails in the ground are a natural monopoly. But it is perfectly feasible to have multiple competing transport companies who move goods and people using the rails.

The present Indian Railways is at the erstwhile DoT stage of development. The incumbent affects policy, which is a natural conflict of interest. Reform proposals will be greeted by scaremongering concerns about safety/stability/security.

Bond Market

RBI is at a DoT stage of development in bond market infrastructure. There is a monopoly exchange (NDS) and a monopoly depository (SGL), both of which are run by RBI. There is a monopoly clearing corporation (Clearing Corporation of India Ltd.; CCIL) which is an external corporation. Policy is made by the incumbent, hence concerns about safety/stability/security arguments are used to block reforms. Telecom-style reforms are required, which separate out policy from regulation of a competitive industry, and remove RBI from an ownership role of SGL and NDS.

The question of competition really boils down to two issues: privatisation and regulation.

In the area of privatisation, our strategy needs to go closer to that adopted in countries like the UK and Germany, which had well developed capital markets, as compared with that chosen in Latin America or former-socialist countries, which lacked capital markets. This would focus on the creation of widely held and board-governed companies, with dispersed shareholding, rather than emphasising strategic sales. Thus our main plan needs to be to continually sell shares through disinvestment, and foster modern corporate governance, for PSUs which are going concerns.

However, there is clearly an important set of defunct PSUs where the only task is that of selling off the assets (typically land) to the highest bidder. Since the buyer of the PSU is also saddled with considerable obligations, such as taking on a workforce, when these auctions take place, negative bids should be permitted.

These issues all link up with the role and mandate of the Competition Commission. To promote competitive markets, there is a need for institutional oversight solely focused on competition policy. The Competition Commission needs to be made functional as early as possible.

In the area of regulation, the important big problems which need to be clarified are those of architecture and implementation.

The problem of architecture is that of mandate. Many of our traditional structures are riddled with conflicts of interest, thus inducing poor decisions and conduct by the regulator.

The second task is that of implementation. Once an agency has been clearly separated out, with a clear mandate and free of conflicts of interest, how best should it function? How should it recruit staff, and how should it pay them? How should it be transparent and consultative? How can we ensure that no firm or group of firms is able to capture the agency? These are the tasks of a sound implementation.

Cities as Engines of Growth

The floods in Bombay were a big reminder to all of us that the single biggest gap in India's infrastructure is now urban infrastructure. Similarly, India has a priceless asset, in the congregation of brilliant people in Bangalore. The whole world envies the intellectual strength that we have, in Bangalore. But we are squandering that Bangalore is dying a slow death owing to bad urban infrastructure.

Over the last 10 years, we have roughly understood how to solve problems like roads, telecom, airports, ports and electricity. We know that if we merely carry through the consensus found today amongst thinking people, these problems will be solved. The one big area where progress has not yet begun is railways, but I am optimistic that the force of ideas will lead to changes there also. In this sense, I think we can see the light at the end of the tunnel in these areas.

In contrast, with urban infrastructure, we have not even begun.

The crisis is bigger than meets the eye, because contrary to popular perceptions, India is neither a primarily rural nor a primarily agricultural economy. Let me show you some numbers:

- Only 20.38 per cent of GDP comes from agriculture.[12] In other words, roughly 80 per cent of GDP comes from non-agriculture.

  The share of agriculture has been dropping, at an accelerating pace. From 1965-66 to 1983-84, over a period of 18 years, the share of agriculture dropped by 11 percentage points. In contrast, the last drop of 8 percentage points took place from 1996-97 to 2005-06 (9 years). We may predict that within 10 years, the share of agriculture will be down to 10 per cent.
- We are not even a particularly rural economy as far as population shares go. A key problem here is that of measurement. Take any town, like Poona or Lucknow. We know that there is an endless urban sprawl outside the town, reaching into land that is classified as 'rural'. The population density in this urban sprawl, outside the official administrative definition, is many many times higher than rural population densities.

  Many 'villages' of a few thousand people are really towns, which are misclassified as 'rural'.

  If you merely count the people living in the cities, based on the 2001 census, you get a gross underestimate of the extent of urbanisation.
- But is a large chunk of our labour force engaged in agriculture? Using the Indian Retirement, Earnings and Savings (IRES) database, we find that of the earners of India, the occupational breakdown is: 30 per cent in agriculture, 25 per cent in small firms, 29 per cent self-employed, 9.7 per cent in government and 6.3 per cent in big firms. This picture is inconsistent with the popular belief that a dominant fraction of India's population practices agriculture.

These estimates reflect the structure of the 364 million earners of the country. In other words, they suggest that there are 109 million earners who derive their livelihood from agriculture. The IRES database does not offer the occupational structure of unpaid family labour, which may lean towards agriculture to a greater extent.[13]

These facts suggest that in thinking about India, with an eye forward on the next 10 years, we must focus on non-agricultural sources of livelihood in 500 cities. India's growth will come out of focusing on urban production of industry and services. But this requires sound urban infrastructure in these 500 cities, and particularly in the 20 megapolises.

What has gone wrong with our urban infrastructure? Some people have argued that urban public goods are underfunded. I do not believe that is a key answer. Electricity distribution, water, sanitation, and solid waste are all problems where user charges can be easily applied. They should really be 'off-balance sheet' when it comes to the operation of the state. When a household in Bombay pays his electricity bill, it goes to a private distribution company, and this is not part of the budget.

Once these user charges are out of the picture, it does not take a lot of money to run cities well. A combination of the property tax plus fiscal transfers, delivered to the correctly structured management team, will do the task.[14] Our mistakes today are: (a) we do not handle the fiscal transfers correctly and (b) there is no correctly structured management team.

In terms of fiscal architecture, we are going in the correct direction by the increasing emphasis on only two major taxes: the income tax and the GST. Taxes such as octroi interfere with transactions and should be eliminated. The problem today is that the revenue stream from GST and income tax would not directly reach cities. The authors of our Constitution did not envisage the distinction between the needs of a 'state' as a big geographical area as opposed to the needs of a 'city' as a concentrated group of people.

The second problem is that of a clear management team. Bombay needs a Mayor who is comparable to the Mayor of New York, in terms of having complete power and complete accountability. But when numerous state level agencies perform functions on Bombay, the accountability and problem solving is diffused. Why is Bangalore doing so badly? My main answer is: there is no one person in charge.

This problem is not unique to India. Writing about New Orleans in the aftermath of Hurricane Katrina, in the article 'Breakdowns Marked Path from Hurricane to Anarchy' in *The New York Times* of 11 September 2005 said:

> As the city become paralysed both by water and by lawlessness, so did the response by government. The fractured division of responsibility—Governor Blanco controlled state agencies and the National Guard, Mayor Nagin directed city workers and Mr. Brown, the head of FEMA, served as the point man for the federal government—meant no one person was in charge. Americans watching on television saw the often-haggard governor, the voluble mayor and the usually upbeat FEMA chief appear at competing daily news briefings and interviews.

How do we address this fragmentation of authority? I believe Delhi is the correct role model here. Delhi is a city state. It is a state, hence it fits well into the old ideas in the constitution. Fiscal transfers from the centre directly reach Delhi, which does not happen with any other city in India. And the Chief Minister of Delhi is in charge of everything that happens in Delhi. There is no separation between the needs of a state and the needs of the city. Sheila Dixit is really the 'empowered' mayor of Delhi. She is the only mayor in India that you have heard of. She wins or loses elections based on what happens in Delhi, not what happens in outlying districts.

I believe that this clarity of authority and accountability is a significant part of the reason why, in the last 20 years, while numerous cities in India have gone downhill, Delhi has actually done rather well.

I believe that such limited surgery, while leaving the fiscal architecture untouched, would set the stage for urban renewal in India in a meaningful sense. It is a much more feasible approach, when compared with the problems of reformulating the fiscal architecture.

Rethinking How Public Goods are Produced and Delivered

Prime Minister Manmohan Singh has eloquently talked about the need to shift focus from outlays to outcomes. The Indian State excels at spending a lot of money, at piously initiating new programmes. But over the years, we know that barring a few special cases, most programmes deliver very little bang for the buck.

The government is supposed to be the agent of the people, taking taxes from the people and delivering public goods in return.[15] But the Indian State is a poor agent of the Indian people, delivering public goods of inadequate quality and quantity.

Posing It as a Principal-Agent Problem

The best way to obtain insights, and formulate sound policies, on these questions is to think of the situation as a 'principal-agent problem'. The principal here is the citizen. The agent is the state. The citizen pays taxes, and in return wants to get some public goods. The citizen recruits the state as a contractor for the purpose of producing public goods. In order to achieve this, the principal needs to constrain the agent to effectively deliver public goods. The agent—like any contractor—likes to not have accountability, prefers to enrich his cronies, and get re-elected all the same.

The present dismal state of public goods in India may be traced to two problems:

- There is an inadequate focus of 'top management' upon public goods.
- When the state does spend on genuine public goods, there is not adequate attention to obtaining the best bang for the buck.

The principal-agent problem can be better solved through a two-part strategy. First, for a series of public goods, we should contract-out the provision of public goods, and only pay for results. Second, that will free up the state to focus on the core which cannot be contracted out, which is the problem of law and order and contract enforcement.

I would like to use education as a case study, and explore these themes at some length.

Elementary Education from Class 1 till Class 12

The dominant focus of public expenditure on education should be focused on class 1 to 12. Here, the current mentality involves government running schools. The government recruits a teacher—often a party worker of the party ruling the state government at that point in time—and hopes that some teaching will also take place. This has been tried for 50 years and has not worked.

One bogey that we need to get out of the way is the question of adequacy of funding. The total spend of GoI on education, summing across centre and states, divided by the number of children from age 4 till age 15, works out to roughly ₹ 4,000 per child per year. Conversations with any headmaster of a school in India will reveal that it is perfectly feasible to obtain good quality schooling, if you are willing to pay fees of ₹ 4,000 per child per year. This is a generous level of expenditure.

Intensification of the existing system of education, by levying an 'education cess' and trying to spend more on education, is surely not the way to strengthen education in India.[16] The recent policy effort leading to the education cess highlights the bankruptcy of thinking about education in India. Sending more money down dysfunctional institutional channels will do nothing to improve educational outcomes, i.e., what children learn.[17]

The puzzle lies in not spending more, but in rethinking incentives and the role of the state. There is certainly a role for the state to ensure that every child goes to school from class 1 to class 12.[18] But this is not best achieved by teachers who are government employees.

I think the right answer is for government to fund scholarships.[19] Imagine that all schools were private. Imagine that the government announced that it would pay ₹ 2,000 per child per year to the school where any child was enrolled. Parents would be free to 'top this up' by paying an additional amount, and buying the services of a school that charged over ₹ 2,000 per year. But every parent would be a consumer armed with the power to spend ₹ 2,000 per child per year.

Parents are well incentivised to compare alternative schools, and put their child in the best one available. Nobody cares more about the welfare of a child than the parent. This will induce competition between schools. Parents would perform the monitoring, evaluation and resource allocation functions that are conspicuously absent when teachers are state employees. When the scholarship flows based on the decision of the parent, parents are empowered. They are customers, and every school will take heed of the wishes of poor people who are parents.

Paying for Results

This approach—a traditional scholarship/voucher system—is very good. It would be a huge step forward when compared with the present Indian school system. But I think we can improve it further. What do we really want out of an education? We do not just want a child to go spend a year at school. We want results! We want the child to learn at school. We crave for the impact of education on the skills and thinking capacity of the child. Educationists like to focus on years of schooling. Economists worry about what the child actually learned in those years.[20]

We must only pay for results. To do this, we need to build a system of standardised tests of reading, writing and mathematics which can be administered to every class at the end of the year. Think of this as a thin monitoring infrastructure, either directly run by the state, or contracted out to external agencies by the state.[21] The school can be paid a bonus based on the scores achieved by the students. The average bonus paid out should be calibrated to work out to ₹ 2,000 per child per year.[22]

This is a framework which will solve the principal-agent problem between citizens and the state, between the parent and the educationist. If parents do not choose a given school for their children, there is no reason for money to flow to that school. The scholarship should be linked first to school choice of parents. Half of our educational expenditure should flow down this channel.

But even more, we should only pay for results. The remaining half of our educational expenditure should be a bonus that is based on test scores. When the school is paid in proportion to test scores of the children, it will have an incentive to focus on teaching, not just on being a day care for children.

The state role will hence reduce to obtaining results of standardised tests of reading, writing and mathematics to all classes of students all over the country, and paying out scholarship + bonus to all managers of schools.

Intuitively, what such reform achieves is shifting away from the 'the long route of accountability' of teachers, through the political system, to a short leash of two layers of accountability: first, through parents who choose which school their children go to and second, through payments which are proportional to how well the students fare at tests.

Departing from the Practices of Industrial Countries

So far I have only talked about education, but I think this approach—contracting out + paying for results—will work well for solving many public goods. This is one area where I believe we should diverge substantially from the institutional arrangements used in some industrial countries.

The experience of the UK and the US involved hundreds of years of effort at perfecting the 'long route of accountability', of building a state where government employees and the state at large was held accountable by the political process. The UK and the US have fairly well functioning elementary schools, even though their teachers are employees of the government and not paid bonuses based on test scores.[23]

However, in India, we are faced with an extreme crisis on the lack of accountability of the state. The state is an errant contractor, who cares little about working for the people, about genuinely producing public goods. It may take decades to refashion the educational system, so as to give incentives to employees of the government to do their work. The cost of this delay will be profound, given where we are in India's demographic transition. Hence, a contracting out approach, coupled with paying for results, will be more effective under Indian conditions. It can be rolled out easily and can rapidly have an impact on public goods.

The approach of contracting-out and paying for results will not, however, work for the most important public good of all: law and order, and contract enforcement. These will have to be the task of the state machinery of police and judiciary.[24] The benefit of extensive contracting out is that it will free up the 'top management time' of every government to focus on the first task of the state, which is the police and the judiciary.

The Case for a Direct Attack on Poverty

In the new India, poverty must become history, by promoting inclusive growth and improved governance. Towards this, incentive-compatible policies and improved institutional architecture will play a key role. We now have a new tool, in the form of IT, which can help deliver more rapid progress in improving governance in general, and poverty removal in particular.

Given decades of failure and policy mistakes on questions of poverty, it is important to reiterate, from first principles, the importance of the goal of a direct, state-sponsored attack on the extremities of deprivation in the country.

The first set of arguments is moral. The extremities of deprivation that are found in pockets of the country are reprehensible. Any of us could have had the misfortune of being born under such circumstances. A minimal degree of transfers from the state can make a great difference to human happiness, at a minimal cost to the economy.

The second set of arguments relate to political economy. It is in India's best interest if these extremities of poverty are addressed as a matter of state policy. It will help the poor bring up children who can then become full-fledged participants in society, instead of leaving festering poverty traps. Our goal should be to improve the probability of intergenerational class mobility, which is the most desirable feature of an open and equitable society.

There is no question that the most powerful anti-poverty programme of all is a high GDP growth rate. GDP growth has been vastly more effective in reducing poverty in India and in China than any government programme. There is no question that our minds should be primarily focused on obtaining high GDP growth. There is no meaningful trade-off between growth and equity; our eyes must be firmly fixed on the task of rapidly achieving a 10-fold increase in per capita GDP, which is the most powerful tool for transforming the lives of the poor.

But over and above this, it appears fair to me that 1 per cent of GDP should be delivered to the poorest 10 per cent of the population. At present, this is a sum of ₹ 30,000 crore, spread over 10 crore people, giving ₹ 3,000 per person per year, or ₹ 15,000 per year for a family of 5, or ₹ 7,500 per person for two workers in the family.

Over the years, GDP growth will generate a powerful increase in the rupee value of 1 per cent of GDP, thus delivering bigger and bigger transfers to the bottom 10 per cent. The challenge lies in finding ways to do this effectively.

The third set of reasons why thinking about poverty programmes matters lies in the larger ramifications. In India today, numerous policies get distorted in the name of poverty alleviation. This mindset is clearly a mistake. We should not contaminate hard-headed thinking, focused on the most-effective poverty programme called growth. An effective set of poverty programmes should free up other policy discussion, and make possible more rational policies which are focused on growth.

Table 18.1

India's Income Distribution (End-2004)

Percentile	*Total Annual Income (₹)*
0	0
10	11,000
20	17,000
30	21,600
40	27,000
50	35,000
60	42,000
70	55,000
80	72,000
90	108,000
100	

Who are the Poor?

Before we embark on any discussion about poverty programmes, it is important to obtain some empirical evidence on who are the poor. The IRES database offers information about a random sample of 42,000 earners as of November/December 2004. At the time, there were roughly 360 million earners and 60 million unpaid family labour in India. The characteristics of unpaid family labour were not measured by IRES; these may range from housewives in affluent homes, to family workers of farmers who own land, to the destitute.

The words 'poor' and 'rich' are only dimly understood in the Indian public policy discourse, and it is important to have empirical evidence about what these ends of the spectrum constitute. Table 18.1 shows the distribution of income among the 360 million earners. We may define the bottom 10 per cent of this distribution as the poor. This corresponds to individuals who earned below ₹ 11,000 per year. If there are a large number of workers who are engaged in unpaid family labour, who are also earning below ₹ 11,000 per year, then using this cutoff will capture more than 10 per cent of workers.

This is shown graphically in Figure 1, which shows the distribution of income as seen in IRES. The vertical line is at ₹ 11,000 per year. The puzzle of poverty programmes lies in correctly identifying the individuals who are in the left tail, and delivering a successfully transfer to them.

In this, two important aspects need to be borne in mind. The first is that the income distribution seen in Figure 18.2 is painted afresh in the real economy every month. Every month, a new curve comes about, and a different set of people are found in the left tail. The challenge of a poverty programme is to correctly identify these people, and continually respond to the fact that this list of people is changing continuously.

Figure 18.2

Distribution of Total Annual Income in IRES (End-2004)

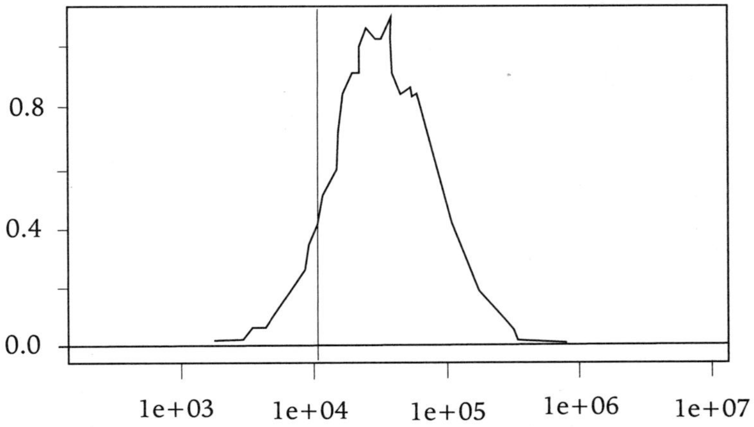

The second aspect is that of geographical distribution. We may visualise a map drawn every month, showing the density of poverty incidence across the districts of India. Every month, a new map comes about, and the poor are found at a different set of locations. The challenge of a poverty programme is to correctly identify these people and continuously respond to the fact that the spatial characteristics of poverty are continuously changing.

Thinking across time, the goal of a poverty programme is to be self-adjusting, self-targeting and self-liquidating. A self-adjusting programme adjusts to the vagaries of weather and seasonal wage fluctuations: more people in a certain district fall in the left tail after a drought. A self-targeting programme is one where people who are in poverty self-select themselves to avail of the programme, and individuals who are not in the left tail do not obtain transfers. Finally, a self-liquidating programme is one which ceases to exist when poverty is eliminated. As an example, there is nobody in Goa who falls in the left tail of the Indian income distribution; hence there should be zero enrolment into a poverty programme in Goa.

Table 18.2

Occupational Structure of the Poor

Occupation	*Number (million)*
Subsistence Farming	0.03
Other Traditional Farming	0.27
Dairy	0.05
Agricultural Labour	1.47
Skilled Wage Labour	0.18
Semi/Unskilled Wage Labour	0.61
Salaried Employee (SME)	0.13
Salaried Employee (Large Firms)	0.12
State Government	0.03
Own Trading Firm	0.14
Self-Employed	0.28
Home-based	0.23
Total	3.6

In terms of location, 3 out of the 10 per cent of the earners in the bottom decile are urban. Hence, sound thinking on poverty programmes will need to address the urban poor also. Interestingly enough, in an unexpected kind of symmetry, 3 out of the 10 per cent of the top decile are rural. Both these statements challenge our stereotypical interpretations of urban *versus* rural.

Table 18.2 shows the occupational structure of the poor. Virtually none of them are members of a trade union.

Existing Efforts Fail to Reach the Poor

Myriad programmes, and policy decisions, have been taken based on the goal of poverty alleviation. But the rude fact is that most of these so-called pro-poor programmes actually get captured by the upper middle class.

- The massive system of state intervention in agriculture is focused on rich farmers. The poor do not use free electricity, or sell to the PDS (public distribution system). Most of the fertiliser subsidy goes to the owners of fertiliser factories.

- The poor use neither LPG (liquefied petroleum gas) nor kerosene.
- The entire system of 'small savings' helps rich people avoid taxes.
- Employees' Provident Fund Organisation (EPFO) members have a median income of ₹ 60,000 while the median income of those outside EPFO is ₹ 30,000. What is worse, 12 per cent of the accounts of EPFO account for 85 per cent of the assets. These richest 12 per cent of EPFO members thus capture almost all of the state subsidy to EPFO.
- The poor are unlikely to have a home with a water connection, so subsidised piped water favours the rich.
- The rich disproportionately capture access to free government hospitals such as AIIMS.

Our thinking about welfare programmes for the poor should be blessed with a profound skepticism about what we have done so far. None of the above elements of policy need to be retained, now that we understand how their incidence actually falls very differently from the claimed 'pro-poor' or 'pro-people' bias. We can save enormous amounts of public money, and remove distortions in numerous parts of the economy, by eliminating all these poorly thought out programmes.

Employment Guarantee

Employment guarantee looms large as an efficient way to deliver money to the poor. The core claim of the employment guarantee (EG) is that rich people do not self-select themselves to work in the hot sun, doing manual labour at a low wage. I believe this core claim. A person needs to be in dire straits in order to utilise the EG.

The EG has three strengths: It is self-targeting, self-adjusting and self-liquidating. It is self-targeting in that rich people do not opt for the EG. It is self-adjusting in that people get in and out of EG programmes depending on the season, or drought, in a way that does not happen with traditional anti-poverty programmes.[25] Finally, it is self-liquidating. If you tried to pay ₹ 40 per day in most of Gujarat or Maharashtra, nobody would show up to work. But in Orissa, ₹ 40 per day is still attractive to the poor. When Orissa reaches the present level of affluence of Gujarat, the flow of resources through the EG will subside.

A well-run EG programme holds the promise of being able to dynamically identify individuals in the left tail, taking into consideration their fluctuating numbers and geographical distribution.

The price at which the government stands ready to buy matters greatly, as we know from our unhappy experiences with the PDS. I think a price like ₹ 30 per day makes sense, and present debates on the EGA have already gone into the dangerous terrain of ₹ 60 per day. Once a nationwide capacity to implement EGA is in place, the price can be gradually adjusted so as to stick with the goal of spending 1 per cent of GDP.

The puzzle of a poverty programme is to locate individuals in the left tail of the income distribution as of today. This is achieved by having a single price for the EGA in the full country. A single price for the EGA defines the vertical line in the income distribution; the EGA is attractive to everyone in the left tail, regardless of where they are physically located. By this reasoning, it is a highly flawed design to have regional variation of the price paid by EGA. There are roughly zero poor people in Goa. It is highly incorrect to have a high-priced EGA programme operating in Goa. Given the spatial distribution of poverty in India, it is to be expected that when the EGA is in operation, the individuals who participate in it will be clustered in perhaps 100 districts.

There are many concerns about the corruption that could go along with the implementation of the EGA. I recognise these threats, and see in them an argument to do more in terms of administrative implementation. We need to learn from our dismal failures, design the schemes better, have better transparency and more monitoring. I remain optimistic that the EG is a sound anti-poverty programme.

While EG is a very effective idea in many ways, it has a few important weaknesses as well. EG is really effectively only in rural areas. It is difficult to conceive of labour-intensive public works in cities to help the urban poor. EG is a highly inefficient way to build public works. If contracts were, instead, given out to build roads, then better roads would get built at a lower price. EG distorts labour markets. Low labour costs would exert effects through 'equalising differences,' attracting firms to produce in a poor area. The introduction of EG elevates wages and reduces the entry of firms. In the worst case, if the prices are set wrong (e.g., ₹ 60 per day), EG can actually increase unemployment.

Schemes Based on Cash Transfers

In an ideal world, economists would favour the negative income tax as the ideal tool for delivering money to the poor. This is an elegant scheme with the minimal frictions. However, this approach can have a negligible role in India at present, given the large informal sector and the small penetration of income tax.

In Latin America, and in some other countries, the poor have been given electronic debit cards, using which 'conditional cash transfers' (CCTs) are delivered to them. A rough sketch of this scheme is as follows:

- Under this scheme, poor women (only) are given cards.
- At banks and using ATM (automated teller machine) machines, cards can be used to extract cash, ₹ 100 at a time. In addition, the cards work as debit cards at modern retail stores.
- At the local level, government employees, NGOs and political workers transparently make a list—a subset out of electoral rolls—of those who are eligible for cards. These lists are placed into public domain. The role of the local government is only to identify poor women and deliver cards to them.
- The lists of women and their cards are sent up to the Ministry of Finance at the centre, which would disburses money—₹ 500 per month—directly into cards.

A key strength of this system is that there is a hard budget constraint. If we decide there are 10.8 crore poor people, and we decide to pay ₹ 1,000 per person, we know that exactly ₹ 10,800 crore can be spent, and we have a single database about who is receiving money.

The 'conditional' aspect of the CCT system is that the women receiving transfers are required to keep their children in school and get regular health check-ups.

Under present conditions, some difficulties in implemention of such a scheme, on an all India basis, are visible. But there are already some policy experiments underway in different parts of the country exploring such systems. I am certain that given advances in IT, and India's competency in scaling up IT systems, we should be able to design and implement such schemes which can—one day—replace employment guarantee type of schemes.[26]

The CCT system has worked well in Latin America. However, at present in India, it appears that the EG will be more effective at identifying poor people.

Social Insurance

Social insurance has been attempted on a large scale in many countries in the last few decades. There is an increasing clarity that it is an ineffective mechanism, where the bulk of the benefits are captured by the rich, and at great costs to society. The welfare programmes of the US and UK have contaminated incentives for individuals and firms on a massive scale. This is an area where we need to depart greatly from Anglo-Saxon capitalism.

Let me start with pensions. The US has a giant, insolvent system named 'social security.' It is a defined-benefits system. The world over, defined-benefits pension systems have collapsed. Some have collapsed sooner, and good governance has helped some linger on for more years. But defined-benefits pensions are fundamentally wrong in terms of inducing bad incentives, contaminating the political system, and introducing gigantic risks for public finance.

India has done well by moving towards an individual account, defined contribution system in the form of the New Pension System (NPS).[27] The introduction of the NPS needs to be followed through by the creation of a formal pensions regulator, the Pension Fund Regulatory and Development Authority (PFRDA), to ensure that the NPS benefits from regulation and supervision.

The EPF programme of the EPFO is also a defined contribution system. The only defined benefit schemes in operation are the erstwhile civil servants pension (which no longer applies for new recruits in most of the country), and the 'EPS' programme of the EPFO. Once the latter is controlled, India will be free of the dangers of defined benefits.

Under defined contributions, individuals tend to build up substantial assets over their life span in their individual accounts. These accounts are personal wealth. As an illustration, a young person who earns ₹ 25,000 a year, who contributes ₹ 10 per day for 250 days per year into the NPS, and makes sound decisions about his asset allocation is likely to achieve a pension wealth of ₹ 2 lakh to ₹ 3 lakh in 2005, corresponding to a pension of ₹ 2,000 per month to ₹ 3,000 per month.

When a person has wealth, this can be used to address the two other major consumption shocks, which relate to unemployment and health. A person at an income of ₹ 2,000 per month who faces a spell of six months of unemployment needs a loan of ₹ 6,000 in order to drop down to a 50 per cent benefit when unemployed. Similarly, an extreme health shock for this person would probably cost ₹ 10,000 to ₹ 20,000.

These are small magnitudes, when compared with the scale of pension accumulation. These kinds of financial depth can be obtained through loans against pension assets. Since these loans would be fully collateralised, they would have interest rates like 7 per cent to 9 per cent. Such loans—which are not withdrawals—give individuals financial depth, to cope with shocks, but do not contaminate the lifetime accumulation of pension wealth.

In this fashion, we can set up a new system, where young people are forced into the NPS, and this helps them to cope with old age, health and spells of unemployment. This system would fully avoid the mistakes of the US and the UK on these questions. Indeed, these lines of thought are consistent with what forward-looking thinkers are proposing for where the US and the UK should be headed.[28]

Towards Better Policy Design

At present, it appears that EG is the most powerful anti-poverty weapon in our arsenal. EG has many problems, and our first task is to strengthen the administrative capacity to make it work well. We have to be careful about policy mistakes, such as high wage rates and differential wages across different regions. We have to be careful about administrative capacity.

In addition, we need to be concerned about the genuine difficulties of a well-implemented EG, and perhaps over a 10-year horizon, move towards some kind of CCT system in addition to the EG.

One of the great insights of the theory of economic policy making is that for making policies effective, the number of policy instruments should be more than the policy objectives. In other words, we should not seek to achieve two objectives with only one policy instrument. Unfortunately, this is forgotten too often, particularly in the areas of pricing of intermediates such as power, petroleum products or fertiliser. Prices are most effective in meeting the objective of efficient allocation of resources. Unfortunately, we have tended to also use them for redistributive purposes. We have ended up achieving neither redistribution nor efficient allocation.

The price system should be used for efficient use of resources. For redistribution, we should use fiscal policy. There is an additional point in this regard, which is relevant at least in India and this relates to discretionary policies. Our experience shows that, like entropy, discretionary policies tend to deteriorate. Hence, even policies for poverty eradication or promoting livelihood security, as far as possible, should have a built-in sunset clause, so that the policies can be compulsorily reviewed from time to time.

I have no doubt that there is a judicious mix of cash transfers and employment guarantee can be very effective tools for delivering resources to the poor. At the same time, this should free up other aspects of public policy to do the right thing, in a hard-headed way, to maximise growth, without worrying about redistribution.

New thinking about poverty programmes is important because it should free our minds. Once poverty programmes are properly implemented, in our minds, we should be saying: we have delivered x per cent of GDP to poor people, with correct targeting. After this is out of the way, in every other area of economic policy, our focus should be on just one thing: to make India grow fast, for there is no more-powerful anti-poverty programme than economic growth.

Corporate Governance

The Corporation in India's Growth Strategy

Sometimes, it is felt that the corporate sector is but a peripheral part of economic development. For millennia, individuals organised themselves as teams for undertaking tasks such as hunting or agriculture. The incentive structures that lay below these teams were based on repeated games and kinship.

As Hicks (1969) observed, the demands made on teams changed decisively with the industrial revolution. For the first time in human history, production could be organised as teams using immense scales of capital and labour, and delivering enormously lower costs in return. Institutional innovations were required, in order to obtain incentive compatible pooling of large amounts of capital and labour into the firm. England's success in the industrial revolution was as much related to James Watt and the steam engine as it was to the limited liability company and the stock market, for the latter made big firms possible to engage in mechanised production.

Three inter-related features are of essence to economic growth: bringing large amounts of capital to bear on a single unit of production, utilising modern technology with a specialised workforce, and harnessing economies of scale. Each of these features is intimately linked to the corporation.

Hence, the corporate sector is not a peripheral part of economic development. It lies at the core of India's transition into a modern market economy. Perfecting the institution of the corporation is not merely about protecting the interests of a few million shareholders. If we seek a future for India with high economic growth, then we have to understand how to foster corporations which utilise capital efficiently.

The field of corporate governance is about a few core ideas:

- The management team does not own a company.
- The shareholders are the owners of the company.
- The management team is only an agent acting on behalf of the shareholders.
- The shareholders should recruit a management team of their choice.
- The cashflows received by every share should be identical.
- If the management team, or a subset of shareholders, extracts monetary or non-monetary benefits from the firm which are not equitably delivered to all shareholders, this is plain theft.

It is important for us to focus the entire discussion of CG (corporate governance) upon the prevention of theft and opportunistic behaviour by corporate insiders. Our challenge is that of creating practices, laws, regulations and supervisory capacity which translates these core ideas into ground reality.

I would like to draw attention to the issue of 'the control premium'. When a controlling interest in a firm is sold by the erstwhile management team to a new management team, it is common, in India, for the transaction to take place at a price much higher than the secondary market price of the shares. This difference is called 'the control premium'. The control premium is made in a pure market process, and it is measured accurately. Investment bankers like to boast about a large control premium, and the pink papers glorify a transaction with a large control premium.

But to an economist, large values of a premium in a control transaction raise concerns about theft by insiders. If CG is sound, all shareholders receive identical cashflows; there are no special benefits that accrue to a man who controls the firm. In this case, the premium only reflects the extent to which the assets of the acquired firm will generate better cashflows in the merged entity.

If insiders receive bigger cashflows compared with minority shareholders, then while the public market may believe that there is a certain NPV (net present value) of dividends, the incumbent managers of the firm may value shares at a much higher value. They would thus need to be paid a big premium in order to be willing to leave. The buyer of these shares could then settle down to enjoying the same private benefits of control.

Episodes with a large control premium are glorified in the mass media, but they reflect poorly upon the state of CG in India.

Macroeconomic Benefits of Sound Corporate Governance

Before I get to these issues, I want to dwell on the macroeconomic benefits of sound CG.

CG debates are sometimes portrayed as being about protecting the helpless individual investor. I would like to remind all of us that the individual investor is not as helpless as we might think. If he feels that his interests are not being taken care of, he will lose interest in the public securities markets. It is when the individual investor is empowered, in terms of both voice and vote, that we will obtain a far-reaching shift in the portfolio allocation of households, away from real estate and gold, towards equity. Such a shift will have macroeconomic consequences. When vast pools of capital are available to the equity market, the required rate of return will be lowered. More projects will get funded, and India's growth will accelerate.

Similar issues apply with foreign investors. India will obviously benefit from vast quantities of foreign portfolio capital coming into the country, and speeding up India's growth. Corporate governance matters in this process at two levels:

Combating 'Home Bias'

First, there is a well-known 'home bias' amongst investors, whereby international diversification takes place to an extent which is much smaller than is rational. An efficient portfolio for a US investor should have roughly 50 per cent of international assets, but at present, international assets are somewhat below 20 per cent.[29] One factor driving home bias, and inadequate portfolio flows to poor countries, is CG. When India improves our CG, this will serve to combat home bias in Organisation for Economic Co-operation and Development (OECD) countries, and thus increase the flow of capital coming into the country.[30]

Stability of Foreign Capital

A second aspect is that of stability of foreign investment. In the East Asian Crisis, one aspect of capital flight was questions of CG. If foreign investors are confident that the interests of minority shareholders are adequately taken care of, then foreign capital will be more stable.

Elements of an Indian Response

I would like to offer a few ideas on how we should approach the CG question.

Another Bipolar Hypothesis

When the managers of a firm have a very high shareholding in the firm, their interests are aligned with those of the minority shareholders. When the managers have a very small shareholding, they are vulnerable to a takeover. The most difficult period is the intermediate regime. Many times, CG discussions in India assume that all family-dominated firms have serious problems. This stance needs to be replaced by a more nuanced, bipolar view.

The Basic Pressures of the Market are in Place

Price discovery in the Indian equity market is dominated by retail investors: of the total equity turnover of ₹ 86.3 trillion in 2004, ₹ 5.5 trillion came from institutional investors. Price discovery primarily takes place on the derivatives market. In September 2005, which was the most active month of equity derivatives trading ever, just 6.95 per cent of the turnover came from institutional investors. This illustrates the domination of retail investors in price discovery.

Retail investors are fairly sensitive to CG issues. Anecdotal evidence suggests that firms which have avoided theft or opportunistic managerial practices have obtained systematically higher valuations from the market. Through this, over time, a greater proportion of capital will be controlled by the firms which are effective at overcoming CG problems. Our task is to strengthen this basic process.

Market Discipline

The most powerful forces that can be brought to play are those of market discipline. Sometimes, CG discussions visualise an Orwellian State that will micro-manage all listed firms and check the incidence of theft. Such developments will damage our political system, and fail to block theft.

The most important forces that can be brought into play are those of market discipline:

- Steadily strengthening disclosure will make it harder for insiders to conceal theft. As an example, the US quarterly disclosures are dramatically superior to those taking place in India. Similarly, there are clauses in existing law making it possible for firms to ignore disclosure of many excellent schedules in the corporate annual reports. These gaps in our disclosure policies need to be closed.
- For the 130 companies where stock futures trading is available, rational speculators can short sell a stock, and thus exert market pressure to drive down the valuation of a badly run company. For the remaining companies, where derivatives trading is not available, there is a need to establish the institutional mechanisms for short selling, so as to achieve the same kinds of market pressure.
- So far, India has seen a polite M&A (mergers and acquisitions) market, where consenting management teams enter into transactions. We need to go beyond this, to the next step, of hostile takeovers. This is the most powerful weapon for strengthening CG. Suppose a company suffers from acute theft by insiders, and the NPV of cashflows coming out to independent shareholders works out to ₹ 100 per share. A new management team can engage in a lower degree of theft, and pay ₹ 150 per share to the shareholders.
- A vital part of enabling this is rational voting by institutional shareholders. FIIs are already a valuable and rational force who can play a role of encouraging takeovers. In addition, Indian institutional investors need to write down detailed manuals about how they will respond to takeover offers,

so as to reduce the extent of political interference when a takeover does arise, and encourage the growth of hostile takeovers, who should not assume that institutions will always vote with the incumbent.

- A US style framework of checking against insider trading will help close an avenue through which insiders can obtain excess cashflows as compared with public shareholders, and remove the conflict of interest where insiders who benefit from insider trading have an incentive to do badly on disclosure, which damages CG.
- If the foundation of CG is the principal-agent problem between shareholders and employees of the firm, then progress on labour market contracting is an essential part of overcoming these conflicts. Employees of corporations need to move much more towards performance-linked labour contracting, where performance is rewarded with bonuses and valuable stock option exercise, and lack of performance leads to wage stagnation and dismissal. Job security, stability of wages and above-market wages are all aspects through which insiders extract cashflows at the expense of public shareholders.
- Competitive markets will help reduce CG difficulties. If a firm is under brutal competitive pressure, then it will have to buy raw materials at the lowest price available on the market. It will be unable to pay higher prices in a related party transaction. Thus, the competition agenda is important to CG. Conversely, the biggest dangers of weak CG are in monopolistic industries, where there is free cash flow to steal.

Avoid a Mechanical Mentality

Traditional corporate insiders in India have had an incentive of shifting the CG focus to superficial 'checkbox compliance'. The attempt is to divert attention on CG from the fundamental principal-agent problem, and the question of the myriad kinds of theft, to a mechanistic compliance checklist such as having x number of independent board members, y number of board meetings, etc. A ramification of this is the 'corporate governance rating' which seeks to measure whether such mechanistic rules are complied with.

It is important to remember that CG is about theft or opportunistic practices by insiders, which takes myriad subtle forms. It is not possible to check CG by focusing on mechanistic rules and their compliance. In my reckoning, one large control premium in a year means more than a hundred laudatory CG ratings in the year. Market discipline will achieve a better focus on theft than checkbox compliance.

Integrity

Finally, I want to talk about something which is unfashionable with economists, but is an important part of India's progress, and this is integrity. In our debates about public policy, we like to focus on markets and transactions, and that should certainly be our first line of attack. But over and above this, I believe that culture counts. Our goal should be to build good practices as a matter of culture.

CG is not so much about courageous decisions by a few people placed in dramatic moments, as a stubborn streak of integrity in many people, who are quietly shaping organisations and culture every day. As Yevgeny Yevtushenko says in his poem about the intellectual in a communist country titled "Talk", in so strange a time, common integrity could look like courage. I feel this way about a lot of Indian public policy questions today. What we need most is not a charismatic character making a courageous decision in a moment of history; what we need most is many people exhibiting a stubborn streak of commmon integrity in everyday life.

The top decile firms with good CG practices in India are not focused on checkbox compliance. They have integrity. Markets have steadily rewarded them with outstanding valuations, and thus supported their growth. The individuals who live this life of high integrity every day are the unsung heroes of India's economic growth. We must treasure such good behaviour, and try to grow the circle of individuals and firms with high integrity.

How Far-reaching has the Liberalisation of the 1990s been?

For many people, the concerns of this lecture appear a little outdated, because it is felt that India is firmly on the path to becoming a market economy. It is sometimes felt that enormous progress has been made, and if we just keep going for a few more years, the big problems will be solved.

I believe this is an incorrect position. A little progress has been made in some areas. In most areas, the number one problem that continues to bedevil us is the question of right sizing the state.

In the period after 1991, we have made huge progress on a growing private sector. New firms like Infosys have sprung up out of thin air. PSUs like VSNL have been privatised. One might have thought that the share of PSUs in the total output of large firms in India has diminished. Also, given all the focus on the private sector, ranging from TELCO all the way to the lively young firms in software, we tend to think that the private sector is prominent.

Figure 18.3

Share of PSUs in Output of Large Firms

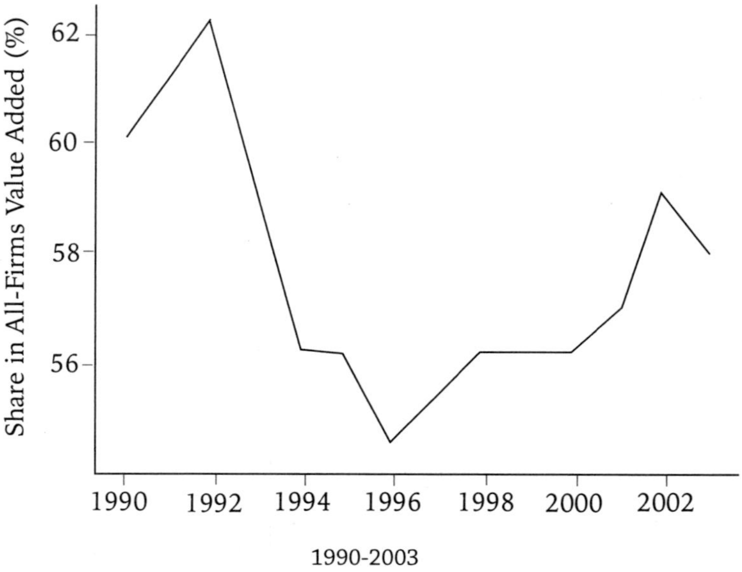

This is, unfortunately, not how the facts pan out. Centre for Monitoring Indian Economy Pvt. Ltd. (CMIE) tracks all the large firms in India. In 1991-92, a full 62.2 per cent of the output (i.e., the value added) of all firms put together came from the 233 PSUs then present. The share of PSUs dropped to 57.9 per cent in 2002-03.[31]

So despite all the greatness of our entrepreneurship, and all the incredible energy of our private sector, more than half of the output of large Indian firms, as of 2002-03, came from PSUs. The decline of the share of PSUs is taking place at a glacial pace of 0.4 per cent per year.

If these trends continue, then we will get to a mere 50:50 split between PSUs and private companies, in the CMIE database, in 2022-2023. I'm sure that the share of the private sector, in the output of Chinese firms, will cross 50 per cent before ours does. And a share of 50 per cent is hardly good enough; in most modern market economies, there is no such thing as a PSU. Our goal should be an 95:5 breakdown between the private and public sectors.

The main point of this lecture has been to argue that this state of affairs, and the pace of change, is not good enough. India needs to go faster, on the enterprise of constructing a modern market economy.

Can it be?

Is this broad agenda politically feasible? I believe it is an attainable direction for India. The interests of the vast majority of our citizens are aligned with this agenda, for it will give us an India which has high growth, an egalitarian India which is a meritocracy, an India where public goods are of high quality and quantity for all citizens.

There is a cynical view that India is incapable of any reforms that hurt a vociferous group, no matter how small. But recent years have shown that this pessimism is misplaced. Let me show you two striking examples:

Tariff Reforms

I believe nothing was harder than cutting tariffs. Every rich industrialist in the country was opposed to cutting tariffs.

But Manmohan Singh, Yashwant Sinha, Jaswant Singh and P. Chidambaram all manfully fought on the subject of cutting tariffs, and the tariffs have indeed been substantially done away with.

Exemption Raj

For years, Indian taxpayers were drugged with every conceivable type of tax exemption. It was considered politically impossible to remove these exemptions. There was an uproar when removal of 'exemption raj' was first proposed. But there has been enormous success in—one by one—removing the exemptions, and forcing all Indian citizens to pay their taxes, fair and square.

So when we look at other areas, I feel it is possible to achieve change. Areas like the GST and restructuring the administration of cities appear hard, but once we have a consensus on the direction, India does achieve profound change over the medium term.

In an open society, nothing matters more than ideas. India has responded to the force of ideas in recent decades, taking on many a holy cow. I vividly remember when disinvestment began in the early 1990s, and I used to say that the logical destination is privatisation. This used to make many people hot and flustered. But the privatisation was inexorably logical, and sure enough, India has moved forward on right sizing the public sector.

Can labour law be reformed? Yes, for there are only 10 million trade union members in India, with a hardline core of 1.37 million workers who take their trade union membership seriously.[32] As politicans understand the fundamental contradictions between the interests of 1080 million people in India, as opposed to the vociferous 1.37 million hardline trade union members, change is inevitable. As we have seen, even the Communist Party of India (Marxist) [CPI(M)] has prohibited some kinds of strikes in West Bengal.

The world changes, and none of us can afford to be irrational, or refuse to change our positions when the data change. As the Chief Minister of West Bengal, Shri Buddhadeb Bhattacharya said, "Marxists are not fools". I am sanguine that in an open society like ours, more policy debate will lead to knowledge-based policies and accelerate reforms including labour reforms.

Conclusion

Public policy in India is at the crossroads. The old orthodoxy of socialism has decisively lost ground in the minds of the younger generation, which is now the majority of the population. But a fully articulated alternative has not been articulated nor has it been internalised. In order to bridge the gulf between ideas and action, there is a need to start from first principles, and fully think through the role of the state in India in the coming decade.

We should take great pride in the transformation that has been achieved in India in the last 20 years or so. But as I ponder over this, I have felt something was missing. In this lecture, I have tried to envision what India would look like, as a modern market economy.

My main point is that we need to move beyond state capitalism as the organising principle for the economy, and we need to craft the idea of a New India as an advanced, modern market economy. Towards this, we can draw upon the experience of successful market economies, while differing from them in important ways.

As emphasised earlier, we are at the threshold of a Golden Age of growth, but this historic window of opportunity is available to us only for the next two decades or so. This great demographic dividend will come to an end as surely and as inevitably as the arrow of time. Hence, there is an urgency for us to accelerate reforms, starting with transforming our mindset and marching towards an advanced modern market economy by going beyond the paradigm of state capitalism.

Notes

1. Last year, I did the K.R. Narayanan lecture at the Australian National University (ANU) on this theme. My talk was titled "India: On the Growth Turnpike." It can be accessed at *http://rspas.anu.edu.au/papers/narayanan/2004oration.pdf*.
2. Economic policy of the 1969-1976 period consisted of enormous powers being usurped by the state. India witnessed an unprecedented increase in control raj. Let me run through the big events of this seven-year period:

   Small Scale Industry Reservation: In 1969, the policy of explicitly reserving certain items for production by small companies was created.

   Industrial Disputes Act (IDA): Factories with over 1000 workers used to require government permission for layoffs. The size threshold was amended in 1976 to 300. In 1982, when Indira Gandhi was back in power, this was further reduced to 100. Bibek Debroy, Director of (*http://www.rgfindia.com/*) Rajiv Gandhi Institute for Contemporary Studies, has drawn attention to the most odious part of the Industrial Disputes Act (IDA), which is Chapter V-B which was introduced into the IDA in 1976. Through this, firms require prior permission of the government before layoffs, retrenchment and closure.

FERA: Draconian currency controls and restrictions on foreign investment came about when the Foreign Exchange Regulation Act (FERA) was passed in 1973. An army of 7,286 *babus* at RBI continues to operate hundreds of rules that meddle with India's engagement with the world.

Urban Land Ceilings: On 17 February 1976 the Urban Land Ceiling Act was passed. It covered 73 towns and cities and imposed a ceiling of 500 to 2000 square metres on urban land holdings. Incidentally, this was a state subject, but the Constitution allows the Parliament to pass a bill if more than two states agree, and this path was chosen during the emergency.

MRTP: The Monopolies and Restrictive Trade Practices (MRTP) bill was proposed in 1967. It became an act and came into force from 1 June 1970. The MRTP Act, which gave huge powers to the government, sought to check the expansion of large industrial houses with assets over ₹ 1 crore in businesses where their share in the market exceeded 33 per cent. The MRTP Act has mercifully been scrapped; it was replaced by the Competition Act in 2002.

Bank Nationalisation: Indira Gandhi nationalised all big banks in 1973.

The Fraser Institute in Canada computes measures of economic freedom across countries and across years. Their score for economic freedom for India dropped sharply from 4.9 in 1970 to 4.1 in 1975. It went back up to 4.8 in 1990, and rose strongly thereafter to a level of 6.4 in 2003.

3. Countries such as the US have put inter-state commerce explicitly into the constitution. Fiscal policy in the US has to adapt to the fundamental principle that the state shall never interfere with inter-state commerce. Our constitution does not have a comparable provision, hence special efforts are needed in order to achieve India as a unified market.
4. See Time for a Two-level VAT by Amaresh Baghchi, *Business Standard*, 6 September 2005.
5. It might be useful to point out that the Twelfth Finance Commission has intruded upon the autonomy of states when forcing them to accept fiscal responsibility.
6. A search for India dysfunctional fiscal federalism gave 16,400 hits on *http://www.google.com and 101 hits on http://scholar.google.com.*
7. See Shah and Patnaik (2005).
8. Foreign firms are mostly free to bring FDI into India. Foreign individuals and institutional investors are able to bring portfolio investment into India. Indian firms are able to take FDI and portfolio investment out of the country. Dishonest individuals in India are able to diversify globally, using illegal transfers of capital outside the country.

   The incidence of capital controls, thus, falls most upon the honest resident individual.
9. For an eloquent exposition of the difficulties and distortions caused by capital controls, see Forbes (2005).
10. An additional facet of this concerns the loss of effectiveness of fiscal policy. Given India's difficulties with fiscal discipline, there is a strong case for relatively rigid fiscal rules. These will inevitably limit the extent to which fiscal policy can possibly be countercyclical. In addition, to the extent that a country has an open economy, the effect of fiscal policy is diluted.

    In this context, monetary policy looms large in the macro stabilisation of the country. It is doubly important to not lose the weapon of monetary policy owing to currency pegging.
11. With half a trillion dollars moving across the border in a year, the greatest risk we may face is that of continuing to use policies which are founded on the assumption of a closed economy.

12. As CMIE projections for 2005-06 show:

Component	*₹ Crore*	*Per Cent to GDP*
Agriculture & Allied	6,16,108	20.38
Industry	8,33,672	27.58
Mining & Quarrying	84,760	2.8
Manufacturing	4,94,531	16.36
Elect., Gas, Water	61,812	2.04
Construction	1,92,028	6.35
Services	15,73,736	52.06
Trade, Hotel, Trans., Comm.	7,35,402	24.33
Finance, Real Estate, etc.	4,11,154	13.6
Social, Personal Services, etc.	4,23,454	14.01
GDP at Factor Cost	30,22,937	100.0

13. Detailed occupational data from the IRES database is as follows:

Category	*Proportion (%)*
Agriculture	30.07
Subsistence Farming	0.57
Mechanised Farming	1.41
Other Traditional Farming	15.97
Dairy	1.33
Agricultural Labour	10.79
Self-employed	28.63
Entrepreneur	12.24
Entrepreneur sans Premises	3.60
Small Manufacturer	0.44
Medium Manufacturer	0.03
Professional	1.08
Home-based	2.09
Others	9.14
Small Firms	25.25
Skilled	8.44
Semi-skilled/unskilled	11.10
Firm < 10 Workers	5.72
Big Firms	6.34
Firms 10-19 Workers	1.62
Firms > 20 Workers	4.72
Government	9.71
Central	2.96
State	6.75

14. Some have argued that a strong increase in property tax is of essence in funding urban infrastructure. The international experience shows that there is almost no country where the urban property tax exceeds 1 per cent of GDP. Hence, while property tax enforcement is surely important, cities also do need to tap into fiscal flows from the centre, which after all has access to the two most efficient taxes, which are the GST and the income tax.

15. One of the great contributions of the discipline of economics is a sharp and technical definition of what is a public good. The careful use of this definition needs to be made by all who think about the Indian State.

    A public good is something which is 'non-rival' and 'non-excludable'.

    'Non-rival' means that the consumption by one person does not reduce the quantity available to another person. In other words, when one more child is born in India, and is safe owing to the Indian defence forces, the amount of public safety does not go down owing to the arrival of this child. Hence, we say that defence is non-rival.

    'Non-excludable' means that it is not possible to exclude a person from benefiting from the public good. When one more child is born in India, it is not possible to deprive the child of the benefits of our defence expenditures. Hence, defence expenditure is non-excludable.

16. Surjit Bhalla ('Model of Governance: Let Them Eat Snakes', in *Business Standard*, 26 June 2004) has documented a natural experiment which gives us an opportunity to measure the impact of higher educational expenditure over the 1983-1999 period:

	Bihar	*West Bengal*	*Rest of India*
Rise in per-student expenditure (%)	107	160	37
Enrolment (%)			
1983	34	50	50
1999	49	68	73

    Similar results obtain for male/female disparities in enrolment also.

    Many countries, such as Sri Lanka, have educational expenditure as per cent of GDP which is similar to that of India, but have much better outcomes. This kind of evidence points a finger at how India spends on education, not how much.

17. Going beyond education, qualitatively similar arguments apply in numerous other areas. As an example, in the case of health, virtually all cross-country variation in child mortality can be explained by six variables: per capita GDP, a measure of income distribution, female education, a dummy variable for predominantly Muslim countries, an index of ethnolinguistic diversity, and five region dummies. After controlling for these, the size of public expenditure on health has a negligible impact upon child mortality. This calls to question the effort to improve health outcomes by spending more on health. The focus has to be on incentives and institutions, not outlays.

    See Filmer *et al.*, 2000.

18. Education from class 1 to class 12 has characteristics of a public good because there is a non-rival and non-excludable benefit to everyone when a child becomes educated. As an example, educated children make better voters, and everyone benefits. Everyone is better off when a country has universal education till the 12th standard, and a large army of unskilled labour ceases to exist.

19. These are also known as 'education vouchers.'

20. The empirical literature has shown dismal results on the benefits of higher economic growth from higher resources spent on education. Part of this problem may be that additional years in school are leading to very little new knowledge in the mind of the child. See Easterly (2002).

21. As an example, the Educational Testing Service (ETS) is a large testing system in the US which is a private body. In India, the NSE runs a computerised testing system named NCFM, which is fully removed from the State.

22. These scores should be publicised, to help parents achieve better school choice.
23. However, there are scholars abroad who have profound concern about the lack of accountability amongst UK and US school teachers. As an example, see If India can... why can't we? by James Tooley in New Statesman, September 2001, an article which argues that the public sector UK educational system has much to learn from the pressures faced by teachers in private schools in India.
24. As Lant Pritchett and Michael Woolcock have pointed out, the hardest problems of producing public goods are those where the government employees have discretion, and there is a large number of transactions. Law and order fits this description: judges and policemen interact with the citizenry through a large number of transactions, and have a great degree of *de facto* discretion. Achieving sound outcomes for such problems requires a prime focus on law and order on the part of the media and the political system.

    See Pritchett and Woolcock (2004).
25. The EG programme has one valuable feature. It is a kind of government expenditure which goes up in a bad year and goes down in a good year. This makes it an 'automatic stabiliser'; it helps fiscal policy become counter-cyclical and thus damp the fluctuations of the economy.
26. See Shah (2005a).
27. See Shah (2005b).
28. Feldstein (2005).
29. By the same yardstick, an efficient portfolio for an Indian investor should have over 50 per cent of international assets, but at present, international assets are somewhat below 1 per cent. India also suffers from an acute case of 'home bias'.
30. See Dahlquist *et al.* (2002). "Corporate Governance and the Home Bias", October.
31. PSUs are laggards in releasing financial information. As of September 2005, while 373 firms had released results for 2002-03, only 289 firms had released information for 2003-04 and just 50 firms had released data for 2004-05. Hence, we use 2002-03 as the last year for which the bulk of PSUs are observed.
32. Using the IRES database, we find that 2.7 per cent of earners are members of trade unions. This gives the estimate of 10 million individuals who are trade union members.

    We find that 0.38 per cent of earners say that they would 'definitely' entrust their trade union leaders with their savings. This 0.38 per cent of India's earners can be considered to be the hardline members of trade unions. The full distribution is:

Response	*Percentage of Earners*
Definitely	0.38
Might Trust	0.32
Given a Choice, would not like to	0.56
Definitely Not	1.08
Don't Know	0.36
All Trade Union Members	2.71

It is fascinating to see that just 14 per cent of trade union members (i.e., 0.38 out of 2.71) would 'definitely' trust their own trade union leaders with handling worker's money.

References

Dahlquist, Magnus, Lee Pinkowitz, Rene M. Stulz and Rohan Williamson (2002). "Corporate Governance and the Home Bias", October.

Easterly, W. (2002). "Barren Land", *Education Next* 2(3), Fall 2002.

Feldstein, Martin (2005). "Rethinking Social Insurance", *NBER Working Paper* 11250. March.

Filmer, Deon, Jeffrey S. Hammer and Lant H. Pritchett (2000). "Weak Links in the Chain: A Diagnosis of Health Policy in Poor Countries", *World Bank Research Observer* 15(2): 199–224. August.

Forbes, Kristin (2005). "The Microeconomic Evidence on Capital Controls: No Free Lunch", October, *http://www.nber.org/papers/w11372*.

Pritchett, Lant and Michael Woolcock (2004). "Solutions when the Solution is the Problem: Arraying the Disarray in Development", *World Development* 32(2): 191–212.

Shah, Ajay (2005a). "Improving Governance using IT Systems".

———. (2005b). "A Sustainable and Scalable Approach in Indian Pension Reforms", October.

Shah, Ajay and Ila Patnaik (2005). "India's Experience with Capital Flows: The Elusive Quest for a Sustainable Current Account Deficit", *NBER Working Paper* 11387, May, *http://www.nber.org/papers/w11387*.

October 26, 2005.

Economic Developments in India, Vol. 105.

19

MANMOHAN SINGH

India's Future

Opportunities and the Challenges

I belong to a generation that was shaped by our freedom struggle and by our efforts at nation building. Freedom gave us hope. Independence gave us courage. Democracy gave us rights and responsibilities. And nation-building defined our charter. Ours was a generation that lived through nearly half a century of slow growth, low industrial development, frequent famines and little social mobility. That India still exists for many of our brothers and sisters, but for fewer and fewer of them.

Having lived through a past that was very different, my generation constantly tends to compare it with our present. And the stark fact is that, as a generation, we have experienced a transformation in our own lives that in our youth we never even imagined was possible. There are millions of Indians like me, who have spent their childhood in a milieu of little hope, and have then lived a lifetime of sweeping transformation. This is not a function of the passage of time alone, but of a combination of the effort, enterprise and aspirations of the people of India, as also the leadership and guidance provided by various governments at the Centre and in the States.

After half a century of zero growth between 1900 and 1950, we saw the annual rate of growth rise to 3.5 per cent. When we realised that other developing countries were overtaking us and had found new routes to development, we too changed our course in the early 1990s. In the past two decades, the rate of growth more than doubled to an average rate of over 7.0 per cent per annum and the Indian economy was put on an upward growth trajectory.

Naturally, there will be periods of ups and downs. The economic cycle presents us years of high performance and years of modest performance. But the important thing to note is that highs are getting higher and so are the lows. Today, many people feel dissatisfied with an annual rate of growth of 5.0 per cent, while for more than two decades after our Independence, 5.0 per cent was the target rate of growth of our five year plans.

Through all the ups and downs in the face of global challenges and despite the burden of past policy mistakes, our economy is on a rising growth trajectory. This is the first lesson I draw from stepping back and looking at The Emerging Big Picture.

However, economic growth, social change and political empowerment have brought in their wake the new aspirations of an entirely new generation of Indians. This has contributed to growing impatience for faster growth and even better quality of life. These aspirations and ambitions are exerting pressures on governments to deliver more, perform better and be more transparent and more efficient.

A "Revolution of Rising Expectations" is underway and I welcome it.

What is truly significant though, if one steps back and looks at the big picture, is that our democratic political system has been responsive to these expectations. Governments have been elected and re-elected in every state of our Republic through peaceful, fair and efficiently organised elections within the context of an India that is changing faster than ever before.

Once in a while, public anger may spilover onto our streets and into the media, but India's 'silent majority' exercises its franchise in legitimate democratic ways to secure change.

Over the past two years, some well-meaning and concerned citizens have tried to spread cynicism by accusing the entire political class of being corrupt and anti-people. Many began to suggest that democracy had not served India well. They attacked the institution of Parliament by refusing to respect Parliament's judgement. Did that turn our people against democracy? Did that make them despair about the electoral system? No. Look at the voter turnout at every election over the past two years and in the just concluded assembly elections.

Even in the face of churning ambitions and rising expectations, the people of our country choose to vote and secure change through democratic means. This is the second important lesson I draw when I look at the Big Picture.

Faced with the challenge of meeting the rising aspirations of our people and of ensuring the political sustainability of high growth, we defined a new strategy of growth that is widely termed as 'inclusive growth'. Making our growth processes socially and regionally inclusive has been the touchstone of our government's policies. Our strategy of inclusive growth has six elements:

First is what I have often called 'A New Deal for Rural India'—investment in rural development, rural infrastructure—especially roads and electricity—rural health and education and remunerative prices for rural produce. We called this 'Bharat Nirman'.

Second, increased public and private investment in education and health care, with a focus on the education and health of young girls and young women.

Third, livelihood, food and energy security for the poor.

Fourth, a more transparent and responsive government made answerable to people through the Right to Information (RTI).

Fifth, investment in skills and support for private enterprise, especially small and micro enterprises.

And sixth, public investment in public transport, especially urban mass transportation.

Taken together, these interventions have made our growth processes more socially inclusive.

I cannot deny that there remain many challenges and problems and weaknesses in implementation. Our biggest challenge in trying to sustain this process of inclusive growth has been to bring rates of inflation down and keep the fiscal deficit under control. These remain a challenge and I admit that they are being seriously addressed.

Any sudden acceleration of growth, as we saw in the period 2004-2008, creates imbalances that can contribute to inflation. Such growth can also create opportunities for personal enrichment and that distorts governance and creates social resentment. Rising economic growth has helped to liberate millions of Indians from chronic poverty, reducing the incidence of poverty, but it has also widened social and economic inequalities. Our Strategy of Inclusive Growth has sought to blunt the edge of such disparities.

This is the third lesson I draw from looking at the Big Picture.

Let me now examine the Big Picture with respect to national security and international affairs. The media, quite understandably, report on events as they occur. Any lapse on the part of security forces and the intelligence and law and order machinery comes in for understandable criticism. We have been victims of premeditated acts of terror and each time terrorists attack us, there is widespread anger and despair.

In considering the Big Picture, I urge you to keep two things in mind. One, a terrorist has to succeed only once to cause pain to the innocent people, while the security forces have to succeed every minute of every day to prevent such terror attacks. By this yardstick, we must appreciate the dedication and commitment of our security forces and intelligence agencies in preventing many, many more attacks.

More importantly, I have always viewed the challenge of terrorism in India as one of preventing the ideologues of terrorism from creating divisions among the people of our great country and pitting one Indian against another. The objective of a terror attack is not just to kill innocent people, it is not just to create fear, but in fact to cause hate. It is to use such killing to create mutual distrust between people of different faiths. Creating communal tension, communal conflict and communal divisions in India is the ultimate objective of terrorism.

Every time the people of our country respond to terror attacks as one people, as Indians and not as Hindus or Muslims or Sikhs or Christians, we defeat the forces of terrorism. We challenge the ideology that feeds terrorism.

If we only look at the number of terror attacks on India in quantitative terms, we may feel despondent. However, if we consider the fact that, over the past decade, such acts of terrorism have failed to generate communal conflict, we feel more hopeful. Terrorism is being defeated in the minds of our people because they are refusing to respond to such attacks in the manner in which the ideologues of terror want them to.

This is the fourth lesson I draw from the Big Picture view of contemporary India.

Finally, look at India and the world.

I entered the world of politics in the midst of a crisis. In 1991, India was confronted by two challenges on the external front. Most of you will only recall the external payments crisis of 1990-91. But this payments crisis occurred against the backdrop of an even bigger challenge—the breakdown of the global bipolar order.

As the Finance Minister in 1991, I had to worry not only about reducing the fiscal deficit and reviving economic growth, but also about stabilising the rupee and ensuring access to adequate foreign exchange. The latter challenge was rendered particularly acute on account of the shifts in global power balances as a result of developments in the former Soviet Union and Eastern Europe.

Under the leadership of Prime Minister Narasimha Rao, we took momentous decisions both with respect to our economic policies and with respect to our foreign policy. Prime Minister Narasimha Rao launched what has come to be known as India's 'Look East Policy', linking India to the new growth engines of Asia. We liberalised our trade and investment rules to help us re-integrate with the global economy. In doing this, we were inspired by the experience of many East and South-East Asian countries.

Since then, we have faced multiple challenges on the external front. But whether it is dealing with sharp escalations in food and energy prices, or the Asian financial crisis in 1997-98 and the Trans-Atlantic financial crisis in 2008-09, or the rise of China as a global mega-trader and changing power balances in the global and regional trading regimes, we have managed to protect India's core economic and foreign policy interests

In facing these challenges, special mention must be made of Indian professionals and entrepreneurs who have made a mark for themselves around the world. Brand India is slowly but surely coming to be recognised all over the world. Millions of Indian professionals, skilled workers and entrepreneurs are today welcomed around the world.

This ability to deal with the challenges of globalisation and build new bridges with a range of countries has helped India emerge as a global player. But, in the past few months, Indian business leaders have been worried. I understand their anxieties about our red tape, our tax laws and administration, our regulations and procedures. I have often found it tough to deal with these challenges because of a lack of political consensus on the reforms we need to bring in. Yet, I must say, despite all these problems, Indian business and enterprise has demonstrated its ability to cope with competition.

The widening global footprint of Indian professionals and entrepreneurs is, therefore, altering the priorities of our foreign policy. In 1991, I had said that the emergence of India as an economic powerhouse was an idea whose time had come. Over these past two decades, this idea has shaped our relations with the world, with all major powers, with our Asian neighbours and across the Indian subcontinent.

This is the fifth lesson I draw from the Big Picture.

As I said to our heads of missions from around the world at their annual conference last month, our foreign policy is defined by our developmental priorities. The single most important objective of Indian foreign policy has to be to create a global environment conducive to the well-being of the people of India. I believe the experience of the past two decades tells us that greater integration with the world economy is benefiting India and enabling our people to realise their creative potential. The world wants India to do well.

Even as we strengthen our relations with all the major powers, we are doing more to become an active member of the emerging Asian economic community. India's voice is heard with respect in all important international forums.

India is on the move. Indians are on the move. As India rises, there are challenges to deal with. Our real challenges are at home, and ups and downs are part of life. We all know that. But we have never allowed ourselves to be overwhelmed by twists and turns in our lives. We have never allowed these challenges to weaken our faith in ourselves, in our democracy, in the principles that define our democracy and in India's destiny.

This unyielding spirit of the Indian people is what we must celebrate at all times. Governments come and governments go. We are all birds of passage, actors on different stages. But this great nation of ours is one of the oldest civilisations known to humanity and the birthplace of some of the world's greatest religions and wisest philosophies. This ancient land of ours has witnessed the flowering of the human spirit time again and again. India will continue to rise and, in doing so, will help everyone rise.

This is the Big Picture as I see it.

For the short period, we mortals occupy the places we do, let us strive to do our best, for India, for the world, for humanity.

PM's address at the Hindustan Times Summit, December 6, 2013.

Economic Developments in India, Vol. 192.

20

C. RANGARAJAN

Needed, a Growth Commission

AN organisation to look at the basic issues confronting the economy, and to prepare a broad framework on how long-term issues can be resolved, is still a necessity.

There is a need to evaluate and restructure every organisation as circumstances change and the Planning Commission is no exception. Restructuring an organisation can be of two types. One approach takes the functions of the organisation as a given and proceeds to restructure it to make it more effective to fulfil those functions. The second approach is more fundamental. It questions the very basis of the organisation and focuses on the relevance of the basic functions it has been performing. It is the second type of restructuring that we are talking about in relation to the Planning Commission.

Relevance now

The Planning Commission has a distinguished past. Many eminent men and women have adorned the position of Deputy Chairman and Member. The question that is posed now is about its relevance in the current circumstances. The Planning Commission now performs three types of functions. First and foremost, it draws a blueprint for the country's economic development over a five-year period. It also outlines a detailed strategy for achieving the goals and objectives enshrined in the blueprint which we call the Plan. The Plan exercise outlines not only how the broad macroeconomic parameters are expected to move, but also a sector wise analysis of what needs to be done. After approval of the Five Year Plan, the Planning Commission in consultation with the Finance Ministry also determines the annual plan. The determination of the 'size' of the annual plan of each state is a major exercise and has been a cause of much irritation.

"Through a broad range of discussions, the commission should prepare a road map which will be acceptable to both the Centre and the States."

Second, flowing from its function of determining the size of plans for states, the Planning Commission allocates funds to states, the distribution of which has again been a contentious issue.

Third, the Planning Commission has a key role in the formulation of various policies and programmes. It critically assesses the individual programmes of ministries. Major projects are also assessed and approved by it. It is this function which resulted in a parallel unit corresponding to every ministry being established in the Planning Commission. It would be useful to analyse which of these functions remain relevant and which of them can be discarded or transferred to other authorities within the government.

Ushering in Faster Growth

Planning was perceived in the 1950s as the most appropriate tool for ushering in faster economic growth. The strategy for achieving this was discussed at great length, particularly at the time of the formulation of the Second Five Year Plan. This was consistent with the thinking at that time that the state must have control over the 'commanding heights.'

Times have changed. In the post-liberalisation period, the concept of planning itself has undergone a change. We have moved, at best, to an era of indicative planning. The blend of public and private investment has tilted in favour of the private sector. While planning of the type we had in the first five decades after Independence has no relevance, an organisation to look at the basic issues confronting the economy, and preparing a broad framework on how long-term issues can be resolved, is still a necessity. If there is an acceptable framework on what the critical issues are and how they should be tackled, it will provide a suitable basis for policy formulation.

While the state may play a diminishing role, it still plays a critical role in the economy. In the infrastructure sector, it still has a dominant role. If the centre and states agree on a broad framework through discussions, it would facilitate the adoption of better policies. Such an organisation will be something more than a think tank. Through a broad range of discussions, it should prepare a road map which will be acceptable to both the centre and the states. Thus, the task of preparing a blueprint for the country over a certain period is essential and should continue to be performed. Also, there are issues which cut across ministries, such as energy, transport, water or environment. In terms of policy formulation, this commission can take a holistic view and offer advice.

The second function of allocating resources among states is somewhat debatable. There is a strong view that the Finance Commission is the appropriate constitutional authority for allocating resources. Of course, the Planning Commission has also been following a formula for allotting funds among states, but the quantum of transfer of funds through this mechanism has been diminishing. Much larger funds from the centre flowed through the centrally sponsored schemes and this was performance-based. Given the states' aversion, it may be best that this function is fully entrusted to the Finance Commission.

The third function of evaluating projects and giving approval has also raised many controversies. The ministries regard the implementation of projects as their prime responsibility and very often consider the Planning Commission as a hindrance.

While having a 'second look' is always an advantage, leaving this task entirely to the ministry seems appropriate. The Planning Commission has been looking at restructuring itself. In fact, the Committee on Public Expenditure Management, of which I was the Chairman, had made the point that the distinction between plan expenditure and non-plan expenditure should go, and the Planning Commission should take a comprehensive look at public expenditure in the key sectors. The result of making a distinction between plan and non-plan expenditures has been that we have had situations of hospitals without doctors and schools without teachers because one is treated as plan and the other as non-plan. In fact, within the present structure of the Planning Commission, the federal element could have been enhanced, if, besides central ministers, some chief ministers were also included as members. This would have given it a national character.

The current practice of 'approval' by the National Development Council has also not been satisfactory. Even when some Chief ministers differed on the strategy, very few changes were made. At the end of a long day of discussions, the plan is taken as approved.

A task that must continue, as we move ahead, there are critical problems facing the economy. Ensuring a faster rate of economic growth with equity is not an easy task. Environmental considerations have emerged as a serious concern. Therefore, an integrated look at the problems faced by the country over a five-year period is very much required. Thus, the need for an organisation for formulating ideas on how to shape the economy over a certain time frame will be helpful. This was the task which the Planning Commission was performing with some success and this must continue.

If the word 'planning' is reminiscent of an earlier period, it may be substituted by 'development' or 'growth.' The other two functions performed by the Planning Commission now can be delegated to other authorities in the government. The allocation function can go to the Finance Commission and project evaluation can be taken care of by strengthening the ministries. Thus, a National Development Commission or Growth Commission, which is charged with a mandate to prepare a blueprint with goals and objectives to be achieved over a defined period, may still be the need of the hour. This document can then be discussed by the National Development Council, a political body.

The Hindu, August 28, 2014.

21

SHANKAR ACHARYA

Ten Myths of Indian Economic Policy

ECONOMIC policy in India, and perhaps in many other countries, is constrained by powerful prevailing myths and prejudices. Sometimes these myths simply reflect lazy thinking or an apparent immunity to facts. Sometimes they are shored up by strong vested interests, sometimes all three. Whatever the reason, it is hard to dispute the potency of myths in economic policy making. Here are my 10 favourites, some old, some new.

Higher minimum support prices (MSPs) for food grains are good for farmers. Not so. Yes, they are good for a powerful minority of farmers who have sizable marketable surpluses and ready access to government procurement programmes. But the majority of Indian farmers (especially poorer marginal farmers) are hurt by higher food prices for the simple reason that they are net buyers of foodgrains. And when you add in tens of millions of landless labourers. It is quite clear that inexorably higher MSPs for wheat and rice are often quite damaging for rural households.

The move to a Goods and Services Tax (GST) will reduce the burden of taxation. I hope not! Or the already massive fiscal deficit will soar higher. The more thoughtful government pronouncements do speak of a reform which is revenue-neutral or even revenue-enhancing. But there are many who tout the illusory prospect of a lower tax burden. The underlying logic of this reform is not tax relief but rather relief from distorted economic incentives and avoidable hassles and uncertainties, which are embedded in the current system of multiple indirect taxes.

There is no role for monetary policy when inflation is driven by supply shortfalls. Not quite. The truth is that the extent and duration of an inflationary bout triggered by a supply shock (such as drought) do depend on the degree of accommodation offered by monetary policy. If liquidity is excessive, the inflationary consequences will be greater; if liquidity is tighter, price increase will be less. Of course, the act of tightening monetary policy can reduce output expansion. Hence, the trade-off between inflation and growth is a live issue even when the initial shock is from the supply-side. And then there is the problem of expectations; if monetary policy stands pat in the face of supply-induced inflation, then inflationary expectations can fuel the fire.

Our labour laws protect labour. Quite the opposite. Present laws over-protect a tiny minority (about 5% of India's 450 million plus labour force, not counting government employees) at the expense of the vast majority of workers. By making it extremely difficult to retrench workers in the organised sector, our present laws massively discourage the employment of new workers in organised enterprises. In effect, our laws are very anti-employment and lead to huge underutilisation and 'casualisation' of our most abundant resource, low-skill labour.

The exchange rate only matters to exporters. This is a common misperception, even among trained economists. Actually, the exchange rate is the single most important price in the economy, which powerfully influences the relative profitability of all tradable goods and services *versus* non-tradables (like haircuts in Delhi or restaurant meals in Mumbai). Thus, an appreciation of the rupee (*versus* foreign currencies) not only makes exports less profitable but also hurts an even greater range of import substitutes, that is goods and services produced for our home market in competition with imports from abroad.

Reducing fiscal deficits hurts growth. In the present 'stimulated' environment, there is much anxiety that a reduction in the current record high fiscal deficits [over 10% of GDP (gross domestic product)] will hurt growth. The massive deficits of 2008-09 and 2009-10 were perhaps justifiable in the face of contractionary effects of the global crisis. But these deficits are neither sustainable nor desirable. Actually, the Indian economy has grown fastest during periods when deficits were being reduced (1992-1997 and 2003-2008) and slower when deficits were expanding (1997-2002). This is because less government borrowing usually facilitates more productive private investment.

Subsidies on food, fuel and electricity mainly help the poor. Not so. The food subsidy mainly helps better-off farmers and consumers in only four or five states where the public distribution system (PDS) has effective coverage. The great majority of India's poor do not have effective access to subsidised food grains. Many studies have shown that the huge subsidies on petrol, diesel, LPG (liquefied petroleum gas) and kerosene mainly accrue to better-off urban households [all those fuel-guzzling cars and SUVs (sports utility vehicles)]. The large state subsidies on electricity for agriculture have helped to thoroughly undermine the development of a viable electricity distribution network and kept our villages in darkness. In contrast, note how the rapid spread of mobile telephony did not need subsidies.

Foreign capital inflows are always good for our economy. Twenty years ago, most Indians believed the opposite that all private foreign capital inflows were bad and somehow designed to impoverish us. In the last two decades, the conventional 'wisdom' has swung to the opposite extreme. In fact, as both the Asian crisis of 1997-98 and the global financial crisis of 2008-09 have amply demonstrated foreign capital inflows into a developing country can be a mixed blessing. Specifically, for India, the capital inflow surge of 2005-2008 posed serious problems of an overly appreciated exchange rate, excess domestic liquidity and an asset price boom. The more thoughtful of our policy makers, including the then Reserve Bank of India (RBI) Governor Y.V. Reddy, grasped the need for capital account management in such situations.

Private provision of infrastructure can effectively substitute for government. Private-public partnerships (PPPs) are the ruling *mantra* of the day. Since the government has failed badly in providing adequate power, roads, ports, water, sanitation and so forth, we must turn to PPPs for our deliverance. Or so runs the new myth. Of course, there is a big and useful part that the private sector can play in building up our infrastructure. But the experience from all over the world suggests that the government must continue to play the major role in this area. In particular, PPPs cannot substitute for effective governance in infrastructure provision. Indeed, there is a growing body of experience which suggests that the governance requirements of PPPs are pretty high, if we are not to fall prey to the rip-offs of crony capitalism.

The trader (or middle man) is at the root of many of our economic problems. This is one of our really hoary and hairy myths. Whenever the rate of inflation rises, governments blame rapacious traders and deploy regulations to control their stocking and other activities. The truth is traders are essential to the efficient functioning of an economy. Commerce is the lifeblood of economic activity. Of course, individual traders exploit whatever monopoly power circumstances grant them to maximise their profits. But the problem does not lie with traders. It rests with the circumstances and policies which nurture national or local monopolies and oligopolies. The best antidote to monopolistic exploitation is competition. And that is best nurtured through better connectivity (transport and communication) and reduction of regulations and levies, which fragment markets and raise barriers to competition, whether from abroad or at home.

Unfortunately, myths have of a life of their own.

Business Standard, January 14, 2010.

Economic Developments in India, Vol. 146.

22

Y.V. REDDY

Financial Globalisation, Growth and Stability

An Indian Perspective

Financial Sector Reforms

In India, reforms to improve efficiency and soundness of the financial sector started early in the reform cycle that commenced in 1991—in some ways anticipating the gains that would accrue from the resultant flexibility in product and factor markets. However, the process of strengthening of the functioning of the financial institutions in terms of prudential framework, operational efficiency and regulatory/supervisory regimes has been gradual. It was also calibrated with the development of money, forex, government securities and equity markets. At the same time, the pace and content of reforms in banking, financial and external sectors are closely aligned with the progress in reforms in the real and fiscal sectors and in the public sector as a whole, considering in particular that the banking sector in India is dominated by the public sector. Our attempts to align the financial sector with the global best practices do take into account progress achieved in public policy in regard to similar alignments in related areas, especially the real sector flexibilities, fiscal health and overall governance standards.

In the Indian context, considerable weight is currently accorded by the Reserve Bank of India (RBI) to price and financial stability while recognising its twin objectives of growth and stability. The large segments of the poor tend to reap the benefits of high growth with a time lag while the rise in prices affects them instantly. Further, we recognise the limited capacity of the poor to bear risks that may occur in the real sector by virtue of developments in the financial sector, in the absence of social security mechanisms and public safety net.

Let me illustrate with two examples of emphasis on stability in relation to financial institutions and financial markets. First, the centrality of the banking sector, especially the retail deposit base and credit disbursement, is maintained while gradually expanding the practice of diversified universal banking. Second, in regard to financial markets, in view of a persisting, though moderating, high combined (i.e., federal and provincial debt together) public debt to GDP ratio of over 70 per cent, coupled with current levels of fiscal deficits, almost the whole of sovereign debt, mostly at fixed interest rates, is denominated in domestic currency and is held almost entirely by residents. A small component is open to foreign institutional investors (FIIs) and multilateral/bilateral agencies. At the same time, the government securities market is well developed and is paving the way for the healthy development of an expanding corporate bond market.

Capital Account Liberalisation

Liberalisation of the capital account has been a gradual process with a distinction being made between households, corporates and financial intermediaries, along with the recognition of a hierarchy of preferences for capital flows. The equity markets are more liberalised, relative to debt markets. Experience has shown that investment in equities, especially in terms of foreign direct investment (FDI), may bring in collateral benefits such as technological and organisational know-how. There is, therefore, considerable openness in regard to equity along with active management of external debt.

While the policy readily recognises the benefits of liberalisation of trade, it constantly weighs the risks and rewards based on both domestic developments and global conditions in regard to management of capital account. Thus, the process of liberalisation of the capital account reckons the pace of concomitant developments in domestic financial sector, fiscal health and flexibilities in the real sector.

Capital Account Management

It is possible to argue that just as 'stabilisation funds' take care of current account shocks, capital account management and market interventions are justifiable to take care of cognisable capital account shocks.

A continued focus on financial market development and its sophistication would, no doubt, mitigate the challenge of capital flows in the medium term. However, it is important to recognise that maturation of financial markets takes time. Hence, sometimes capital flows may have to be managed through other instruments in the short term, while continuing to work on development of the financial markets.

Increase in absorptive capacity of the economy could be a mitigating factor in the context of large inflows. It is not easy, however, to develop absorptive capacity of an economy in the short run and in any case it is very difficult to calibrate the absorptive capacity of an economy to match capital flows if they happen to be volatile. Furthermore, the level of current account deficit (CAD) in respect of emerging market economies that is generally considered as sustainable by the global financial markets may be lower than the sheer volume of capital inflows in these economies.

It is sometimes suggested that encouraging outflows would be a good solution to manage surging inflows. While there is some merit in this approach, liberalising outflows may not be of great help in the short run because a more liberalised regime generally attracts higher inflows. Hence, such a policy has to be combined with other measures which could help to effectively manage the flows.

In implementing a calibrated process of liberalisation of capital account, coterminous with developments in other sectors, there are several issues that are addressed in regard to managing capital flows in the short run. These are: (a) whether the capital flows are judged to be large and lumpy; (b) whether they are assessed to be temporary; (c) the limits to effectiveness of interventions if the exchange rate movements are unidirectional; (d) the desirable extent of sterilisation, considering costs and the available instruments; and (e) above all, the likely impact of the relevant policy stance and procedural measures on the exchange rate expectations. Needless to say, monetary and exchange rate and reserve management are rendered complex in the context of the well known 'trilemma', especially in the current global environment.

Monetary Policy

Monetary policy recognises the growing importance of global factors but the domestic developments play a dominant role. No doubt, the structural transformation underway and the continued significance of public sector in financial sector as well as notable prevalence of administered interest rates make the tasks particularly complex. While there has always been a dual mandate of the RBI, it has, in recent years, successfully articulated a self-imposed tolerance limit of five per cent on headline inflation. The tightening of monetary policy commenced in October 2004 and there have been seven increases of 0.25 per cent in the repo rates till March 2007, to address early signs of possible overheating during the period. To meet the challenges of excess liquidity on account of surge in capital flows, the cash reserve ratio in regard to banking system has been increased in ten instalments since September 2004 till date, aggregating three hundred basis points. Currently, there are acute policy dilemmas arising from global food and energy prices as also from financial market turbulence that need to be factored-in in evolving appropriate policy responses.

Supervision of Banks

In recent years, partly reflecting the buoyant economy, credit growth has been very high, particularly, in select segments and the asset prices have been accelerating. The RBI made it clear that while it does not have a view on the market valuations, it would like to sensitise the banking system to the potential risks of rapid escalation in prices. The actions taken since December 2004 to address these issues include increase in risk weights in respect of housing loans and sensitive sectors *viz.*, commercial real estate and capital market exposure. Further, since November 2005, provisioning requirement for standard advances, except for agriculture and SMEs, was increased, while the increases in respect of sensitive sectors were steeper. Several procedural and suasive measures, and supervisory review processes over select banks were also undertaken to sensitise them in this regard. In particular, the RBI's concerns about credit quality in the expansion phase of credit, the recourse to non-deposit resources to fund their assets, the uncomfortable loan-to-value ratios and excessive reliance on wholesale deposits were repeatedly expressed, and this has been followed up with interactions with select banks, as needed. As a result, overall credit growth as also advances to sensitive sectors have since moderated. The RBI has been urging the banks to also monitor carefully larger unhedged foreign exchange exposures of their corporate clients.

In view of the tendency of some of the banks to utilise non-banking financial companies (NBFC) as conduits to channelise funds leading to regulatory arbitrage and discomfort, limits on both direct and indirect exposures were imposed and transparency in their relationship with banks was insisted. Further, supervisory review process has been undertaken in regard to the few banks that rapidly expanded their off-balance sheet exposures so as to secure supervisory comfort.

As regards complex financial products, the structured credit market is in its infancy. Both mortgage-backed and asset-backed securities are in vogue, but in the light of differing market practices and concerns relating to accounting, valuation and capital adequacy treatment of such products, the RBI issued guidelines on securitisation of standard assets in February 2006. Permitting introduction of credit derivatives, currency futures as well as interest rate futures with modified product design in India are under active consideration and the process of extensive consultations with market participants is underway.

Regulatory Focus on Liquidity

The overall liquidity in the system is actively managed by the RBI mainly through the operation of Liquidity Adjustment Facility on a daily basis in addition to sterilisation through several instruments.

While the RBI has prescribed prudential guidelines for asset liability management by the banks and they have flexibility in devising their own risk management strategies as per Board-approved policies, subject to regulatory limits on mismatches prescribed for short-term time buckets, the RBI has taken steps to mitigate risks at the system level as well.

RBI had, early on, recognised the risks of allowing access to the unsecured overnight market funds to all categories of entities and, therefore, restricted the overnight unsecured market for funds only to banks and primary dealers.

Like other supervisors, the asset liability management guidelines for dealing with overall asset-liability mismatches have been issued by the RBI. Since excessive reliance on call money borrowings by banks could cause systemic problems, prudential limits in relation to net worth have been stipulated on both lending and borrowing in call money market in addition to those on inter-bank liabilities.

The guidelines on securitisation of standard assets have laid down detailed regulations on provision of liquidity support to special purpose vehicles (SPVs). It *inter alia* enables grant of liquidity facility, by the originator or a third party, to help smoothen the timing differences faced by the SPV between the receipt of cash flows from the underlying assets and the payments to be made to investors. The liquidity facility is subject to certain conditions to ensure that the liquidity support was only temporary and gets invoked only to meet cash flow mismatches and for absorbing losses. Any commitment to provide such liquidity facility is to be treated as an off-balance sheet item and attracts 100 per cent credit conversion factor as well as 100 per cent risk weight.

Select Issues

Keeping in view the Indian experience and recent global developments, I will venture to pose some select issues for consideration. First, arguably globalisation had helped to bring down inflationary pressures. An interesting issue would be as to whether globalisation of trade has contributed more to such a process than globalisation of finance or whether it is a combined effect. China's manufacturing industry and to some extent, India's services sector, have admittedly contributed to the downward inflationary pressures while more recent upward pressures on prices of food and fuel do not suggest significant role for finance relative to trade. The impact of extensive use of derivative instruments in respect of commodity trade on oil and food prices is still indeterminate.

Further, as illustrated by China and perhaps India, major contributors to the price moderation so far, consequent upon global integration, have remained relatively less open on capital account and have a moderately integrated financial sector.

Second, the link between open capital account and growth performance is not fully confirmed by the experience of the two largest emerging markets, though such a link is not entirely refuted either. In view of limited experience so far, it is also useful to explore the link between movement in asset prices and financial integration *vis-à-vis* trade integration. In any case, the assumption that a managed capital account generates adverse sentiments in financial market is not fully borne out so far by the two aforesaid examples which experience large capital inflows. This points to the need for assigning greater weight to macro-economic fundamentals than to the state of capital account openness.

Third, recent turbulence in financial markets/institutions and the importance of harmonised and coordinated response of public policies indicate the significance of counter-cyclical fiscal and monetary policies. Is it possible to argue that similar harmonisation between monetary policy and prudential policies would be of some value as part of counter cyclical measures?

Fourth, in regard to regulation and supervision over banks, it is useful to explore whether the special status of banks in the financial system and the need for active coordination among regulators/ supervisors needs to be reaffirmed. Further common persons in most of the societies would like to have a set of institutions where almost total safety of funds is assured and these traditionally are the banks. Hence, if the concept of reasonable expectation in public policies is accepted in regard to banks (as evidenced by the experience with Northern Rock), the pre-eminence of depositors' interests come out prominently. In this light, a reassessment of 'originate-to-distribute' models, off balance sheet items and liquidity requirements of banks may warrant a closer examination in regard to banks. Moreover, the debate on financial innovation and regulation has to be considered in terms of potential and systematic relevance of such innovations besides the capabilities for bringing them effectively under the regulatory umbrella. The extent of relevance of reputational risks in the conduct of the banking business relative to the past may also be worth considering.

Fifth, relative to trade in goods, externalities are more prevalent in regard to financial sector, especially the banking sector. Hence, some regulation is essential and it tends to be national. However, the financial flows are rapid due to modern technology and could be quite substantial, but in view of global scale, it becomes extremely difficult to identify or enforce the rules of origin in regard to financial flows. In this regard, the scope of and limit to global harmonisation of banking regulations in a convincing and enforceable manner may have to be continuously assessed so that the national regulators appropriately build into their regulatory regimes the requisite global requirements and domestic compulsions of reasonable expectation from the common person that ought to govern the public policy.

Sixth, currently there appear to be simultaneous challenges from several angles to the conduct of monetary policy emanating from recent financial turbulence. These relate to abrupt and large shifts in monetary policy measures of the major economies, major realignments in exchange rates within a short period and unprecedented inflationary pressures due to food and energy prices. These warrant significant and innovative ways of cooperation among the central bankers.

Finally, from a purely academic perspective, it may not be out of place to explore the issues concerning international policy coordination including the political economy considerations, in terms of interaction between governments and the financial sector, which may have been influenced by not only by the growing importance of finance but also the cross-border linkages in the financial flows. Recent debates on the Northern Rock, Sovereign Wealth Funds and financial innovations being ahead of regulation are symptomatic of this broader issue. If I recall, Prof McKinnon and Prof Jagdish Bhagwati, among others, had alluded to some of these aspects some years ago.

Remarks made at the International Symposium of the Banque de France on Globalisation, Inflation and Monetary Policy, Paris, March 7, 2008. Available online at *www.rbi.org.in*.

Economic Developments in India, Vol. 124.

23

DUVVURI SUBBARAO

India and the Global Financial Crisis

What Have We Learnt?

BY all accounts the 2008-09 crisis has been the deepest financial crisis of our times. It has taken a devastating toll on global output and welfare. Arguably, the fundamental causes of all financial crises are the same—global imbalances, loose monetary policy and high levels of leverage driven by 'irrational exuberance'. In that respect, this crisis has been no different.

Where this crisis has been different, however, is in its manifestation. Most recent crises had occurred in individual emerging economies or regions, and they were, at their core, traditional retail banking or currency crises. The countries in trouble could be rescued by multilateral interventions; besides, the advanced countries provided a buffer for trade and financial support. In contrast, this crisis originated in the most advanced economy, the United States, and hit at the very core of the global financial system. With virtually no buffers to fall back on, the crisis rapidly engulfed the whole world. Much to their dismay, emerging market economies too were soon pulled into the whirlpool.

How was India Hit by the Crisis?

India was no exception. We too were affected by the crisis. Output growth which averaged 9.5 per cent per annum during the three-year period 2005-2008 dropped to 6.8 per cent in the crisis year of 2008-09. Exports which grew at 25 per cent during 2005-08 decelerated to 12.2 per cent in the crisis year (2008-09) and declined by 2.2 per cent in 2009-10. In the pre-crisis years, we had capital flows far in excess of our current account deficit (CAD). In contrast, during the crisis year, net capital flows were significantly short of the

CAD and this put downward pressure on the rupee. The exchange rate depreciated from ₹ 39.37 per dollar in January 2008 to ₹ 51.23 per dollar in March 2009.

Notwithstanding our sound banking system and relatively robust financial markets, India felt the tremors of the tectonic shocks in the global financial system. The first round effects came through the finance channel by way of sudden stop and then reversal of capital flows consequent upon the global deleveraging process. This jolted our foreign exchange markets as well as our equity markets. Almost simultaneously, our credit markets came under pressure as corporates, finding that their external sources of funding had dried up, turned to domestic bank and non-bank sources for credit.

By far the most contagious route for crisis transmission was the confidence channel. For weeks after the Lehman collapse in mid-September 2008, everyday there was news of yet another storied institution crashing. In this global scenario of uncertainty, the lack of confidence in advanced country markets transmitted as hiccups to our markets too. The net result was that all our financial markets—equity, debt, money and foreign exchange markets—came under varying degrees of pressure. Finally, the transmission of the crisis through the real channel was quite straightforward as the global recession that followed the financial crash resulted in a sharp decline in export demand for our goods and services.

Why was India Hit by the Crisis?

There was dismay in India that we too were affected by the crisis, and this dismay arose mainly on two counts. First, the exposure of our banks to toxic sub-prime assets was marginal and their off balance sheet activities were limited, and so, the argument went, we should not have been affected by a financial sector crisis that originated from these causes. Second, India's growth is driven by domestic demand and a drop in external demand, it was contended, should have caused no more than a small dent in output growth. Yet the crisis hit us, and did so more ferociously than we thought possible. The reason for this is globalisation: India is more integrated into the global system than we tend to acknowledge. Let me illustrate that point with some broadbrush numbers.

India's two-way trade (merchandise exports plus imports), as a proportion of GDP (gross domestic product), more than doubled over the past decade: from 19.6 per cent in 1998-99, the year of the Asian crisis, to 40.7 per cent in 2008-09. Note that global trade declined by 11 per cent in 2009 as a result of the crisis in contrast to a robust average growth of 8.6 per cent during the previous few years 2004-2007. Such a sharp collapse in world trade had an impact on our export demand demonstrating that our trade integration was quite deep.

If our trade integration was deep, our financial integration was even deeper. A measure of financial integration is the ratio of total external transactions (gross current account flows plus gross capital account flows) to GDP. This ratio had more than doubled from 44 per cent in 1998-99 to 112 per cent in 2008-09 evidencing the depth of India's financial integration. In sum, the reason India was affected by the crisis, despite mitigating factors, is its deepened trade and financial integration with the world.

Managing Globalisation

What the experience of the crisis demonstrated clearly was the power of globalisation. Globalisation is a double edged sword; it opens up incredible opportunities but also poses immense challenges. India surely benefited from opening up to the world but had also incurred costs on that count. The challenge for India, and indeed for all emerging market economies (EMEs), is really to minimise the costs and maximise the benefits of globalisation.

Lessons of Crisis

A lot is being written about how this crisis has been too important to waste, how we should learn the lessons of the crisis and apply them in a Schumpeterian creative destruction mode. Some people have, however, questioned the wisdom of drawing lessons even before the crisis is fully behind us. When Zhou Enlai, former Chinese Prime Minister, was asked what he thought of the French

Revolution, he said it was too early to say. Historians who take a long view may agree with Zhou Enlai but practical policy makers do not enjoy that luxury. So, let me use the opportunity of this platform to draw out eight big picture lessons of the crisis.

Lesson 1: In a Globalising World, Decoupling does not Work

The crisis challenged many of our beliefs, and among the casualties is the decoupling hypothesis. The decoupling hypothesis, which was intellectually fashionable before the crisis, held that even if advanced economies went into a downturn, EMEs would not be affected because of their improved macroeconomic management, robust external reserves and healthy banking sectors. Yet the crisis affected all EMEs, admittedly to different extents, bringing into question the validity of the decoupling hypothesis.

Some analysts argue against such an outright dismissal of the decoupling hypothesis and suggest a more nuanced evaluation. Recent IMF research[1] in fact illustrates that the transmission of distress from advanced economies to EMEs took place in three distinct phases. The first phase runs from the time early signs of the crisis appeared in mid-2007 till the Lehman collapse in September 2008. During this period, the growth performance of EMEs outshone that of advanced economies indicating decoupling. The second phase, starting with the Lehman collapse till the first quarter of 2009 was one of 'recoupling' when advanced economies pulled EMEs too into the downturn. The third phase started in the second quarter of 2009 when EMEs started recovering from the crisis ahead of advanced economies suggesting a shift once again to decoupling.

So, have EMEs decoupled from the advanced economies? The answer has necessarily to be nuanced. A useful way to visualise decoupling in the wake of the crisis is to distinguish between 'trend' and 'cycle' decoupling. 'Trend' decoupling is reflected by the widening gap between the trend rates of growth of EMEs and of advanced economies. This is evidently owing to the growing weight of domestic

1. Llaudes, Ricardo, Ferhan Salman and Mali Chivakul (2010). "The Impact of the Great Recession on Emerging Markets", *IMF Working Paper* 237, October.

factors, mainly consumption, in the EMEs' growth process. However, given that there is still significant integration between the two groups of countries, cycles are still coupled. From a 'lessons' perspective, what this means is that EMEs should focus on strengthening domestic drivers of demand and instituting automatic stabilisers to buffer themselves against cyclical shocks from advanced economies.

Lesson 2: Global Imbalances Need to be Redressed for the Sake of Global Stability

No crisis as complex as this has a simple or a single cause. In popular perception, the collapse of Lehman Brothers in mid-September 2008 will remain marked as the trigger of the crisis. At one level that may well be true. Indeed, I can visualise future text books in finance dividing the world into 'before Lehman' and 'after Lehman'. But if we probe deeper, we will learn that at the heart of the crisis were two root causes—the build-up of global imbalances and developments in the financial markets over the last two decades. And received wisdom today is that these two root causes are interconnected, and that financial market developments were in a sense driven by the global imbalances.

Global macro imbalances got built-up because of the large savings and current account surpluses in China and much of Asia in wake of the East Asian Crisis a decade ago. These were mirrored by large increases in leveraged consumption and CADs in the US. In short, Asia produced and America consumed. Between the US consumption boom and the Asian savings glut, there is a raging debate on what was the cause and what was the effect. Regardless, the bottom line is that one was simply the mirror of the other and the two share a symbiotic relationship.

And how did these imbalances build up? The answer lies in globalisation—globalisation of trade, of labour and of finance. The world witnessed a phenomenal expansion in global trade over the last three decades; global trade as a proportion of global GDP increased from 34 per cent in 1980 to 51 per cent in 2007, just before the crisis hit us.[2] Globalisation of finance was even more prolific, especially

2. Calculations based on IMF Direction of Trade Statistics, June 2010.

over the last decade. For the world taken together, the ratio of foreign assets and foreign liabilities to GDP rose from 133 per cent in 1994 to over 300 per cent in 2008.[3] The impact of globalisation of labour was by far more striking. Emerging Asia added nearly three billion to the world's pool of labour as it integrated with the rest of the world over the last two decades thus hugely improving its comparative advantage. Together, the three dimensions of globalisation—trade, finance and labour—helped emerging Asia multiply by a factor its exports to the advanced economies. The result was large and persistent current account surpluses in the Asian economies and corresponding CADs in the importing advanced economies.

The chain of causation from these imbalances to the financial crisis is interesting although not obvious. As Asia accumulated savings and simultaneously maintained competitive exchange rates, the savings turned into central bank reserves. Central banks, in turn, invested these savings not in any large, diversified portfolio but in government bonds of the advanced economies. This in turn drove down risk-free real interest rates to historically low levels triggering phenomenal credit expansion and dropping of the guard on credit standards, erosion of credit quality and search for yield, all of which combined to brew the crisis to its explosive dimensions.

It is argued that if the US Fed had refused to supply the incipient demand for liquidity in the late 1990s and early 2000s, higher interest rates could have prevented the borrowing boom and the follow-on widespread deterioration of financial standards and the subsequent meltdown. But this also would have meant lower growth in the US and the rest of the world. The short point is that even as macroeconomic imbalances should not be allowed to proliferate, it is necessary to balance the need for global economic growth against the disruptions which follow the unwinding of such imbalances.

So, where do we go from here? The G-20 is now actively engaged in the challenging task of redressing structural imbalances in the global economy. At their Pittsburgh Summit in September 2009, the G-20 leaders agreed on a 'Framework for Strong, Sustainable and Balanced

---

3. Calculations based on IMF *Balance of Payments Year Book*, 2010.

Growth' and committed to a 'Mutual Assessment Process' (MAP) which is a peer review of each country's progress towards meeting the shared objectives underlying the framework. Recognising that global imbalances which had narrowed during the crisis started widening again in the exit phase, driven mainly by the uneven recovery around the world, the G-20 resolved that promoting external sustainability should be the focus of the next stage of the MAP and entrusted this task to a Framework Working Group (FWG).

India is privileged in co-chairing, together with Canada, the FWG for managing the task of developing the indicative guidelines for assessing and addressing persistent global imbalances. The FWG has adopted a two-stage approach: a limited number of indicators will guide the initial assessment process, while a broader set—including qualitative ones—will be used in the second stage to inform an in-depth external sustainability assessment. The success of this initiative is critical for redressing the problem of global imbalances.

Lesson 3: Global Problems Require Global Coordination

The crisis demonstrated the interconnectedness of the world through trade, finance and confidence channels. What originated as a bubble in the US housing sector soon snowballed into a crisis and radiated in two different ways—first, in a geographical sense, from the US to other advanced economies and then to the rest of the world, and second, in a sectoral sense, from housing to all productive sectors. Even as each country started dousing the fires on its own, it was soon realised that the effort was in vain and that global coordination is a necessary condition for managing a global crisis.

From that perspective, the London G-20 Summit in April 2009 will go down in history as a clear turning point when the leaders of the world showed extraordinary determination and unity. Sure, there were differences, but they were debated and discussed and compromises were made without eroding the end goal—that is to end the crisis. This resulted in an agreed package of measures having both domestic and international components but all of them to be implemented in coordination, and indeed in synchronisation where necessary. The entire range of crisis response measures—

accommodative monetary stance, fiscal stimulus, debt and deposit guarantees, capital injection, asset purchases, currency swaps—all derived in varying degrees from the G-20 package.

Now, as we exit from the crisis, there are concerns and apprehensions that the vaunted unity that the G-20 had shown during the crisis is dissipating. But might it also be a tad unrealistic to expect the degree of unity shown in managing the crisis to also be shown in addressing 'peace time' issues? The focus of G-20 now is to flesh out the agenda for economic and financial restructuring at national and international levels so that the world can prevent, or at any rate minimise the probability of, another crisis of the type we have gone through. Differences of opinion, when the agenda is so broad, are not only to be expected, but may in fact have a positive influence in determining what is collectively optimal.

The common thread running through the entire G-20 agenda is the need for global cooperation in solving our most pressing problems of today. The crisis has taught us that no country can be an island and that economic and financial disruptions anywhere can cause ripples, if not waves, everywhere. The crisis also taught us that given the deepening integration of countries into the global economic and financial system, uncoordinated responses will lead to worse outcomes for everyone.

The global problems we are facing today are complex and not amenable to easy solutions. Many of them require significant and often painful adjustments at the national level. Because short-term national interests conflict with globally optimal solutions, it is quite understandable that there are differences of views within the G-20. We must remember though that in a world divided by nation-states, there is no natural constituency for the global economy. At the same time, the global crisis has shown that the global economy as an entity is more important than ever and that global coordination to solve global problems is critical.

Lesson 4: Price Stability and Macroeconomic Stability do not Guarantee Financial Stability

The years before the crisis were characterised by steady growth and low and stable inflation in advanced economies and rapid growth and development in EMEs. The so called 'Great Moderation' prompted a growing consensus around the view that the best practice in monetary policy framework is the pursuit of a single target (price stability) by means of a single instrument (short-term policy interest rate). The success of the Great Moderation fortified the argument that price stability is a necessary and (a nearly) sufficient condition for economic growth and for financial stability. Central bankers believed that they had discovered the holy grail.

That sense of triumph was deflated by the unravelling of the crisis. As the global financial sector came to the brink of a collapse even in the midst of a period of extraordinary price stability, it became clear that price stability does not necessarily guarantee financial stability.

Indeed the experience of the crisis has prompted an even stronger assertion—that there is a trade-off between price stability and financial stability, and that the more successful a central bank is with price stability, the more likely it is to imperil financial stability. The argument goes as follows. The extended period of steady growth and low and stable inflation during the Great Moderation lulled central banks into complacency. Only with the benefit of hindsight is it now clear that the prolonged period of price stability blindsided policy makers to the cancer of financial instability growing in the underbelly.

A dominant issue in the wake of the crisis has been the role of central banks in preventing asset price bubbles. The monetary stance of studied indifference to asset price inflation stemmed from the famous Greenspan orthodoxy which can be summarised as follows. First, asset price bubbles are hard to identify on a real time basis, and the fundamental factors that drive asset prices are not directly observable. A central bank should not therefore second guess the market. Second, monetary policy is too blunt an instrument to counteract asset price booms. And third, central banks can 'clean up the mess' after the bubble bursts. The surmise therefore was that the cost-benefit calculus of a more activist monetary stance of 'leaning against the wind' was clearly negative.

The crisis has dented the credibility of the Greenspan orthodoxy. The emerging view post-crisis is that preventing an asset price build up should be within the remit of a central bank. Opinion is divided, however, on whether central banks should prevent asset bubbles through monetary policy action or through regulatory action. On one side, there is a purist view questioning the efficacy of resorting to monetary tightening to check speculative bubbles. Opposed to this is the argument that a necessary condition for speculative excesses is abundant liquidity, and that controlling liquidity which is within the remit of monetary policy should be the first line of defence against 'irrational exuberance'.

No matter how this debate settles, a clear, if also disquieting, lesson of the crisis is that price stability and macroeconomic stability do not guarantee financial stability.

Lesson 5: Microprudential Regulation and Supervision Need to be Supplemented by Macroprudential Oversight

The crisis has clearly demonstrated that a collection of healthy financial institutions does not necessarily make a healthy financial sector. This is because there are complex interconnections in the financial sector across banks, other financial institutions, markets and geographies, and a problem in any part of the system can rapidly transmit through the system, cascade across layers and develop into a crisis. Systemic safety can also be jeopardised by procyclicality. As the crisis demonstrated, there is a strong collective tendency among financial entities to overexpose themselves to the same type of risk during an upturn and become overly risk averse during a downturn. Importantly, individual institutions, and indeed microprudential oversight too, fail to take into account the spillover impact of the actions of the rest of the financial system on them. This raises the paradox of the fallacy of composition. What is good from an individual institution's point of view can become disruptive, and even destructive, if all institutions act in a similar way.

That a bubble that started in the US housing sector snowballed into a major crisis is a vivid illustration of the risks arising from the interconnectedness of the global financial system and the risks of procyclicality. The lesson clearly is that as much as microprudential supervision is necessary, it needs to be supplemented by macroprudential oversight to prevent systemic risk building up.

Macroprudential oversight requires both analytical sophistication and good judgement. Regulators need to be able to analyse the nature and extent of risk and be able to make informed judgement on when and what type of countercyclical buffers they must impose. Both type I and type II errors—imposing buffers too early out of excessive caution or delaying imposition of buffers till it is too late to avert an implosion—can be costly in macroeconomic terms.

Lesson 6: Capital Controls are not only Unavoidable, but Advisable in Certain Circumstances

As EMEs started recovering from the crisis earlier than advanced economies, they also began exiting from the crisis driven accommodative monetary stance ahead of the advanced economies. This multi-speed recovery and the consequent differential exit have triggered speculative capital flows into EMEs resulting in currency appreciation unrelated to economic fundamentals. This poses complex policy management challenges. Currency appreciation erodes export competitiveness. Intervention in the forex market to prevent appreciation entails costs. If the resultant liquidity is left unsterilised, it could potentially fuel inflationary pressures. If the resultant liquidity is sterilised, it puts upward pressure on interest rates which not only hurts competitiveness, but also, in a curious variation of the Dutch disease, encourages further flows.

Capital inflows far in excess of a country's absorptive capacity could pose problems other than currency appreciation. Speculative flows on the lookout for quick returns can potentially lead to asset price build up. Also, in the current juncture, one of the driving forces behind hardening commodity prices in recent months is the excess liquidity in the global system which has possibly triggered financialisation of commodities.

Quite unsurprisingly, the old debate about whether capital controls are a legitimate policy option has resurfaced again. This is a debate that has traditionally frowned on moderation. Critics maintain that capital controls are distortionary, largely ineffective, difficult to implement, easy to evade and that they entail negative externalities. On the other hand, supporters of capital controls argue that controls preserve monetary policy autonomy, save sterilisation costs and tilt the composition of foreign liabilities toward long-term maturities and ensure macroeconomic and financial stability.

The debate on capital controls resurfaced after the Asian crisis of the mid-1990s, especially as one of the root causes of the crisis was the open capital accounts of the East Asian economies. However, as the Asian economies recovered in quick order, regained their export competitiveness and started building up external reserves for self-insurance, the debate was not pursued to its logical conclusion, and the orthodoxy that capital controls are undesirable persisted.

The recent crisis has, however, been a clear turning point in the worldview on capital controls. Notably, the IMF put out a policy note (Ostry *et al.*, 2010) in February 2010 that reversed its long-held orthodoxy that capital controls are inadvisable always and everywhere. The note has referred to certain 'circumstances in which capital controls can be a legitimate component of the policy response to surges in capital flows'. The World Bank (2009) and the *Asian Development Bank Outlook-2010* too echoed these views.

A useful way of assessing the capital account management of an EME is to draw a distinction between 'strategic' and 'tactical' controls. Strategic controls would involve defining a long-term policy indicating the *inter se* preference, or the hierarchy of preferences as it were, across different types of capital flows and the controls that will be deployed to operationalise that policy. Strategic controls give stakeholders a clear and predictable framework of rules to make informed choices and to manage risks, and they give policy makers sufficient levers to calibrate the flows; in essence they define the boundaries of the playing field. Tactical controls, on the other hand, introduce barriers into the playing field itself. They are deployed opportunistically to stem a surge in inflows or outflows. By their very nature, tactical controls introduce a new element of uncertainty into the calculations of both domestic and foreign stakeholders.

India's approach to capital account management is typically strategic. For example, we have an explicitly expressed preference for long-term over short-term flows and equity over debt flows, and we have used both price-based and quantity-based controls to operationalise this policy. We have, of course, periodically recalibrated elements of the strategy in pursuit of capital account liberalisation. An important lesson from India's experience is that even with relatively large swings in capital flows during the crisis, the pressure to use tactical controls did not build up because the strategic controls provided automatic buffers.

Even as we debate what EMEs should or should not do to manage excess capital flows, we should remember that to the extent that lumpy and volatile flows are a spillover from policy choices of advanced economies, managing capital flows should not be treated as an exclusive problem of emerging market economies. How this burden is to be shared raises both intellectual and practical challenges. The intellectual challenge is to build a better understanding of the forces driving capital flows, what type of policy instruments, including capital controls, work and in what situations. The practical challenge is the need to reach a shared understanding on a framework for cross-border spillovers of domestic policies in capital-originating countries, and the gamut of policy responses by capital receiving countries.

Lesson 7: Economics is not Physics

A few months into the crisis, the Queen happened to be at the London School of Economics and asked a perfectly sensible question: 'how come none of the economists saw the crisis coming'. The Queen's question resonated with people around the world who felt that they had been let down by economics and economists. As economists saw their profession discredited and their reputations dented, the economic crisis soon turned into a crisis in economics.

What went wrong with economics? It now seems that by far the most egregious fault of economics, one that led it astray, has been to project it like an exact science. The charge is that economists suffered from 'physics envy' which led them to formulate elegant theories and models—using sophisticated mathematics with impressive quantitative finesse—deluding themselves and the world at large that their models have more exactitude than they actually did.

Admittedly, in a limited sense there may be some parallels between economics and physics. But similarity in a few laws does not mean similarity in the basic nature of the academic discipline. The fundamental difference between physics and economics is that physics deals with the physical universe which is governed by immutable laws, beyond the pale of human behaviour. Economics, in contrast, is a social science whose laws are influenced by human behaviour. Simply put, I cannot change the mass of an electron no matter how I behave but I can change the price of a derivative by my behaviour.

The laws of physics are universal in space and time. The laws of economics are very much a function of the context. Going back to the earlier example, the mass of an electron does not change whether we are in the world of Newton or of Einstein. But in the world of economics, how firms, households and governments behave is altered by the reigning economic ideology of the time. To give another example, there is nothing absolute, for example, about savings being equal to investment or supply equalling demand as maintained by classical economics but there is something absolute about energy lost being equal to energy gained as enunciated by classical physics.

In natural sciences, progress is a two-way street. It can run from empirical findings to theory or the other way round. The famous Michelson-Morley experiment found that the velocity of light is constant led to the theory of relativity—an example of progression from practice to theory. In the reverse direction, the ferocious search now under way for the Higgs Boson—the God particle—which has been predicted by quantum theory is an example of traversing from theory to practice. In economics, on the other hand, where the human dimension is paramount, the progression has necessarily to be one way, from empirical finding to theory. There is a joke that if something works in practice, economists run to see if it works in theory. Actually, I don't see the joke; that is indeed the way it should be.

Karl Popper, by far the most influential philosopher of science of the 20th century, propounded that a good theory is one that gives rise to falsifiable hypotheses. By this measure, Einstein's General Theory was a good theory as it led to the hypothesis about the curvature of space under the force of gravity which indeed was verified by scientists from observations made during a solar eclipse from the West African islands of Sao Tome and Principe. Economics on the other hand cannot stand the scrutiny of the falsifiable hypothesis test since empirical results in economics are a function of the context.

The short point is that economics cannot lay claim to the immutability, universality, precision and exactitude of physics. Take the recent financial crisis. It is not as if no one saw the pressures building up. There were a respectable number of economists who warned of the perilous consequences of the build-up of global imbalances, said that this was simply unsustainable and predicted a currency collapse. In the event, we did have the system imploding but not as a currency collapse but as a melt down of the financial system.

We will be better able to safeguard financial stability both at global and national levels if we remember that economics is a social science and real world outcomes are influenced at a fundamental level by human behaviour.

Lesson 8: Having a Sense of Economic History is Important to Prevent and Resolve Financial Crises

Let me finish with the last lesson which is on a larger canvas—that having a sense of economic history is important to prevent and to resolve financial crises. In their painstakingly researched book, *This Time is Different: Eight Centuries of Financial Folly* (2009), Kenneth Rogoff and Carmen Reinhart argue that every time a crisis occurs and experts are confronted with the question of why they could not, based on past experience, see it coming, they would argue that past experience was no guide as circumstances had changed. Yet this 'this time is different' argument does not hold. Reinhart and Rogoff put forward impressive evidence showing that over 800 years, all financial crises can be traced to the same fundamental causes as if we learnt nothing from one crisis to another. If only teaching in economics had included a study of economic history, perhaps we can avoid repeating history, never mind as a farce or a tragedy.

References

Ostry, Jonathan D., Atish R. Ghosh, Karl Habermeier, Marcos Chamon, Mahvash S. Qureshi and Dennis B.S. Reinhardt (2010). "Capital Inflows: The Role of Controls", *IMF Staff Position Note*, SPN/10/04, February 19.

World Bank (2009). *Global Monitoring Report 2009: A Development Emergency*. Washington DC.

K.R. Narayanan Oration at the South Asia Research Centre of the Australian National University, Canberra, June 23, 2011.

Economic Developments in India, Vol. 163.

24

RAKESH MOHAN

Global Financial Crisis

Causes, Impact, Policy Responses and Lessons

THE intensification of the global financial crisis, following the bankruptcy of Lehman Brothers in September 2008, has made the current economic and financial environment a very difficult time for the world economy, the global financial system and for central banks. The fallout of the current global financial crisis could be an epoch changing one for central banks and financial regulatory systems. It is, therefore, very important that we identify the causes of the current crisis accurately so that we can then find, first, appropriate immediate crisis resolution measures and mechanisms; second, understand the differences among countries on how they are being impacted; and, finally, think of the longer term implications for monetary policy and financial regulatory mechanisms.

A legion of both policy makers and scholars are at work analysing the causes of the crisis and findings both immediate and longer term solutions (for example, the de Larosiere Report, 2009; the Turner Review, 2009; the Geneva Report, 2009; the Group of Thirty Report, 2009; the IMF Lessons paper, 2009b). I can only attempt some conjectures, raise issues and identify some possible directions in which we should move.

What I will attempt to do is to provide my interpretation of the unfolding of the present global financial crisis; how it is affecting us; why the Indian financial sector has been able to weather the crisis relatively well; the analytics of our policy response; and finally, some implications of its longer lasting effects.

Global Financial Crisis

Genesis of Global Financial Crisis

The proximate cause of the current financial turbulence is attributed to the subprime mortgage sector in the US. At a fundamental level, however, the crisis could be ascribed to the persistence of large global imbalances, which, in turn, were the outcome of long periods of excessively loose monetary policy in the major advanced economies during the early part of this decade (Mohan, 2007; Taylor, 2009).

Global imbalances have been manifested through a substantial increase in the current account deficit (CAD) of the US mirrored by the substantial surplus in Asia, particularly in China, and in oil exporting countries in the Middle East and Russia (Lane, 2009). These imbalances in the current account are often seen as the consequence of the relative inflexibility of the currency regimes in China and some other EMEs. According to Portes (2009), global macroeconomic imbalances were the major underlying cause of the crisis. These saving-investment imbalances and consequent huge cross-border financial flows put great stress on the financial intermediation process. The global imbalances interacted with the flaws in financial markets and instruments to generate the specific features of the crisis. Such a view, however, offers only a partial analysis of the recent global economic environment. The role of monetary policy in the major advanced economies, particularly that in the US, over the same time period needs to be analysed for a more balanced analysis.

Following the dot-com bubble burst in the US around the turn of the decade, monetary policy in the US and other advanced economies was eased aggressively. Policy rates in the US reached one per cent in June 2003 and were held around these levels for an extended period (up to June 2004) (Figure 24.1). In the subsequent period, the withdrawal of monetary accommodation was quite gradual. An empirical assessment of the US monetary policy also indicates that the actual policy during the period 2002-2006, especially during 2002-2004, was substantially looser than what a simple Taylor Rule would have required (Figure 24.2). "This was an unusually big deviation from the Taylor Rule. There was no greater or more persistent deviation of actual Fed policy since the turbulent days of the 1970s. So there is clearly evidence that there were monetary excesses during the period leading up to the housing boom" (Taylor, *op.cit.*). Taylor also finds some evidence (though not conclusive) that rate decisions of the European Central Bank (ECB) were also affected

Figure 24.1

Effective Federal Fund Rate in the US

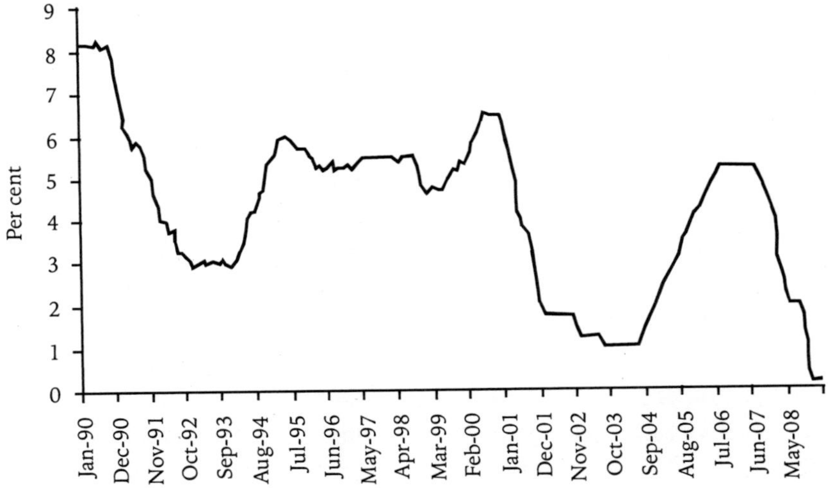

Figure 24.2

Monetary Policy Rates: Deviation from the Taylor Rule

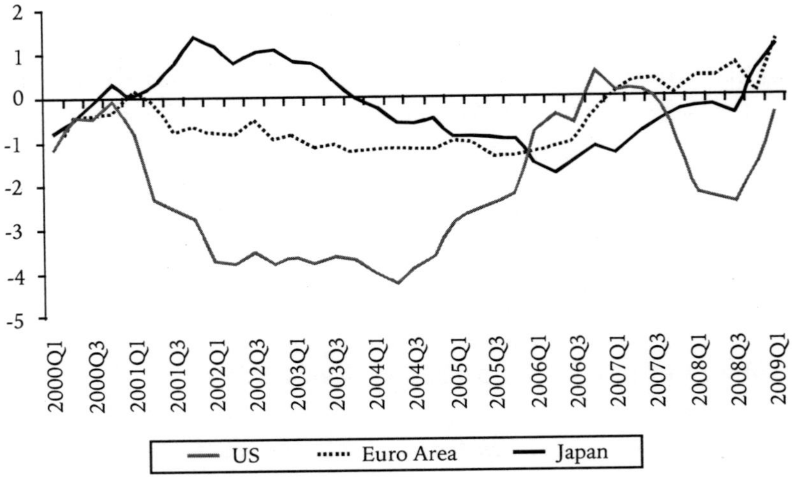

by the US Fed monetary policy decisions, though they did not go as far down the policy rate curve as the US Fed did.

Excessively loose monetary policy in the post dot-com period boosted consumption and investment in the US and, as Taylor argues, it was made with purposeful and careful consideration by monetary policy makers. As might be expected, with such low nominal and real interest rates, asset prices also recorded strong gains, particularly in housing and real estate, providing further impetus to consumption and investment through wealth effects. Thus, aggregate demand consistently exceeded domestic output in the US and, given the macroeconomic identity, this was mirrored in large and growing CADs in the US over the period (Table 24.1). The large domestic demand of the US was met by the rest of the world, especially China and other East Asian economies, which provided goods and services at relatively low costs leading to growing surpluses in these countries. Sustained current account surpluses in some of these emerging market economy (EMEs) also reflected the lessons learnt from the Asian financial crisis. Furthermore, the availability of relatively cheaper goods and services from China and other emerging market economies (EMEs) also helped to maintain price stability in the US and elsewhere, which might have not been possible otherwise. Thus, measured inflation in the advanced economies remained low, contributing to the persistence of accommodative monetary policy.

The emergence of dysfunctional global imbalances is essentially a post-2000 phenomenon and which got accentuated from 2004 onwards. The surpluses of East Asian exporters, particularly China, rose significantly from 2004 onwards, as did those of the oil exporters (Table 24.1). In fact, Taylor (*op.cit.*) argues that the sharp hike in oil and other commodity prices in early 2008 was indeed related to the very sharp policy rate cut in late 2007 after the subprime crisis emerged.

It would be interesting to explore the outcome, had the exchange rate policies in China and other EMEs been more flexible. The availability of low priced consumer goods and services from EMEs was worldwide. Yet, it can be observed that the Euroarea as a whole did not exhibit large CADs throughout the current decade. In fact,

Table 24.1

Current Account Balance

(Per cent to GDP)

Country	*1990-1994*	*1995-1999*	*2000-2004*	*2005*	*2006*	*2007*	*2008*
China	1.4	1.9	2.4	7.2	9.5	11.0	10.0
France	0.0	2.0	1.3	-0.6	-0.6	-1.0	-1.6
Germany	-0.4	-0.8	1.4	5.1	6.1	7.5	6.4
India	-1.3	-1.3	0.5	-1.3	-1.1	-1.0	-2.8
Japan	2.4	2.3	2.9	3.6	3.9	4.8	3.2
Korea	-1.0	1.9	2.1	1.8	0.6	0.6	-0.7
Malaysia	-5.2	1.8	9.8	15.0	16.7	15.4	17.4
Philippines	-4.0	-2.8	-0.7	2.0	4.5	4.9	2.5
Russia	0.9	3.5	11.2	11.0	9.5	5.9	6.1
Saudi Arabia	-11.7	-2.4	10.6	28.7	27.9	25.1	28.9
South Africa	1.2	-1.3	-0.7	-4.0	-6.3	-7.3	-7.4
Switzerland	5.7	8.8	10.8	13.6	14.5	10.1	9.1
Thailand	-6.4	1.0	4.2	-4.3	1.1	5.7	-0.1
Turkey	-0.9	-0.8	-1.6	-4.6	-6.0	-5.8	-5.7
United Arab Emirates	8.3	4.6	9.9	18.0	22.6	16.1	15.8
United Kingdom	-2.1	-1.0	-2.0	-2.6	-3.4	-2.9	-1.7
United States	-1.0	-2.1	-4.5	-5.9	-6.0	-5.3	-4.7
Memo:							
Euroarea	n.a.	0.9@	0.4	0.4	0.3	0.2	-0.7
Middle East	-5.1	1.0	8.4	19.7	21.0	18.2	18.8

Note: (-) indicates deficit.

@: 1997-1999.

Source: International Monetary Fund (2009c). World Economic Outlook Database, April.

it exhibited a surplus except for a minor deficit in 2008. Thus, it is difficult to argue that the US large CAD was caused by China's exchange rate policy. The existence of excess demand for an extended period in the US was more influenced by its own macroeconomic and monetary policies, and may have continued even with more flexible exchange rate policies in China. In the event of a more flexible exchange rate policy in China, the sources of imports for the US would have been some countries other than China. Thus, it is most likely that the US CAD would have been as large as it was—only the surplus counterpart countries might have been somewhat different. The perceived lack of exchange rate flexibility in the Asian EMEs cannot, therefore, fully explain the large and growing CAD in the US. The fact that many continental European countries continue to exhibit surpluses or modest deficits reinforces this point.

Apart from creating large global imbalances, accommodative monetary policy and the existence of very low interest rates for an extended period encouraged the search for yield and relaxation of lending standards. Even as financial imbalances were building up, macroeconomic stability was maintained. Relatively stable growth and low inflation have been witnessed in the major advanced economies since the early 1990s and the period has been dubbed as the Great Moderation. The stable macroeconomic environment encouraged underpricing of risks. Financial innovations, regulatory arbitrage, lending malpractices, excessive use of the originate and distribute model, securitisation of subprime loans and their bundling into AAA tranches on the back of ratings, all combined to result in the observed excessive leverage of financial market entities.

Components of the Crisis

Most of the crises over the past few decades have had their roots in developing and emerging countries, often resulting from abrupt reversals in capital flows, and from loose domestic monetary and fiscal policies. In contrast, the current ongoing global financial crisis has had its roots in the US. The sustained rise in asset prices, particularly house prices, on the back of excessively accommodative monetary policy and lax lending standards during 2002-2006 coupled with financial innovations resulted in a large rise in mortgage credit to households, particularly low credit quality households. Most of these loans were with low margin money and with initial low teaser payments. Due to the 'originate and distribute' model, most of these mortgages had been securitised. In combination with strong growth in complex credit derivatives and the use of credit ratings, the mortgages, inherently subprime, were bundled into a variety of tranches, including AAA tranches, and sold to a range of financial investors.

As inflation started creeping up beginning 2004, the US Federal Reserve started to withdraw monetary accommodation. With interest rates beginning to edge up, mortgage payments also started rising. Tight monetary policy contained aggregate demand and output, depressing housing prices. With low/negligible margin financing, there were greater incentives to default by the subprime borrowers. Defaults by such borrowers led to losses by financial institutions and investors alike. Although the loans were supposedly securitised and sold to the off balance sheet special institutional vehicles (SIVs), the losses were ultimately borne by the banks and the financial institutions wiping off a significant fraction of their capital. The theory and expectation behind the practice of securitisation and use of derivatives was the associated dispersal of risk to those who can best bear them. What happened in practice was that risk was parcelled out increasingly among banks and financial institutions, and got effectively even more concentrated. It is interesting to note that the various stress tests conducted by the major banks and financial institutions prior to the crisis period had revealed that banks were well-capitalised to deal with any shocks. Such stress tests, as it appears, were based on the very benign data of the period of the Great Moderation and did not properly capture and reflect the reality (Haldane, 2009).

The excessive leverage on the part of banks and the financial institutions (among themselves), the opacity of these transactions, the mounting losses and the dwindling net worth of major banks and financial institutions led to a breakdown of trust among banks. Given the growing financial globalisation, banks and financial institutions in other major advanced economies, especially Europe, have also been adversely affected by losses and capital write-offs. Inter-bank money markets nearly froze and this was reflected in very high spreads in money markets. There was aggressive search for safety, which has been mirrored in very low yields on Treasury bills and bonds. These developments were significantly accentuated following the failure of

Lehman Brothers in September 2008 and there was a complete loss of confidence.

The deep and lingering crisis in global financial markets, the extreme level of risk aversion, the mounting losses of banks and financial institutions, the elevated level of commodity prices (until the third quarter of 2008) and their subsequent collapse, and the sharp correction in a range of asset prices, all combined, have suddenly led to a sharp slowdown in growth momentum in the major advanced economies, especially since the Lehman failure. Global growth for 2009, which was seen at a healthy 3.8 per cent in April 2008, is now projected to contract by 1.3 per cent (IMF, 2009c) (Table 24.2). Major advanced economies are in recession and the EMEs—which in the earlier part of 2008 were widely viewed as being decoupled from the major advanced economies—have also been engulfed by the financial crisis-led slowdown. Global trade volume (goods and services) is also expected to contract by 11 per cent during 2009 as against the robust growth of 8.2 per cent during 2006-07. Private capital inflows (net) to the EMEs fell from the peak of US$ 617 billion in 2007 to US$ 109 billion in 2008 and are projected to record net outflows of US$ 190 billion in 2009. The sharp decline in capital flows in 2009 will be mainly on account of outflows under bank lending and portfolio flows. Thus, both the slowdown in external demand and the lack of external financing have dampened growth prospects for the EMEs much more than that was anticipated a year ago.

Volatility in Capital Flows: Implications for Emerging Market Economies

Monetary policy developments in the leading economies not only affect them domestically, but also have a profound impact on the rest of the world through changes in risk premia and search for yield leading to significant switches in capital flows. While the large volatility in the monetary policy in the US, especially since the beginning of this decade, could have been dictated by internal compulsions to maintain employment and price stability, the consequent volatility in capital flows impinges on exchange rate movements and more generally, on the spectrum of asset and

Table 24.2

Global Economic Outlook for 2009

(Per cent)

Indicator	*Month of Forecast*											
	April 2008		*July 2008*		*October 2008*		*November 2008*		*January 2009*		*April 2009*	
	2008	*2009*	*2008*	*2009*	*2008*	*2009*	*2008*	*2009*	*2008*	*2009*	*2008*	*2009*
1. Global Growth	3.7	3.8	4.1	3.9	3.9	3.0	3.4	0.5	3.4	0.5	3.2	-1.3
(a) Advanced Economies	1.3	1.3	1.7	1.4	1.5	0.5	1.0	-2.0	1.0	-2.0	0.9	- 3.8
(b) EMEs	6.7	6.6	6.9	6.7	6.9	6.1	6.3	3.3	6.3	3.3	6.1	1.6
2. World Trade Volume	3.7	3.8	4.1	3.9	3.9	3.0	4.1	-2.8	4.1	-2.8	3.3	-11.0
3. Consumer Price Inflation												
(a) Advanced Economies	2.6	2.0	3.4	2.3	3.6	2.0	3.5	0.3	3.5	0.3	3.4	-0.2
(b) EMEs	7.4	5.7	9.1	7.4	9.4	7.8	9.2	5.8	9.2	5.8	9.3	5.7

Note: @: Volume growth in goods and services.

Source: *World Economic Outlook*, various issues, IMF.

commodity prices. The monetary policy dynamics of the advanced economies thus involve sharp adjustment for the EMEs.

Private capital flows to EMEs have grown rapidly since the 1980s, but with increased volatility over time. Large capital flows to the EMEs can be attributed to a variety of push and pull factors. The pull factors that have led to higher capital flows include strong growth in the EMEs over the past decade, reduction in inflation, macroeconomic stability, opening up of capital accounts and buoyant growth prospects. The major push factor is the stance of monetary policy in the advanced economies. Periods of loose monetary policy and search for yield in the advanced economies encourage large capital inflows to the EMEs and *vice versa* in periods of tighter monetary policy. Thus, swings in monetary policy in the advanced economies lead to cycles and volatility in capital flows to the EMEs. Innovations in information technology (IT) have also contributed to the two-way movement in capital flows to the EMEs. Overall, in response to these factors, capital flows to the EMEs since the early 1980s have grown over time, but with large volatility (Committee on Global Financial System, 2009).

After remaining nearly flat in the second half of the 1980s, private capital flows jumped to an annual average of US$ 124 billion during 1990-1996.[1] With the onset of the Asian financial crisis, total private capital flows fell to an annual average of US$ 86 billion during 1997-2002. Beginning 2003, a period coinciding with the low interest rate regime in the US and major advanced economies and the concomitant search for yield, such flows rose manifold to an annual average of US$ 285 billion during 2003-2007 reaching a peak of US$ 617 billion in 2007 (Figure 24.3). As noted earlier, the EMEs, as a group, are now likely to witness outflows of US$ 190 billion in 2009—the first contraction since 1988. Amongst the major components, while direct investment flows have generally seen a steady increase over the period, portfolio flows as well as other private flows (bank loans, etc.) have exhibited substantial volatility. While direct investment flows largely

1. The data on capital flows are based on World Economic Outlook Database (April 2009) of the IMF (2009c).

reflect the pull factors, portfolio and bank flows reflect both the push and the pull factors. It is also evident that capital account transactions have grown much faster relative to current account transactions, and gross capital flows are a multiple of both net capital flows and current account transactions. Also, large private capital flows have taken place in an environment when major EMEs have been witnessing current account surpluses leading to substantial accumulation of foreign exchange reserves in many of these economies.

Figure 24.3

Capital Flows to Emerging Market Economies

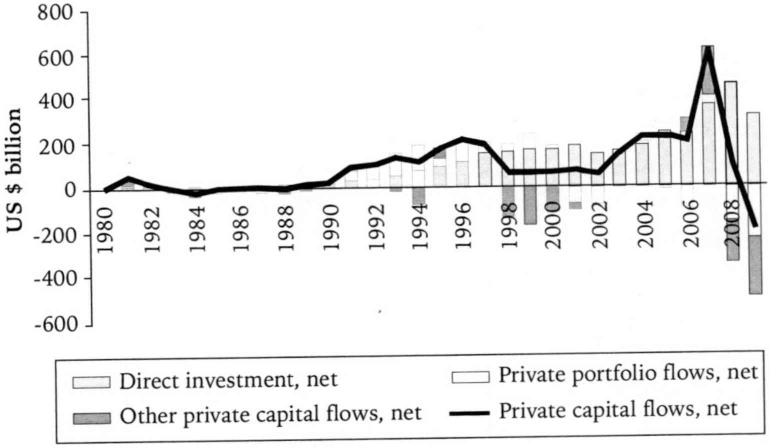

Source: World Economic Outlook Database (April 2009), IMF (2009c).

As noted earlier, the policy interest rates in the US reached extremely low levels during 2002—one per cent—and remained at these levels for an extended period of time, through mid-2004. Low nominal interest rates were also witnessed in other major advanced economies over the same period. The extremely accommodative monetary policy in the advanced economies was mirrored in the strong base money expansion during the period 2001-02—shortly before the beginning of the current episode of strong capital flows to EMEs. As the monetary accommodation was withdrawn in a phased manner, base money growth witnessed correction beginning 2004.

However, contrary to the previous episodes, capital flows to the EMEs continued to be strong. The expected reversal of capital flows from the EMEs was somewhat delayed and finally took place in 2008. Similarly, the previous episode (1993-1996) of heavy capital inflows was also preceded by a significant expansion of base money during 1990-1994, and sharp contraction thereafter. This brief discussion highlights the correlation between monetary policy cycles in the advanced economies on the one hand, and pricing/mispricing of risk and volatility in capital flows on the other hand. At present, monetary policies across the advanced economies have again been aggressively eased and policy interest rates have reached levels even lower than those which were witnessed in 2002. Base money in the US more than doubled over a period of just six months between June and December 2008. Given such a large monetary expansion and given the past experiences, large capital inflows to the EMEs could resume in the foreseeable future, if the unwinding of the current monetary expansion is not made in a timely fashion.

In rapidly growing economies such as India, high real GDP growth needs concomitant growth in monetary aggregates, which also needs expansion of base money. To this extent, the accretion of unsterilised foreign exchange reserves to the central bank's balance sheet is helpful in expanding base money at the required rate. However, net capital flows and accretion to foreign exchange reserves in excess of such requirements necessitate sterilisation and more active monetary and macroeconomic management. Thus, large inflows of capital, well in excess of the current financing needs, can lead to high domestic credit and monetary growth, boom in stock market and other asset prices, and general excess domestic demand leading to macroeconomic and financial instability. Abrupt reversals in capital flows also lead to significant difficulties in monetary and macroeconomic management.

While in principle, capital account liberalisation is expected to benefit the host economy and raise its growth rate, this theoretical conjecture is not supported by the accumulated empirical evidence. Despite an abundance of cross-section, panel and event studies, there is strikingly little convincing documentation of direct positive impacts of financial opening on the economic welfare levels or growth rates of developing countries. There is also little systematic evidence that financial opening raises welfare indirectly by promoting collateral reforms of economic institutions or policies. At the same time, opening the financial account does appear to raise the frequency and severity of economic crises (Obstfeld, 2009). The evidence appears to favour a hierarchy of capital flows. While the liberalisation of equity flows seems to enhance growth prospects, the evidence that the liberalisation of debt flows is beneficial to the EMEs is ambiguous (Henry, 2007; Committee on Global Financial System, 2009).

Reversals of capital flows from the EMEs, as again shown by the current financial crisis, are quick, necessitating a painful adjustment in bank credit and collapse of stock prices. Such reversals also result in the contraction of the central bank's balance sheet, which may be difficult to compensate with accretion of domestic assets as fast as the reserves depletion. These developments can then lead to banking and currency crises, large employment and output losses, and huge fiscal costs. Thus, the boom and bust pattern of capital inflows can, unless managed proactively, result in macroeconomic and financial instability. Hence, the authorities in the EMEs need to watch, closely and continuously, financial and economic developments in the advanced economies on the one hand and actively manage their capital account on the other.

To summarise, excessively accommodative monetary policy for an extended period in the major advanced economies in the post dot-com crash period sowed the seeds of the current global financial and economic crisis. Too low policy interest rates, especially the US, during the period 2002-2004 boosted consumption and asset prices, and resulted in aggregate demand exceeding output, which was manifested in growing global imbalances. Too low short-term rates also encouraged aggressive search for yield, both domestically and globally, encouraged by financial engineering, heavy recourse to securitisation and lax regulation and supervision. The global search for yield was reflected in record high volume of capital flows to the EMEs; since such flows were well in excess of their financing requirements, the excess was recycled back to the advanced economies, leading to depressed long-term interest rates. The Great Moderation over the preceding two decades led to under-pricing of risks and the new financial and economic regime was considered as sustainable. The combined effect of these developments was excessive indebtedness of households, credit booms, asset price booms and excessive leverage in the major advanced economies, but also in EMEs. While forces of globalisation were able to keep goods and services inflation contained for some time, the aggregate demand pressures of the accommodative monetary started getting reflected initially in oil and other commodity prices and finally onto headline inflation. The consequent tightening of monetary policy led to correction in housing prices, encouraged defaults on subprime loans, large losses for banks and financial institutions, sharp increase in risk aversion, complete lack of confidence and trust amongst market participants, substantial deleveraging, and large capital outflows from the EMEs. Financial excesses of the 2002-2006 were, thus, reversed in a disruptive manner and have now led to the severest post-war recession. In brief, the large volatility in monetary policy in the major reserve currency countries contributed to the initial excesses and their subsequent painful correction.

Impact on India

Initial Impact of the Subprime Crisis

The initial impact of the subprime crisis on the Indian economy was rather muted. Indeed, following the cuts in the US Fed Funds rate in August 2007, there was a massive jump in net capital inflows into the country. The Reserve Bank of India (RBI) had to sterilise the liquidity impact of large foreign exchange purchases through a series of increases in the cash reserve ratio and issuances under the Market

Stabilisation Scheme (MSS).[2] With persistent inflationary pressures emanating both from strong domestic demand and elevated global commodity prices, policy rates were also raised. Monetary policy continued with pre-emptive tightening measures up to August 2008.

The direct effect of the subprime crisis on Indian banks/financial sector was almost negligible because of limited exposure to complex derivatives and other prudential policies put in place by the RBI. The relatively lower presence of foreign banks in the Indian banking sector also minimised the direct impact on the domestic economy (Table 24.3). The larger presence of foreign banks can increase the vulnerability of the domestic economy to foreign shocks, as happened in Eastern European and Baltic countries. In view of significant liquidity and capital shocks to the parent foreign bank, it can be forced to scale down its operations in the domestic economy, even as the fundamentals of the domestic economy remain robust. Thus, domestic bank credit supply can shrink during crisis episodes. For instance, in response to the stock and real estate market collapse of early 1990s, Japanese banks pulled back from foreign markets—including the United States—in order to reduce liabilities on their balance sheets and thereby meet capital adequacy ratio requirements. Econometric evidence shows a statistically significant relationship

2. In view of sustained large capital flows, the finite stock of government securities with the RBI and the absence of the option of issuing central bank securities under the RBI Act, a new scheme, MSS, was introduced in April 2004 to manage the large capital flows. Under this scheme, the RBI has been empowered to issue government Treasury Bills and medium duration dated securities exclusively for sterilisation purposes, so as to manage liquidity appropriately. The proceeds collected under MSS auctions are kept in a separate identifiable cash account with the RBI, and are used for redemption and/or buyback of securities issued under the MSS. The payments for interest and discount on MSS securities are not made from the MSS Account, but shown in the government budget transparently. The MSS securities are indistinguishable from normal government Treasury Bills and dated securities in the hands of the holders. The introduction of MSS has succeeded broadly in restoring LAF to its intended function of daily liquidity management (see Mohan, 2006). MSS operates symmetrically as a store of liquidity: it helps to absorb excess liquidity in times of large capital flows and to inject liquidity in periods of reversals in capital flows. Thus, balances under MSS rose from around ₹ 39,000 crore at end-January 2007 to around ₹ 1,75,000 crore by end-May 2008 in the face of large capital flows; in the subsequent period, with reversals in capital flows, MSS balances came down to around ₹ 88,000 crore by end-March 2009 and helped maintain adequate rupee liquidity in the system.

Table 24.3

Share of Banking Assets Held by Foreign Banks with Majority Ownership, 2006

(Per cent)

Country	*0–10*	*Country*	*10–30*	*Country*	*30–50*	*Country*	*50–70*	*Country*	*70–100*
Algeria	9	Moldova	30	Senegal	48	Rwanda	70	Madagascar	100
Nepal	9	Honduras	29	Congo	47	Côte d'Ivoire	66	Mozambique	100
Guatemala	8	Ukraine	28	Uruguay	44	Tanzania	66	Swaziland	100
Thailand	5	Indonesia	28	Panama	42	Ghana	65	Peru	95
India	5	Cambodia	27	Kenya	41	Burkina Faso	65	Hungary	94
Ecuador	5	Argentina	25	Benin	40	Serbia and Montenegro	65	Albania	93
Azerbaijan	5	Brazil	25	Bolivia	38	Cameroon	63	Lithuania	92
Mauritania	5	Kazakhstan	24	Mauritius	37	Romania	60	Croatia	91
Nigeria	5	Pakistan	23	Burundi	36	Niger	59	Bosnia-Herzegovina	90
Turkey	4	Costa Rica	22	Seychelles	36	Mali	57	Mexico	82
Uzbekistan	1	Malawi	22	Lebanon	34	Angola	53	Macedonia	80
Philippines	1	Tunisia	22	Nicaragua	34	Latvia	52	Uganda	80
South Africa	0	Mongolia	22	Chile	32	Jamaica	51	El Salvador	78
China	0	Sudan	20	Venezuela	32	Zimbabwe	51	Zambia	77
Vietnam	0	Morocco	18	Georgia	32	Namibia	50	Botswana	77
Iran	0	Colombia	18	Armenia	31	Kyrgyzstan	75		
Yemen	0	Malaysia	16	Poland	73				
Bangladesh	0	Jordan	14	Bulgaria	72				
Sri Lanka	0	Russia	13	Paraguay	71				
Ethiopia	0	Egypt	12						
Togo	0								

Note: 1. A bank is defined as foreign owned only if 50 per cent or more of its shares in a given year are held directly by foreign nationals. Once foreign ownership is determined, the source country is identified as the country of nationality of the largest foreign shareholder(s). The table does not capture the assets of the foreign banks with minority foreign ownership.

2. World Bank staff estimates based on Bankscope data.

Source: World Bank (2008).

between international bank lending to developing countries and changes in global liquidity conditions, as measured by spreads of interbank interest rates over overnight index swap (OIS) rates and US Treasury bill rates. A 10 basis-point increase in the spread between the London Interbank Offered Rate (LIBOR) and the OIS sustained for a quarter, for example, is predicted to lead to a decline of up to 3 per cent in international bank lending to developing countries (World Bank, 2008).

Impact of Lehman Failure

Balance of Payments: Capital Outflows

There was also no direct impact of the Lehman failure on the domestic financial sector in view of the limited exposure of the Indian banks. However, following the Lehman failure, there was a sudden change in the external environment. As in the case of other major EMEs, there was a sell-off in domestic equity markets by portfolio investors reflecting deleveraging. Consequently, there were large capital outflows by portfolio investors during September-October 2008, with concomitant pressures in the foreign exchange market. While foreign direct investment (FDI) flows exhibited resilience, access to external commercial borrowings and trade credits was rendered somewhat difficult. On the whole, net capital inflows during 2008-09 were substantially lower than in 2007-08 and there was a depletion of reserves (Table 24.4). However, a large part of the reserve loss (US$ 33 billion out of US$ 54 billion) during April-December 2008 reflected valuation losses.

The contraction of capital flows and the sell-off in the domestic market adversely affected both external and domestic financing for the corporate sector. The sharp slowdown in demand in the major advanced economies is also having an adverse impact on our exports and industrial performance. On the positive side, the significant correction in international oil and other commodity prices has alleviated inflationary pressures as measured by wholesale price index (WPI). However, various measures of consumer prices remain at elevated levels on the back of continuing high inflation in food prices.

Table 24.4

Trends in Capital Flows

(US$ billion)

Component	*Period*	*2007-08*	*2008-09*
Foreign Direct Investment to India	April-February	27.6	31.7
FIIs (net)	April-March	20.3	-15.0
External Commercial Borrowings (net)	April-December	17.5	6.0
Short-term Trade Credits (net)	April-December	10.7	0.5
Total Capital Flows (net)	April-December	82.0	15.3
Memo:			
Current Account Balance	April-December	-15.5	-36.5
Valuation Gains (+)/Losses (-) on Foreign Exchange Reserves	April-December	+ 9.0	-33.4
Foreign Exchange Reserves (variation)	April-December	76.1	-53.8
Foreign Exchange Reserves (variation)	April-March	110.5	-57.7

Fiscal Impact

Government finances, which had exhibited a noteworthy correction starting 2002-03, came under renewed pressure in 2008-09 on account of higher expenditure outgoes due to: (i) higher international crude oil prices (up to September 2008) and the incomplete pass-through to domestic prices, (ii) higher fertiliser prices and associated increase in fertiliser prices, (iii) the Sixth Pay Commission award and (iv) debt waiver scheme. The fiscal stimulus packages involving additional expenditures and tax cuts have put further stress on the fisc. Reflecting these factors, the Central government's fiscal deficit more than doubled from 2.7 per cent of GDP in 2007-08 to 6.0 per cent in 2008-09, reaching again the levels seen around the end of the 1990s. The revenue deficit at 4.4 per cent of GDP will be at its previous peak touched during 2001-02 and 2002-03. Primary balance again turned into deficit in 2008-09, after recording surpluses during the preceding two years (Table 24.5). Net market borrowings during 2008-09 almost trebled from the budgeted ₹ 1,13,000 crore to ₹ 3,29,649 in the revised estimates (actual borrowings were ₹ 2,98,536 crore as per RBI records) and are budgeted at ₹ 3,08,647 crore (gross borrowings at ₹ 3,98,552 crore) in 2009-2010.

Table 24.5

Key Fiscal Indicators of the Central Government

(Per cent to GDP)

Year	*Gross Fiscal Deficit*	*Gross Primary Deficit*	*Revenue Deficit*
1	2	3	4
1990-91	7.8	4.1	3.3
1991-92	5.6	1.5	2.5
1992-93	5.3	1.2	2.5
1993-94	7.0	2.7	3.8
1994-95	5.7	1.3	3.1
1995-96	5.1	0.9	2.5
1996-97	4.8	0.5	2.4
1997-98	5.8	1.5	3.0
1998-99	6.5	2.0	3.8
1999-2000	5.4	0.7	3.5
2000-01	5.7	0.9	4.1
2001-02	6.2	1.5	4.4
2002-03	5.9	1.1	4.4
2003-04	4.5	0.0	3.6
2004-05	4.0	0.0	2.5
2005-06	4.1	0.4	2.6
2006-07	3.5	-0.2	1.9
2007-08	2.7	-0.9	1.1
2008-09 RE	6.0	2.5	4.4
2009-10 BE	5.5	1.8	4.0

Note: RE: revised estimates; BE : budget estimates.

1. Negative (-) sign indicates surplus.
2. Oil and fertiliser bonds issued during 2008-09 were 1.8 per cent of GDP.

In view of the renewed fiscal deterioration, the credit rating agency Standard and Poor's has changed its outlook on long-term sovereign credit rating from stable to negative, while reaffirming the 'BBB' rating. If bonds issued to oil and fertiliser companies are taken into account, the various deficit indicators will be even higher. Moreover, in order to boost domestic demand, the government has announced additional tax sops subsequent to the interim vote-on-account budget putting further pressure on fiscal position. Thus, while the slowdown in the domestic economy may call for fiscal stimulus, fiscal manoeuvrability is limited.

According to the IMF, based on measures already taken and current plans, it is estimated that government debt ratios and fiscal deficits, particularly in advanced economies, will increase significantly. For the G-20 as a whole, the general government balance is expected to deteriorate by 3½ per cent of GDP, on average, in 2009. While the fiscal cost for some countries will be large in the short-run, the alternative of providing no fiscal stimulus or financial sector support would be extremely costly in terms of the lost output (IMF, 2009b).

Impact on the Real Economy

Reflecting the slowdown in external demand and the consequences of reversal of capital flows, growth in industrial production decelerated to 2.8 per cent in 2008-09 (April-February) from 8.8 per cent in the corresponding period of 2007-08. On the other hand, services sector activity has held up relatively well in 2008-09 so far (April-December) with growth of 9.7 per cent (10.5% in the corresponding period of 2007-08). Services sector activity was buoyed up by acceleration in 'community, social and personal services' on the back of higher government expenditure. Overall, real GDP growth has slowed to 6.9 per cent in the first three quarters of 2008-09 from 9.0 per cent in the corresponding period of 2007-08. On the expenditure side, growth of private final consumption expenditure decelerated to 6.6 per cent from 8.3 per cent. On the other hand, reflecting the fiscal stimuli and other expenditure measures, growth in government final consumption expenditure accelerated to 13.3 per cent from 2.7 per cent.

Financial Regulatory Policies to Manage Financial Stability: Why the Indian Financial Sector has Weathered the Storm?

As the preceding discussion shows, it is apparent that the Indian banks and financial system had only negligible direct exposure to the type of toxic assets that have contaminated the Western countries' banking system. Bank's credit quality remains of high quality. Although bank credit growth was quite high at around 30 per cent per annum during 2004-2007, it would appear that there was no significant relaxation of lending standards. Bank's loans to individuals for housing have been backed by prudent loan-to-value ratios. However, in view of the rapid credit growth to certain sectors, the RBI had pre-emptively tightened prudential norms (provisioning requirements and risk weights) for these sectors in order to safeguard financial stability; provisioning norms for standard assets were also raised across the board except for agriculture and small and medium enterprises (SMEs). These tightened provisioning norms and risk weights have now been rolled back in the wake of slowdown in order to ensure flow of credit to the productive sectors of the economy. This 'dynamic provisioning' approach has facilitated adequate buffers within the banking system. Such 'dynamic provisioning' is now being advocated as general practice internationally. Therefore, unlike the banking system in the Western world, domestic banks have not recorded losses so far and there has been no need for any government bailout.

Bank balance sheets remain healthy and adequately capitalised. The capital to risk assets ratio (CRAR) of all scheduled commercial banks (SCBs) taken together was 13.0 per cent at end-March 2008, well-above the regulatory requirement of 9.0 per cent. No SCB has CRAR below 9 per cent. Of the 79 SCBs, 77 banks had CRAR above 10 per cent, while 2 banks had CRAR between 9 and 10 per cent. Asset quality of the domestic banks also remains satisfactory with net NPAs being only 1.0 per cent of net advances and 0.6 per cent of assets at end-March 2008 (Table 24.6).

A more rigorous assessment of the health of commercial banks, recently undertaken by the Committee on Financial Sector Assessment (CFSA) (Chairman: Dr Rakesh Mohan) (RBI, 2009), also shows that the commercial banks are robust and resilient. The single-factor stress tests undertaken by the CFSA reveal that the banking system can withstand significant shocks arising from large potential changes in credit quality, interest rate and liquidity conditions. These stress tests for credit, market and liquidity risk show that Indian banks are generally resilient. Given the ongoing financial crisis and its likely impact on the Indian economy, the CFSA conducted stress tests for the end of September 2008. Under the worst-case scenario [150% increase in gross non-performing assest (NPAs)], the overall capital adequacy position of the banking sector would have declined to 10.6 per cent in September 2008—still well-above the regulatory requirement of 9 per cent. Thus, even under the worst case scenario, CRAR remains comfortably above the regulatory minimum.

Table 24.6

Key Indicators of Scheduled Commercial Banks in India

Item	*2004-05*	*2005-06*	*2006-07*	*2007-08*
Capital to Risk-Weighted Assets Ratio (CRAR) (per cent)	12.8	12.3	12.3	13.0
Of which: Tier I CRAR (per cent)	8.4	9.3	8.3	9.1
Net Non-Performing Assets (per cent to net advances)	1.9	1.2	1.0	1.0
Net Non-Performing Assets (per cent to assets)	0.9	0.7	0.6	0.6
Net Profits (per cent to assets)	0.9	0.9	0.9	1.0
Net Interest Margin (per cent to assets)	2.8	2.8	2.6	2.3

Source: Report on Trend and Progress, 2007-08, RBI.

Growth in bank credit remained strong up to October 2008 but has decelerated since. The financial system is working normally and accordingly there has been no need for any enhancement of government guarantee for bank deposits or banks' other liabilities. In view of the strong balance sheets and the transparency in the operations, there is no mistrust between banks and the interbank money market has been working throughout the period normally (Table 24.7). Volumes in the money market have in fact grown over the past few months. There was some volatility in the call money rate, but this resulted from the sudden reversal in capital flows and resulting tightening of liquidity in September-October 2008. Thus, the Indian banking system is displaying none of the distresses that the Western banking system has exhibited since the start of the subprime crisis.

Table 24.7

Activity in Money Market Segments
(Average Daily Volume [One Leg])

(in ₹ crore)

Year/Month	*Call Money*	*Repo Market (Outside RBI)*	*CBLO*	*Total (2+3+4)*
1	2	3	4	5
Year				
2006-07	10,863	8,419	16,195	35,477
2007-08	10,697	13,684	27,813	52,194
2008-09	11,218	14,330	30,776	56,324
Month				
Apr.-08	9,758	14,966	38,828	63,552
May-08	9,740	14,729	36,326	60,795
June-08	10,854	11,262	35,774	57,890
July-08	12,368	8,591	23,669	44,628
Aug.-08	11,704	10,454	22,110	44,268
Sept.-08	11,690	10,654	20,547	42,891
Oct.-08	14,497	9,591	16,818	40,906
Nov.-08	10,906	15,191	24,379	50,476
Dec.-08	10,820	16,943	32,261	60,024
Jan.-09	9,248	18,053	31,794	59,095
Feb.-09	11,121	19,929	38,484	69,534
Mar.-09	11,909	21,593	43,819	77,321

The resilience of the Indian financial sector in the face of the worst global financial crisis since the 1930s can also be attributed to our approach to financial globalisation. The key features of our approach have been reflected in a full, but gradual opening up of the current account but a more calibrated approach towards the opening up of the capital account and the financial sector. As far as the capital account is concerned, whereas foreign investment flows, especially direct investment inflows are encouraged, debt flows in the form of external commercial borrowings are generally subject to ceilings and some end-use restrictions. Macro ceilings have also been stipulated for portfolio investment in government securities and corporate bonds. Capital outflows have also been progressively liberalised. Along with the calibrated approach to opening of the capital account, we have also practised prudential regulation, particularly of banks to manage financial instability.

The financial sector, especially banks, is subject to prudential regulation, with respect to both liquidity and capital. A number of initiatives have been taken by the RBI over the past 5-6 years with a view to mitigating liquidity risks, at the very short end, systemic level and institution level *viz*.: (i) participation in the overnight unsecured overnight money market has been restricted to banks and primary dealers (PDs) and ceilings have been stipulated on their borrowing and lending operations in this market; (ii) prudential limits have been imposed on banks on their inter-bank liabilities in relation to their net worth; (iii) asset-liability management guidelines have been framed that take cognisance of both on and off balance sheet items; and (iv) a detailed policy on the provision of liquidity support to special purchase vehicles (SPVs) has been outlined in the guidelines on securitisation of standard assets.

With the objective of further strengthening capital requirements, the credit conversion factors, risk weights and provisioning requirements for specific off-balance sheet items including derivatives have been reviewed. Furthermore, in India, complex structures like synthetic securitisation have not been permitted so far. Introduction of such products, when found appropriate would be guided by the risk management capabilities of the system.

Detailed guidelines have been issued by the RBI on the implementation of the Basel II framework covering all the three pillars. Minimum CRAR of 9 per cent has been prescribed. Banks have been advised to bring Tier I CRAR to a minimum of 6 per cent before end-March 2010. All foreign banks operating in India and

Indian banks having a presence outside India migrated to Basel II by March 31, 2008 and all other SCBs have migrated to Basel II by March 31, 2009.

Apart from normal prudential requirements on banks, additional prudential measures in respect of exposures to specific sectors, such as real estate, housing loans to individuals and consumer credit, have been successively imposed, on the lines of dynamic provisioning. Furthermore, the regulation and supervision of non-banking finance companies (NBFCs) was tightened by reducing regulatory arbitrage *vis-à-vis* the banking sector. The regulatory requirements are also higher in the case of deposit-taking NBFCs *vis-à-vis* the non-deposit-taking ones which has helped to contain leverage in this sector.

Thus, a number of prudential measures were put in place incrementally over the past five years in order to maintain stability in the Indian financial system and these measures in conjunction with the overall cautious approach to financial and external sector liberalisation have contributed to domestic macroeconomic and financial stability.

Our Response to the Unfolding Impact of the Crisis

As noted earlier, the main impact over the past few months, especially following the collapse of Lehman Brothers in September 2008, has been the outcome of the reduction in net capital inflows and the significant correction in the domestic stock markets on the back of sell-off in the equity market by foreign institutional investors (FIIs). The reduced foreign funding and the lacklustre domestic capital market had put pressures on some segments of the financial system, such as NBFCs and mutual funds. A substantial proportion of collections of mutual funds reflected bulk funds from the corporate sector under the money market schemes, partly reflecting tax and other regulatory arbitrage. As alternative sources of funding dried up and also due to the substantial correction in stock prices, there were large redemption pressures on mutual funds. While the mutual funds promised immediate redemption, there assets were relatively illiquid. Maturity mismatches between assets and liabilities of mutual funds further aggravated the problems. Drying up of funds with mutual funds, which in turn were provider of funds to other sectors, further accentuated the flow of funds. Consequently, all the pressure for fund availability came to rest on banks: from the corporate sector unable to get external funds or equity, from NBFCs and from mutual funds; and the perception of a credit crunch emerged.

Reserve Bank's Policy Response: Analytics

In view of the lower level of capital inflows, there were some pressures in the foreign exchange market. Consistent with its policy objective of maintaining orderly conditions in the foreign exchange market, the RBI sold foreign exchange in the market. While foreign exchange sales attenuated the mismatch in the foreign exchange market, these operations drained liquidity from the rupee market and accentuated pressures on the rupee liquidity. Accordingly, the RBI has been proactively managing liquidity since mid-September 2008 to assuage the liquidity pressures through a variety of measures. The cash reserve ratio (CRR) was reduced from 9 per cent (September 2008) to 5 per cent by early January 2009 injecting nearly ₹ 1,60,000 crore of primary liquidity in the system. Fresh issuances under MSS were stopped and buyback of existing MSS securities was also resorted to inject liquidity into the system. Buybacks were timed with government market borrowing programme. Following the amendment to the Memorandum of Agreement on the MSS, ₹ 12,000 crore was transferred to the government cash account from the MSS cash account. Reflecting the various operations, MSS balances declined from ₹ 1,75,362 crore at end-May 2008 to around ₹ 88,000 crore by end-March 2009. Other measures taken by the RBI in response to the global financial crisis include cut in the statutory liquidity ratio (SLR), opening of new refinancing windows, refinance to SIDBI and EXIM Banks, and clawing back of prudential norms in regard to provisioning and risk weights. The measures to improve forex liquidity included increase in interest rate ceilings on non-resident deposits, and easing of restrictions on external commercial borrowings and on short-term trade credits.

Simultaneously, in view of the adverse impact of the global slowdown on the domestic economy, policy rates were also cut—the reverse repo rate by 425 basis points from 9.00 per cent to 4.75 per cent and the reverse repo rate by 275 basis points from 6.00 per cent to 3.25 per cent. However, it may be noted that, at present, the reverse repo rate (the lower band of the liquidity adjustment facility (LAF) corridor) is the operational policy rate, whereas, in the period prior to mid-September 2008, the repo rate (the upper band of the LAF corridor) was the operational policy rate. The effective policy rate has, thus, seen a larger cut of 575 basis points from 9.00 per cent in mid-September 2008 to 3.25 per cent now. This is mirrored in the money market interest rates [weighted average of call, market repo and collateralised borrowing and lending obligation (CBLO)] falling from 9.3 per cent in September 2008 to 3.8 per cent in March 2009 (2.8% as on April 22, 2009).

While in 2007 and previous years, large capital flows and their absorption by the RBI led to excessive liquidity, which was absorbed through sterilisation operations involving LAF, MSS and CRR. During 2008, in view of reversal in some components of capital flows, fresh MSS issuances were initially scaled down and then reversed. The MSS operates symmetrically and acts as a store of liquidity and hence, has the flexibility to smoothen liquidity in the banking system both during episodes of capital inflows and outflows. The existing set of monetary instruments has, thus, provided adequate flexibility to manage the evolving situation. In view of this flexibility, unlike central banks in major advanced economies, the RBI did not have to dilute the collateral requirements to inject liquidity. LAF repo operations can, however, be limited by the excess SLR securities held by banks.

Furthermore, in view of the large government market borrowing programme, the RBI has been conducting purchases of government securities under its open market operations (OMO) as warranted by the evolving monetary and financial market conditions. On March 26, 2009, the RBI announced a calendar for OMOs for the first half (April-September 2009) of the fiscal year. Taking into account the expected unwinding of MSS securities of ₹ 42,000 crore during April-September 2009 and other factors in view, the RBI announced that it intended to purchase government securities of ₹ 80,000 crore under OMOs during the first half. The OMO calendar and amounts are indicative and the RBI will have the flexibility to make changes in the amount of OMO depending on the evolving liquidity conditions and its other operations. These actions reflect the need for close coordination between government debt management and monetary policy operations. This can be done smoothly in our case since the RBI also acts as the debt manager for the government.

Analytically, the various policy actions by the RBI since mid-September 2008 have been aimed at offsetting the contraction caused to its balance sheet due to fall in its foreign assets. Policy initiatives have aimed at expanding domestic assets on the RBI's balance sheet through open market operations, scaling back of MSS, refinance facilities, regular operations under LAF and special market operations for oil bonds. The central bank balance sheet is the ultimate source of money and credit creation and expansion in the economy. It is therefore important that the central bank balance sheet and the monetary base/reserve money continue to expand so as to meet the normal monetary requirements of a growing economy consistent with price stability. The reduction in CRR is expected to increase the money multiplier. The various monetary and liquidity measures, taken together, have released actual/potential liquidity amounting to over ₹ 4,90,000 crore since mid-September 2008 (about 9% of GDP) (Table 24.8). In brief, the proactive policy initiatives to avoid contraction of the RBI balance sheet coupled with the increase in the money multiplier are aimed at ensuring non-inflationary growth of money supply in the economy to support the needs of the real economy. Despite large capital outflows and the concomitant sales of foreign exchange by the RBI and the depletion of its assets side, the RBI was able to substitute them with equivalent domestic assets so as to stabilise the growth of reserve money. Year-on-year growth in reserve money (adjusted for changes in the CRR) was 19.0 per cent at end-March 2009 as compared with 25.3 per cent in the previous year. Reserve money expansion, thus, remains consistent with the growth requirements of the Indian economy and long-run trends. In contrast to the trends in major advanced economies (discussed next), there has been no excessive expansion of reserve money. Hence, the issue of unwinding and exit of the current excessively accommodative monetary and liquidity policies, which is of extreme concern in the major advanced economies, is not relevant for us in view of the consistent growth in reserve money.

Table 24.8

Actual/Potential Release of Primary Liquidity (Since Mid-September 2008)

(₹ crore)

Measure/Facility	*Amount*
Monetary Policy Operations (1 to 3)	
1. Cash Reserve Ratio (CRR) Reduction	1,60,000
2. Open Market Operations	68,835
3. MSS Unwinding/De-sequestering	97,781
Extension of Liquidity Facilities (4 to 8)	
4. Term Repo Facility	60,000
5. Increase in Export Credit Refinance	25,512
6. Special Refinance Facility for SCBs (Non-RRB)	38,500
7. Refinance Facility for SIDBI/NHB/EXIM Bank	16,000
8. Liquidity Facility for NBFCs through SPV	25,000
Total (1 to 8)	4,91,628
Memo:	
Statutory Liquidity Ratio (SLR) Reduction	40,000

Monetary Aggregates in Major Advanced Economies: Recent Trends

In this regard, the recent behaviour of US monetary aggregates is interesting. With interest rates approaching near zero levels, the US Federal Reserve has resorted to aggressive quantitative easing as reflected in its expansion of balance sheet. In view of the continuing strains in the US financial markets, the Fed's major policy tools—lending to financial institutions, providing liquidity directly to key credit markets and buying longer-term securities—represent a use of the asset side of the Fed's balance sheet, that is, they all involve lending or the purchase of securities. According to the Federal Reserve, these policies provide it the flexibility to continue to push down interest rates and ease credit conditions in a range of markets, despite the fact that the federal funds rate is close to its zero lower bound. The Fed prefers to dub this approach as 'credit easing'—rather than terming it as 'quantitative easing', the policy approach used by the Bank of Japan from 2001 to 2006. While both approaches involve an expansion of the central bank's balance sheet, in a pure quantitative easing regime, the focus of policy is the quantity of bank reserves (liabilities of the central bank); the composition of loans and securities on the asset side of the central bank's balance sheet is incidental. In contrast, the Federal Reserve's credit easing approach focuses on the mix of loans and securities that it holds and on how this composition of assets affects credit conditions for households and businesses (Bernanke, 2009). The Bank of England is also now doing similar quantitative easing.

Reflecting the massive liquidity injection operations, monetary base in the US almost doubled between June 2008 and December 2008. Over the same six-month period, money supply (M2) and bank credit increased by only 6 per cent. M2 money multiplier correspondingly fell from 8.8 to 4.9 over the same period. Thus, even as the Fed expanded its balance sheet significantly, money supply and bank credit appeared to maintain their normal growth. This can be attributed to the fact that banks, rather than employing such additional liquidity pumped by the Federal Reserve into the system, have preferred to keep these funds as excess reserves with the Fed itself. Banks' deposits with the Federal Reserve jumped from around US$ 90 billion to US$ 839 billion between June and December 2008. Thus, all the efforts of the Fed to accelerate the pace of credit and monetary aggregates in the US economy have been largely offset by the increased holdings of commercial bank deposits with the Fed. As noted earlier, the strong growth in monetary base holds the potential to increase capital flows to the EMEs with lags. Since December 2008, there has been some moderation in the expansion of monetary base and pick-up in money supply growth (Table 24.9).

Table 24.9

Recent Behaviour of Monetary Aggregates in the US

(US$ billion)

	Dec.07	Mar.-08	Jun.-08	Sep.-08	Dec.-08	Feb.-09
1. Monetary Base	847	861	863	936	1669	1587
Of which:						
Bank Reserves	92	97	94	160	839	758
2. M1						
3. M2	7415	7599	7648	7782	8124	8238
4. Bank Credit	9206	9495	9403	9573	9975	9824
5. M2 Money Multiplier	8.7	8.8	8.9	8.3	4.9	5.2
Memo:	Year-on-Year Growth (%)					
Monetary Base	1.2	1.5	1.4	9.9	97.0	85.2
M2	5.6	6.9	6.1	6.3	9.6	9.3

Source: Monetary Trends (April 2009) and FRED database, Federal Reserve of St. Louis.

Credit Growth in India: Perceptions and Reality

In view of the changed environment due to capital outflows and risk aversion, there was a substantial shrinking of non-bank sources of funding in India—such as domestic capital markets, funding from NBFCs and mutual funds and external funding in the form of commercial borrowings and America Depository Receipt/Global Depository Receipt (ADRs/GDRs) (Table 24.10). Accordingly, there was a sudden rush for bank credit from the various sectors of the economy and there were perceptions of credit crunch. Moreover, in view of incomplete pass-through to domestic petroleum prices in the first half of 2008-09 (before the sharp correction in international crude oil prices), there was a large demand from petroleum companies for bank credit. For almost similar reasons, fertiliser companies also had a large resort to bank credit. Reflecting these factors, growth in non-food bank credit (y-o-y) accelerated to around 30 per cent by October 2008. Nonetheless, there was a perception that there was credit crunch during this period, which could be attributed to a large decline in non-bank sources of funding. The slowdown of the manufacturing sector and a temporary build-up in inventories as well as liquidity problems faced by mutual funds and NBFCs during this period added to an increased demand for bank credit. At the same time, there might have been an increase in precautionary demand for bank credit in the last quarter of 2008 in view of the heightened uncertainties. The cumulative impact of all these demand pressures was reflected in acceleration of non-food bank credit from around 25-26 per cent in the quarter July-September 2008 to around 30 per cent in October 2008. Accordingly, a number of steps were taken by the RBI to make available adequate rupee and forex liquidity and to ensure adequate flow of credit.

Table 24.10

Flow of Resources to the Commercial Sector

(*₹ crore*)

Item	*2007-08*	*2008-09*
1	*2*	*3*
A. Adjusted Non-Food Bank Credit Commercial Banks (1+2)	4,44,807	4,14,902
1. Non-Food Credit	4,32,846	4,06,287
2. Non-SLR Investments	11,961	8,615
B. Flow from Other Major Sources (3+4)	3,35,698	2,64,138
3. Domestic Sources	1,72,338	1,50,604
4. Foreign Sources	1,63,360	1,13,534
C. Total Credit (A+B)	7,80,505	6,79,040

Note: Data are provisional.

Source: RBI (2009b).

Non-food bank credit growth has, however, moderated from the peak of around 30 per cent in October 2008 to around 18 per cent by end-March 2009. This could be attributed to both demand and supply factors. The demand-side factors include the significant moderation in industrial activity over the past few months, the substantial correction in international commodity and raw material prices and the still elevated bank lending rates. On the supply side, some risk-aversion on the part of the banks could have reduced the availability of bank credit. The cumulative impact of deceleration in bank credit, relatively strong deposit growth and various measures by the RBI to increase liquidity is mirrored in the RBI's LAF operations—switch from an average net repo (injection) of around ₹ 45,600 crore in September 2008 to an average net reverse repo (absorption) of around ₹ 43,000 crore during January-March 2008.

Stickiness in Bank Deposit and Lending Rates

While the policy rates have been substantially eased since early October 2008, some rigidity has been observed in banks' deposit and lending rates. Banks deposit and lending rates continue to be high albeit some easing has been witnessed in the past few months. This rigidity could be attributed to a variety of factors. First, while headline inflation in terms of wholesale price index has seen a significant easing over the past few months (from around 12% in September 2008 to 0.3% by end-March 2009), it is largely due to the substantial decline in international crude oil prices and some reduction in domestic prices of administered oil products. Food articles inflation in the WPI continues to remain at high levels (6%). Reflecting high food inflation, various measures of consumer price inflation—which have a relatively higher weight for food items *vis-à-vis* WPI—also remain at elevated levels (around 10-11%). Second, the interest rate on small savings continues to be administered and any reduction in interest rates on bank deposits can make bank deposits relatively unattractive, which could lead to some deceleration of growth in bank deposits. Third, the bulk of banks' time deposits continue to be at fixed interest rates. While interest rates on incremental time deposits are coming down, the average cost of deposits will remain high till the maturing deposits get renewed. This, in turn, constrains an immediate substantial reduction in lending rates. Thus, for a variety of factors, bank lending rates are expected to exhibit only a gradual softening, which impedes monetary transmission.

Tables 24.11

Measures of Inflation in India

(Per cent)

	March 2008	*June 2008*	*September 2008*	*December 2008*	*March 2009*
Wholesale Price Inflation					
All Commodities	7.8	12.0	12.1	5.9	0.3
Of which:					
Primary Articles	9.7	11.0	12.0	11.6	3.5
Fuel	6.8	16.3	16.5	-0.7	-6.1
Manufactured Products	7.3	10.9	10.5	6.2	1.4
Consumer Price Inflation					
Agricultural Labourers	7.9	8.8	11.0	11.4	10.8 (Feb.)
Rural Labourers	7.6	8.7	11.0	11.4	10.8 (Feb.)
Urban Non-Manual Employees	6.0	7.3	9.5	9.8	9.9 (Feb.)
Industrial Workers	7.9	7.7	9.8	9.7	9.6 (Feb.)

Conclusions and Lessons

The global financial crisis can be largely attributed to extended periods of excessively loose monetary policy in the US over the period 2002-2004. Very low interest rates during this period encouraged an aggressive search for yield and a substantial compression of risk-premia globally. Abundant liquidity in the advanced economies generated by the loose monetary policy found its way in the form of large capital flows to the EMEs. All these factors boosted asset and commodity prices, including oil, across the spectrum providing a boost to consumption and investment. Global imbalances were a manifestation of such an accommodative monetary policy and the concomitant boost in aggregate demand in the US outstripping domestic aggregate supply in the US. This period coincided with lax lending standards, inappropriate use of derivatives, credit ratings and financial engineering, and excessive leverage. As inflation began to edge up reaching the highest levels since the 1970s, this necessitated monetary policy tightening. The housing prices started to witness some correction. Lax lending standards, excessive leverage and weaknesses of banks' risk models/stress testing were exposed and bank losses mounted wiping off capital of major financial institutions. The ongoing deleveraging in the advanced economies and the plunging consumer and business confidence have led to recession in the major advanced economies and large outflows of capital from the EMEs; both of these channels are now slowing down growth in the EMEs.

Monetary Policy and Asset Prices

The conventional wisdom is that, even if the monetary authority can *ex ante* identify an asset bubble, the typical monetary policy actions—changes of 25 or 50 basis points—would be insufficient to stop the bubble. It has been argued that only substantial hikes in policy rates could prick the bubble but this would be at a substantial cost to the real economy. The influence of interest rates on the speculative component of asset prices is unclear from both a theoretical and empirical perspective (Kohn, 2008). In the context of the current global financial crisis, with deleterious impact on growth and employment and significant fiscal costs, the issue of relationship between monetary policy and asset prices needs to be revisited. It can be argued that the output losses of a preemptive monetary action might have been lower than the costs that have materialised from a non-responsive monetary policy. At least, a tighter monetary policy could have thrown sand in the wheels and could have reduced the amplitude of asset price movements. As asset prices bubbles are typically associated with strong growth in bank credit to certain sectors such as real estate and stock markets, preemptive monetary actions could be reinforced by raising risk weights and provisioning norms for sectors witnessing very high credit growth. For both monetary and regulatory actions to be taken in tandem, it is important that both the functions rest with the central banks. In this context, the recent trend of bifurcation of monetary policy responsibility from regulatory responsibility appears to be unhelpful (Mohan, 2006b). On balance, it appears that preemptive and calibrated monetary and regulatory measures would be better than an inertial monetary policy response. Such an approach can help in mitigating the amplitude of the bubble in both the upswing and the downswing of the cycle and contribute to both macroeconomic and financial stability. This view seems to be gaining ground. As the IMF in its recent assessment notes: "Central banks should adopt a broader macroprudential view, taking into account in their decisions asset price movements, credit booms, leverage, and the build up of systemic risk. The timing and nature of pre-emptive policy responses to large imbalances and large capital flows needs to be re-examined" (IMF, 2009b).

It thus appears that the sharp swings in monetary policy, especially periods of prolonged accommodation, in the advanced economies are the underlying causes of the ongoing global financial crisis. While until recently, the Great Moderation since the early 1990s—reduction in inflation and reduction in growth volatility—had been attributed, in part, to the rule-based monetary policy, it now appears that volatility in monetary policy can also have the side-effect of creating too much volatility in financial markets and financial prices, which can then potentially feed into the real economy with dangerous consequences, as indicated by the ongoing global financial crisis.

Management of Capital Flows by EMEs

Large volatility in capital flows to EMEs has been a recurrent feature of the global economic landscape since the early 1980s. Periods of large capital inflows, well above the financing need, have been followed by a sudden drying up of capital flows. Such large swings in capital flows over a very short period of time impose significant adjustment costs and large output and employment losses on the EMEs. As is well-known, capital flows reflect both push and pull factors. The push factors are critically dependent upon the stance of monetary policy in the advanced economies, a factor over which domestic authorities have no control. In view of these factors, it would be better for the EMEs to manage their capital account. Contrary to the theoretical expectation, empirical evidence does not find any support that free capital movement leads to higher economic growth. While benefits from external debt flows remain unproven, equity flows, especially FDI, are found to be beneficial. This suggests a relatively liberal regime for direct investment flows. Progress in the liberalisation of debt flows, especially short-term debt flows, by EMEs would depend upon greater macroeconomic stability, convergence of inflation levels and development of financial markets.

Issues in Financial Regulation

Finally, the current global financial crisis has again shown that markets can fail and such market failures have huge costs. The financial system is prone to excesses, given the high leverage of banks and other financial institutions. Within the financial system, banks are 'special', whether locally or foreign-owned, because they effectively act as trustees of public funds through their deposit taking activities and are the lynchpins of the payment systems. The speed with which a bank under a run collapses is incomparable with any other organisation. A failure of one bank can have a strong contagion on the rest of the banks, even if they are healthy. In this age of globalisation, as the current crisis has revealed, the lack of confidence in banks in one country can also have a contagion on banks in the rest of the world. It is because of this that many governments in EMEs had to guarantee the deposits in their banking systems during the later part of 2008. Given the risks to financial stability, governments in advanced economies had to bail out their largest banks and financial institutions. The notion that markets will take care of weaknesses has once again been proven wrong. So far, the focus of banking regulation globally has been on capital adequacy. As this crisis has shown, liquidity issues are equally important and it is appropriate to note that, in India, we have focused our attention on these issues as well. Given the complex inter-linkages between banks and non-banks and the move towards conglomerates, it is important that regulatory arbitrage loopholes are fixed to avoid regulatory arbitrage. It is in this context that we have tightened the regulatory regime in regard to NBFCs over the past few years in a phased manner. It is, therefore, important that banks and other financial sector players are well-regulated, while permitting them the necessary flexibility to grow and expand and meet the financing needs of a growing economy. A host of other issues such as accounting, auditing and compensation have also received attention in the aftermath of the global financial crisis. All these issues are engaging the active attention of policy makers and academia alike around the world (G-20, 2009). In view of the fast pace of technological and financial innovations, regulatory authorities would have to follow an approach that would have to be dynamic and adjust in response to the changing economic environment.

References

Bernanke, Ben (2009). "The Crisis and the Policy Response", Stamp Lecture at London School of Economics, January 13. Available at *http://www.federalreserve.gov/newsevents/speech/bernanke20090 113a.htm*

Committee on Global Financial System (2009). *Report of the Working Group on Capital flows to Emerging Market Economies* (Chairman: Rakesh Mohan). Basel: Bank for International Settlements.

Federal Reserve Bank of St. Louis (2009). *Monetary Trends*. April.

Group of Thirty (2009). "Financial Reform: A Framework for Financial Stability" (Chairman: Paul A. Volcker). Washington DC.

Geneva Report (2009). "The Fundamental Principles of Financial Regulation", *Geneva Reports on the World Economy* 11 (by Markus Brunnermeier, Andrew Crocket, Charles Goodhart, Avinash D. Persaud and Hyun Shin).

G-20 (2009). "Working Group on Enhancing Sound Regulation and Strengthening Transparency" (Co-Chairs: Tiff Macklem and Rakesh Mohan).

Haldane, Andrew (2009). *Why Banks Failed the Stress Test*?. Bank of England.

Henry, Peter Blair (2007). "Capital Account Liberalisation: Theory, Evidence, and Speculation", *Journal of Economic Literature* XLV, December.

International Monetary Fund (2009a). "Group of Twenty: Note by the Staff of International Monetary Fund", January.

———. (2009b). "Initial Lessons of the Crisis", February.

———. (2009c). *World Economic Outlook* Database, April.

Kohn, Donald (2008). "Monetary Policy and Asset Prices Revisited", Remarks at the Cato Institute's 26th Annual Monetary Policy Conference, November 19. Available at *http://www.federalreserve.gov/newsevents/speech/kohn20081119a.htm.*

Lane, Philip (2009). "Global Imbalances and Global Governance", Paper presented at the *Global Economic Governance: Systemic Challenges, Institutional Responses and the Role of the New Actors*. Brussels. February.

de Larosiere Report (2009). "Report of the High-Level Group on Financial Supervision in the EU" (Chairman: Jacques de Larosiere). Brussels.

Mohan, Rakesh (2006a). "Coping with Liquidity Management in India: A Practitioner's View", *Reserve Bank of India Bulletin*, April.

———. (2006b). "Evolution of Central Banking in India", *Reserve Bank of India Bulletin*, June.

———. (2007). "India's Financial Sector Reforms: Fostering Growth while Containing Risk", *Reserve Bank of India Bulletin*, December.

Portes, Richard (2009). "Global Imbalances", in Mathias Dewatripont, Xavier Freixas and Richard Portes (ed.) (2009), *Macroeconomic Stability and Financial Regulation: Key Issues for the G20*. London: Centre for Economic Policy Research.

Obstfeld, Maurice (2009). "International Finance and Growth in Developing Countries: What Have We Learned?", *Working Paper 14691*. Cambridge, MA: National Bureau of Economic Research.

Reserve Bank of India (2009a). "India's Financial Sector: An Assessment", Committee on Financial Sector Assessment (Chairman: Rakesh Mohan), March.

———. (2009b). "Macroeconomic and Monetary Developments during 2008-09", April.

Taylor, John (2009). "The Financial Crisis and the Policy Responses: An Empirical Analysis of What Went Wrong", *Working Paper* 14631, January, National Bureau of Economic Research.

Turner Review (2009). "The Turner Review: A Regulatory Response to the Global Banking Crisis" by Lord Turner, Chairman, Financial Services Authority, UK.

World Bank (2008). *Global Development Finance 2008: The Role of International Banking*. World Bank.

Address delivered at the RBI-BIS Seminar on "Mitigating Spillovers and Contagion—Lessons from the Global Financial Crisis", at Hyderabad on December 4, 2008, at the International Chambers of Commerce at New Delhi on January 16, 2009, at the Yale School of Management, Yale University, on April 3, 2009 and at the 7th Annual India Business Forum Conference at London Business School, London, on April 23, 2009. Available online at *www.rbi.org.in*.

Economic Developments in India, Vol. 137.

25

V.S. VYAS

Changing Contours of Rural India

Causes and Consequences

I

I will start with identifying some of the developments which have made profound impact on rural economy in our country; spell out the outcome of these changes i.e., strength they have imparted and distortions they have led to; and finally suggest few critical areas where we should focus.

Among several important forces of change, I will focus on four major developments that are shaping the contemporary rural economy and society. These are: (i) increased connectivity, (ii) spread of formal education, (iii) plethora of government programmes with large funds and numerous functionaries, and (iv) emergence of *panchayats* as powerful political institutions. Let me say a few words on each one of these.

Increased Connectivity: The most important among the recent developments is the growing accessibility in the rural areas. The existence of an isolated, inaccessible, village is now becoming a rarity. Attempt to link all villages with all-weather roads started in right earnest in the year 2000 with the Pradhan Mantri Gram Sadak Yojana, which stipulated providing at least a paved road initially to villages above the population of 1,000, and eventually to all villages above 500 inhabitants. This programme got a fillip, as it became a component of the ambitious Bharat Nirman Programme. In more recent years, nation's flagship programme for rural India [Mahatma Gandhi National Rural Employment Guarantee Act (MGNREGA)] has also contributed significantly to the road-building programme. The net result is that more than three-fourth of Indian villages are connected with roads where a motorised vehicle can ply. Most of these roads are fair weather roads and the vehicles plying on them are ramshackle buses and lorries, but the connectivity is assured for overwhelmingly large majority of the villages. This has resulted in phenomenon of rural urban continuum, a situation that is now observable in many parts of the country, and not only in Kerala.

The impact of greater connectivity on the rural economy is far reaching. In a series of studies, which the Ministry of Rural Development had instituted in 2006 in eight states to assess the impact of road connectivity on agriculture, it was brought out that on every aspect of agricultural production and marketing, it had made substantial and positive difference. Better connectivity has also led to increase in non-farm employment opportunities, in small industries, trade and services. Of course, this has also enabled urban enterprises to introduce their products and services in the rural areas with much ease, most of the times at the cost of local artisans and traditional service providers.

More than surface connectivity, it is the spread of telecommunication which is changing the face of rural India. The country has recorded one of the fastest growth of telephony in the world, and the rural areas have their adequate share. According to the Telecom Authority of India, by July 2013, there were more than 904 million telephone subscribers in India, of these nearly 40 per cent, roughly 360 million, were in the rural areas, and the number of the rural subscribers is rapidly increasing. A farmer ploughing a field or transporting his product to nearby market with his cell phone glued to his ear is not an unusual sight. With extension of broadband facilities under the ambitious National Optical Fiber Network and spread of information technology (IT) applications, rural India is undergoing a veritable communication revolution.

Spread of Formal Education: Other major development taking place in the rural India is the spread of formal education. During last few decades, education landscape of the rural India has changed beyond recognition. Now there is a school practically in every village, with near universal enrollment of children of school-going age. (However, retention of the boys and girl in the schools after first few years and quality of education are still the major problems, as I will observe later.) Even now difference between the literacy rates in the urban (83.6% male and 73.6% female in 2009-10) and the rural India (70.6% male and 53.3% female, in the same year) is significant, but it is fast narrowing. Sarva Shikhshya Abhiyan has covered whole of India, including the rural areas, making it easier for the boys and girls to have elementary education. The schemes such as 'mid-day meal' have further helped in the enrollment of the boys and girls in the schools. The Right to Education Act, which came in force from April 2010, aiming at eight years of compulsory education to all children, will further accelerate the spread of education in the rural areas.

All levels of educational institutions are spreading rapidly in the rural areas. There is a primary school at walking distance in large parts of the country. Number of secondary schools is burgeoning. practically every *taluka/tehsil/*town has a college. Apart from the government efforts, private sector is making its presence felt in education field. Even in the rural areas, privately run 'English-medium' schools are becoming ubiquitous. An all-India survey conducted in 2005 found that 21 per cent of the rural children were enrolled in private schools (Desai *et al.*, 2010). Since then, the proportion must have risen significantly. Presence of the private sector is more prominent in the secondary level institutions. Twelfth Plan has noted that nearly half of the secondary schools in the country are sponsored by the private sector. With the increase in the number of secondary schools and colleges in the rural areas, the number of people passed out from these institutions has also increased. By 2009-10, 18.8 per cent of rural male and 10.3 per cent of rural female had education up to secondary level and above [National Sample Survey (NSS), 66th Round, 2009-10].

Admittedly, infrastructure of the educational institutions in the rural areas is grossly inadequate, they are under-staffed and the quality of teaching is appalling. Schooling in most of these institutions does not open the 'gateway to knowledge,' yet the students who go through these institutions, especially those who get secondary and college education, imbibe different worldview than their parents. They may not acquire higher knowledge, but their aspiration level changes. Due to lack of relevance and poor quality, spread of education in the rural India might not have made any measurable impact on the production processes or employment opportunities but it has resulted in truly distinguishable consumption pattern and living style, bringing rural population, particularly the youth, closer to their urban counterparts.

Large Influx of Public Servants: Pace of change in the rural area has accelerated with massive intrusion of the public institutions and their functionaries. Historically, state administration ended at the district level with a few functionaries, mainly the revenue and police officers, stationed at the lower level. The picture is completely changed now. With government assuming a major role in economic and social development, a plethora of programmes and schemes are located in the administrative units below the district, right up to the village level. Departments of Health, Education, Social Security, Women Empowerment and many more have their functionaries in villages. Other development departments, irrigation, power, roads, to name a few, have also their presence in the villages.

Apart from the government departments, increasingly a number of public agencies are being located in the rural areas. Post offices already had a very wide coverage of the rural areas. Fair price shops, numbering thousands, have been located in the rural areas. Now more than one-fourth of the villages, 1,60,000 out of nearly 6 lakh villages, have branches or correspondents of commercial banks. There are more than 1,00,000 cooperative credit societies located in the rural areas. Overall nearly 2,68,000 banking outlets have been set up in the villages as on March 2013 (Chakrabarty, 2013). A large number of NBFCs, chit funds and insurance companies have located their offices or appointed agents in the rural areas. In every part of the country, hundreds of public functionaries are working in the units below a district, in *taluka/tahsils* headquarters and even in villages. Way back in 1980, as a part of Indian Institute of Management, Ahmedabad's (IIMA's) project on Rural Development for Rural Poor, we conducted a survey in a backward *tehsil* of Devagarh, Rajasthan. We found that there were 27 agencies working in that *tehsil* accounting for 570 functionaries. Similar results were obtained in our survey of a backward *taluka* of Dharampur, Gujarat. Since then the number of the agencies and their staff located in the rural areas must have increased many fold.

I am not commenting on the development role or the efficiency or probity of these functionaries. What I wish to point out is that this army of officials is acting as change agent in the rural areas with their distinct life style and higher spending power. Most of these functionaries are urban, educated youth who import urban values and urban life style in the rural areas. Their higher spending power impacts on the production and employment structure in the rural areas. As their number is progressively increasing, their impact on the rural society is also becoming more pronounced.

Emergence of Panchayats as Power Centre: A profound change has occurred in the rural life with the enactment of the 73rd amendment to the Constitution, which provided the constitutional status to three-tier Panchayati Raj Institutions (PRIs), at the district, block and village levels. There are about 2,44,000 village *panchayats*. Several features of this institution have introduced significant changes in the rural life, especially at the village level. For example, there is a provision for regular meetings of the village general assembly, *gram sabha*, regular election of the *panchayats*, 50 per cent reservation for women in the *panchayats,* etc. All these are meant to give power to villagers including women. It is true that only a minority of the *panchayats* lives up to their constitutional responsibility, but in every state, some sections of more alert or more resourceful persons are assuming power through this route.

There is a constitutional provision to delegate 26 important functions of the state, such as education, health, social services, etc., to these institutions. Not all the states in the country have delegated these functions to *panchayats* but a beginning has been made in several states. With the delegation of these responsibilities, there is a demand for giving funds and functionaries to carry out various activities. The *panchayats* now have large funds at their disposal and sizable number of employees under their supervision.

More important than the delegated function, the 'agency' function has made them very powerful institutions. A number of government schemes, the most important among these being MGNREGA, are executed by the *panchayats*. For a few other central schemes, funds are directly given to the *panchayats*, bypassing the states. It is not uncommon to find a village *panchayat* handling annual budget of ₹ 80-100 millions. Such large sums of money spent in the villages under the supervision of the elected representatives have changed the environment in the villages as well as status of the elected *panchs*. Huge amounts under the control of the *panchayats* have not necessarily lead to more efficient or more honest use of money, but it has given rise to a new breed of leaders in the village with substantial power.

II

Let us now look into how these changes have affected the village society. Cumulative effect of these developments is reflected, principally, in the monetisation of the rural economy, changes in the structure and composition of rural workforce, and increasing prosperity along with growing income differentiation in the rural areas.

Penetration of market: Because of easy transport and communication facilities, commercialisation has made deep inroads in the rural area. In the main economic activity in the rural area, i.e., agriculture, which accounts for 66.5 per cent of the rural workforce, share of purchased inputs is progressively increasing. An earlier symbol of Indian agriculture, a farmer walking behind a wooden plough drawn by a pair of bullocks with a family member assisting in the farming operations has to be replaced by a farmer driving a tractor, using large amounts of purchased inputs and hiring labour for major farm operations. Farming which was principally depending on family labour and family-owned inputs has now become an activity largely depending on purchased inputs and services. Amount of expenditure on fertilisers, pesticides, purchased seeds, diesel and electricity is increasing year after year.

At the output level, shift to commercialisation is even more pronounced. High-value, market-oriented products of allied sectors to agriculture, namely horticulture, dairying and animal husbandry, poultry and fishery, already account for 50 per cent of the total value of the output of agriculture, and their share is progressively increasing. In the crop sector also, so-called 'commercial crops,' e.g., cotton, oilseeds, sugar cane, etc., are acquiring a dominant share, relegating food grain production to a secondary place. Because of the increased share of the purchased inputs and larger proportion of output for sale in the market, agriculture's backward as well as forward links with the rest of economy are becoming ever stronger (Mythili and Hara, 2013).

Compared to the inputs and products, the consumption pattern has become even more market oriented. In the consumption basket of the rural families, share of non-food, non-agricultural commodities and services is dominating. Picture of self-reliant (for production) and self-sufficient (in consumption) rural households has become outdated. Market forces are impacting on their livelihood as well as household economy with ever increasing intensity. The lesson is clear. While formulating macro policies for credit, trade, pricing, etc., their impact on rural livelihood and rural consumption cannot be ignored.

Changing Composition of Workforce: Easy accessibility has facilitated market penetration in the rural area; it has also impacted on the composition of workforce. An immediate result has been the growing feminisation of agriculture. Man folk leaving villages in hordes every morning for a nearby town in overcrowded buses for wage labour and returning in the evening with paltry earning is a common sight in large parts of the country. Meanwhile, the women have to look after the households as well as their small farms. Actual work on the farms by women is underestimated if one takes into account only the 'principal source of income' criterion. In 2012-13 on MGNREGA sites in the country as a whole, women accounted for 51 per cent of labour days, and in seven states, including Kerala, Goa, Tamil Nadu, Rajasthan and Andhra Pradesh, the proportion of women workers was more than the national average. Thus, wage-paid labour on MGNREGA may be their principal source of income, but women manage most of the small family farms, mostly as unpaid family workers.

Another factor changing the composition of workforce, in this case a tilt towards more elderly people, is the result of the spread of education in the rural areas. It is not only when the youth, especially boys, are in the school that they are not available for work, even after the rudimentary schooling they are reluctant to work on farm. The fact of progressively feminisation of farming is now well recognised. A less appreciated, though an equally important, phenomenon is the growing proportion of aged among the workers. NSS 60th Round has shown that the proportion of the rural male workers in the age group of 60 and above has increased from 70 per 1,000 workers in 1999-2000 to 77 in 2009-10. The increase in the proportion of female rural worker in the same age group during that period was from 72 per 1,000 to 81 per 1,000. The reverse phenomenon, i.e., declining proportion in the workforce, is observed in the 20-29 age group. If the present trend continues, proportion of aged in the rural workforce may become higher still as the 'education' spreads in the rural areas, making youth reluctant to work on farms.

Diversification of Occupational Structure: With all these developments, one sensitive indicator of change, namely, diversification of occupational structure, does not seem to have changed much. The dependence on agriculture as the main source of livelihood has declined from 58 per cent to 51 per cent over a decade, from 2001 to 2011. For a fast developing economy, averaging GDP growth of 8-9 per cent per year does not appear as a remarkable change. However, it does not reflect fully the changes that are taking place in rural occupational structure. For example, there has been a significant change in the composition of the agricultural workforce. For example, proportion of 'workers' in the agricultural workforce is progressively increasing and the proportion of 'farmers' is declining.

This increase in the proportion of workers should be viewed, as I will explain later, in the context of diminution of the size of holdings. Available evidence suggests that larger proportion of scheduled castes (SCs), scheduled tribes (STs) and minority community household are changing their principal source of livelihood, i.e., cultivation, to farm and non-farm labour (NSS 60th Round).

Equally significant changes have taken place in the composition of workforce in the rural non-agricultural sectors. The number of workers engaged in the small household enterprises, i.e., in traditional arts and crafts, is declining. Rural workers engaged in trade, transport and construction have increased. Prosperity of a section of rural society and the changing life style of the rural households have affected the occupational composition in the non-farm sector in the rural area. Taking advantage of these developments, the organised sector, including large multinational corporations (MNCs), from soft drink makers to white goods manufacturers, has also penetrated in the rural areas to push their wares.

Increasing Prosperity and Growing Differentiation: On the whole, rural areas have benefited from these changes. Rural incomes have increased, poverty has been reduced, productivity in agriculture has improved, and terms of trade have gone in favour of agriculture. Whether in terms of income per hectare or in terms of income per worker, there is an improvement over a period of time. Apart from the favourable stance of the policy directly impinging on agriculture, such as minimum support prices (MSPs), subsidised inputs and credit, the overall economic reforms, e.g., privatisation and trade liberalisation, have also benefited agriculture sector (see Vyas, 2001).

The overall picture of rural prosperity, however, hides substantial misery and deprivation of a section of rural people. There is wide differentiation in wealth and income in the rural society. Based on NSS consumption data, a recent study has concluded that inter-personal inequality has increased in the country as well as in the rural areas (Motiram and Vakulabharanam, 2013). In the rural areas, sharp and persistent inequality can be observed between farm and non-farm sector in the rural area, between rainfed regions and irrigated agriculture, and between marginal farmers and the middle and the large farmers. The marginal and the small farmers are particularly handicapped. As I have elaborated elsewhere ("Marginalised Sections of Indian Agriculture—the Forgotten Millions," Presidential Address to 48th Conference of Indian Society of Labor Economics), while they are at a serious disadvantage in the market place, the government schemes also leave them to their fate. The official figures on rural poverty, 33.8 per cent (in 2009-10) of the total households, do not take into account the households who are only marginally above the poverty line and are vulnerable to a shock, market-induced, natural, familial or personal. In terms of numbers, the disadvantaged sections in the rural area far outweigh those who have benefited from the developments, I have mentioned above.

A powerful factor contributing to the income as well as social differentiation is the politicisation of the rural society. The starting point is the election to *panchayats*, which carries not only prestige but also control over vast resources. It also facilitates contacts with state bureaucracy and managers of the public institutions, and ensures benefits that can be obtained from such contacts. Political parties also like to make foothold in the rural area by controlling the *panchayats* directly, or by proxies. Ensuing competition for power aggravates the differentiation in the rural society.

The problem of 'rural-urban divide' is voiced at several forums; however, equally serious problem of 'rural-rural divide' does not receive as much attention. As a matter of fact, benefits of state policies and programmes are pre-empted by a section of the rural society, while the rest have to remain contained with paltry relief.

III

The changes discussed above have affected different sections of rural society in different ways. While a number of geographically and socially well-placed households had all the positive advantages from these changes, many others have been left behind and even become losers. To ensure that the gains are shared more equitably, the strategy adopted by Dr Kurien in developing AMUL has a great relevance in the present context. As I understand it, there are three pillars of this strategy: organisation of the producers, taking advantage of the existing and the potential demand, and emphasis on human resource development.

Organisation of the Poor: The reasons why the marginalised groups of the rural society are not able to take advantage of the recent developments are: (i) the high transaction cost involved and (ii) weak bargaining power. With collective action, the poor can largely overcome these disadvantages.

We have experience with different forms of organisations for collective action, e.g., self-help groups (SHGs), cooperatives, producers companies, etc. Not many of these organisations have succeeded for long period of time. But there are examples of successful collectivities. SEWA group of organisations started by Smt Ela Bhatt and AMUL pattern of milk cooperatives initiated by Dr Kurien are two examples of the successful collective organisations known all over the country. There are other organisations of the marginalised groups in different parts of the country some initiated by the producers themselves, others sponsored by the civil society groups or the government.

All these groups exhibit some common features. The basic units of the successful collective entities are small homogeneous groups of members; there is a dedicated 'agency' to initiate and support them for a length of time; there are distinct gains in productivity and/ or realisation of higher value for their products; there is sufficient stress on capacity building. It needs to be emphasised that in present circumstances, homogeneous groups of small producers with joint efforts to cater to their needs will not only increase their bargaining power and income, but also provide foundation for an efficient and equitable rural structure. We have now sufficient experience of working with different models of collective organisations, and should be able to adapt them to the given circumstances

Exploiting the Market for Goods and Services: It was Dr Kurien's genius that he put market orientation of cooperative efforts at the central place. Both farm and non-farm producers in the rural economy have suffered because of faulty marketing system. Gap between the prices received by the farmers and the prices paid by the final consumer is one of the most important indicators of its deficiency. This gap is not because of the value added at different stages of the marketing chain but largely because of leakages, wastage and high margins charged by the intermediaries. Such gaps are wider in the perishable products like fruit and vegetables, milk and dairy products. The small farmers feel the incidence of market imperfection more seriously.

Initially, the milk producers of the Kaira district, and latter dairy farmers all over the country who were members of Anand pattern of dairy cooperatives, could receive a fair share in the consumers' rupee mainly because of astute marketing (which also included processing) by their cooperatives. For most of the farm produce, especially for the high value products, aggregate demand is not a problem. With the burgeoning demand, the product mix and quality of the products on the one hand and the marketing arrangements on the other have become very important to maximise producers' income. Reforms in marketing are as important as the investment in rural infrastructure. In fact both can go together to enhance the value of the produce and income of the producers.

For non-farm products, especially those produced by the artisans in small enterprises, marketing is of paramount significance, not only for receiving signals about the effective demand for their products, but also for claiming a higher share in consumers' spending. Today the artisans and craftsmen are the most disadvantaged sections in the rural areas because of the cheap products available from urban organised sector due to easy accessibility, exacerbated due to inefficient marketing of their products.

For strengthening the market chain and making it more producers friendly, government intervention is needed, particularly in strengthening marketing infrastructure. The producers have also to be trained to operate efficiently in today's more complex markets. Latter has become relatively easy with the spread of IT in the villages, which can reduce the information asymmetry, one of the principal causes of inefficient marketing. For small producers in the farm as well as in the non-farm sectors, marketing is an important element in what C.K. Prahalad in his seminal work, 'The Fortune at the Bottom of the Pyramid,' has called "the ecosystem of wealth creation."

Development of Human Resources: Dr Kurien laid great emphasis on development of human resources at all levels. Importance of human development as a measure of progress was recognised in our plans. Growth with justice was a recurring theme in our plan documents.

This objective has been made more explicit in the Twelfth Plan with the emphasis on 'inclusive growth.' Of the three main components of human development highlighted by the United Nations Develoment Programme's (UNDP's) *Human Development Reports*, namely, 'Income, Education and Health,' I have already commented on the growth of income and status of poverty in the rural area. Let me say a few words on the other two major components of human development, namely, education and health.

Education: Investment in creating educational facilities has increased phenomenally. As I had mentioned earlier, the infrastructure for education has been strengthened all over the country. This has brought about a profound change in the rural areas in terms of access to elementary, and to an extent secondary, and higher education. Yet several problems remain. There is a serious problem of 'exclusion' of weaker sections of society, particularly the SCs and STs, and minority. There is a problem of 'dropouts,' with the retention period in the schools limited to hardly 3 years. And above all, there is the problem of quality. Extensive surveys of rural educational institutions have shown that not only the quality of teaching is very low, there is no sign of improvement. Further, in the case of secondary and higher education, the students are not equipped for gainful employment. Skill deficit, which is common in the country, is more glaring in the rural areas. These problems have to be tackled to give true benefits of the large and growing investment in education in the rural areas.

Health and Nutrition: Situation in regard to health and nutrition, another critical element for human development, is disappointing in the country; it is worse in the rural areas. We have not been able to meet the modest targets for reducing infant and maternal mortality set as a part of Millennium Development Goals (MDGs). Our record in correcting malnutrition is highly disappointing. On all indicators of health and nutrition, the rural areas are far below the desirable norms. Investment in health infrastructure seems to be inadequate, even in comparison to some other developing countries. But it is not the only, or even primary, factor coming in the way of achieving satisfactory results. There seem to be some basic lacunae in the design of the projects and programmes and more so in the delivery systems.

Human development is a goal in itself as Amartya Sen has said in relation to education. Even to keep the present phase of rural prosperity continuing, improvement in human resources is a pre-requisite more so, if we wish to move towards a more egalitarian society. Again, it is not primarily because of dearth of investment or shortage of programmes and schemes, the basic fault lies with the delivery system.

It is easy to explain failure of delivery to the inefficiency of bureaucracy or imperfections of market, but one wonders why with the power given to *panchayats* to supervise various programmes of education and health, the situation has not changed. Explanation would go beyond economic logic. The nature of social organisations at local level has to be understood and the scope for change has to be defined. For these purposes, academics and professionals can play an important role, as advocates as well as activists. Dr Kurien had visualised that role when he started the experiment of the Spear Head Teams for expanding the cooperative movement in the dairy sector. In this as in several other aspects of rural development, there is much to be learnt from the ideas and actions of this remarkable leader.

References

Chakrabarty, K.C. (2013). "Financial Inclusion in India: Journey so far and Way Forward", *RBI Bulletin*, October.

Desai, Sonalde B., Amaresh Dubey, Brij Lal Joshi, Mitali Sen, Abusaleh Sharif and Reve Vanneman (2010). *Human Development in India*. New Delhi: Oxford University Press.

Motiram, Sripad and Vamsi Vakulabharanam (2013). "Indian Inequality: Pattern and Changes, 1993-2010", in *India Development Report 2012-13*.

Mythili, G. and Nitin Hara (2013). "Sectoral Linkages, Multipliers and the Role of Agriculture", in S. Mahendra Dev (ed.) (2013), *India Development Report 2012-13*. New Delhi: Oxford University Press.

Vyas, V.S. (2001). "The Second Round of Reforms in Agriculture", *Dantwala Memorial Lecture*. Indian Economic Association.

Second Dr Verghese Kurien Memorial Lecture, Anand, December 13, 2013.

Economic Developments in India, Vol. 193.

26

ASHOK GULATI and SURBHI JAIN

India's Second Green Revolution

AGRI-TRANSFORMATION that occurred during 2004-05 to 2011-12 was certainly the most remarkable change that happened since the beginning of economic reforms in 1991, and perhaps even one of the best spells for agriculture since Independence. Consider the following facts: over the seven-year period of 2004-05 to 2011-12, the real agri-GDP (gross domestic product) per worker engaged in agriculture increased by a whopping 51 per cent compared to just stagnant, nay marginally lower (by -1.3%) agri-GDP per worker during the preceding five years, 1999-2000 to 2004-05, and only 21 per cent during 1993-94 to 1999-2000, as Figure 26.1 shows. Call it agri-growth with human face.

Figure 26.1

Agri-GDP per Worker

(In ₹ at 2004-05 Prices)

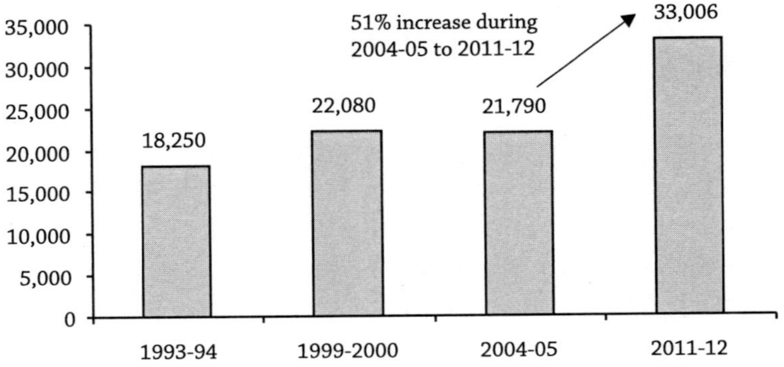

Note: 1. Agri-GDP for 2011-12 is the revised estimate released by the Central Statistics Office (CSO).

2. Employment in agriculture has been estimated from the National Sample Survey Organisation (NSSO) data on permanent and usual status of workers engaged in agriculture applied to interpolated population between the population censuses of 1991, 2001 and 2011. The rural-urban population for 1993-94 is based on 1991 census, for 1999-2000 and 2004-05 based on 2001 census, and 2011-12 based on 2011 census.

The big-bang 51 per cent rise in agri-GDP per worker was presumably propelled by an even more impressive increase of 71.5 per cent in net fixed capital stock per worker in agriculture during 2004-2011. No wonder, with each worker better equipped with capital, growth in per worker agri-incomes has accelerated by leaps and bounds, which was never witnessed earlier. This had the most salutary impact on rural poverty ratio (estimated by Tendulkar's poverty line), which decreased almost three times faster during 2004-05 to 2011-12 (by 2.3% points per annum) than during 1993-94 to 2004-05 (declining by just 0.7% points per annum). This pace of decline in poverty ratio is robust and will broadly hold, no matter how one defines poverty levels. Isn't faster poverty reduction one of the most important policy aims of any government in India? And if that is delivered, why don't we give credit to the policy and stay its course even more rigorously? The problem is poor communication of complex policies and processes that triggered this capital accumulation in agriculture, propelling per worker agri-GDP growth, and fall in rural poverty. Let us try to decipher some of this complexity.

Investments and accumulation of capital in any sector lay down the foundation of growth and prosperity of that sector. Investments in Indian agriculture as a percentage of agri-GDP have been fluctuating, but broadly hovered around 10-12 per cent during 1980-81 to 2003-04. However, since 2004-05, it had a clear structural break, and by 2011-12, it is now hovering around 20 per cent of agri-GDP. It is coupled with first time drop in absolute number of workforce engaged in agriculture (by about 31 million) during 2004-05 to 2011-12 (as per NSSO). Both are most fundamental and welcome changes in Indian agriculture since decades, as they equip the agri-workers with more capital and thus raise labour and land productivity. And, that is what seems to have happened.

But what triggered the investments in agriculture? It may be noted that in 2011-12, almost 85 per cent of investments in agriculture came from the private sector. Our econometric analysis of this over the period 1990-91 to 2011-12 reveals that private investments respond strongly to the price ratio of agriculture to non-agriculture commodities, and also to the public sector investments in agriculture. But the elasticity of private investments in agriculture with respect to price ratio is almost three times higher than with public sector investments. So, it is basically the relative prices that have been the game changers. Call it the terms of trade impact.

How did it happen? Gradual integration of agriculture to global economy has been a part of the overall liberalisation policy since the 1991 economic reforms. In 1990-91, agri-trade (imports plus exports) was less than 5 per cent of agri-GDP, which increased to more than 18 per cent by 2012-13. What this indicates is that our domestic agri-prices cannot be insulated from global prices for long. What happens to commodity prices in global economy percolates to domestic economy, albeit with a little lag. The global food prices have been increasing since 2003-04, first gradually but then with an almost volcanic eruption in 2007-08. By 2011-12, global food prices as measured by the Food and Agriculture Organization of the United Nations (FAO's) food price index (with 2002-04=100) stood at 230 and then declined marginally to 210 by 2013. Our domestic food price index (with 2004-05=100) stood at 175 in 2011-12, and continued to rise to 210 by the end of 2013. Both food price indices show a remarkable convergence at 210 by 2013. It shows clearly that our agri-prices are very much aligned to the movements in global prices.

What this means in a two-sector economy was that relative prices improved in favour of agriculture, triggering private investments in agriculture, raising productivity and incomes, and ultimately reducing rural poverty at an unprecedented pace.

But it had a side effect too. Food inflation in India at double digits for the last five years seems to be taking a political toll. Onion price spike in 2013, which was more of a seasonal than an inbuilt trend, seems to dominate the news, while the fastest increase in per worker agri-GDP and the fastest accumulation of capital in agriculture and most dramatic fall in rural poverty during 2004-2011 all go unnoticed. Call it lack of effective communication of policies, programmes and consequent burial of their benefits.

Financial Express, February 10, 2014.

Economic Developments in India, Vol. 193.

27

C.P. CHANDRASEKHAR and JAYATI GHOSH

The Industrial Recession

New or Ongoing?

THE industrial slowdown is now accepted as a fact by most policy makers and observers of the Indian economy. Yet officials and commentators seem to blame it on external factors: most obviously, the global financial crisis originating in the US economy, the consequent economic slowdown and now, recession in the US, the European Union (EU) and other developed country markets, and the associated impact upon exports.

Causes for Concern

It is certainly true that the bad news from abroad—which shows no signs of easing up—has impacted upon domestic stock markets, investor expectations, and the exporting industries in particular. But it is also unfortunately the case that our own economy has been showing several causes for concern even before that external bad news started pouring in. There was the accelerating inflation, which particularly hit food and other items of essential consumption, and recently exacerbated by the increase in petrol prices. In addition there have been signs of decelerating growth, especially in industrial activity, and these cannot be ascribed only to reduced export orders, but are more likely to have domestic causes.

Consider the index of industrial production, presented in Figure 27.1 (with base year 1993-94). The general index peaked in March this year, fell quite sharply thereafter, and subsequently has been more or less flat at the lower level.

This pattern essentially reflects the behaviour of the manufacturing index, which accounts for around 80 per cent of the weight of the general index. Such a pattern tends to be obscured by the standard way of presenting the industrial growth data, in terms of year-on-year (y-o-y) monthly rates.

What is especially disconcerting is the evidence on electricity production, which shows hardly any increase at all but simply fluctuations around a flat trend for the past 18 months. Since electricity still remains substantially undersupplied, and its shortage can create supply bottlenecks for other production, this stagnation is worth noting.

Figure 27.1

Index of Industrial Production

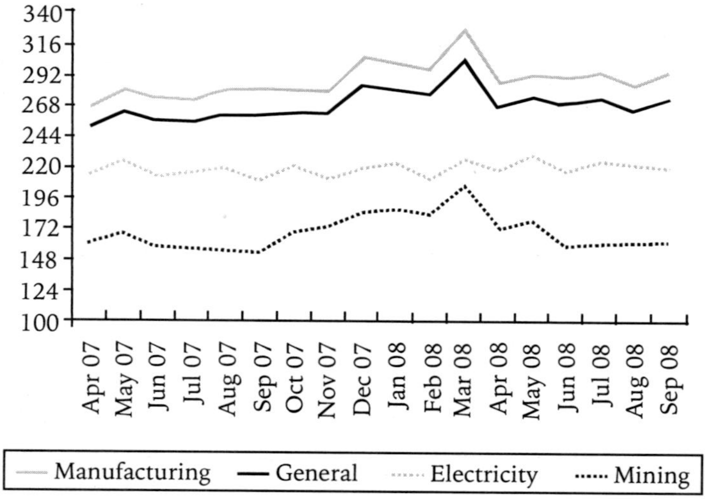

Slowdown Across Sectors

The use-based classification of industrial production suggests that the slowdown in growth is spread across several important sectors. Figure 27.2 provides the evidence on recent trends in production in the basic, capital goods and intermediate industries. Once again, both basic goods and intermediate goods, which have strong backward and forward linkages with other industrial activity, have been stagnant and hardly increased at all over the past one and a half years. The production of capital goods shows much greater volatility, with a sharp increase in March 2008 but decline thereafter from that peak.

Figure 27.2

IIP for Basic and Capital Goods

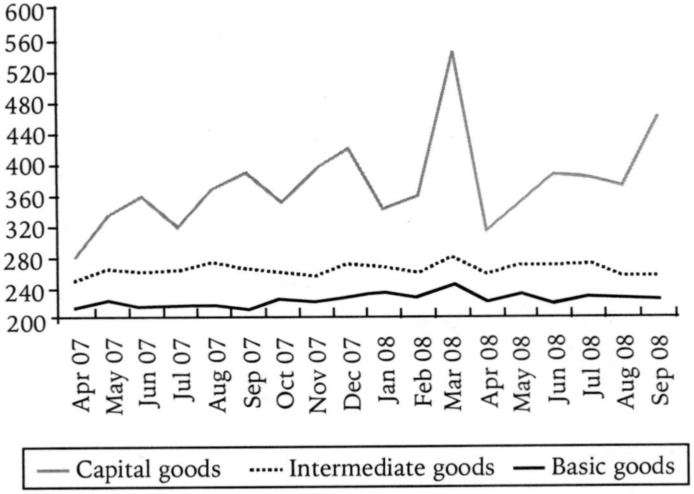

Consumer goods are the most likely—and the first—to be directly affected by slowing demand in domestic and export markets. Figure 27.3 shows that this too is not a recent problem, but one which has been clearly evident in the economy at least since the beginning of the current calendar year.

Figure 27.3

IIP for Consumer Goods

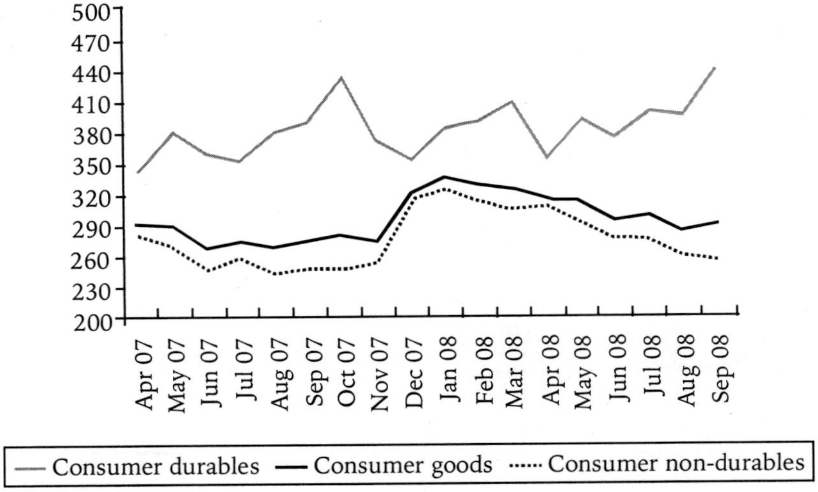

The production of consumer non-durable goods, which account for the bulk of consumer goods (with more than 80% weight) peaked in January 2008 and have fallen continuously since then. Consumer durables, on the other hand, had benefited from a credit-financed boom that had elements of unsustainability that are eerily similar to the US credit-driven consumption boom.

The significant expansion of retail credit, especially credit card debt and hire purchase schemes, had generated demand for consumer durables and automobiles, but such credit-driven expansion became increasingly problematic as interest rates increased and lenders became more concerned with the viability of this rapidly growing consumer debt.

Table 27.1

Year-on-Year Growth of IIP for Particular Sectors

(in per cent)

	Sept. 2008	*Apr.-Sept. 2008-09*
Food Products	5.2	-1.4
Beverages, Tobacco and Related Products	11.7	23.3
Cotton Textiles	-9.3	-0.5
Wool, Silk and Man-made Fibre Textiles	1.4	-0.2
Jute and other Vegetable Fibre Textiles (except Cotton)	-0.4	-5.5
Textile Products (including Wearing Apparel)	-1.9	3.8
Wood and Wood Products; Furniture and Fixtures	-9.7	-10.4
Paper & Paper Products, and Printing, Publishing and Allied Industries	8.3	3
Leather, and Leather & Fur Products	-8.6	-0.3
Basic Chemicals and Chemical Products (except Products of Petroleum & Coal)	-3.6	61
Rubber, Plastic, Petroleum and Coal Products	-3.4	-4.2
Non-metallic Mineral Products	-0.6	0.6
Basic Metal and Alloy Industries	5.6	6.2
Metal Products and Parts, except Machinery and Equipment	12.8	1.3
Machinery and Equipment other than Transport Equipment	16.1	9.8
Transport Equipment and Parts	16.8	12.8
Other Manufacturing Industries	10.5	-1.1

Table 27.1 shows that this deceleration was widely spread across different manufacturing sectors. Indeed, only the chemicals, machinery and transport equipment sectors appear to still be growing, albeit at slower rates.

Explaining the Trend

What explains this trend of deceleration even before the outbreak of the global financial crisis? One partial explanation can be found in Figure 27.4, which shows the movement of imports and exports over the same period. It is evident that exports have been growing throughout this period, and so a fall in aggregate export demand cannot yet be blamed for the domestic industrial deceleration, although it may indeed have an adverse impact soon. But the explosion in imports is also worth noting, and that suggests import competition could have affected domestic production of many manufactured goods.

The rapidly growing import bill is only partly a result of the high oil prices that prevailed over most of 2007 and the early part of 2008. Non-oil imports also increased, aided not only by more liberalised trade but also by the appreciation of the rupee in 2007.

Figure 27.4

Exports and Imports

(Rs. crore)

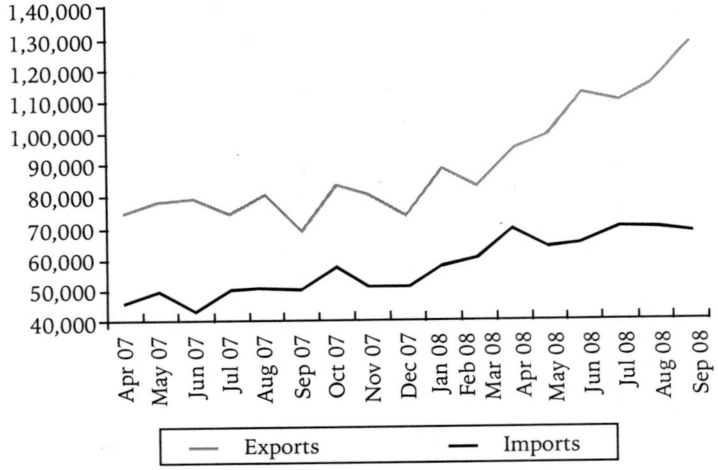

Table 27.2

Year-on-Year Increase in Import Values for April-May 2008

(in per cent)

Total Imports	38.51
POL Imports	73.61
Non-oil Imports	23.51
Textile Products, incl. Garments	19.28
Chemical Products	56.53
Med. & Pharma Products	37.77
Artificial Resins & Plastics	47.85
Metal Goods	89.44
Machine Tools	83.41
Non-elec. Machinery	47.54
Elec. Machinery	58.02
Electronic Machinery	19.65
Transport Equipment	25.62
Professional Equipment	57.05
Other Miscellaneous Imports	28.95

Table 27.2 shows that non-oil imports for the period April-May 2008 compared to the same period in 2007, increased by nearly a quarter. Within that, certain sectors showed very high rates of increase in import values, much more than the growth of domestic production, suggesting some amount of import penetration in a wide range of manufacturing sectors.

This in turn suggests that the deceleration of industry may have resulted from the inability of the Government to ensure the macro management of the economy in a complex global situation. The rush of foreign capital into India was acutally sought by the Government, whether in the form of (subsequently fickle) portfolio investments or by encouraging Indian corporates take on more external commercial loans.

This inflow led to upward pressure on the rupee, and this combined with trade liberalisation to encourage more import penetration. Some of this must definitely have damaged activity and employment among Indian producers, especially the small-scale producers who still account for around one-third of manufacturing GDP and much more than two-third of manufacturing employment.

Then, the global rise in food and fuel prices was allowed to impact upon prices in India. In response to this, instead of managing these specific items, the Government raised interest rates as an anti-inflationary measure. This had the effect of further damaging the prospects for industrial activity. All this happened before the subsequent outflows of capital led to a rapidly depreciating rupee—but by then the damage had been done.

Macro Mismanagement

It is pointless to blame external forces, because none of these processes was necessary within India. There was no need to encourage and then suffer the effects of mobile capital flows that brought in resources that were not even going to be used. Instead, capital inflows could simply have been controlled to prevent upward pressure on the exchange rate.

Inflation could have been managed by first recognising the essentially speculative and, therefore, temporary nature of the global fuel and food price rises, and then addressing the specific management of these sectors within the economy.

Unfortunately this previous mismanagement has worse consequences than simply the evident industrial deceleration. It has also weakened the economy even before it faces the full impact of the global recession and the financial turmoil.

Business Line, November 18, 2008.

Economic Developments in India, Vol. 132.

28

R. NAGARAJ

Indian Investments Abroad

What Explains the Boom?

THE year 2006 will probably end on a unique note, with private capital outflow from India exceeding inflow of foreign direct investment (FDI). According to Dealogic, a consultancy firm tracing cross-border investments, in the first nine months of 2006, investment outflow from India was estimated to be $7.2 billion, up from $4.2 last year (*Financial Times*, October 3, 2006).

What started as a trickle in 2000 has grown into a flood with Tata Steel catapulting itself to become the world's fifth largest steel manufacturer by acquiring the Anglo-Dutch company, Corus. This has been closely followed by Videocon Industries acquiring Daewoo's electronics manufacturing facility in South Korea to become the self-proclaimed 'Indian Multinational'.

According to news reports, prior to the Corus deal, the Tata group alone had made 28 overseas acquisitions since 2000, investing $1.4 billion in eight major acquisitions spread across the world in industries ranging from steel to beverages (*Wall Street Journal*, October 7, 2006). The recently released *World Investment Report* 2006 notes that India is not alone in experiencing a boom in outward flow; this is true of developing countries as a whole. However, while most of the investments from developing countries are into other developing countries and in services, recent Indian acquisitions have been, one, mainly in the advanced economies and, two, the acquisitions are now concentrated in manufacturing (software being the exception). Cumulative capital outflow from India between 2000 and 2005 was $8.1 billion.

Since 2001, Indian firms have made 30 to 60 overseas acquisitions per year, as per the Centre for Monitoring the Indian Economy's

(CMIE) information on international acquisitions and mergers. About 40 per cent of them are of less than $10 million each. Ten deals are of a value of over $100 million each, while financial information regarding 38 per cent of the acquisitions is unavailable.

Software Focus

Software is the single largest industry of acquisition, followed by pharmaceuticals and the automotive industry. Over 40 per cent of the acquisitions are made in the US, followed by continental Europe, the UK and Asia, in that order. Although information technology (IT) and the information technology enabled services (ITES) industry leads the number of acquisitions from India, these are quantitatively small in value. About 300 Indian firms are reported to have set up representative offices in London, and India currently ranks third in FDI inflow in the UK. London is apparently the first port of call; this is natural given the long-standing business and social connections, and access to its financial market and commercial expertise.

Although capital outflow from India appears large, it is still modest by international standards. According to the *World Investment Report (WIR) 2006*, FDI outflow from India ranked only 88th in 2005 in world outward FDI, up from 94th in 2000. Even among the developing economies, Indian investments are modest as the country does not figure in the top 15 outward FDI countries. Of course, these are figures for 2005, and Indian acquisitions abroad have exploded in 2006 with big ticket items like the Tata-Corus and Videocon-Daewoo deals. This is likely to make India leap in the rankings for 2006.

After netting out investments between China and Hong Kong, the two countries together would account for a substantial share of capital outflow from the developing economies, that is, many times the value of investments from India. While much of China's investments are in search of oil fields and industrial raw materials to sustain its rapid growth, India's investments, in contrast, are seeking markets for their products in developed economies, in the manufacturing sector and in mature industries, like machinery, automotives, textiles and pharmaceuticals.

What explains the boom in FDI from India? There are domestic reasons and international factors propelling outward flows, and industry-specific factors have also contributed to the trend.

In the face of investment and trade policy reforms, Indian industry underwent a major restructuring in the 1990s—lay-offs and retrenchments, domestic mergers and acquisitions, hike in promoters' equity holdings to ward-off threats of hostile takeovers, and so on. There was a surge by incumbent firms in fixed investment to expand manufacturing capacity and distribution networks to face external competition. But with the sharp downturn after 1995-96, the industrial sector was saddled with huge excess capacity. This experience taught Indian business the perils of excessive dependence on the domestic market in an increasingly open economy. The bigger and more successful Indian companies also sought to establish businesses abroad so that they would not be dependent on the fortunes of a single (i.e., domestic) market. In this gloomy scenario, the success of Indian software firms demonstrated India's advantage of low-cost skilled workforce in exploring international market.

One of the decisions the government took during the depressed investment scenario (operative from the mid-1990s until 2002-03) was to allow Indian firms to invest abroad up to twice their domestic net worth, enabling them to target acquisitions in advanced countries where industrial assets were available at a discount on account of the global economic downturn in the early 2000s. In principle, such acquisitions allowed firms to combine their low production costs at home with low interest rates in international capital markets to emerge as low-cost producers accessing the world market. By acquiring running businesses, they got ready access to customers and markets, closely knit supply chain networks and consumers' brand loyalty. Such investments have enabled Indian firms to produce labour-intensive parts/sub-assemblies/processes in India and use the factories and firms in advanced countries to undertake capital or technology-intensive investments in their business. The speed with which Indian firms went overseas over the past five years was also perhaps driven by the desire to get a toe-hold in a variety of markets divided into trading blocs.

However, the foundation for overseas expansion was laid a long time ago. It is well worth remembering that given the large size of the domestic market, India had acquired international competitiveness in many industries, mainly based on the low-cost of skilled workforce. It is worth recalling the words of late Sanjaya Lall, who in 1982, described TELCO (now Tata Motors) as "...(the) first real automotive multinational to emerge from the Third World with its own trade and technology..." (Lall, 1982).

Positive Externalities

Now in the 2000s, in an increasingly open world economy, large and efficient firms in India would want to expand overseas, to secure external markets, to extend their intangible assets like brand names into newer territories. For example, Asian Paints, which has been setting up plants or acquiring paint-making factories and firms abroad for some time now, has apparently emerged as the world 10th largest producer operating in 24 countries. This follows its acquisition of Berger International in Singapore in 2003. Asian Paints' efficient manufacturing and distribution systems seem to be the source of its success. As the firm has developed technology to produce paint intermediaries, export of these goods add value to the firm. Such overseas expansion could, in principle, have a positive externality as it augments domestic production capability, promotes backward and forward linkages, and also increases employment opportunities.

Coming to industry-specific reasons, in pharmaceuticals many firms have proven their capability to produce generic drugs at a fraction of world prices. This is clearly the result of the Patents Act of 1970 (that promoted process patenting and facilitated reverse engineering), and import substituting industrialisation that encouraged local technology and skill development. Indian firms now perceive an opportunity to produce a large number of drugs that are going-off patent. Although it may be cheaper to produce many of these drugs in India, by acquiring firms abroad they get access to the prescription drug markets, which are often restricted to firms belonging to the country or trading bloc like the European Union (EU). Getting access to specialised R&D (research & development) firms to speed up the drug discovery process is another reason for such investments.

In the case of the automotive spare parts industry, some efficient domestic firms have received international recognition for quality (e.g., Deming award for Sundaram Fasteners) that gives them access to firms like General Motors. As the automotive industry has a tightly knit supply chain across the world, Indian firms perceive their growth prospects in becoming a part of such supplier networks to original equipment manufacturers (OEM). Bharat Forge and Sundaram Fasteners are two examples of such suppliers. Although most Indian suppliers at the moment operate at the low end of the spectrum, they expect to move up the value chain to supply complete sub-assemblies with the help of their external acquisitions.

In telecom, the boom in the telecommunication industry in the second-half of the 1990s created huge capacity, but with the collapse of the dot-com bubble and the implosion of firms like Tyco and WorldCom, a significant amount of surplus capacity became available. As the prices of these 'unlit' fibre optic cable network plummeted, large Indian telecom firms like Tata, VSNL and Reliance have competed to get hold of the networks to augment long distance telephony and data transfer capacity to meet the growing requirement of the IT and ITES industry. In IT, after the late-1990s bust, many firms have set up new offices and made outright purchase of software firms abroad to move up the value chain, building on their strength of low-cost and credibility of their services. After the 2001 terrorist attacks in the US, Indian software companies are apparently investing in 'mirror sites' or parallel locations in places like Singapore to ensure uninterrupted services to their clients in the west. Many of these acquisitions in the US are mainly from non-resident Indians (NRIs), perhaps reflecting prior business and social ties.

Risk Factors

The great Indian outward movement does not, however, mean success is guaranteed. While internationalisation of business represents natural progression in an open economy, it faces many risks and uncertainties. Allowing large domestic enterprises to tap the international market for funds to fuel the acquisitions exposes them to the volatilities of the global financial markets with attendant risks. Many of the recent large acquisitions are predominantly financed by debt finance (leveraged buyouts), raised from the global capital market; success depends on augmenting cash flow in international currency to service the huge debt. In the event of an economic downturn—which is not a question of if but when—servicing such debts could pose serious challenge for these firms. Moreover, the experience from developed countries suggests that about one-third of mergers and acquisitions fail to add value to the firm and the shareholders. More fundamentally, industrial organisation literature suggests that it is still an open issue about whether or not corporate mergers improve efficiency and profitability (Scherer, 2006).

What are the policy implications of growing outward investment from India? Given the scarcity of industrial resources in relation to India's size, there is perhaps a need for strategic initiatives to encourage public and private sector firms to seek scarce natural resources, including energy, to facilitate industrial development at home. Since the policy makers in their preoccupation with market-oriented reforms during the last one and a half decades took their eyes off energy security, there is now an urgent need to refocus on India's long-term investments in exploration and development of mineral and energy resources, just as China has done to invest in Australia and more recently Africa. For this purpose, it may be desirable to be open to forming joint ventures with firms in developed economies to acquire technology and design capabilities.

More recently, with oil prices reaching unprecedented levels over the past two years, Indian policy makers have begun to emulate China and make frantic effort to acquire oil and gas exploration rights to ensure energy security. Public sector firms like Oil and Natural Gas Corporation Ltd. (ONGC) have also made considerable investments to acquire oil fields in countries like Sudan, Russia, Vietnam and Kazakhstan to augment supply of petroleum for domestic use. Some Indian firms, public and private, have also picked up stakes in mining operations in Australia.

Access to long-term finance at reasonable interest rates is imperative to enable Indian firms to exploit external opportunities. Development finance institutions need to open special windows to promote international business—just like China's policy banks systematically do so for their domestic firms. Exim Bank of India has a window for this purpose, but it appears a feeble and nominal initiative to be of much consequence. Given the sizeable foreign exchange reserves of $160 billion, India could probably consider setting up an investment arm like the Temasek Holdings of the Singapore government to strategically invest globally to secure resources for rapid industrialisation and access to external markets.

The boom in the outward investments is likely to increase external pressure on India to quickly reduce tariffs and dismantle the remaining restrictions on capital inflows. Calibrating these moves without foregoing the interests of the vast unincorporated sector enterprises and the rural economy would remain a challenge for policy makers.

References

Lall, Sanjaya (1982). *Developing Countries as Exporters of Technology*. London: Macmillan, p.41.

Scherer, F.M. (2006). "A New Retrospective on Mergers", *Review of Industrial Organisation*, Spring.

An abridged and updated version of the San-Ei Gen lecture delivered at the University of Edinburgh Management School and Economics, November 2005. *Economic and Political Weekly*, November 18, 2006.

Economic Developments in India, Vol. 107.

29

RAGHURAM G. RAJAN

The Five Pillars of RBI's Financial Sector Policies

THESE are challenging times for the Indian economy, but I have dwelt on those near-term challenges elsewhere. Let me turn instead to the opportunities we have to make India a far better place than it is today, focusing in particular on finance.

Much of the world is ageing, facing the demographic tax of having to pay for an increasingly elderly population with a shrinking work force. Much of the world has run out of easy paths to growth. Having built infrastructure everywhere and exploited natural resources to their fullest, many countries are left with building bridges to nowhere to stimulate growth. Much of the world is also well-educated, well-fed, and well-connected through roads, telecommunications and finance. India is unlike the rest of the world. Our population is young, our infrastructure inadequate, and too many Indians are poorly educated, poorly fed and poorly connected. But this is precisely why our low hanging opportunities for betterment are plentiful in the coming years. All we need to do is to pluck them.

So if it is so easy, why are we not there already? This is an important question, but I don't want to go into the political economy of underdevelopment today. Suffice it to say that India is battling the internal interests that held it back in the past. While victory is not assured, we have made sufficient progress that we can look ahead to what we need to do in the next few years to put ourselves firmly back on the path of strong and sustainable growth.

Some would say we need to focus on manufacturing. Others point to the industries we do not have, such as electronics or computer chips, and say that is what we need. Echoes of industrial planning seem to be heard once again in the corridors of power. I am worried because we seem to be reverting to a dialogue of protection and subsidies that we left behind long ago. Our industrial sector is no longer an infant that needs to be mollycoddled. While we should not enter into free-trade agreements that give foreign manufacturers an undue advantage, that is no reason for us to now respond by giving domestic manufacturers protection. We must remember that one domestic producer's advantage from protectionist profits is paid for by the consumer, or shows up as another domestic producer's cost disadvantage.

Instead of targetting specific industries for governmental attention, which risks bringing back all the baggage of the Licence Permit Raj that we have left behind, let us focus on improving the conditions for growth for all. Our measure of success should be the jobs that are created, not by giving government subsidies or protections to labour-intensive industries or sectors but by developing a facilitating, though competitive, environment that will result in the emergence of the best solutions.

This requires a disciplined focus on four issues:

1. We need to improve the quality of our infrastructure, especially the logistical support and power that industry and services need. Grand plans are on the anvil, such as, the Delhi-Mumbai Industrial Corridor. We need to complete such projects on time, and within budget. The success of the New Delhi Metro suggests that timeliness and cost control are not foreign to the Indian psyche.
2. Our youth need education and training for the jobs that will be created. Some of this will be higher degrees, not just computer science but also design or civil engineering. Some of it will be appropriate vocational education that teaches them to be good plumbers and electricians rather than unemployable low-skilled engineers. Teaching our citizens can be a stepping stone to teaching the world. India can be at the forefront of providing mass technology-enabled education laced with appropriate human inputs to the world.

3. We need better business regulation. This does not always mean less regulation but it means regulation that is appropriate to the objective and that is enforced. I am told that factories in one state are still required to have a snake trap on the factory floor by law, a law that has not been changed since the days factories were surrounded by jungles. The lack of change may be sheer inertia, but it may be more sinister rent-seeking. All too often, we have too much regulation on the books and too little regulation in practice, with the worst of the regulated finding unscrupulous ways around the regulation while the honest are stymied. We have strong labour laws in theory that are meant to protect employees, but in practice we have a very flexible system with no incentive for firms to invest in their workers or hold on to them, and no loyalty towards the firms from workers. This needs to be changed if we are to have more skilled manufacturing jobs.
4. And finally, we need a better financial system, which will finance the needed infrastructure and the expansion of every producer ranging from the *kirana* shop owner to the industrialist even as it allows households to save safely with positive real returns, insure themselves against health emergencies or old age costs, and borrow at low cost to finance consumption. Importantly, the financial system should not require constant subsidies to bail it out.

Five Pillars of Reserve Bank of India's (RBI's) Developmental Measures

In the rest of this talk, I want to focus on what we at the RBI are doing to improve the financial system. We plan to build the RBI's developmental measures over the next few quarters on five pillars. These are:

1. Clarifying and strengthening the monetary policy framework.
2. Strengthening banking structure through new entry, branch expansion, encouraging new varieties of banks, and moving foreign banks into better regulated organisational forms.

3. Broadening and deepening financial markets and increasing their liquidity and resilience so that they can help allocate and absorb the risks entailed in financing India's growth.
4. Expanding access to finance to small and medium enterprises, the unorganised sector, the poor, and remote and underserved areas of the country through technology, new business practices, and new organisational structures, that is, we need financial inclusion.
5. Improving the system's ability to deal with corporate distress and financial institution distress by strengthening real and financial restructuring as well as debt recovery.

Let me elaborate on each of these measures a little.

First, we are among the large countries with the highest consumer price inflation in the world, even though growth is weaker than we would like it to be. Much of the inflation is concentrated in food and services sectors. Our households are turning to gold because they find financial investments unattractive. At the same time, many industrial corporations are complaining about high interest rates because they cannot pass through their higher costs into higher prices for their products.

We can spend a long time debating the sources of this inflation. But ultimately, inflation comes from demand exceeding supply, and it can be curtailed only by bringing both in balance. We need to reduce demand somewhat without having serious adverse effects on investment and supply. This is a balancing act, which requires the RBI to act firmly so that the economy is disinflating, even while allowing the weak economy more time than one would normally allow for it to reach a comfortable level of inflation. The weak state of the economy, as well as the good *kharif* and *rabi* harvest, will generate disinflationary forces that will help, and we await data to see how these forces are playing out. No single data point or number will determine our next move.

I think the market understands what we are trying to do. But we do need a more carefully spelled out monetary policy framework than we have currently. Action on the framework will follow the submission of the Dr. Urjit Patel Committee report, which is expected to submit its report by end December 2013.

Second, we have already announced measures to free bank branching, and to incentivise foreign banks to incorporate domestically. Going forward, we have to give our public sector banks, which are a national asset, the means to improve their competitiveness. Many of them have made enormous strides in the last decade—for instance, the extent to which they have digitised their operations is extremely praiseworthy—but because competition in the banking sector is likely to increase in the next few years, they cannot rest on their laurels. In the coming months, we will discuss with stakeholders in public sector banks about what needs to be done to further improve their stability, efficiency and productivity.

Third, we need to enlist markets in the aid of banking. Liquid markets will help banks off load risks they should not bear, such as interest rate or exchange risk. They will also allow banks to sell assets that they have no comparative advantage in holding, such as long-term loans to completed infrastructure projects, which are better held by infrastructure funds, pension funds and insurance companies. Liquid markets will help promoters raise equity which is sorely needed in the Indian economy to absorb the risks that banks otherwise end up absorbing. Rather than seeing markets as being inimical to the development of the banking sector, we have to see them as complimentary—of course, this requires you bankers to build on your risk management capabilities so that you can use markets effectively.

In the coming weeks, we will roll out more recommendations of the Gandhi Committee report to improve the liquidity and depth of the government security (G-Sec) market. We will then turn to money markets and corporate debt markets. We will introduce new variants of interest rate futures and products like inflation indexed certificates, and work to improve liquidity in derivative markets.

Fourth, we have to reach everyone, however remote or small, with financial services. Financial inclusion does not just mean credit for productive purposes, it means credit for health care emergencies or to pay lumpy school or college fees. It means a safe means of remunerated savings, and an easy way to make payments and remittances. It means insurance and pensions. It means financial literacy and consumer protection.

We have made great strides in inclusion, but we are still some distance from our goal. We have adopted a branch-based strategy for inclusion, but it is not enough. Too many poor people in so-called 'overbanked' urban areas still do not have access to banking services. We have many experiments under way to use technology, mobile phones, new products such as mobile wallets, and new entities as business correspondents to link people up to the formal financial system. Much as with cell phones where we created a frugal Indian model, we need a frugal, trustworthy and effective Indian model for financial inclusion. The Dr. Nachiket Mor Committee is helping us think through possible models, and I am hopeful that when we outline measures based on its recommendations, our fine banks, non-banking financial companies (NBFCs), IT companies and mobile players will rise to the occasion. At a more detailed level, we have set up committees like the Sambamurthy Committee to advise us on how to expand mobile banking in India through encrypted SMS-based funds transfer in any type of handset.

I should emphasise the need for banks like the ones represented in this room to move beyond simply opening bank accounts to ensuring that poor customers are confident and comfortable enough to use them. Innovation in reaching out to the underserved customer, rather than simply posting higher numbers in branches or bank accounts opened, has to be part of our efforts.

And last but not least, we have to deal better with distress: the natural, and worst, way for a bank management with limited tenure to deal with distress is to 'extend and pretend' to evergreen the loan, hope it recovers by miracle, or that one's successor has to deal with it. The natural incentive for a promoter to deal with distress is to hold on to equity and control despite having no real equity left, and to stand in the way of all efforts to resolve the underlying project while hoping for an 'Act of God' to bail him out. Not all bankers and promoters succumb to these natural incentives but too many do.

We have to ensure that the system recognises financial distress early, takes steps to resolve it, and ensures fair recovery for lenders and investors. We could wish for a more effective judicial process or a better bankruptcy system, but while we await that, we have to improve the functioning of what we have. In the next few weeks, we will announce measures to incentivise early recognition, better resolution, and fair recovery of distressed loans. We will focus on putting real assets back to work in their best use. Here again, you bankers have a critical role to play by fighting the natural incentives that are built into the system. You have to help those with genuine difficulty while being firm with those who are trying to milk the system. The RBI will help you with every means at our disposal.

Let me conclude. We are going through a period of great cynicism about what India can do. That cynicism does not just permeate the foreign press and their audiences, but also infects our domestic debate. Every policy is greeted with suspicion and scrutinised for evidence of malfeasance. With no upside to making decisions, it is no wonder that decision making has slowed. The solution, however, cannot come through inaction but through action, action that is, and is seen to be, purposeful, unbiased and effective. No doubt mistakes will be made, but if the weight of clean actions builds up, the miasma of suspicion that pervades our society today will ebb. The RBI intends to play its part in making this happen.

Speech at BANCON 2013 held at Mumbai, 15 November, 2013. RBI Monthly Bulletin December 2013.

Economic Developments in India, Vol. 192.

30

P. CHIDAMBARAM

Capital Account Management and Macro-Prudential Regulation for Financial Stability and Growth

IN India, we have experienced many systemic crises in finance. These included problems such as the stock market scandal of 1992. It extended to the bond market as well. That experience motivated us to strengthen the framework for financial regulation in India and the construction of well-governed infrastructure institutions such as the National Stock Exchange (NSE), the National Securities Depository Ltd. (NSDL), the depository and the Clearing Corporation of India Ltd. (CCIL), the clearing corporation. Since 1992, we have also weathered the global crisis of 2008. In the period immediately after the bankruptcy of Lehman Brothers, India was one of the most affected emerging markets. The money market experienced great turmoil and the short-term rate went beyond the band between the repo rate and the reverse repo rate. Money market mutual funds were forced to do fire sales. Corporate treasuries pulled out their money. The bond market collapsed under the burden of the fire sales and became illiquid. The Reserve Bank of India (RBI) had to set up an emergency mechanism to give liquidity to mutual funds.

Over 5 years later, the dust has settled and it all seems easy, what we did in 2008. But it was not easy. For those of us who lived through that period, we know that we were really tested. I wish to congratulate all the people who worked on understanding and addressing that crisis with rapid thinking and responses, day after day, and some times through the night, through that difficult period. Contrary to popular perception, the government and the RBI worked together closely at that time. These experiences have motivated much soul searching on the subject of systemic risk and I would like to take this opportunity to summarise our thinking on four points.

First, some systemic crises are born out of blunders in the fundamentals of financial regulation. Financial regulation is about three problems: consumer protection, micro-prudential regulation and resolution. The institutional framework governing the financial sector in India has been built up over a century. The Financial Sector Legislation Reforms Commission reviewed the scene and it concluded and I quote:

> There are over 60 Acts and multiple rules and regulations that govern the financial sector. Many of the financial sector laws date back several decades when the financial landscape was very different from that seen today. For example, the Reserve Bank of India (RBI) Act and the Insurance Act are of 1934 and 1938 vintage respectively. Financial economic governance has been modified in a piecemeal fashion from time to time without substantial changes to the underlying foundations. Over the years, as the economy and the financial system have grown in size and sophistication, an increasing gap has come about between the requirements of the country and the present legal and regulatory arrangements.

Given that legal framework, many but not all systemic crises were born of blunders on those foundations. As an example, better micro-prudential regulation may have stopped the stock market scandal of 1992 in its tracks. Our first port of call is therefore to strengthen our foundations. The draft Indian Financial Code, presented by the Commission, envisages a lot of new work on all three fronts including the construction of a brand new resolution corporation.

Second, deep and liquid markets are shock absorbers. When mutual funds faced large redemptions on money market mutual funds, they ran into trouble because we failed to build a deep and liquid bond market. The currency market would have experienced less trouble after Lehman collapsed if we had a deep and liquid currency market. We should never lose sight of the importance of deep and liquid markets as shock absorbers. We have done a decent job with the equity market, but there is a big unfinished agenda with the bond-currency-derivative nexus.

Three, systemic risk is all about the woods and not the trees. Nobody who thinks a lot about any one sector can understand systemic risk, which involves complicated interactions of all sectors. Persons, who are experts on any one sector, say for example mutual funds, may not understand the interconnection between Indian multinationals and the Lehman shock and the treasury balances held by Indian firms with mutual funds and the fire sales on the bond market. This requires a new kind of thinking, what we call a financial system thinking which will be elusive to people who think about one sector at a time or one firm at a time.

Four, in order to improve policy coordination and to undertake system-wide actions, we responded to these experiences by constructing a Council of Regulators: the Financial Stability and Development Council, FSDC for short. This is a mechanism for all financial regulators to meet, exchange information and coordinate strategies. The Ministry of Finance is part of the FSDC and the FSDC is intended to ensure coordination of the use of fiscal resources if such a moment should arise. FSDC, since it was set up, has already improved communication between all regulators. It is our sincere hope that it will increasingly play this coordination role, better and with sharper focus. We are working to strengthen databases and technical capabilities at FSDC so far as to make it a full-blown systemic risk agency. Towards this, we intend to construct the financial data management centre envisaged by the Commission. In the future, if you face a situation like 2008 again, FSDC will be the war room.

I would like to end with a note of caution and before that I would like to identify the fault lines that we have discovered in the last few years. These fault lines, once more or less hidden, are now evidently open in the form of, as Financial Sector Legislative Reforms Commission (FSLRC) says, lack of legal clarity on responsibility and powers of regulators, inter-regulatory disputes, regulator-regulated court battles, adventurism of market participants, and the growing shadow banking and shallow financial sector. Given these fault lines, in the aftermath of the global crisis, we find that legislatures world wide have rushed to create new agencies and confer them with additional powers to ensure that no systemic crisis takes place. Is that the way to go forward? Our foundations of knowledge in this field are only emerging. For a comparison, central banks that printed paper money experienced all sorts of problems until the late 1970s or early 1980s, by which time, the body of knowledge on monetary policy was strong enough to support the smooth working of monetary policy. In the same way, should we not be careful about creating new agencies or giving them new powers and using them without adequate evidence in the field of systemic risk? There is profound need for more scientific knowledge and more experience. We should make the most of our limited data on systemic risk and we should be constantly skeptical and questioning about the evidentiary base based on such a short time. I think we should apply a hippocratic oath 'Above all, do no harm.' We should be mindful when we use the new powers in the field of systemic risk.

Inaugural Speech of Finance Minister at the CAFRAL Conference, January 13, 2014.

Economic Developments in India, Vol. 195.

31

MANMOHAN SINGH

Indian Economic Crisis and the Fall of Rupee

THE movement of the exchange rate of the Indian rupee recently has been a matter of concern. The rupee has depreciated sharply against the dollar since the last week of May. There are concerns, and justifiably so, of the impact this would have on our economy.

What triggered the sharp and sudden depreciation was the markets' reaction to certain unexpected external developments. On May 22, 2013, the US Federal Reserve Bank indicated that it would soon 'taper' its quantitative easing as the US economy was recovering. This led to a reversal of capital flows to emerging economies which are now sharply pulling down not just the rupee, but also the Brazilian real, the Turkish lira, the Indonesian rupiah, the South African rand and many other currencies.

While global factors such as tensions over Syria and the prospect of US Federal Reserve tapering its policy of quantitative easing have caused general weaknesses in emerging market currencies, the rupee has been especially hit because of our large current account deficit (CAD) and some other domestic factors. We intend to act to reduce the CAD and bring about an improvement in the functioning of our economy.

In 2010-11 and the years prior to it, our CAD was more modest and financing it was not difficult, even in the crisis year of 2008-09. Since then, there has been a deterioration, mainly on account of huge imports of gold, higher costs of crude oil imports and recently, of coal. On the export side, weak demand in our major markets has kept our exports from growing. Exports have been further hit by a collapse in iron ore exports. Taken together, these factors have made our CAD unsustainably large.

Clearly we need to reduce our appetite for gold, economise in the use of petroleum products and take steps to increase our exports.

We have taken measures to reduce the CAD. The Finance Minister has indicated that it will be below $70 billion this year, and we will take all possible steps to ensure that outcome. These are already showing results with a declining trade deficit in both June and July. The Government is confident that we will be able to lower our CAD to $70 billion. Our medium-term objective is to reduce the CAD to 2.5 per cent of our gross domestic product (GDP). Our short-term objective is to finance the CAD in an orderly fashion. We will make every effort to maintain a macro economic framework friendly to foreign capital inflows to enable orderly financing of the CAD.

Coming back to the effects of the Rupee depreciation, we must realise that part of this depreciation was merely a needed adjustment. Inflation in India has been much higher than in the advanced countries. Therefore, it is natural that there has to be a correction in the exchange rate to account for this difference. To some extent, depreciation can be good for the economy as this will help to increase our export competitiveness and discourage imports.

There are many sectors which are regaining competitiveness in export markets as a result of the fall in the exchange rate. Over the next few months, I expect the effects of this to be felt more strongly, both in exports and in the financial position of exporting sectors. This in itself would correct the CAD to some extent.

However, foreign exchange markets have a notorious history of overshooting. Unfortunately this is what is happening not only in relation to the rupee but also other currencies.

The Reserve Bank of India (RBI) and Government have taken a number of steps to stabilise the rupee. Some measures have given rise to doubts in some quarters that capital controls are on the horizon. I would like to assure the House and the world at large, that the Government is not contemplating any such measures. The last two decades have seen India grow as an open economy and we have benefitted from it. There is no question of reversing these policies just because there is some turbulence in capital and currency markets. The sudden decline in the exchange rate is certainly a shock, but we will address this through other measures, not through capital controls or by reversing the process of reforms. The Finance Minister has clarified this matter at length, and I take this opportunity to reaffirm our position.

Ultimately, the value of the rupee is determined by the fundamentals of our economy. While we have taken a number of actions to strengthen those fundamentals, we intend to do more.

Growth has slowed down in recent quarters. I expect growth in the first quarter of 2013-14 to be relatively flat, but as the effects of the good monsoon kick in, I expect it to pick up. There are many reasons for this optimism. The decisions of the Cabinet Committee on Investment in reviving stalled projects will start bearing fruit in the second half of the year. The full effects of the growth friendly measures that have been taken over the last six months, such as liberalising norms for foreign direct investment (FDI), resolution of some tax issues of concern to industry and fuel subsidy reform will come into play over the year resulting in higher growth particularly in manufacturing. Exports are also starting to look up as the growth performance of the rest of the world is showing signs of improvement. So I believe growth will pick up in the second half of the fiscal year barring extreme unforeseen eventualities.

There are questions about the size of the fiscal deficit. The government will do whatever is necessary to contain the fiscal deficit to 4.8 per cent of GDP this year. The most growth friendly way to contain the deficit is to spend carefully, especially on subsidies that do not reach the poor, and we will take effective steps to that end.

Inflation measured by the wholesale price index (WPI) has been coming down, even though inflation measured by the consumer price index (CPI) is still too high. The depreciation of the rupee and rise in dollar prices of petroleum products will no doubt lead to some further upward pressure on prices. The RBI will therefore continue to focus on bringing down inflation. The favourable monsoon and the anticipated good harvest will help bring down food prices and ease the task of controlling inflation.

All in all, the macro-stabilisation process which should support the value of the rupee is under way. I expect that as the fruits of our efforts materialise, currency markets will recover.

Even while we go about doing what is necessary, it is important to recognise that the fundamentals of the Indian economy continue to be strong. India's overall public-debt to GDP ratio has been on a declining trend from 73.2 per cent of GDP in 2006-07 to 66 per cent in 2012-13. Similarly, India's external debt is only 21.2 per cent of our GDP and while short-term debt has risen, it stands at no more than 5.2 per cent of our GDP. Our foreign exchange reserves stand at US$ 278 bn, and are more than sufficient to meet India's external financing requirements.

Many foreign analysts worry about banking problems that may arise in the wake of the currency crisis. The Indian banking sector has seen some rise in bad loans. The question that needs to be asked is whether there is a liquidity problem or a solvency problem for the borrowers. My belief is that there is a liquidity problem. Many of the projects are not unviable but only delayed, in contrast to the overbuilding that has characterised the banking sector problems in many other countries. As these projects come on stream, they will generate revenue and repay loans. Our banks are fortunately well capitalised much above the Basel norms and they have the capacity to provide for any non-performing assets (NPAs) until those assets are turned around.

The easy reforms of the past have been done. We have the more difficult reforms to do such as reduction of subsidies, insurance and pension sector reforms, eliminating bureaucratic red tape and implementing Goods and Services Tax (GST). These are not low hanging fruit and they need active political consensus.

It is here that I urge Honourable Members across the political spectrum to reflect on the need of the hour. Many laws that are necessary are held up for lack of political consensus. Reforms such as the GST, which everyone agrees is essential to restore growth and boost revenues, require states to come to an agreement. We need to forge consensus on such vital issues. I urge political parties to work towards this end and to join in the government's efforts to put the economy back on the path of stable, sustainable growth.

There may be short-term shocks to our economy and we need to face them. That is the reality of operating in a globalised economy, whose benefits we have reaped over the last 15 to 20 years. We will need to ensure that the fundamentals of the economy remain strong so that India continues to grow at a healthy rate for many years to come. That we will ensure. We are no doubt faced with important challenges, but we have the capacity to address them. It is at times like these that the nation shows what it is truly capable of.

August 31, 2013.

Economic Developments in India, Vol. 189.

32

ARVIND SUBRAMANIAN

What Saved the Rupee?

THE near-crisis witnessed this year will be the subject of many future exegeses. "History is that certainty produced at the point where the imperfections of memory meet the inadequacies of documentation," says a character in Julian Barnes' Booker-winning novel, *The Sense of an Ending*. Pre-empting the writing of such 'certain' future histories requires exploiting the objectivity that recency provides, to get the facts down, straight and quick.

What happened to the rupee between May and October? What helped? What hindered? The evolution of the rupee, illustrated in the graphs, allows four hypotheses to be tested.

(1) *Raghuram Rajan turned the rupee around:* The popular view is that leadership change at the Reserve Bank of India (RBI) changed the fortunes of the rupee. And there is truth to this. As Figure 32.1 shows, there was a big upward move in the rupee the day after Raghuram Rajan formally took charge as Governor of the RBI. And the upward climb of the rupee has been maintained since Dr Rajan's appointment, helped by his policy announcements and actions. But was this the whole story?

(2) *External events, not domestic actions, played the decisive role*: In this view, the rupee was a victim during the summer of the broader re-assessment of emerging markets, following the US Federal Reserve's (Fed) announcement that it might soon wind down ('taper') its unconventional monetary policy stimulus. By the same token, the rupee would have benefited from the growing doubts after August about the fact or magnitude of the Fed taper.

If this hypothesis were true, one should see broadly similar movements in the currencies of the five major emerging markets that were particularly buffeted by external developments. Figure

Figure 32.1

Evolution of the Rupee (May 22 to October 13, 2013)

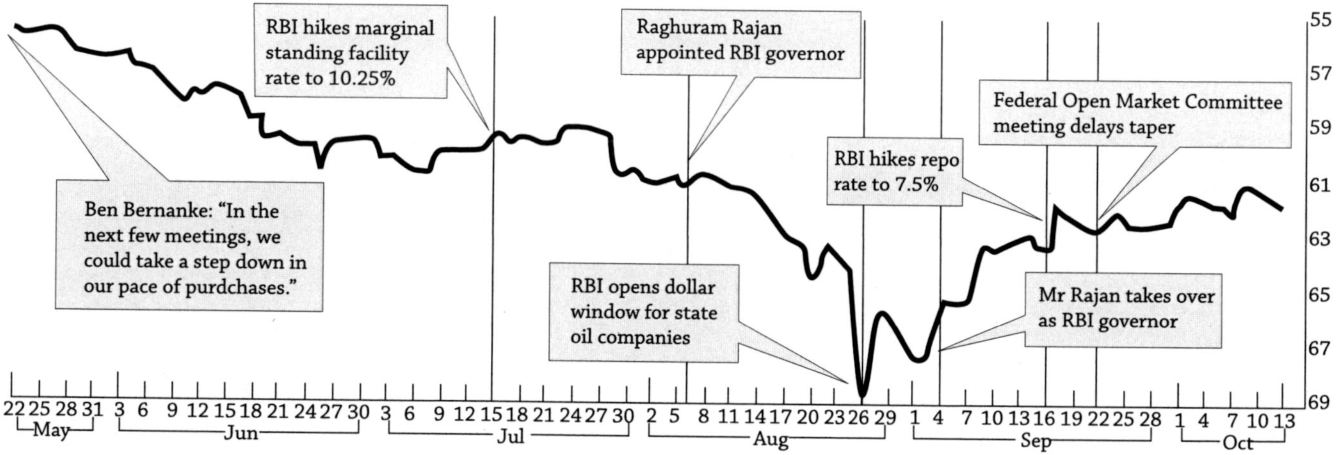

Figure 32.2

Evolution of Five Fragile Emerging Market Currencies (May 22 to October 13, 2013)

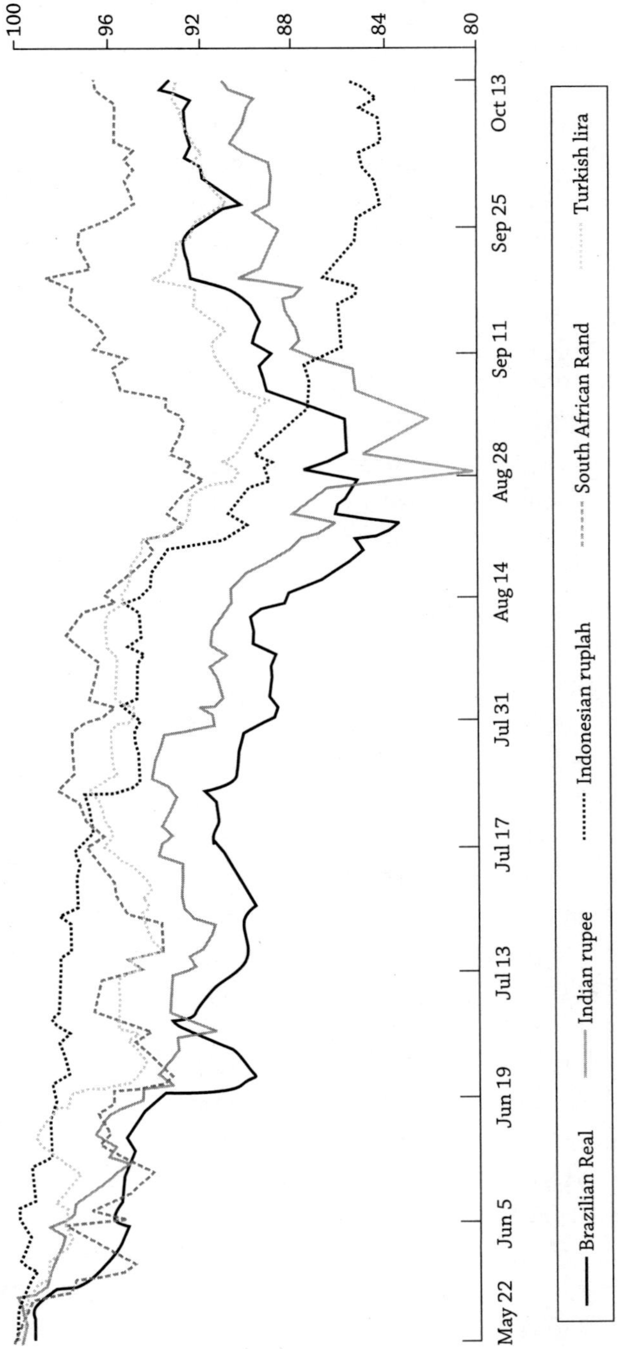

32.2 shows the evolution of the currencies of the five fragile emerging market economies during the same period. There is indeed a broad pattern. All five currencies declined after the Fed's May announcement. And with the exception of Indonesia, all currencies bottomed out around the same period, and have recovered since. The rupee declined more and hence also recovered more. But one could come away from Figure 32.2 with the conclusion that the rupee's exchange rate was broadly shaped by external events, much more so than domestic factors.

(3) *Conventional defence of the rupee through monetary tightening failed*: On July 15, as the rupee started tumbling, the government announced its own peculiar version of monetary policy tightening to defend the rupee. It tightened short-term interest rates (the marginal standing facility) by two percentage points without changing the key policy repo rate. As Figure 32.1 shows, this action had no permanent impact on the rupee, which, after a short blip up, kept sliding till August end. It is true that this policy tightening was half-hearted because officials in the RBI and the Ministry of Finance sent mixed signals about its desirability and durability. In a government securities (G-Sec) auction immediately after the action, the RBI in fact rejected high-interest bids.

The advice given to the government—from outside and within—to target the exchange rate was bad for both substantive and political reasons. The interest rate defence was based in part on the assumption that a depreciation would not help much in improving the current account deficit (CAD). Leading up to the crisis, investment bank peddled this exchange rate pessimism. But such pessimism has not proved warranted elsewhere, and is unlikely to prove valid in India. Indeed, the recent increase in exports and service sector profits and decline in imports may be early signs that the rupee depreciation is beginning to produce the expected effects.

The interest rate defence was also badly designed in focusing only on some lending (short-term and not G-Sec and other bank lending), ignoring the obvious fact that liquidity is fungible. If you have to tighten, that needs to happen across the board. Politically, the advice to tighten was misguided because it was obvious to all market participants that the government was deeply conflicted on raising interest rates. That meant that the interest rate defence was not credible and hence could not be sustained.

(4) *Unconventional defence by lending foreign exchange to public sector oil companies worked:* Look at Figure 32.1 closely, and it is evident that the rupee bottomed out at 68.8 per dollar on August 28, even before the new governor of the RBI took charge. On that day, the government in collaboration with the RBI announced that it would provide dollar loans to the oil companies. Thereafter, the rupee climbed upwards, aided by the fact that the balance-of-payments (BoP) picture started to change significantly in September as gold imports were squeezed and as the economic slowdown took its toll on imports.

But why did the provision of loans to the oil companies work? First, it essentially took the big demand for dollars from these oil companies (about $8.5 billion per month) out of the foreign exchange market, which immediately lifted rupee pressures.

Second, the action was not to sell but to loan dollars to these companies. That distinction was critical. Ordinary sales would have tightened rupee liquidity in the market (because oil companies would have had to give rupees to the RBI in return for dollars). This tightening would again have raised a clamour of disapproval from the private sector and the government based on its adverse growth impact.

The puzzle was why such non-contractionary ('sterilised') foreign exchange intervention worked. The international experience suggests that sterilised intervention to defend a currency, especially during crises, tends to be ineffective or counterproductive. Essentially, the party receiving the foreign exchange can speculate against the currency in many ways; for example, an importer can deposit the foreign exchange overseas while using his rupee funds to pay for his dollar bills. In this case, the loan does nothing to alleviate currency pressures. But it worked in India because the parties receiving the dollars—public sector entities—were liable to moral suasion by the government. Effectively, the RBI had become an import financing company, helping to pay for public sector imports with its foreign exchange reserves.

What can we conclude from all of this? An India-centred perspective on the recent rupee crisis offers two strong lessons. Half-hearted and partial policy tightening in defence of the rupee was an unmitigated failure. Second, a very peculiar Indian case of sterilised intervention—which failed in other crises and is generally proscribed—actually worked.

But a broader cross-country perspective suggests that all the domestic angst and actions may have been overdone because in the end, they were subordinate to external events. Welcome to the new, financially globalised Indian economy, pitfalls, risks and all.

Business Standard, October 17, 2013.

Economic Developments in India, Vol. 194.

33

C. RANGARAJAN

Recent Improvement in the Current Account Deficit

Is it Sustainable?

INDIA'S balance of payments (BoP) has shown several interesting twists and turns in the last few years. In 2010-11, the current account deficit (CAD) rose sharply from 2.8 per cent of gross domestic product (GDP) in the previous year to 4.2 per cent of GDP. In 2012-13, CAD continued to remain high and stood at 4.8 per cent of GDP. The picture looked grim in the first quarter of the current fiscal 2013-14. Even as the CAD remained high, capital flows dried up in the aftermath of the May 22, 2013, statement of the Fed and the rupee depreciated sharply by almost 25 per cent. However, since then, there has been dramatic change in the CAD. The CAD has come down sharply and capital flows have revived. For the year as a whole, the CAD is estimated at 2 per cent of GDP. In this context, three important questions arise: (1) Is the improvement that has been seen in the last two quarters sustainable? (2) In the light of our recent experience, what is the sustainable level of CAD? and (3) What role does the exchange rate play in such a situation?

In the high growth phase of the Indian economy, that is 2005-06 to 2007-08, when the annual rate of growth exceeded 9 per cent, India's CAD remained low. The average for the three years was 1.1 per cent of GDP. The trade deficit as a proportion of GDP was in the region of 6.2-7.4 per cent. There was a substantial surplus on the invisibles account which ranged between 5.0 per cent and 6.1 per cent of GDP. Export growth averaged 25 per cent per annum. Import growth rate was at 31 per cent and invisibles at 31 per cent. This was the time when the world economy was also booming. With the CAD remaining low and with a substantial inflow of capital, the addition to reserves amounted to $170 billion. The exchange rate remained between ₹ 44.3 and ₹ 46.0 to the dollar. During the next three years, the CAD as a proportion of GDP remained around 2.8 per cent of GDP. But the deterioration started in 2011-12, when the CAD rose sharply from $48 billion to $78 billion. Although the increase in the trade deficit was $63 billion, the invisibles growth was strong and the surplus on the invisible account increased by $32 billion. During this year, both export and import growth were strong. But the import growth rate was higher than the export growth rate. The oil import bill went up by $49 billion, as crude oil prices shot up by 31.5 per cent. Gold imports touched a new high at $56 billion. This was an increase of $16 billion over the previous year. The increase in coal imports was $7 billion and that of electronics $6 billion. Thus of the increase in imports of $116 billion, oil, gold, coal and electronics contributed almost $80 billion. In 2012-13, imports remained at a high level but the exports growth rate fell and turned negative. Invisibles also declined and consequently CAD rose to 4.8 per cent of GDP. Both in 2011-12 and 2012-13, despite the fact that the CAD remained high, alarm bells did not ring. That was because of the surge in capital flows. The total quantum of capital flows in 2012-13 was $92 billion which covered not only the CAD but also added $4 billion to the reserves.

In 2013-14, the CAD continued to remain high in the first quarter, i.e., April-June 2013. Gold imports were still running at a high level. Capital flows took a sudden downward turn after the May 22, 2013, Fed statement and the interpretation markets put on it. Portfolio flows turned highly negative. This happened to many other countries as well but, perhaps, India was affected more because of the high level of the CAD. Without going into the various actions taken, we must note that in Quarter 2 and Quarter 3, the CAD came down very sharply. The data on the BoP are now available for the first three quarters of the fiscal year. The CAD fell from $70 billion in the fiscal year 2013 to $31 billion in the current fiscal. Of this dramatic improvement in the CAD of the order of $39 billion, the improvement in invisibles contributed $6 billion and the reduction in the trade deficit was of the order of $33 billion. Looking at the decline in the trade deficit, the increase in exports was $13 billion and the decline in imports was $20 billion. Of this decline in imports, decline in gold alone amounted to $14.6 billion. There was no change in the net oil imports. With the resumption of capital flows both as a result of the special measures taken by the Reserve Bank of India (RBI) and the general improvement in the global climate, capital flows were adequate and the pressure on the rupee has eased.

The reduction in imports seen in the last two quarters, and which has continued into the first two months of the current quarter, seems sustainable. On gold imports, while the substantial drop in imports in the last two quarters may partly have been contributed by certain administrative actions, one can hope for a reduction in imports in gold in the coming years, as inflation moderates. Imports of gold rose sharply, when inflation was hovering around the double digit level. The returns on financial assets were not attractive enough and the demand for gold as an asset increased. As moderation in inflation continues and the returns on financial assets become attractive, the demand for gold as an asset must come down. After all, the imports of gold remained around $30-$40 billion in the years prior to 2010-11. Exports will also benefit as inflation comes down. Competitiveness of Indian exports critically depends upon the relative inflation levels. As regards oil imports, after the sudden rise in 2011-12, they have remained more or less at the same level. International crude oil prices are not expected to rise. As domestic retail prices of petroleum products get adjusted in sync with the international prices, there will be a price effect which may to some extent dampen the demand for oil imports. If the power situation improves, for which there are several indications, the use of diesel for power generation may also come down. On the other hand, as the economy improves, imports of oil as well as capital goods will pick up. As domestic production of coal increases, there can be some moderation in the import of coal. The imports of electronic goods have been rising and the answer to it lies in creating an appropriate production base in the country. Given this set of factors, India's CAD may remain in the range of 2-2.5 per cent of GDP over the next few years.

Is there a need to work towards an even lower level? Recent events have shown that a high CAD may have a sharp effect on the exchange rate, when external conditions change. The post May 22, 2013, events are again a reminder for this. What is the level of deficit which can be financed by normal capital flows? On reasonable assumptions of growth and exchange rate, a deficit of 2.5 per cent of GDP will require capital flows annually of the order of $40-$60 billion in the next few years. This may be around 5 per cent of the capital flows to emerging markets. This level of flows can reasonably be expected to materialise. Nevertheless, it may be prudent to keep the CAD at a slightly lower level by an appropriate domestic policy environment. The policy actions should include the following: (1) Inflation must be tamed and this will ensure export competitiveness and also contain some imports like gold. (2) Fiscal consolidation must be pursued and this will bridge the gap between investment and savings which is in fact the other side of the CAD. (3) Appropriate pricing policies must be in place and this will help to contain oil imports. (4) Policies that can help to increase domestic production of coal must be adopted.

Finally, on the exchange rate. No longer does the CAD determine the exchange rate. Capital flows considerably influence the exchange rate. For example, when we had a high CAD, the exchange rate should have taken a hit. It did not happen because of the large capital flows. But this stored the problem for a later date. Therefore, there is need to watch the real effective exchange rate. In times of strong capital flows, policy makers have to moderate the real appreciation, even though there is a cost to it. In the absence of such interventions, we will have to be prepared for sudden shocks coming from the drying up of capital flows for which we may not be directly responsible. Capital flows have done good for India. But that does not preclude keeping a watch when the flows become very large. Equally important is the need for controlling inflation. In fact in many ways, controlling inflation is the key to ensuring a comfortable BoP situation.

Economic Developments in India, Vol. 197.